Out of My Bone

Out of My Bone

THE LETTERS OF

Joy Davidman

Edited and Introduced by

Don W. King

WILLIAM B. EERDMANS PUBLISHING COMPANY
GRAND RAPIDS, MICHIGAN / CAMBRIDGE, U.K.

Published 2009 by
Wm. B. Eerdmans Publishing Co.
2140 Oak Industrial Drive N.E., Grand Rapids, Michigan 49505 /
P.O. Box 163, Cambridge CB3 9PU U.K.

Printed in the United States of America

15 14 13 12 11 10 09   7 6 5 4 3 2 1

Library of Congress Cataloging-in-Publication Data

Davidman, Joy.
Out of my bone: the letters of Joy Davidman /
edited and introduced by Don W. King.
p.   cm.
Includes bibliographical references and index.
ISBN 978-0-8028-6399-7 (cloth: alk. paper)
1. Davidman, Joy — Correspondence.
2. Authors, American — 20th century — Correspondence.
I. King, Don W., 1951-   II. Title.

PS3507.A6659Z48   2009
813'.52 — dc22
[B]
                              2009000864

www.eerdmans.com

To Rich Gray

Contents

Contents

Acknowledgments

This book began as have many others; that is, the author begins writing one book and along the way discovers that a second book has appeared. In my case, as I was doing research on *Yet One More Spring: A Critical Study of the Works of Joy Davidman,* I managed to collect most of the surviving letters written by Davidman. As I read over the letters, I realized that many readers would find her correspondence both compelling and fascinating. At that moment, *Out of My Bone* was born. About a week later, I decided Davidman's letters would be superbly supported by reprinting her hard-to-find autobiographical essay "The Longest Way Round."

I have many persons to thank for assistance in writing this book. First and foremost, I am thankful to David and Douglas Gresham, who have graciously given me permission to publish their mother's letters and autobiographical essay. I also thank Lyle Dorsett, whose biography *And God Came In: The Extraordinary Story of Joy Davidman* I consulted frequently. Perry C. Bramlett was especially helpful in securing copies of many of Davidman's reviews and poems. Dr. Judith Priestman of the Bodleian Library has been a faithful supporter in all my efforts, as has her colleague, Colin Harris, Reader Services Librarian & Superintendent of the Modern Papers and John Johnson Reading Room. Elizabeth Pearson, the Library Director at Montreat College, and her staff have been endlessly patient and helpful in securing materials. I am grateful as well to the staff at the Marion E. Wade Center, particularly Laura Schmidt, Heidi Truty, Christopher W. Mitchell, and Marjorie Mead, who encouraged my research and made me comfortable during my many visits to the Wade Center. I owe debts of gratitude to Montreat College, for granting me research grants to work on this book, and the Appalachian College Association, for awarding me two summer research grants. I also thank my student assistants, Nathan King and Joanna King, and my colleagues Sue Diehl and Kim McMurtry for reading and correcting early versions of the manuscript. I am most appreciative of the excellent editorial advice of Wm. B. Eerdmans Publishing Company, especially Jon Pott, Vice-President and Editor in Chief, and my editor, Jenny Hoffman. Finally, I owe my wife, Jeanine, a great debt since I spent so many hours away from her while working on this book.

All letters, poems, essays, and other written material by Joy Davidman are copyrighted by David and Douglas Gresham and are used by their permission. In addition, excerpted letters by William L. Gresham are copyrighted by David and Douglas Gresham and are used by their permission. Excerpts of letters by Chad Walsh are used by permission of Damaris (Walsh) McGuire. The following have provided copies of Davidman's letters, and the letters are used by permission: Bodleian Library, Oxford, Special Collections; Papers of Ruth Lechlitner, Special Collections Department, University of Iowa Libraries, Iowa City, Iowa; James Still Papers, 1885-2007, 87M12, Box 24, Special Collections and Digital Programs, University of Kentucky Libraries, Lexington, Kentucky; Jack Conroy Papers, Box 17, folder 894, Midwest Manuscript Collection, The Newberry Library, Chicago; Aaron Kramer Papers, Special Collections Library, University of Michigan; The Marion E. Wade Center, Wheaton College, Wheaton, Illinois; and the William Rose Benét Papers, Yale Collection of American Literature, Beinecke Rare Book and Manuscript Library.

A final note concerns the guidelines I followed in editing the letters. In some cases I have substituted or changed minor marks of punctuation in order to provide greater clarity in the letters; however, I have not altered any of Davidman's original language, including in a very few cases wording that today might be offensive. Davidman on occasion uses the ellipsis mark in her letters in order to suggest a trailing off of thought; in order to avoid confusion that might occur in the minds of readers when seeing the ellipsis mark (since it normally means that material has been left out), I have omitted them from the letters. Davidman frequently emphasizes points in her letters, which I have maintained by use of italics. In footnotes I have tried to identify all correspondents as well as the names of those persons appearing in the texts of the letters whenever possible; in addition, I have provided basic historical background concerning many of the events Davidman alludes to in the letters. In order to fill in important bio-graphical details, I have on occasion inserted explanatory notes between letters (these passages appear in italics). In a few cases it has not been pos-sible to determine with certainty the year of a letter; I have indicated this by placing the year in brackets. Finally, I have identified the sources of the letters using the following abbreviations:

Bod	Bodleian Library
Iowa	University of Iowa Libraries
UK	University of Kentucky Libraries
Newberry	The Newberry Library, Chicago
UM	University of Michigan Library
Wade	The Marion E. Wade Center
Yale	Yale University Library

Introduction

Yet One More Spring

What will come of me
After the fern has feathered from my brain
And the rosetree out of my blood; what will come of me
In the end, under the rainy locustblossom
Shaking its honey out on springtime air
Under the wind, under the stooping sky?
What will come of me and shall I lie
Voiceless forever in earth and unremembered,
And be forever the cold green blood of flowers
And speak forever with the tongue of grass
Unsyllabled, and sound no louder
Than the slow falling downward of white water,
And only speak the quickened sandgrain stirring,
Only the whisper of the leaf unfolding,
Only the tongue of leaves forever and ever?

Out of my heart the bloodroot,
Out of my tongue the rose,
Out of my bone the jointed corn,
Out of my fiber trees,
Out of my mouth a sunflower,
And from my fingers vines,
And the rank dandelion shall laugh from my loins
Over million seeded earth; but out of my heart,

Introduction

*Core of my heart, blood of my heart, the bloodroot
Coming to lift a petal in peril of snow,
Coming to dribble from a broken stem
Bitterly the bright color of blood forever.*

*But I would be more than a cold voice of flowers
And more than water, more than sprouting earth
Under the quiet passion of the spring;
I would leave you the trouble of my heart
To trouble you at evening; I would perplex you
With lightning coming and going about my head,
Outrageous signs, and wonders; I would leave you
The shape of my body filled with images,
The shape of my mind filled with imaginations,
The shape of myself. I would create myself
In a little fume of words and leave my words
After my death to kiss you forever and ever.*[1]

Although best known as C. S. Lewis's wife, Joy Davidman was a gifted writer, publishing a volume of poetry, *Letter to a Comrade* (1938); two novels, *Anya* (1940) and *Weeping Bay* (1950); and *Smoke on the Mountain* (1954), her interpretation of the Ten Commandments. *Letter to a Comrade*, winner of the Yale Younger Poet competition for 1938, appeared to signal the beginning of a significant writing career as Davidman also won in the same year the Russell Loines Memorial award for poetry given by the National Institute of Arts and Letters. *Anya* and *Weeping Bay* received modest but generally favorable critical scrutiny, while *Smoke on the Mountain* continues to be read and quoted by those doing intensive study of the Decalogue. In addition, from April 1938 through July 1945 her poetry, book reviews, and movie reviews appeared regularly in the *New Masses,* the semi-official weekly magazine of the Communist Party of the United States of America (CPUSA).[2]

1. From Joy Davidman's *Letter to a Comrade* (New Haven: Yale University Press, 1938), p. 65.
2. See my "Joy Davidman and the *New Masses:* Communist Poet and Reviewer," *The Chronicle of the Oxford C. S. Lewis Society* 4, no. 1 (February 2007): 18-44. I offer a careful critical analysis of her published works in the working manuscript, *Yet One More Spring: A Critical Study of Joy Davidman.*

These published works, however, are not the sum total of her literary corpus. Although a few of her excerpted letters have appeared, most notably in Lyle Dorsett's *And God Came In*, until now the majority of her surviving letters have remained unpublished.[3] Accordingly, this book publishes for the first time the letters of Joy Davidman. Readers interested in Davidman will find these letters fascinating for at least five reasons.

1. These letters reveal Davidman's persistent search for truth, her curious, incisive mind, but most importantly, her clear and unique voice; hers is an arresting, provocative, and sharply penetrating voice as is evident in her poem "Yet One More Spring."
2. They chronicle Davidman's religious, philosophical, and intellectual journey from secular Judaism to atheism to Communism to Christianity; her very personal engagement in her correspondence with these issues offers key insights into the historical milieu of America in the 1930s and 1940s.
3. Her letters illustrate the struggles of her marriage to William Lindsay Gresham and of maintaining a family life that did not always fit easily with her career goals.
4. Her letters illuminate her relationship with C. S. Lewis and demonstrate her influence upon his later writings, including *Surprised by Joy* and especially *Till We Have Faces*.
5. Her letters expose her mental, emotional, and spiritual state as she confronted the challenge of the cancer that eventually took her life.

To begin, Davidman's letters reflect a definite, clear, unique voice: focused, concentrated, hard, insisting to be heard, earnest, serious, determined, not suffering fools lightly, confrontational, zealot-like, insightful, and penetrating. Her confrontational and demanding voice may have developed in part from the way her father treated her as she was growing up. According to Dorsett, Joseph Davidman, a perfectionist himself, was "incredibly demanding; nothing less than perfection was tolerated in his house."[4] Although Davidman was a prodigy and naturally gifted to excel — as a child she scored extremely high on her IQ test — this only made her father push her even harder. Dorsett writes:

---

3. Lyle Dorsett, *And God Came In: The Extraordinary Story of Joy Davidman* (New York: Macmillan, 1983).
4. Dorsett, *And God Came In*, p. 10.

[Her father's] pressure to perform at peak level never let up. Even meal-time was devoted to discussions of weighty subjects, rather than light and loving family chatter. Because the perfect father could never be wrong, and because Joy was driven to be perfect, too, there was no way that she and her father could take opposite sides on an issue and leave it at that; agreement to disagree was out of the question. Inevitably, discussions evolved into arguments, and arguments eventually led to longlasting resentments.[5]

Her father's unrelenting pressure — amounting almost to brow beating — may have accustomed Davidman to adapting the same kind of tactics in her own approach to argumentation and disputation.

Let me set the context for exploring Davidman's voice in her corre spondence by briefly illustrating it in her early published works.[6] By 1938 she was regularly writing book, theater, and movie reviews — especially the latter — for the *New Masses (NM)*. During her most active period, March 1941 through July 1943, she was publishing a book, theater, or movie review in almost every issue of *NM*. An early book review of Kenneth Porter's volume of poetry, *The High Plains*, on February 7, 1939, illustrates an important element of her voice: a sharp, biting tone. Davidman begins kindly enough: "In an age when so much verse is verbally profuse and emotionally costive, technically dazzling and stale with the pedantry of an Ezra Pound, it is sometimes refreshing to come upon a book wherein purpose and passion somewhat outrun technique." However, her pen cuts a few lines later when she dismisses some of Porter's religious poems; in particular, she says Porter's "The Lord's Supper" rises "to singular heights of silliness . . . with its comparison of a mountain to a sliced cake."[7] In correspondence with Porter later she tried to ameliorate her criticism:

> I was rather hasty in calling "The Lord's Supper" silly, I'm afraid. Looking at it now, I see it was the whole sacramental idea which annoyed me; I'm inclined by nature to call anything sacramental sentimental, being an iron materialist. As for the imagery, I've seen the mountains you speak of and I know the symbolism, but the whole philosophy of the poem is so unlike mine, and so unlike, indeed, that of

5. Dorsett, *And God Came In*, p. 11.
6. For more see "Joy Davidman and the *New Masses:* Communist Poet and Reviewer."
7. "Kansas Poet," *New Masses* 30 (February 7, 1939): 26.

your own later work, that I could wish you had followed your first impulse in not printing it.

Then she admitted her tendency toward pointed criticism: "I must tell you something about that review; it's probably the most favorable I've ever written, for the cat in me comes out in reviewing; and it was originally half of a longer review, the other part of which was devoted to a book which I boiled in oil by way of contrast. But I cut that out, attacked by an uneasy conscience because I knew the book's author" (February 19, 1939).

Davidman's open admission of her aggressive tendency to unsheathe her pen is borne out in many later movie reviews. For example, in one of her most blistering reviews she savages the World War II movie *I Wanted Wings:*

> This reviewer has always considered herself fairly articulate, yet, face to face with *I Wanted Wings*, she feels the poverty of her vocabulary. All the words that describe it adequately are unprintable. . . . [The film] makes no bones about its intentions. It is a recruiting poster in style, sentiment, and static quality. If you imagine yourself compelled to stare at such a poster for two solid hours, you will have some idea of the entertainment value of this juicy offering. . . . Using the crudest of appeals, *I Wanted Wings* alternates uplifting pep talks with uplifted blondes. . . . It is astonishing, indeed, how many women there are in the Air Corps (Hollywood version). They attend court-martials, they stroll across the field cheerfully snapping pictures of bombers, they stow away in airplanes. And they never wear any underwear, or much overwear for that matter. . . . [It] is a limping affair; you find yourself looking closely at the screen to make sure the projector hasn't stopped. There are, of course, some extremely beautiful and intelligent airplanes, that contrast favorably with the human performers. . . . If Miss Veronica Lake ever puts on a brassiere, her acting ability will disappear.[8]

In many of her letters she was similarly candid though not as caustic. For example, in one letter she complained about her life as a mother and housewife — a life that she felt was intellectually and emotionally unfulfilling:

> What I'm mad about is the prevailing notion — even Bill falls into it at times — that, because I'm a woman, it's quite correct for me to be living

8. "Rover Boys on Wings," *New Masses* 39 (April 8, 1941): 28-29.

this vegetable, parasitic life. I'm not suffering from overwork, but from a species of enforced mental and physical idleness; housework fills your time, but damn it, it doesn't make any really satisfactory demands either of your muscles or of your mind. You just get tired in a nasty, irritable sort of way. And you don't have the reward which gives productive work point, for when you have finished your housework there is nothing of any value to show for it and you start right over. In short, as Sherman did not say, socially unproductive labor is Hell. And I resent the contemptuous fashion in which the world demands no more of me — because I'm female. (January 19, 1945)

At times her voice verged on the acidic. For instance, after several letters back and forth with the Communist poet Aaron Kramer, he asked her for an honest critique of his latest poems. I doubt he was prepared for her typed, eleven-page, single-spaced, response. She begins: "If your real desire is not to do the best possible work but only to get personal self-satisfaction out of whatever work you do, then you had better not read past this paragraph." After then offering an extended critique of the philosophic, aesthetic, and literary failures of Communism, she writes:

Brace yourself, boy; here it comes. The trouble with your poetry is sheer unwillingness to get an education. . . . You seem to have little power of self-criticism. There are some fine things . . . but they are side by side with work which no one should be willing to have printed. Worse yet, you have not developed your powers of observation. You seem to regard the visible world merely as a means of making a political point. . . . All you seem able to appreciate in *any* experience is its possible political implication. This is all very well, and it is possible to be a good human being on this basis; but it is not possible to be a good poet. . . . The . . . most serious general point I want to make is that you simply do not know the English language well enough. It is not that you can't write grammatically; you can. But grammar is only the bare bones of a language. Its flesh and blood are generations of association of ideas, so that a word has not only its dictionary meaning but a whole range of emotional values, from the comic to the tragic, the grotesque to the exquisite. Words also have *class* associations; a given word or idiom may stamp you at once as proletarian, middle class, or gentleman — as literate or illiterate; as city-bred or rural, modern-minded or old-fashioned. No doubt you know this in theory. What you have not realized is that your own use of words stamps you, to the eye, say, of an intelligent college senior with a turn for literature — stamps you as a boy trying to make bluff serve instead of education. It is not because you write simply. You don't write simply. You write with an appalling variety of out-of-date bourgeois affectation; words that not even a college professor would use in speech, let alone a worker, come tumbling off your typewriter in all their mid-Victorian lushness. You are wearing the cast-off rags of bourgeois language, and you don't even know it. (January 26, 1948)

While Kramer (in follow-up letters) showed no pique at Davidman's scolding tone, the correspondence between them cooled considerably from this point forward. Her arresting, provocative, and penetrating voice is a constant throughout her correspondence, although it did soften somewhat after her conversion to Christianity.

The second aspect of her letters of note to readers concerns her religious, philosophical, and intellectual journey from secular Judaism to atheism to Communism to Christianity. In her autobiographical essay, "The Longest Way Round," she offers a very fine summary of this journey, noting in particular how disenchanted she eventually became with Communism.[9] In the early 1940s, during the high point of her Communist fervor, she joined the Communist writers' guild, the League of American Writers, and actively promoted their events. In addition, she was on the faculty of the School for Democracy, an anti-fascist, pro-Communist institution in New York City. She wrote Stephen Vincent Benét: "The League [of American Writers] wants me to ask you if you'd care to appear at [our upcoming] antiwar poetry meeting. . . . We're going on record, while we can, against America's entering the war; and we should be grateful if you would consent to read some appropriate poems of your own" (June 3, 1940).

However, by the mid-1940s Davidman rejected Communism, in large part because for the first time she read the books of Marx, Lenin, and Engels. What she found there intellectually appalled her. She wrote a fellow disaffected Communist:

I got an awful shock when I read [Lenin's] *Materialism and Empirio-Criticism*. What possesses us to offer *this* as a statement of our philoso-

9. Joy Davidman, "The Longest Way Round," in *These Found the Way: Thirteen Converts to Protestant Christianity*, ed. David Wesley Soper (Philadelphia: Westminster Press, 1951), pp. 12-26. This essay appears in this book, pp. 83-97.

phy? No wonder we can never get anywhere with educated bourgeois thinkers! The book is pathetic; merely from the standpoint of construction it is rambling, repetitious to idiocy, irrelevant; its language, probably further corrupted by the translator, is of an almost hysterical violence and bad manners. Even the jokes ain't funny; they're just insults. As for its logic, it is unbelievable; the premises are wrong, the conclusions are wrong, and they're all non sequiturs anyway. He does not seem even to have understood the point under discussion, the question of whether sensory reality can be taken as the only or the whole reality; for his whole argument *depends* on the assumption of the absoluteness of sensory reality, and that is just the thing he is supposed to prove. . . . And what is still less defensible, by God, is . . . the endless reprinting, with superstitious reverence, of books like Lenin's *Materialism,* without the slightest attempt to develop Marxism, to use it as a science instead of a revelation from Heaven! Marx-idolatry is not one whit better than Bible-idolatry. It is true that there are tremendous truths in Marx. But so are there in the Bible. The point is not to parrot them, but to *apply* them. (January 21, 1948)

Elsewhere she called Lenin's *Materialism* "surely the world's most unreadable book," exposing Marxism as "philosophically nonsensical, logically unsound, historically arbitrary, and scientifically half false" (October 31, 1948).

Davidman's most detailed explanation for why she left the Party appears in a letter thanking William Rose Benét for having published a poem, "To a Communist":[10]

> You've got it all said, all that I've been working out for myself — very painfully, very much against the grain — for the last few years. It's quite true, I'm afraid, that Marxism is just another of man's hopeless attempts to foresee and control the future, and a crystal ball would have done nearly as well. . . . I wish there were others like you, who know enough to condemn Communism on the *real* ground, that it is false. The press and the politicians resort so freely to abuse, bullying, and plain lying that it almost seems they fear in their hearts that Communism may be true! (October 31, 1948)

In this same letter she indicates that her own movement away from the Party was a direct result of "a direct and shattering experience of God,"

10. *The Saturday Review of Literature* 31 (October 23, 1948): 39.

the experience she details so memorably in "The Longest Way Round." Much of her gratitude in the letter turns upon Benét's not personally attacking lapsed Communists:

> And thank you . . . for giving us credit for our good intentions, no matter what road they paved. For almost all of us had them. I've met a few definitely paranoid Communists, and a few embittered failures, but Lord knows the majority of us were just well-meaning half-educated schlemiels, and none a bigger schlemiel than I. We knew something was wrong with the world, and knew so little else that we were ready to fall for any glib way of putting it right. Some of us had to take the Sacred Writings of Marx and Engels on superstitious trust because we couldn't understand a word of them. Others, like me, were simply too lazy to read them — until we began to wonder if they really proved the case.

Then she offers her own assessment of the CPUSA:

> [It] is nearly dead — membership somewhere under twenty thousand, and much of that in splinter groups cutting each others' throats; three or four splinters are attacking the official Party for not being pro-Russian *enough!* Some of the Party's decline is no doubt due to fear, and some to the good look at Soviet foreign policy we have been getting; whatever they've got there, it doesn't seem to be the New Jerusalem. But mostly, I think, the failure is the Marxist failure in ethics. What brought us to the Party, whether we knew it or not, was the ethic of Christ: Love your neighbor as yourself. The Party's first act was to teach us that Marx recognized only the ethic of self-interest! . . . [The] result was moral confusion — the end justifying the means, as you have pointed out, with its inevitable coarsening and corrupting effect on our characters. Our desire to teach others led to contempt of them, our sense of justice to self-righteousness, our love to hate. Most of us were absurdly gentle people physically, and yet I do not think any of us were fit to trust with power.

She ends the letter: "I knew the comrades and worked with them, and for all their unreasoning fanaticism they were good people in most ways; very good people, if you compare them to the advertising man, the Hollywood executive, the machine politician — all our Pharisees. I didn't leave them in order to run to safety, and I don't like kicking them when they're down."

In "The Longest Way Round" Davidman confesses that in her work for the *NM* she sold her intellectual, artistic, and aesthetic soul in order to support the causes of the CPUSA. She analyzes the death of *NM* in another letter to Benét: "What killed [the *NM*], incidentally was simply the entire incompetence of its editors; they didn't know there was such a thing as a technique of editing, and refused to consider the possibility of learning it. They didn't know anything about their readers and did nothing to find out; their position was that reading *New Masses* was a moral duty, so it didn't have to be interesting." And then she adds: "Since my conversion — I am now, believe it or not, a deaconess of the Presbyterian Church, and it feels odd to say the least. Oy! — since becoming a Christian, I am reveling in my new-found ability to admit my ignorance. In my old world, you just *had* to have an opinion on every conceivable subject that came up; an open mind was a moral offense. You can't imagine what a luxury it is to have no opinions where I have no evidence!" (February 1, 1949). Davidman's admission of pride and hauteur is winsome — that she connects her "new-found" humility with her conversion to Christianity "rings true" and offers compelling anecdotal evidence for the start of a genuinely transformed personality.

A third focus of the letters concerns the struggles of her marriage and the challenges of family life. While the letters do not offer a detailed chronicle of the specific reasons for the breakdown of her marriage to Bill Gresham, they do reveal that his alcoholism and infidelity were important contributing factors. Bill had been consistently sexually unfaithful during the marriage, and his alcoholism was becoming more and more problematic.[11]

Added to these strains on Davidman was the fact that her physical health was not strong in the late 1940s and early 1950s. Dorsett notes that she began to suffer from nervous exhaustion because she was trying to write enough to pay the bills while also caring for her two young boys, David and Douglas.[12] In addition, Dorsett says that she had been very ill leading up to her trip to England in 1952, that she was even hospitalized for a time, and that her doctor had ordered her to get away and rest.[13]

Recovering from illness and fed up with Bill's behavior, Davidman decided to take a break away from him by traveling to England. She also hoped to visit C. S. Lewis, with whom she had been corresponding since

11. Dorsett, *And God Came In*, pp. 55-57, 73-74, 78.
12. Dorsett, *And God Came In*, pp. 57 and 59.
13. Dorsett, *And God Came In*, pp. 79-80.

1950. Dorsett believes that she had already fallen in love with Lewis even before she sailed for England in August of 1952.[14] Just before her return, she received a letter from Bill giving her the news of his latest infidelity: he and Joy's cousin, Renée, had fallen madly in love. In his letter Bill tells Joy that he believes their marriage is effectively over:

> I can understand, I believe, what resolutions you have made about coming home and trying to make a go of our marriage. But I feel that all such decisions are sacrifices of human life on the altar of Will Power, with the women's magazine hacks serving as high priests. I have never yet know[n] will power and determination to "make a go of marriage," to take the place of love in its complete sense. I have tremendous affection for you and have certainly missed you, although I was glad that you were having fun and adventures and seeing all the things you wanted to see. But affection and intellectual camaraderie are not marriage. (late 1952 or early 1953)

Later in the letter he suggests that their lack of sexual intimacy has been a death knell to their marriage: "When physical attraction is gone from a relationship between a man and a woman, all the comradeship in the world will not bring it back, and between you and me it is gone and has been gone for years. I am more than willing to take full responsibility for this if it is a question of responsibility. But people cannot fall in love by will power and they certainly cannot fall back in love by it."

Joy, not surprisingly, was initially furious at this development, blaming Bill rather than Renée. However, she soon reconciled herself to the idea of divorce, writing to Chad Walsh:

> I always took it that divorce was only the last possible resort, and felt I ought to put up with anything I could bear for the children's sake. And I hoped that Bill's adulteries, irresponsibilities, etc. would end if he ever recovered from his various neuroses; also that his becoming a Christian would make a difference. Unfortunately I've been disappointed on both counts. Bill gave up being a Christian as soon as he found out it meant living by a moral code and admitting and repenting one's sins. . . .

---

14. Dorsett writes: "It is likely that Joy was already falling in love with C. S. Lewis. [Her cousin, Renée,] believed that [Joy] had fallen in love with Lewis's mind during their extended period of correspondence, and since Joy's marriage was a shambles, it does not require an overly active imagination to believe this" (*And God Came In*, p. 87).

There's one thing I must say in Bill's defense — my love for him died very suddenly and completely two years ago, as a result of something he did when I was seriously ill. And he knows that; and in his philosophy a marriage is over when the sexual excitement passes. Besides, he's very dependent on admiration, and it must be agonizing for him to live in the same house with a woman who neither loves nor respects him. (February 27, 1953)

The letters also reveal that after their divorce and despite what Joy saw as Bill's irresponsible and sporadic financial support of her and the boys, most often her letters to him were friendly and newsy; moreover, on a number of occasions she offered writing ideas or suggested that they collaborate on writing projects. For example, some of Joy's letters written while she and the boys were living in London vacillate between trying to understand Bill's financial situation and giving way to frustration and impatience.[15] In her letter of January 8, 1954, she wrote: "Your check for $35 came today. From what you tell me I can see that you're doing everything you can. . . . We are tightening our belts as well as we can — peanut-butter sandwiches for lunch — and making up for it at our other meals, which are provided by the house." Two months later she wrote: "Check for $25 arrived. How long is Valley Forge going to last? I am barely able to cover my expenses at this rate, and what I'm going to do about the boys' holiday I don't know. Surely you can get somewhere if you are really working and not just planning to work" (March 8, 1954).

Her frustration and genuine worry got the best of her at times, so she wrote:

Why, no, all is not well with me and the boys. How do you expect it to be, on five-dollar checks? This weekend is Davy's birthday, too; I had hoped you'd do something about that. I'm doing the best I can, and working as hard as I can. But I'm pretty near the end of my tether, Bill, and I can't stand much more of this. So far this year you've sent me about $300, or very little more. I doubt whether you've lived on as little as that. And I certainly can't support myself, let alone two children, on it. (March 25, 1954)

Eventually she threatened legal action (which she never pursued):

15. Their eventual divorce agreement stipulated that Bill would provide $60 a week in financial support.

What in Heaven's name is happening to you? I can't help fearing that you are hitting the bottle again and going completely to pieces; otherwise I cannot understand why you should fail so completely to carry out your obligations. It is hard for me to believe that you can leave your children penniless as you are doing; Heaven knows I ought to know your character, but I didn't somehow expect that. . . . I have had to give up my London place and find a cheaper one here [Oxford]; but we can't live on nothing at all. . . . I don't know what you're trying to do — force me to commit suicide or force me to bring action against you; I don't want to put you in jail, as you very well know, but you're certainly asking for it, and even my indulgence is not going to hold out forever. In short, please send some money at once. And I don't mean pennies. You are now far short of the agreed sum. Sometimes I wonder how you can bear to live with yourself at all; but I suppose you can always find some rationalization or other. (August 19, 1955)

Yet despite her frustrations with Bill, she often encouraged him to let her work with him on writing ideas. For instance, once Bill moved to Florida and started working for the magazine *All Florida,* Joy often sent him ideas for stories, features, and photographs; at one point she suggested he run a contest for writers as a way to drum up contributors for the magazine. Later she lamented: "I imagine that some of the trouble you're having in writing is the same as mine; the difficulty of breaking up a team. We were a good team; we each had what the other lacked, and I hated to dissolve it. A pity that your ego made you resent the collaboration so much" (June 26, 1954). Later she softened a bit and wrote: "If you ever feel it would be any help, don't hesitate to consult me on any plot you're having trouble with, and we can maul it over all night by air-mail! I don't kid myself in these matters — whatever my talents as an independent writer, my *real* gift is as a sort of editor-collaborator like Max Perkins, and I'm happiest when I'm doing something like that" (April 29, 1955).[16]

Fourth, Joy's letters offer insights into her developing relationship with Lewis and how she did eventually become a collaborator with him on the books he wrote during this period. Letters report on her Christmas 1952

16. See Diana Glyer, "Joy Davidman Lewis: Author, Editor and Collaborator," *Mythlore* 22 (Summer 1998): 10-17, 46; Glyer also explores the notion of collaboration among Lewis and other members of the Inklings in her *The Company They Keep: C. S. Lewis and J. R. R. Tolkien as Writers in Community* (Kent, OH: Kent State University Press, 2007).

stay at the Kilns (she says it was "a marvelous time"); Lewis's suggestions for how she could improve *Smoke on the Mountain* (Lewis serving as her collaborator and writing a preface for the English edition); her confessions to Lewis about the state of her marriage; her and the boys' Christmas 1953 stay at the Kilns ("a very relaxed and friendly visit, though physically strenuous enough"); other stays at the Kilns (in part to help ease Joy's financial worries); trips with Lewis and his brother, Warren, to Whipsnade Zoo; jokes among the three of them; how Lewis permitted her to work out of his rooms at Magdalen College, Oxford; her first meeting with J. R. R. Tolkien; and an amusing account of tea at a London hotel with Lewis, Joy, and her parents.

Of special note are her letters that offer details of Lewis's acceptance of a professorship at Cambridge and his move there. Joy attended Lewis's famous inaugural address and wrote to Bill about the event:

> Yesterday I went up to Cambridge for Jack's inaugural address — there was damn near as much fuss about that as a Coronation. I lurked modestly in the crowd and didn't go near him — he was walled about with caps and gowns and yards of recording apparatus. A great success; instead of, as usual with teachers of the humanities, talking about the continuity of culture and pleading for the traditional values, *he* tells 'em the "Old Western Culture" is quite dead, has been supplanted by a machine-culture, we are now living in "post-Christian Europe" and learning about literature from a representative of the older culture like himself is like learning about Neanderthal men *from* one or studying paleontology *from* a live dinosaur. He ended by telling them to study their dinosaur while they could; there wouldn't be any around much longer! He made a remarkably effective case (with which I do not much agree) for the *really* important historic break between cultures coming not with the fall of Rome or the Renaissance but with the rise of science as a power; I don't know how the dons liked it but the students ate it up. But I think, for once, he was sacrificing accuracy in the interests of a good show. (November 30, 1954)[17]

In her July 6, 1954, letter to Bill she mentioned for the first time how she had been assisting Lewis as a collaborator: "I've been reading Jack's autobiography [*Surprised by Joy*] in manuscript and I shan't send them to *his*

---

17. The lecture was later published as *"De Descriptione Temporum,"* in C. S. Lewis, *Selected Literary Essays* (Cambridge: Cambridge University Press, 1969).

old school, Malvern. Wow! He's as violent a satirist as Swift when he wants to be." Later letters show that she earned money doing the typescript for *Surprised by Joy*.[18] Perhaps the clearest picture of how Joy collaborated with Lewis appears in her March 23, 1955, letter to Bill, where she revealed the genesis for what became *Till We Have Faces:*

> Jack has started a new fantasy — for grownups. His methods of work amaze me. One night he was lamenting that he couldn't get a good idea for a book. We kicked a few ideas around till one came to life. Then we had another whiskey each and bounced it back and forth between us. The next day, without further planning, he wrote the first chapter! I read it and made some criticisms (feels quite like old times); he did it over and went on with the next. What I'd give to have his energy!

This letter also offers an inside view of Lewis's writing schedule: "He only writes *half* the day; the other half, he answers letters and writes lectures, which he doesn't count, and by the time *I* get up in the morning (about 8) he has like as not hauled the ashes out of all the stoves, dumped them outside, and gone off to early service. I begin to see the force of your contention that what a writer chiefly needs is a strong back!" A month later she wrote Bill: "Though I can't write one-tenth as well as Jack, I can tell him how to write more like himself! He is now about three-quarters of the way through his new book (what I'd give for that energy!) and says he finds my advice indispensable. Well, it's a very suitable gift for a woman" (April 29, 1955). Joy may also have influenced Lewis's writing of *Reflections on the Psalms*[19] and *The Four Loves*.[20]

The last focus of her letters reveals her physical, mental, emotional, and spiritual state as she battled cancer and other health problems. Joy suffered from serious problems with her teeth almost from her first days in England, but because of the national health system she was able to have her dental work done almost for free; this was a Godsend given her scant financial support from Bill. She also was treated on numerous occasions for thyroid problems. She wrote Bill: "Was round to the thyroid clinic yester-

18. C. S. Lewis, *Surprised by Joy: The Shape of My Early Life* (London: Geoffrey Bles, 1955).

19. C. S. Lewis, *Reflections on the Psalms* (London: Geoffrey Bles, 1958); see Davidman's letters of June 6, 1957; February 4, 1958; and October 29, 1958.

20. C. S. Lewis, *The Four Loves* (London: Geoffrey Bles, 1960).

day; it took five hours — conference with *eight* doctors, two of 'em as famous thyroid men as exist, all poking and prodding me in the eye and neck and elsewhere. Much edified by my original symptoms and the fact that the radium collar hadn't burned me; apparently they've quite given it up here and most people were scarred by it. General conclusion, I'm hypothyroid!" (May 19, 1954). When Bill writes later and tells her his cataract is being treated with radium, she replies: "Nearly twenty years ago I had Dee Ray [radium] all over my face for sinuses, and the eyes still work. Altogether I now regard radium as something to stay away from; you should have heard the thyroid specialists in the London clinic when I told 'em how I'd been treated" (September 13, 1956).

Joy's worst fears about her earlier radium treatment were realized only five weeks later. She wrote Bill and told him of the ordeal that led her to be admitted to Wingfield Hospital, Headington, Oxford, on October 19, 1956:

> I have got something really hellish the matter with my left hip and am being carted off to the hospital this afternoon on a stretcher. I've been increasingly lame for a long time but could walk painfully till last night. Then I fell and wrenched the leg, and now can not use it at all — can only move it with great pain. . . . *But* the prospects are not good. I shan't know definitely for a few days, till they get finished with blood cultures and urine tests. But the X-rays showed the bone looking "moth-eaten" — and they are talking of carcinomas or leukemia. In short, it is fairly probable that I am going to die. I am only moderately afraid for myself. I've been very tired for a long time. But I am alarmed for the boys (I have told them nothing yet, of course). My will appoints Jack and his lawyer as their guardians, and I think it is essential for them to finish their education here — a break now would upset them irreparably. Jack has promised to see to their schooling, and of course I know you will contribute what you can. *Please, please* don't try to get them back to the States.

This crisis was the catalyst for Joy to write for the first time about her civil wedding to Lewis, which had occurred on April 23, 1956, telling Walsh: "One good thing has come of all this — I can now tell you that Jack and I are married; have been for a few months, and are going to publish an announcement soon. When I come out of here I shall go to the Kilns as Mrs. Lewis" (December 3, 1956).

Although Joy knew her condition was extremely serious, she initially tried to put the best face forward, writing in the same letter: "There were three bad days of vomiting after the op. during which physical agony was combined with a strange spiritual ecstasy; I think I know now how martyrs felt. All this has strengthened my faith and brought me very close to God — as if at last I knew all the answers. Jack is terribly upset himself partly because of a lifelong horror of cancer; but he's recovering a bit now." Yet she did have some dark moments, writing Walsh two months later:

> I am in rather a bad state of mind as yet — they had promised me definitely that the X-rays would work; I'd pinned all my hopes to having a year or so of happiness with Jack at least — and instead it seems I shall lie about in hospital with my broken femur waiting for death, and unable to do anything to make my last shreds of life useful or bearable. I am trying very hard to hold on to my faith, but I find it difficult; there seems such a gratuitous and merciless cruelty in this. I hope that all we have believed is true. I dare not hope for anything in *this* world. Miracles may happen, but we mustn't count on them. The worst of it is, I feel perfectly well aside from mild intermittent pain in the leg. I fear all this will be horribly depressing for you; I shall go on praying for the grace to endure whatever I must endure, and perhaps I'll be more cheerful next time I write. Jack is terribly broken-up. How horrible that I, who wanted to bring him only happiness, should have brought him this! Perhaps it would have better for him if he'd never known me, though he says not. (February 5, 1957)

However, only a week later Joy accepted her condition, readied herself for what might be an early death, and reconciled herself to God's will:

> Everything looks much brighter than it did before. For one thing my prayers for grace have been answered. I feel now that I can bear not too unhappily what is to come, and the problem of pain just doesn't loom so large. I'm not at all sure I didn't deserve it after all, and I'm pretty sure that in some way I need it. . . . Jack pointed out to me that we were wrong in trying to accept utter hopelessness; uncertainty is what God has given us for a cross. And from the questions I ask, it does seem that no one really knows what this cancer will do next; the leg cancer is not *of itself* likely to kill me, though others may — and no others have made themselves known as yet. What I dreaded most, lying helpless in hospital for months or years waiting for it, we can avoid. I'll get up, by the aid of will-power and sweat and grace; and if God will let me, I shall walk.

Our family doctor, Humphrey, had been talking to me before I wrote last time; and after a chat with him you always want to rush out and order your coffin. He lost *his* wife by cancer and always takes the darkest view, but even he admitted there was no knowing. (February 13, 1957)

She also added in the letter: "I was very merry last weekend and Jack and I had a gay time in my room with lots of sherry and kisses. *What* a pity I didn't catch that man younger."

Her use of the word "gay" to describe her relationship with Lewis during this otherwise grim time is consistent with Lewis's own account; he wrote Walsh: "You wd. hardly believe how much happiness, not to say *gaiety*, we have together — a honeymoon on a sinking ship" (February 13, 1957).[21] Later Lewis told Dorothy L. Sayers, "my heart is breaking and I was never so happy before: at any rate there is more in life than I knew about" (June 25, 1957).[22] To another correspondent he positively gushed: "We are crazily in love" (July 9, 1957).[23] Joy's letters also document her "second" marriage to Lewis and the well-known service of healing performed by the man who married them, the Rev. Peter Bide. For two and a half years Joy's cancer went into remission, and they enjoyed a happy and comfortable time, including trips to Ireland and Greece. Joy's letters in early 1960 show that her cancer returned with a vengeance, and she died on July 13, 1960, ironically almost coinciding with a visit to England by Bill; in fact, Lewis wrote Bill on July 15, 1960: "Joy died on the 13th July. This need involve no change in your plans, but I thought you should arrive knowing it."[24]

Many other matters are covered by her letters: her own writing projects after her move to England, her drive to find the best possible boarding school for her sons, her initial infatuation but eventual disaffection with dianetics (Bill remained convinced of its value), her cordial relationship with Renée, her love of all things British, her impatience with American politics (and President Eisenhower in particular), and especially her genuine affection for Warren and concern over his alcoholism. There is one aspect of the letters, however, that readers should not expect to find — there

21. C. S. Lewis, *Collected Letters: Volume 3, Narnia, Cambridge, and Joy, 1950-1963*, ed. Walter Hooper (London: HarperCollins, 2006), p. 832; hereafter CL, 3.

22. Lewis, CL, 3, p. 862.

23. Lewis, CL, 3, p. 867.

24. Lewis, CL, 3, p. 1170.

are few letters from Davidman to Lewis or from Lewis to Davidman. Lewis was notorious for not saving letters (he tried to burn the letters sent him three weeks or so after he received them), and most of Lewis's letters to Davidman have not survived.

Finally, Joy Davidman's letters help correct what I believe has become a mistaken view of her: the perception that she was predatory in her pursuit of and eventual marriage to Lewis. For some time now I have been surprised at the negative attitude otherwise compassionate Lewis devotees adopt with regard to Joy; perhaps they are suspicious of her Communist background, embarrassed by her New York brashness, or upset by her winning Lewis's heart. This negative attitude, combined with the fact that most of Lewis's friends did not have many kind things to say about Joy, has relegated Joy to the status of an interloper in the minds of many. This issue deserves more discussion than I can devote to it here, so I will limit myself to the most obvious counterargument — Lewis and his brother Warren absolutely adored Joy. Both men had spent their lifetimes developing very circumspect attitudes toward women, so I find it hard to believe that they were somehow tricked or deceived by Joy. I believe we need to take a more gracious view of Joy than has been granted in the past, seeing her as the woman Lewis loved willingly, completely, and passionately.

I also hope that publishing Joy's letters will bring her more critical acclaim than she currently enjoys. She was a gifted writer in many regards, and her letters are articulate, insightful, and fascinating. They not only supplement what we know of her relationship with Lewis through his own letters and Dorsett's *And God Came In,* but they also reveal a woman who was philosophically informed, intellectually brilliant, and, as a Christian, spiritually perceptive. *Poi si tornò all' eternal fontana.*[25]

---

25. This is the last line of C. S. Lewis, *A Grief Observed* (London: Faber and Faber, 1961), p. 60. It comes from Dante's *Paradiso,* Canto XXXI, 30, and may be translated thus: "Then she turned herself back toward the eternal fountain."

Chronology of Joy Davidman's Life (1915–1960)

April 18, 1915. Helen Joy Davidman is born to Joseph and Jeannette Davidman.

1919. Joy's brother Howard is born.

Joy is brought up in and around New York City with summer vacations to Maine and other New England sites.

By age 12 she is an atheist and a writer.

As a young teenager she suffers from early thyroid problems and is treated with a radium-laced collar that she wears to bed.

1929. Joy finishes high school at age 14.

1930. She matriculates at Hunter College in 1930 and becomes an associate editor for the *Echo,* the college's literary magazine.

1934. She graduates from Hunter College, begins teaching English in local high schools, and matriculates at Columbia University for an MA in English.

1935. She earns her MA from Columbia University.

1936. She continues high school teaching and publishes poems in the important literary journal, *Poetry.*

1938. Joy's volume of poetry, *Letter to a Comrade,* is published to favorable reviews and wins the Russell Loines Memorial award for poetry given by the National Institute of Arts and Letters. Also, after several abortive attempts, she joins the Communist Party of the United States of America (CPUSA) and throws herself into the cause as an editor for its magazine, *New Masses.* She spends the summer at the MacDowell Colony, a writers' retreat in New Hampshire; she returns there in the summers of 1940, 1941, and 1942.

1939. She moves for six months to Hollywood in a failed effort at writing screenplays.

1940. Her novel *Anya* is published.

1941-1943. Her poetry and reviews are appearing almost weekly in the *New Masses.*

1942. She meets William Lindsay Gresham; they are married near the MacDowell Colony on August 2, 1942.

1943. She edits and publishes the *War Poems of the United Nations,* a collection of poems with a strong pro-Communism bias.

March 27, 1944. David Gresham is born; Joy is gradually becoming disillusioned with Communism.

November 10, 1945. Douglas Gresham is born.

1946. Bill Gresham publishes the very successful novel *Nightmare Alley;* using some of the proceeds, Joy and Bill purchase a large farmhouse in New York; Joy is no longer active in the CPUSA. Also, she has a mystical experience that leads her from atheism to theism.

1947. Joy begins reading books by C. S. Lewis and eventually converts to Christianity.

1948. She becomes a member of the Pleasant Plains Presbyterian Church.

1949. She begins corresponding with Chad Walsh; Bill Gresham publishes his second novel, *Limbo Tower.*

January 10, 1950. C. S. Lewis receives his first letter from Joy.

1950. Joy's novel *Weeping Bay* is published.

1951. The autobiographical essay of her conversion, "The Longest Way Round," is published.

August 1952. Her marriage to Bill falling apart, Joy sails for England to visit friends and to meet Lewis.

September 24, 1952. She meets and has lunch with Lewis.

Christmas 1952. She spends Christmas with Lewis and his brother, Warren, at their home near Oxford, the Kilns.

January 1953. She returns to New York and to the eventual breakup of her marriage to Bill.

February 1953. She becomes a member of the Episcopal Church.

November 1953. Joy and her sons arrive in London; Joy believes they can live more cheaply in England than in New York.

Christmas 1953. Lewis and Warren invite the three to spend the holidays at the Kilns.

For the next eighteen months Joy and the boys eke out an existence in London, with the boys going to a boarding school. At the same time, Joy and Lewis spend a good deal of time together; he loves her wit, intellect, sense of humor, and sharp mind.

1954. She publishes *Smoke on the Mountain: An Interpretation of the Ten Commandments*.

August 1955. Joy, probably with help from Lewis, rents a house in Headington, about a mile from the Kilns.

September 13, 1955. Lewis writes his lifelong friend Arthur Greeves that he is thinking of marrying Joy in a civil ceremony.

April 23, 1956. Lewis marries Joy in a civil ceremony; they live separately.

October 18, 1956. Joy falls when her left femur snaps; she is told that she has advanced cancer and that it has spread throughout her body.

December 24, 1956. Lewis makes a public announcement of his marriage to Joy in *The Times*; Joy begins to live at the Kilns.

Lewis, now completely in love with Joy, asks the Bishop of Oxford to conduct a religious wedding; he refuses. In desperation, Lewis asks a former pupil and Anglican priest, Peter Bide, to come to the hospital and offer a prayer of healing; while there Lewis asks Bide to marry them; Bide agrees and marries them in the hospital on March 21, 1957.

Joy recovers, and for the better part of two and a half years they experience real happiness.

July 1958. Lewis and Joy take a wonderful trip by plane to Ireland.

December 1959. Joy's cancer begins to return.

April 3-14, 1960. Lewis and Joy take another delightful trip, this time to Greece.

May 20, 1960. Joy's cancer returns with a vengeance. She is hospitalized again.

July 13, 1960. Joy dies. Lewis later writes a friend: "I never expected to have in my sixties, the happiness that passed me by in my twenties."

September 1962. Bill Gresham dies.

November 22, 1963. Lewis dies peacefully, the same day that John F. Kennedy is fatally wounded in Dallas.

Poet, Zealot, Critic

Letters 1936–1946

To Stephen Vincent Benét[1]

2277 Andrews Avenue
New York, N.Y.
August 18, 1936

Mr. Stephen Vincent Benét
220 East 69th Street
New York, N.Y.

My dear Mr. Benét:

    I did not receive your letter discussing my manuscript *Ashes and Sparks* until my recent return from a vacation trip, and therefore there has been some delay in answering on my part; but I am very glad you thought highly of my work, and I should like to thank you for your encouragement.[2] You mention the influences which have affected my poetry (among which your own is not lacking); I am somewhat uneasily con-

---

1. American writer Stephen Vincent Benét (1898-1943) published poetry, including *Heavens and Earth: A Book of Poems* (1920); novels, including *Young People's Pride* (1922), *Spanish Bayonet* (1926), and *The Devil and Daniel Webster* (1937); and short stories, including *Thirteen O'Clock: Stories of Several Worlds* (1937). His narrative poem about the American Civil War, *John Brown's Body* (1928), won the Pulitzer Prize for poetry in 1929. He provided Davidman invaluable critical advice and later wrote the foreword to her *Letter to a Comrade* (New Haven: Yale University Press, 1938).

2. *Ashes and Sparks* has not survived; it was likely an early version of *Letter to a Comrade*.

I

scious of them nowadays, yet I feel they are fading rapidly from my more ambitious work.

If I am still unpublished in two years' time, I shall take advantage of your invitation to submit another manuscript for the Yale Series of Younger Poets, and I trust I shall then send a manuscript more worthy of your consideration.[3] I'll not weary you with any more conclusion than to say again I am grateful.

Yours very truly,
Joy Davidman

Source: Yale

It was about this time that Davidman decided to join the Communist Party of the United States of America (CPUSA). Joining was not as easy as she thought. According to Oliver Pilat, she first joined the CPUSA at a large meeting of a downtown West Side branch: "The ceremony verged on the casual. The chairman intoned: 'Any new members, any outsiders?'" Davidman and several others took the oath; she waited for something to happen, but no one from the Party contacted her. She took the oath again during a big Communist rally in Madison Square Garden, but again she heard nothing from Party officials. Still determined, she made a third attempt at a branch meeting on lower Fifth Avenue and finally received her membership card in 1938.[4]

3. The Yale Younger Poets prize, established in 1919, is the oldest annual literary award in the United States. The competition is open to any American under forty years of age who has not previously published a volume of poetry. Other notable winners include James Agee, Muriel Rukeyser, Margaret Walker, Adrienne Rich, William Meredith, W. S. Merwin, John Ashbery, John Hollander, James Tate, and Carolyn Forché.

4. For more, see Oliver Pilat, "Girl Communist [Joy Davidman]: An Intimate Story of Eight Years in the Party," *The New York Post*, October 31; November 1-4, 6-11, and 13, 1949 (here November 2).

To Stephen Vincent Benét

1950 Andrews Avenue
New York, N.Y.
April 2, 1938

Dear Mr. Benét,
   I have to thank you not only for your very kind letter of recommendation but also for something more subtle. When one is beset with rejection slips and tormented by distrust of one's work and ability, it is a comforting thing to receive encouragement from a man who knows. And so I am very grateful for your letter; it will justify the sunny moments in which I tell myself how good I am.

Yours truly,
Joy Davidman   *Source: Yale*

To the Editor of the Yale Series of Younger Poets

1950 Andrews Avenue
New York, N.Y.
April 2, 1938

Editor, Yale Series of Younger Poets
Yale University Press
New Haven, Connecticut

Dear Sir:
   I am enclosing a manuscript which I wish to enter in the Yale Series of Younger Poets competition.[5] I am not quite twenty-three years old and have never published a volume of poetry.
   The poems "Resurrection" and "Shadow Dance" have appeared in *Poetry: A Magazine of Verse;* "Spartacus 1938," "Prayer against Barrenness," and "Apology for Liberals" are scheduled to appear at any mo-

---

5. The manuscript version has not survived.

ment in the *New Masses*.[6] No other poems included here have been published.[7]

Yours truly,
Joy Davidman

LETTER TO A COMRADE

Table of Contents

6. *New Masses* (1926-48), the semi-official weekly magazine of the CPUSA, was the literary descendant of two radical periodicals: *Masses* (1911-18) and *The Liberator* (1918-24). Davidman contributed poetry, was poetry editor, and reviewed books, theater productions, and films for *New Masses* 1938-46. For more on this see my "Joy Davidman and the *New Masses:* Communist Poet and Reviewer," *The Chronicle of the Oxford C. S. Lewis Society* 4, no. 1 (February 2007): 18-44.

7. The poems she mentions here were published as follows: "Resurrection," *Poetry* 47 (January 1936): 193-94; "Shadow Dance," *Poetry* 49 (March 1937): 326; "Spartacus — 1938," *New Masses* 27 (May 24, 1938): 19; "Prayer against Barrenness" appeared as "Prayer against Indifference," *New Masses* 28 (August 9, 1938): 17; "Apology for Liberals," *New Masses* 28 (August 16, 1938): 4.

8. Not included in the final version of *Letter to a Comrade*. See her letter of July 25, 1938. The poem is published below for the first time.

9. Not included in the final version of *Letter to a Comrade*. See her letter of July 25, 1938. The poem is published below for the first time.

10. Not included in the final version of *Letter to a Comrade*. See her letter of July 25, 1938.

11. Not included in the final version of *Letter to a Comrade*. See her letter of July 25, 1938; the version printed below on pp. 6–7 is a variant of the version printed in *Poetry* (see n. 7 above).

12. Not included in the final version of *Letter to a Comrade*. The poem is published below for the first time. See her letter of July 25, 1938. Appearing in *Letter to a Comrade* but not in the Table of Contents as given above are six poems: "Survey Mankind," "Sorceress Eclogue," "Near Catalonia" (this also appeared in *New Masses* 29 [October 18, 1938]: 18), "Totentanz," "Againrising," and "Waltzing Mouse."

ARTIFICERS[13]

Cellini made a drinking cup
So fine that from it no one drinks;
Fluted the gold and curled it up,
And set thereon a woman sphinx.

He gave her glitters for her eyes,
Tinseled her skin instead of fur,
Painted her mouth both warm and wise;
The gold is none too good for her.

I will take bronze and make your face,
Or I will carve you out of tree,
And what you have of fire and grace,
That shall you have eternally.

Cellini made his lover small
To grace a cardinal his meat;
But I will build you tall, so tall
The world shall froth about your feet,

And I will paint you on the sky
And set you shining in the air,
And men shall come to read your eye
Or guess the meanings of your hair,

And you shall admirably stand
For other loves, other times,
Gold and immortal from my hand;
All this I give you in my rhymes.

RESURRECTION

Pain cannot contrive for you
Humility beyond your own,
Stripped of your body to the bone;
Passion will not weave anew

13. Not included in the final version of *Letter to a Comrade*. The poem is published here for the first time. See her letter of July 26, 1938.

A fabric more than skeletal
To veil the candor of your skull.

Fire and anger let you rest;
The wind comes where your lips are mute,
Blowing a labyrinthine flute
Out of the caverns of your breast;
Fire and agony depart
From fallen ashes of a heart.

Symbols for the celebrant
Are your sharp and silver feet,
Syllables he shall repeat;
And your light bones lie aslant
Across the sacred shape of days
Carved an eidolon of your praise.

This is the kingdom that you find
When the brave empty eyeholes stare
Impartially against the air;
A little universe defined
By infinite white ribs for bars
Against the struggles of the stars.

This is the power that you hold
Over these worlds of splintered sand;
Your crystal framework of a hand
Can crumple space in hollow cold,
And your small broken fingers roll
The seven heavens in a scroll.

This is the glory that you have;
The broad sun standing overhead
To shape a halo for your head;
Out of the satiated grave
You shine across the fields of breath,
Inviolable lovely death.

Stars of the cold septentrion
Fashion you a diadem;

What is your desire of them?
The planet you arise upon
Lies a jewel at your feet;
Is the taste of kingdom sweet?

Around your finger for a ring
The living seas are lightly curled,
Silver sorrows of a world;
Power is a pleasant thing!
Paint the northern lights to make
A flower of glory for your sake!

Receive the rainbows and the spheres;
Receive the crown for which you cried
Before the slight soul wept and died;
Receive the laughter of the years,
Bestowing lands of living sun
Upon the risen skeleton.

I POET

Cruel bladed words
Wheel in my head;
Wings and swords
And purple blood.

Ever and again the seagull
Falls spread and screaming;
Forever the Roman eagle
Lifts a fierce gleaming.

High stars go over
Silver as death;
Deadly birds hover
To eat my breath.

Wars long since fought
Make splendors and spells;
I keep in my thought
A place of skulls.

WITCH IN THE CITY

Incessant rooftops to the sky
Spatter their insensate cry
Where the planets circling sing;
There on evanescent wing
Miracles of silver and steel
Unimaginably reel
Over cloud and under sun
Till the yellow day is gone.
Then the moon alight and thin,
Fish with an enchanted fin,
Swims into a starry mesh,
Luring soul and loosing flesh
Till the body is of air
Garlanded with comet's hair;
Till the spirit may endure
Images that flower obscure
Over facets of the brain;
Strange concrete of joy and pain,
Hooded horrors out of night;
Then the streets are waste and white,
Pallid doorways to a tomb,
Then apparelled in the gloom
My enfranchised ghost shall fly
Painting death across the sky.

ENDYMION

The upright forest closes
My journey in with bars;
The format night opposes
Geometry of stars

To my intense unreason;
And the wind weaves
An unrelenting prison
With the black shapes of leaves.

Like ghosts in wizard cages,
Entangled in a rune,
My captive spirit rages
And cannot find the moon.

SHADOW DANCE

The hurtful power of flesh
Lends your desire a mesh
And your hatred a blade;
You lunge, where unafraid
I flash and evade.

So you will swirl your net,
Intent to set
Strong toils about my head
And strike me dead,
Who presently am fled

Shifty as little sand
Blown from a closed hand;
Too lunar and thin
To fix upon a pin,
My trophy skin

Will not adorn a wall;
You cast your net, and fall;
Now admirably strain
At the slim noose of pain;
You will not fight again.

GENETRIX[14]

I shall have the making of you in my hands,
I shall make you over again;
I shall breed your body out of the pain of my womb
and put my flesh with it to make it wise.

14. Not included in the final version of *Letter to a Comrade*. The poem is published here for the first time. See her letter of July 26, 1938.

And you shall have again the shape of your head
and the strength crouching in the corners of your eyes.

I shall put your bones together, one by one,
and set your heart beating in the midst of all
and the mouth shall be you that plucks at my breast;
you will live in the eyesockets, and you shall be
a laughter, a small noise, a wordless happiness
closed in my arm, loving my breast and me.

These are your fingers I have joined together;
these are your hands that I have made with care,
these are your feet made new by my love.
Man, you are a new creature, dear and wild
with your new thoughts and your familiar hair,
and being my lover, you shall be my child.   *Source: Yale*

To Stephen Vincent Benét

MacDowell Colony[15]
Peterboro, N.H.
July 21, 1938

Dear Mr. Benét,

I am sending you eight new poems for inclusion in the manuscript. I do not remember whether the original volume contained two poems entitled "Near Catalonia" and "For the Revolution"; if not, I should like to include them. I shall probably cut considerable old work out as soon as I see the table of contents, so there will be room.

I have been thinking hard about the question of a title; I quite see the limitations of *Letter to a Comrade*. But the only other possibilities that occur to me are *In Praise of Iron* and the titles of two poems: "Survey Mankind" and "Waltzing Mouse." I do not like any of these, and I have been wondering if you could help me out by suggesting a suitable name for the book.

---

15. The MacDowell Colony, established in 1907, exists "to nurture the arts by offering creative individuals of the highest talent an inspiring environment in which to produce enduring works of the imagination" (see http://www.macdowellcolony.org). Davidman spent time there in the summers of 1938, 1940, 1941, and 1942.

I don't think it is necessary to divide the book into sections. A question which puzzles me is this; do I have to write to the editors of *Poetry* and the *New Masses* to get their permission to reprint?

The dedication of the book I should like to run as follows:

To

ERNST THAELMANN

who will not know.[16]

I am sorry to give you so much trouble, but you know I am quite inexperienced in these things and need a good deal of assistance.

Yours truly,
Joy Davidman   *Source: Yale*

To Stephen Vincent Benét

MacDowell Colony
Peterboro, N.H.
July 25, 1938

Dear Mr. Benét:

I find that without trying to I agree with you about "Witch in the City," "Endymion," "Shadow Dance," "Resurrection," and "I Poet." By all means leave them out. They are all, I am glad to say, early work; "Resurrection," for instance, was done when I was eighteen, and I suppose it was sentimental affection that prompted me to include it. I am sending you so much additional work — I have written thirty poems since submitting the manuscript — that I wish I could find more of the old stuff that I don't like at all. If I am overcrowding the book, you might also take out the two sonnets and "Obsession."[17]

I trust you've received, by now, the manuscript I forwarded the other day. You'll find two more poems I should like to add in this envelope. I

---

16. Ernest Thaelmann (1886-1944), born in Hamburg, Germany, helped form the German Communist Party in 1920. A fierce anti-fascist, he publicly opposed Nazism, was arrested by the Gestapo in 1933, and was executed in Buchenwald concentration camp on August 18, 1944.

17. Two sonnets, "This Woman" (p. 54) and "An Absolution" (p. 92), as well as "Obsession" (p. 57), appear in *Letter to a Comrade*.

forgot to mention, in my previous letters, that "And Pilate Said" has to be dedicated to Basil Rathbone.[18]

The proofs had best go to my New York address; if I am still at the Colony — I shall stay till September — they will be forwarded. I'm still racking my brains over titles; how about *Bitter Shouting*?

Thank you, once again, for the things you say about my work.

Yours truly,
Joy Davidman

Source: Yale

To Stephen Vincent Benét

MacDowell Colony
Peterboro, N.H.
July 26, 1938

Dear Mr. Benét:

Thank you very much for the preface, which, speechless with pride, I have been showing to my friends here.[19] I do not think any more could be said for my poetry than you have done. I am glad you prefer the original title, for I find myself unable to think of the book by any other.

And I am very glad of what you say about "Twentieth Century Americanism"; you have put in *a few* words exactly what I was trying to do, and I did not know whether I had accomplished it.[20] You are right too about "Artificers"; I think the Elinor Wylie poem was consciously in my mind as I wrote it.[21] If you think it should be left out, I wish you would take it out; that goes for "Genetrix" too. I am sending you a revised table of contents, and I should like to give you a free hand in making any rearrangements or omissions you think necessary.

18. "And Pilate Said" (p. 89), with the dedication, appears in *Letter to a Comrade*. South African actor Basil Rathbone (1892-1967) appeared on stage and in many movies; he was best known for his film portrayals of Sherlock Holmes.

19. See "Foreword" (pp. 7-9) in *Letter to a Comrade*. The opening line is: "Here is what an intelligent, sensitive, and vivid mind thinks about itself and the things of the modern world."

20. The poem appears in *Letter to a Comrade*, pp. 25-28.

21. American poet and novelist Elinor Wylie (1885-1928) later married William Rose Benét, the brother of Stephen Vincent Benét.

Never mind about the title I suggested yesterday; I don't like it. And thank you for your good wishes about the novel; it's practically done.

Yours truly,
Joy Davidman

Source: Yale

To James B. Still[22]

1950 Andrews Avenue
New York, N.Y.
September 1, 1938

Dear Jim,

I want to tell you how much I liked your story in the *[Saturday Evening] Post* this week.[23] You know it was, except for the poem you showed me, the first thing of yours I had read. But it was not a surprise to me; somehow I expected you to write like that, with that admirable trick of understatement and quiet strength and precision of detail. I understand now what you meant when you described the time you spent over each sentence. There wasn't a bit of casual description in the story you hadn't thought about and made a part of the whole. I wish I could do so much with so few words; I'm apt to splash colors about like an impressionist painter.

As you can see, I'm home now; I hope you are, and that you'll write me. New York, much as I love it, doesn't keep me yet from missing the [MacDowell] Colony. Those last two weeks or so, after you left, I didn't do much work except for finishing my play and two or three poems;[24] but I had a high time improving my beer-drinking and sitting for my portrait. Charlotte Blass did it; and it came out very well — a sort of female Thinker brooding over beer.[25] (For the record, may I add that I never got drunk?)

Have you heard from John Fletcher?[26] Charlie May sent me one let-

22. James B. Still (1906-2001) was a poet, short story writer, and novelist who lived most of his life in Knott County, Kentucky. He and Davidman met while attending the MacDowell Colony together in the summer of 1938.
23. "Bat Flight," *Saturday Evening Post* 211, no. 10 (September 3, 1938): 12-13, 50-51.
24. The play has not survived.
25. The portrait has not survived.
26. John Gould Fletcher (1886-1950) was an American imagist poet profoundly influ-

ter, and then the heat must have got her; I haven't heard since.[27] I was feeling rather sour the morning I answered her, however, and my letter must have been a masterpiece of unstrung nerves. I think I'll write again with better grammar and self-control. If you're in touch with John at all, remember me to him, will you?

Do you remember our pet detestation, Barbara? She complained to me after you'd gone that you hadn't seemed to like her; seemed quite upset about it. She said she'd had a real talk with you on the last day, however. I got to like her better later, though she never stopped being a strain on my nerves. That vitality of hers was real I guess; it was merely that her idea of life was giving everyone a noisy good time with no chance to think. Anyhow, she had a sort of generous ease which most of the men got to like a lot. She never stepped on anybody's pet corns because she hadn't the subtlety to see that sore spots were there. In short, she wasn't an artist, and most of the artists were grateful.

I don't think there were any big Colony happenings you missed. Jeff Levy — do you remember him? — rounded out the season neatly by sprinting to breakfast, slipping on a pebble, wrenching an arm and breaking his ankle in two places. He became a pale and interesting invalid and was shoveled out of the Colony. Otherwise, no major events.

Good Lord, Jim! What awful prose style I've used in this letter! I should adopt your carefulness   only I am so lazy that then I'd never write letters at all. Send me an answer, anyhow!

Sincerely,
Joy Davidman   *Source: UK*

Letter to a Comrade *won the Yale Younger Poets Award for 1938 and the Russell Loines Prize for poetry given by the National Institute of Arts and Letters for 1939.*[28]

---

enced by post-impressionist art and music. His *Selected Poems* won the Pulitzer Prize in 1939.

27. Charlie May Hogue Simon was Fletcher's second wife.

28. For reviews of *Letter to a Comrade,* see R. P. Blackmur, "Nine Poets," *Partisan Review,* Winter 1939, p. 112; Dorothy Emerson, "Three Young Poets," *Scholastic* 34 (May 27, 1939): 27E; Desmond Hawkins, Review of Joy Davidman's *Letter to a Comrade, Spectator* 162 (May 19, 1939): 868; Ruth Lechlitner, Review of Joy Davidman's *Letter to a Comrade, New York Herald Tribune Books,* December 25, 1938, p. 2; C. A. Millspaugh, "Among the New

To William Rose Benét[29]

1950 Andrews Avenue
New York, N.Y.
February 8, 1939

Dear Bill,

Thanks for the congrats — I have bought Charlotte's picture of me with some of the award and everybody's happy except my friends the Yale Press — did you ever see a Press weeping? Something like [an] elephant with toothache [drawing of weeping elephant with toothache inserted and the words: "Tuskache (not as nice as yours but recognizable I hope"]. All the tears are on account of *[The] Saturday Review [of Literature]* not reviewing me, says the Yale Press, and would I write you a tearful letter?[30]

Could you come to [a] concert at Town Hall with me next Tuesday night? We've got to sit in a box and impress the audience and you'd look beautiful in a box.

Joy   *Source: Yale*

To Kenneth W. Porter[31]

1950 Andrews Avenue
New York, N.Y.
February 19, 1939

Dear Mr. Porter,

I was rather hasty in calling "The Lord's Supper" silly, I'm afraid.

Books of Verse," *Kenyon Review* 2 (1940): 363; Review of Joy Davidman's *Letter to a Comrade, Times Literary Supplement* [London], October 14, 1939, p. 599; Muriel Rukeyser, Review of Joy Davidman's *Letter to a Comrade, New Republic* 98 (March 8, 1939): 146; Dorothy Ulrich, Review of Joy Davidman's *Letter to a Comrade, New York Times Book Review*, August 6, 1939, p. 4; and Oscar Williams, Review of Joy Davidman's *Letter to a Comrade, Poetry* 54 (April 1939): 33.

29. William Rose Benét (1886-1950), along with several others, established the *Saturday Review of Literature* in 1924. He was a prolific writer, and his book of autobiographical verse, *The Dust Which Is God* (1941), won a Pulitzer Prize for poetry in 1942.

30. Here the letter contains Davidman's drawing of her face weeping.

31. Kenneth W. Porter (1905-1981) was a poet and historian.

Looking at it now, I see it was the whole sacramental idea which annoyed me; I'm inclined by nature to call anything sacramental sentimental, being an iron materialist.[32] As for the imagery, I've seen the mountains you speak of and I know the symbolism, but the whole philosophy of the poem is so unlike mine, and so unlike, indeed, that of your own later work, that I could wish you had followed your first impulse in not printing it.[33] I put some in my own book which now rise appallingly to haunt me, and I should have done worse if Stephen Benét hadn't (bless him) sternly taken the horrors out.[34]

Isn't it an embarrassment to you, even more than it is to me (most of whose work is the creation of three years) to find your early ideas contradicting the later ones in the shape of verse? I think I said something in my review about the contrast between the ironic force of your "social" poems with the simple sensuousness of some of the others; a contrast particularly interesting to me since I have changed in the same way.[35] As recently as

32. Davidman is referring to her book review of Porter's *The High Plains* (New York: The John Day Co., 1938), "Kansas Poet," *New Masses* 30 (February 7, 1939): 26-27.

33. Here is Porter's "The Lord's Supper" (*The High Plains*, p. 37):

We have received our daily bread,
and now our souls as well are fed.

A mountain, like a half-sliced cake,
rests on the tray of a silver lake,

and for a napkin, crisp and white,
linen He wove of snow last night.

A blue grape on a heavenly vine,
Sky will serve us airy wine.

Our souls now know a great content:
we have received the Sacrament.

34. In an April 2, 1981, letter to Chad Walsh, Porter writes: "Ms. Davidman was, I think, rather too generous in her epistolary comments. Her reasons, as given in her letter, for objecting to 'The Lord's Supper' are illuminative of her views at the time, but although the poem may not have been 'silly' — the adjective she withdrew — it simply was not a very good poem without, perhaps, being positively bad and I *shouldn't* have included it. I had no editor like Steve Benét" (source: Wade).

35. In her review she had written:

In an age when so much verse is verbally profuse and emotionally costive, technically dazzling and stale with the pedantry of an Ezra Pound, it is sometimes refreshing to come upon a book wherein purpose and passion somewhat outrun technique. . . . [Some poems] show a fiery sympathy with victims of the world's wrong and pain

17

the beginning of the War in Spain I was conscious of no interest beyond a faint wish that the aggressors would make a quick job of it and end the bloodshed; and now — well, as you say, Salud![36] I must tell you something about that review; it's probably the most favorable I've ever written, for the cat in me comes out in reviewing; and it was originally half of a longer review, the other part of which was devoted to a book which I boiled in oil by way of contrast. But I cut that out, attacked by an uneasy conscience because I knew the book's author.

Thanks for the good wishes — more power to you too. Who the hell is this Jerome J. Rooney anyway?[37]

Comradely,
Joy Davidman

Source: Wade

To Stephen Vincent Benét

1950 Andrews Avenue
New York, N.Y.
March 1, 1939

Dear Mr. Benét,

You've helped me so much already that I ought to let you alone; but it's always the nice guys who get pestered. Could you write me a letter of recommendation for Yaddo?[38] They sent me what I thought was an invi-

---

which did not come to Mr. Porter readymade from headlines, but rather with slow processes of growth and thought. And although the nature poems of the book are conventional in subject, they convey so vividly the feeling of Kansas earth and sun as to raise Kenneth Porter's passion for his native plains to the level of authentic poetry. ("Kansas Poet," pp. 26-27)

36. In the Spanish Civil War (1936-39) the supporters of the fascist General Francisco Franco rebelled against the newly and legally elected Popular Front, a progressive government with pro-Communist leanings. The bloody conflict eventually attracted volunteer soldiers from outside Spain who supported the Popular Front; these soldiers were known as the International Brigade, and they fought valiantly, but in the end ineffectively. William L. Gresham saw service during the conflict as a member of the International Brigade.

37. Jurist John Jerome Rooney (1866-1934) was also a poet; his *The Men Behind the Guns* was privately printed in 1934, and his *Collected Poems* appeared after his death (New York: Dodd, Mead & Company, 1938).

38. Located in Saratoga Springs, New York, Yaddo is an artists' community founded in

tation, and overwhelmed by the honor I changed my plans for the summer and accepted; now they want recommendations. So I'd be very grateful if you'd send me a brief note I could forward to them.

The Yale Press tells me they're planning to reprint *Letter to a Comrade;* my mother claims it's all her work. She walks into all the bookstores asking for it, and then looks terribly, terribly hurt when it isn't there. But the other evening she marched into a place breathing fire, and came out meekly two minutes later with a neat parcel under her arm. They soaked her the full two dollars for it too.

Have you noticed the way half the reviewers crib from your introduction?

Yours sincerely,
Joy Davidman   *Source: Yale*

Within a short time of joining the CPUSA, Davidman, eager to use her talents as a writer to help the Party, looked for a way to help. With the literary success of Letter to a Comrade *she thought she might be a useful tool. Since she had been reading* New Masses *for some time, particularly the poetry, she eventually made her way to the offices of* NM *and offered her services. Almost immediately she was brought on board as a poetry editor. Initially it appeared that she would make her primary contribution to* NM *as a poet. Although she was only twenty-three years old, her poem "Strength through Joy" appeared in the April 5, 1938, issue of* NM.[39] *However, poetry was not the primary literary contribution Davidman made to* NM; *instead, it was her facility as a book, theater, and movie reviewer — especially the latter — that best portrayed her contribution to the cause. Indeed, during her most active period as a writer and editor for* NM, *March 1941 through July 1943, she was publishing a book, theater, or movie review in almost every issue.*[40]

1900. Its mission is "to nurture the creative process by providing an opportunity for artists to work without interruption in a supportive environment" (see http://www.yaddo.org). There is no record that Davidman attended Yaddo in 1939; this may be in part because by July 1939 she was living in Hollywood as a screen writer for Metro-Goldwyn-Mayer Pictures.

39. For a discussion of this poem and others, see "Joy Davidman and the *New Masses:* Communist Poet and Reviewer."

40. There is one notable gap in Davidman's publications in *NM:* June 1939 through December 1940. The primary cause of this gap was her six-month move to Hollywood in

To Kenneth W. Porter

1950 Andrews Ave.
New York City
March 31, 1939

Dear Kenneth Porter,

. . . . . Forgive the dots; they're unintentional, my typing being erratic this morning as a result of lecturing to the Poetry Society last night.[41] Good God, what an assemblage of pathetic hangers-on of the arts. I mentioned politics and was nervously shushed, which reminded me of [George Bernard] Shaw's criticism of polite conversation, that it excluded the only two topics worth discussing; religion and politics.[42] But how the blazes do people expect to write poetry in a vacuum? I told 'em so, but I imagine each listener mentally excepted himself from my accusations.

Thanks for dating your poems for me; I wish everyone did, it's essential for a complete understanding. I've written the dates into the book. About reviewers — don't you find their praise as annoying as their blame? I've been lucky myself; prepared myself heroically for attack, sealed myself into an armor of indifference — and then they patted me on the back. Next time they'll really cut loose. But the only thing that got me angry, was to have Oscar Williams (who is surely the world's worst poet) tell me he'd made his debut as poetry reviewer by slamming me for [my ideas about] Poetry and go on to say that if I followed his instructions I might

---

summer 1939 — an abortive attempt to write movie screenplays. Since she had been initially unpaid at *NM*, the $50 a week offered by MGM as a part of its Junior Writer Project was very attractive. In 1940 she was busy working on another volume of poetry, *Rise and Shine* (see her letter to Still of February 15, 1940) as well as correcting the proofs of *Anya* (see her letter to Benét of May 20, 1940). In addition, she spent the summer of 1940 at the MacDowell Colony, so she was probably focusing on creative work rather than Party work. Finally, she may have been "burned out" by the Hollywood experience and simply needed time off. For more on this, see Pilat, "Girl Communist [Joy Davidman]," November 6, and Dorsett's *And God Came In.*

41. The Poetry Society was founded in 1910. Members have included Robert Frost, Langston Hughes, Edna St. Vincent Millay, Marianne Moore, Wallace Stevens, John Ashbery, Louise Glück, Rita Dove, Brenda Hillman, Stanley Kunitz, Sharon Olds, Robert Pinsky, and James Tate (see http://www.poetrysociety.org).

42. George Bernard Shaw (1856-1950) was perhaps the foremost playwright of his generation; among his best known plays are *Man and Superman* (1905), *Major Barbara* (1905), *Pygmalion* (1913), and *Saint Joan* (1923).

some day learn to write.[43] I had just rejected his awful masterpieces at *New Masses,* but was too kind to tell him so. One of his latest lines, I think, beats anything yet: "God lets the planets fall out of his hair." Dandruff? Bugs?

Do you come to New York at all? If so you may be interested in the Auden-MacNeice-Isherwood symposium at the Keynote Club, 201 W. 52 St. that the League of American Writers is holding on April 6, 8:30 P.M. I'm arranging it myself, so I yell about it everywhere. [W. H.] Auden is the curiousest specimen of English method it has ever been my luck to encounter.[44] By the way, would you be interested in joining the League of American Writers?[45] It's the logical organization for writers with leftwing sympathies, the only one which really takes United Front action. We've just published, for instance, a pamphlet listing anti-Semitic people and publications in this country with their interrelations; a shocking list.

Thanks for the low-down on Jerome J. Rooney.

dosvedanye tovarishch[46]

Joy Davidman   *Source: Wade*

---

43. Oscar Williams (1900-1964) was the pen name of Ukrainian poet Oscar Kaplan. Immigrating with his parents in 1907, Williams became primarily an anthologist of poetry; his many texts include *Little Treasury of Modern Poetry* (1952) and *Immortal Poems of the English Language* (1964).

44. W. H. Auden (1907-1973) was among the most important literary figures of the twentieth century. In addition to poetry, he wrote essays, plays, and operettas. Among his notable works are *Poems* (1930), *On This Island* (1937), *Another Time* (1940), *Nones* (1951), *The Shield of Achilles* (1955), *About the House* (1967), and *City without Walls* (1973). His *Age of Anxiety* (1947) won a Pulitzer Prize, and he won the Bollingen Prize for poetry in 1954.

45. The League of American Writers, formed in 1935, was a writers' organization closely aligned with the Communist Party of the United States of America. For more see Franklin Folsom, *Days of Anger, Days of Hope: A Memoir of the League of American Writers, 1937-1942* (Boulder: University Press of Colorado, 1994).

46. "Farewell comrade" in Russian.

To Lina[47]

1950 Andrews Ave.
New York, N.Y.
April 28, 1939

Dear Aunt Lina,

Grippe has prevented me from writing to you until now about Aaron Kramer's little book, which I enjoyed very much.[48] I wish you would show his cousin this letter as a token of my appreciation.

I often have the task of discussing young poets' work; but it is not often so great a pleasure as in this instance. The boy has astonishing command of technique for one so young; not that his poems are without the clumsiness of youth, but what awkwardness there is, for the most part consists in a slight excess of rhetoric and a tendency to expand an idea too far; both qualities which he will certainly outgrow, for he is, fundamentally, a very fine poet. At an age at which the best of us are usually experimenting with cautious lyric flights he has already developed a keen sense of the dramatic in poetry (I should imagine he will make a good prose writer also) and has graduated from preoccupation with form to a bold handling of significant content. Some of the poems could not be improved on; I liked "Tired" tremendously — it's extremely hard to write a fine poem in four lines.[49] And I can tell by the dates that he has been growing steadily; "Have You Felt the Heart," "Rose," "Smiles and Blood," are extraordinarily powerful,[50] tho' all

47. Surname unknown.

48. Aaron Kramer (1921-1997) was a poet, translator, and literary critic. His works include *The Poetry and Prose of Heinrich Heine* (1948), *The Prophetic Tradition in American Poetry* (1968), *Melville's Poetry: Toward the Enlarged Heart* (1972), and *Neglected Aspects of American Poetry* (1997). Selections of his poems appeared along with those of Davidman and others in *Seven Poets in Search of an Answer*, ed. Thomas Yoseloff (New York: Bernard Ackerman, 1944). The book Davidman is referring to here is *The Alarm Clock* (sponsored by Branches 25 and 134 of the International Workers Order and the Young Communist League of Bensonhurst; privately printed, 1938).

49. Here is the entire text of "Tired" (*The Alarm Clock*, p. 20):

> Tired are my feet, that felt today the pavement;
> Tired are my ears, that heard of tragic things —
> Tired are my eyes, that saw so much enslavement;
> Only my voice is not too tired. It sings.

50. "Have You Felt the Heart of America," pp. 38-40; "The Epitaph for a Rose," pp. 18-19; "Smiles and Blood," pp. 22-23.

three could stand cutting; the last two really should end at the bottom of the first page. There are others, but I won't go into them in detail.

The best thing about Aaron Kramer's work is that it unites proletarian themes with proletarian language.[51] You have no idea how rarely one finds a so-called Workers' Poet who writes in language the workers can understand. I do not mean to imply that workers are slow-witted, they aren't; but when T. S. Eliot, Ezra Pound, and their imitators in the Left Wing write verse they make it a puzzle-exercise for those who have had their sort of education and know all their private jokes.[52] Pound, the disgusting idiot, stated recently that Italy was the true seat of culture because there the writer addressed himself to an audience of a few hundred.

I was once a sinner in that direction myself, though never as much as some, and have only recently succeeded in stating my verse in direct terms. I'm going to copy here a poem I wrote last night to show you what I mean; you used to claim I was too involved:

Ten Dead Workers

I
Over this blood
Stretch the blank shroud,
Modestly cover it;
Lest it offend
Comfortable men,
Put flowers over it;
Use for its sheath
The funeral wreath.

II
Lest your blood cry
Loud to the listening sky,
Lest it breed riot,
Their money spent
On careful print
Will keep it quiet,

51. For more on proletarian literature, see "Joy Davidman and the *New Masses:* Communist Poet and Reviewer."

52. T. S. Eliot (1888-1965) was a highly gifted literary critic, dramatist, and editor/publisher and the most influential twentieth-century modernist poet. Ezra Pound (1885-1972) was a controversial poet and critic widely believed to have pro-Nazi sympathies.

Disguise its flavor
For their breakfast paper.

III
Lie still, you dead,
Wrapped in the heavy bed;
Lie cold and meek.
Your graves possess
In decent humbleness;
They will not hear you speak.
The living speak your word
And will be heard.[53]

Forgive the screwy typing. I think anyone can understand what I say here, and I think too it is worth saying. And that's what I like about the Kramer boy's work; it achieves poetry with ordinary words and conversational diction, the best and the hardest way of achieving it.

A little professional advice may help him; let him try sending his work to the *New Masses, New Anvil, Common Sense, The Wheel* — which can be reached at League of American Writers, 381 Fourth Ave. These encourage young writers far more than the more conservative & opulent magazines. By the way, I'm planning to give a poetry-writing course in the League's Writers School next fall; that, or something like it, might be useful to him.[54]

Thank you, and will you thank Mrs. Jacobs, for the booklet. I hope you and Simon are well.[55]

Yours affectionately,
Joy Davidman   *Source: UM*

53. This poem is published here for the first time.

54. Although I cannot document whether Davidman did teach the course she refers to here, later she was on the faculty of the School for Democracy, an anti-fascist, pro-Communist institution in New York City. Records show that for the fall 1943 term she taught "Poetry Workshop."

55. A note at the top of this letter, presumably in the hand of Aaron Kramer, gives the following: "Joy Davidman's response to *The Alarm Clock*. The cousin to whom her letter was shown, and who in turn let me copy it, is Fanny Jacobs, a fellow-teacher of 'Aunt Lina' and my own 3rd grade teacher. Note her 'new' poem given here" (source: UM).

From spring to fall of 1939 Davidman moved to Hollywood at the invitation of Metro-Goldwyn-Mayer to be a part of an experimental young scriptwriters' program, the Junior Writer Project. As the two letters below suggest, Davidman was miserable during her time in Hollywood.

To James B. Still

221 South Arnaz Drive
Beverly Hills, California
July 18, 1939

Dear Jim,

    Look at where I am![56] It's horrible. I'm a New Yorker, used to crowds, strangers, loud noises and sudden explosions — but not to this. I should like to hide in your rhubarb patch. All you have ever heard about Hollywood is true; not only are the people mad, dishonest, conscienceless, and money-grubbing, but they are all these things at the top of their voices. There is a continuous rapid-fire rattle of talk at a Hollywood party, louder than any machine-gun. Perfect strangers rush over, wave their drinks in your face, tell you discreditable stories about their best friends (who are always famous stars), remark that Joan Crawford Is Slipping, and announce how much they paid for their clothes, manicure, and cigarette holders.[57] Intelligence is measured by the raucousness of the laugh and the speed of the wise-crack. Genius is measured by the expensiveness of the automobile and the number of screen credits. (Screen credits are an invention for giving each of one hundred writers a share of the responsibility in a bad picture.)

    You are growing beans and corn; I am entangled in a nest of cement. I am writing this from a studio; there are thirty sound stages all around me with films flowering on each. I don't like it. But it pays for my food and drink — reasonably well too. I never got money before for doing nothing; but although I've tried to work here, it's impossible. I get the work done, and nobody cares. As for finding someone to read it, [it is impossible].

---

56. The letterhead features a picture of a lion's head within a circle. Above the circle is "Loew's Incorporated: Ars-Gratia-Artis." Below the circle is: "Metro-Goldwyn-Mayer Pictures, Culver City, California."
57. Joan Crawford (1908-1977) was a popular MGM film star in the 1930s and 1940s.

I wish you'd write me more. I'm homesick for the peace and quiet of the subway in this terrible flat city full of pink and green stucco and frowsy palms. I wish I could be in New York to see you. I can't leave here for six months — not then, unless they throw me out (which they probably will). I expected you North in April; was looking forward to it. Why on earth did they ever want me here anyhow?

How I would like a log house deep in the hills just now, and a chance to work at my own work. I've finished a new book of poems though; to be called *Red Primer*.[58] You won't see it for a while, however. I've been following your short stories; the one about the little school teacher who was shot ("Bat Flight," isn't it) will stay with me all my life. Have you heard from the Fletchers? They seem to have dropped me. Isn't it fine about John's Pulitzer Prize?

Green grow the rashes, O. Do they still? Write me.

Yours,
Joy Davidman   *Source: UK*

To Dorothy[59]

221 South Arnaz Drive
Beverly Hills, Calif.
July 19, 1939

Dear Dorothy,

How are you Easterners doing? Is there still civilization in Ypsilanti? There isn't here. As you will see from the sunburst lion overhead, I am a slave of the films now, degraded past all recognition.[60] Every day at lunch I have to strain Robert Taylor out of my soup.[61]

Every horror you have ever heard about Hollywood seems to be true. God knows there's plenty of heartlessness in the writing game and plenty of fakes; but out here they're the rule. Most of us in New York were decent people living lives that made sense; but something seems to happen

58. This book has not survived.
59. Identity unknown.
60. The letterhead is the same as the previous letter.
61. Robert Taylor (1911-1969) was a popular male film star in many MGM films of the 1930s and early 1940s.

even to human beings here. Of course most of those here aren't human beings; they're bright boys whose poppas are down to the last yacht, so
they're making a bit of extra cash to redeem the old palace from the mort-
gage. But there are a few who were once Marxists, and who have turned
into collectors of swanky houses, expensive phonographs, beautiful auto-
mobiles, and who announce the price they paid for everything the minute
you meet them. O I do not like this place.

The actors aren't really so bad though; the ones I have met around
here are hardworking and seem normal. It's the writers, producers, direc-
tors, etc. Fortunately my immediate boss is a swell person, and I enjoy
working with him; but none of the writing I do is very likely to be looked
at by a producer. In six months the company can kick me out of here if it
wants to. I am looking forward to it. God, I'm homesick. Write me.

Yours,
Joy Davidman   *Source: Wade*

To James B. Still

1950 Andrews Avenue
New York, N.Y.
February 15, 1940

Dear Jim,

New York is a foot deep under snow this morning and I love it. The
film business fired me with many compliments two months ago; the
consensus of opinion was that I didn't take kindly to "consultation."
Once, in a moment of emotion, I said No to a producer, so they were
right. I'm too much of an egoist to listen to anyone tell me how to write;
I wouldn't take it from [John] Steinbeck,[62] let alone some degenerate illiterate of a producer whose knowledge of America is gleaned from
glimpses he gets from an airliner. Have you ever spent any time with the
disgusting rich? I used to think there was no sort of human being I
couldn't understand and get along with. But I've learned otherwise; I

---

62. Novelist and short story writer John Steinbeck (1902-1968) wrote mostly about
simple people confronting insurmountable problems. His best-known works include *Of
Mice and Men* (1937), *The Grapes of Wrath* (1939), and *East of Eden* (1952).

can't even talk to café society without losing my temper. Towards the end of my Hollywood career I used to run off at night and prowl through the mountains and canyons (with a knife in my belt for protection, but all I ever met was a stray cat and an unhappy hoptoad). The mountains are good, although disfigured with film stars' Tudor mansions and French chateaux.

Anyhow I rushed home howling with joy, and have been kissing skyscrapers and subway trains ever since. It's beautiful to be in a place where there's snow, and although I've had three attacks of grippe I go out and wallow in it. In Los Angeles the only sign of winter is that the film stars appear in heavier furs.

I've sold my novel to Macmillan — it happened when I was still in California, and I gloated over my writer-colleagues, none of whom were capable of producing more than a ten-page screen story.[63] It's going to come out next August or September. As for the poetry, it's called *Rise and Shine* now, and I'm waiting for the Yale Press opinion on it.[64]

Your novel is taking New York by storm.[65] Everybody's talking about it, even an aunt of mine who usually never hears about a book till someone hits her over the head with it. I've seen enthusiastic reviews, even in the *New York Sun,* which is Morgan's paper and officially disapproves of *Grapes of Wrath* and *Abraham Lincoln.*[66] I've just got my Social Security money, and I'm going downtown to buy it. As for Fadiman's opinion (I've met him; he's a bit of a left-winger and not a bad sort) it is only too true as far as MGM goes — *Gone with the Wind* is their standard idea of Southern life.[67] But other studios are sometimes more honest, and you might easily get several offers. I'll write you again as soon as I've read the novel. Don't expect help from the Roosevelt government, though, for mountaineers or anyone. The official solution for such problems is now Go and fight for dear little Finland, Mr. Morgan's nickel mines, and the sacred cause of capitalism.

---

63. Davidman is referring to her novel, *Anya* (New York: Macmillan, 1940).

64. In her July 18, 1939, letter to Still she said this volume of poetry was entitled *Red Primer;* it has not survived.

65. James B. Still, *River of Earth* (New York: Viking Press, 1940).

66. Davidman is referring to John Steinbeck's *The Grapes of Wrath* (New York: Viking Press, 1939) and Carl Sandburg's *Abraham Lincoln: The War Years* (New York: Harcourt, Brace, 1939).

67. Clifton P. Fadiman (1904-1999) was an essayist, broadcaster, and literary and film critic.

Have you heard from the Fletchers at all? They have ignored me for about a year. As for you, Mr. Still, I hope for an answer inside of a month. Come to New York again this year; I'll show you the city, my new hair-do, and my collection of Oriental knives.

Yours,
Joy

Source: UK

To Stephen Vincent Benét

1950 Andrews Avenue
New York, N.Y.
May 20, 1940

Dear Mr. Benét,
    Here is my new book as it stands today, stripped of everything except *what* I really like; but a good deal may happen to it in the next few months.[68] I'd have sent it along much earlier, but it was in a state of flux and I was busy correcting proofs on my novel and wishing I could afford to rewrite it.[69]
    Do you think it's good enough to print as it stands, or ought I to wait a while? If there are any changes you can suggest, I wish you'd tell me.
    Hope you're all well; my regards to Mrs. Benét. Tell Rachel [Benét's daughter] to try the chocolate bars with the rum flavoring.

Yours,
Joy Davidman

Source: Yale

---

68. This manuscript, *Rise and Shine* (see the previous letter), has not survived.
69. Davidman is referring to her novel, *Anya*.

To Stephen Vincent Benét

League of American Writers
381 Fourth Avenue
New York, N.Y.
June 3, 1940

Dear Mr. Benét,

Thanks enormously for your letter. It came just when I was feeling that I'd never be any good as a poet so had better stick to prose, at which I'd never be any good either. I don't feel at all like that now. But I don't suppose I need tell you how much pleasure your letter gave me; I think you knew it would. (Grammar twisted, but sentiments sincere; emotion always confuses my style.)

The League wants me to ask you if you'd care to appear at an antiwar poetry meeting, to be held on Thursday, June 20, at 8:30 in the evening. We're going on record, while we can, against America's entering the war; and we should be grateful if you would consent to read some appropriate poems of your own (some of those in *Burning City*, for instance).[70]

We will notify you of the place of the meeting as soon as it is decided. If you cannot appear, would you authorize us to read some of your poems, or send us some you would like read?

Thanks again for everything.

Sincerely,
Joy Davidman

Source: Yale

In July 1940, Davidman's novel Anya *was published by Macmillan.*[71]

American novelist and writer William Lindsay Gresham (1909-1962) married Davidman on August 2, 1942, in Peterborough, New Hampshire, near the MacDowell Colony. Gresham, who had spent time serving as a volunteer

---

70. Stephen Vincent Benét, *Burning City* (New York: Farrar & Rinehart, 1936).

71. For reviews of *Anya*, see John Cournos, Review of Joy Davidman's *Anya*, *New York Times*, July 14, 1940, p. 7; Dorothy Frye, Review of Joy Davidman's *Anya*, *Boston Transcript*, August 10, 1940, p. 2; Alfred Kazin, Review of Joy Davidman's *Anya*, *New York Herald Tribune Books*, July 14, 1940, p. 2; Review of Joy Davidman's *Anya*, *Christian Century* 57 (July 10, 1940): 879; Review of Joy Davidman's *Anya*, *New Republic* 103 (August 12, 1940): 222; and N. L. Rothman, Review of Joy Davidman's *Anya*, *Saturday Review of Literature* 22 (July 13, 1940): 10.

freedom fighter in the Abraham Lincoln Brigade during the Spanish civil war in the mid-1930s, had joined the CPUSA at about the same time as Davidman. Other than their mutual interest in the CPUSA, there was little to connect Gresham and Davidman. He was a southerner from Baltimore, a gentile, and something of a gypsy; she was a big-city northerner, ethnically Jewish, and very much at home in New York. However, by all accounts he was a charmer, so this may help explain how it was that he quickly won Davidman's heart. Perhaps another important thing that brought them together initially was their mutual commitment to establishing careers as writers.[72]

To Ruth N. Lechlitner[73]

The Dial Press, Inc.
432 Fourth Avenue,
New York
October 28, 1942

Dear Miss Lechlitner,
Enclosed is a prospectus describing *War Poems of the United Nations,* our forthcoming anthology of anti-Axis poems from all over the world.[74] This collection will, of course, include the work of outstanding poets of the United States. As a symbol of America's solidarity with the other anti-Axis forces, we are asking leading American poets to undertake the translation into English verse of original material in other languages. Literal prose translations will be supplied with the originals.
May we invite you to submit for consideration war poems you have written? May we also count on you to undertake some of the translations?

72. For more on the steps leading to this marriage, see Lyle Dorsett, *And God Came In,* pp. 51-57.
73. Ruth N. Lechlitner (1901-1989) was a poet and journalist whose work appeared in *New Masses.*
74. The book was eventually published as *War Poems of the United Nations,* ed. Joy Davidman (New York: Dial Press, 1943). In addition to editing the book, Davidman published the following poems: "Fairytale" and "Trojan Women"; "For My Son" (under the name Megan Coombes-Dawson); "Four Years After Munich" and "Peccavimus" (both under the name Haydon Weir); "For Odessa" (by Boris Veselchakov, adapted by Joy Davidman); "The Young Pioneers" (by A. Bezmensky, adapted by Joy Davidman); and "Snow in Madrid" (reprinted from *Letter to a Comrade*).

If so, please let us know which foreign languages you prefer to work from, if any, and how many poems you will translate.

The sooner this volume appears in print, the more valuable it will be as a morale builder. A prompt reply will, therefore, be very much appreciated.

Thank you for your cooperation.

Yours very truly,
Joy Davidman
Editor

Source: Iowa

Goebbels's Missing Link [An Open Letter to *New Masses* Readers][75]

March 23, 1943

No idea of Herr Doktor Goebbels has ever been too grotesque for our American fascists to ape.[76] Two words from the wizened little monkey in Berlin, and Martin Dies starts cutting monkeyshines in Congress.[77] It would appear that Dr. Goebbels has imitators in Hollywood as well; for his racist propaganda, in its filthiest form, is expressed in a picture planned by Universal Studios.

Hollywood's treatment of the Negro has usually been ill-informed and ill-natured to an outrageous extent. *Captive Wild Woman,* however, out-Herods Herod. Among the more brutal and unprincipled exponents of southern lynch law there used to be a theory that the Negroes were the mythical Missing Link. Possible only to minds of the ultimate degree of illiteracy, this idea was used as a sort of warped justification of the bestialities inflicted upon helpless Negroes. But it was too grotesque to survive long except among the most virulent poll taxers.

It is a shock, therefore, to discover that Universal Studios is planning to resurrect the Missing Link idea, in conformance with Nazi racial theories by which only that non-existent animal, the Aryan, is quite human. In *Captive Wild Woman,* apparently a horror quickie of even more incoher-

75. This letter appeared in the *New Masses* 46 (March 23, 1943): 29.

76. Joseph Goebbels (1897-1945) was the German propaganda minister under Adolf Hitler and the Nazis.

77. Martin Dies (1900-1972) was a congressman from Texas who was fiercely anti-Communist. In May 1938 his congressional resolution created the House Special Committee on Un-American Activities.

ence than usual, the inevitable Mad Doctor decides to turn a female go-rilla into a human being. By itself this would be merely silly; but someone had the idea of making that human being into a Negro girl! Lest you should conceivably miss Dr. Goebbels' point, the final script leads the girl up to a mirror while she is giving way to her "lower emotions" — namely jealousy. As the emotions get lower, her skin grows darker, until she re-lapses through stages of subhumanity into the gorilla again!

Sheer illiteracy, though it explains some Hollywood phenomena, can hardly be the sole cause of this piece of fascist propaganda. It is tempting to suggest that the gentlemen responsible, in trying to reduce human be-ings to the ape level, were looking for company in their own misery; but it is more to the point to ask who gave them their orders? And it is still more to the point to see that those orders are countermanded by the American people. This film has not yet been released, has not even been publicized; its makers no doubt intend to slip it over quietly as a routine horror melo-drama. They can be stopped.

Protest to the OWI [Office of War Information] as well as to Univer-sal Studios should be effective in throttling Dr. Goebbels' apes. Mean-while, one might suggest to the gentlemen responsible for *Captive Wild Woman* that, if they must hunt for a Missing Link, they might try to find one between themselves and decent humanity.[78]

To Rosemary Benét

New Masses
461 Fourth Avenue
New York, N.Y.
April 14, 1943

Dear Mrs. Benét,

At Mr. William Rose Benét's suggestion, I'm sending you a copy of my article on Stephen Benét which appeared in the March 30 issue of *New Masses*.[79]

You probably won't remember meeting me, and I scarcely knew your

78. The movie was released on June 4, 1943.

79. Stephen Benét died March 13, 1943, and Davidman's tribute to him appeared as "Stephen Vincent Benét," *New Masses* 46 (March 30, 1943): 23-24.

husband personally; but he did a great deal for me, both through being my editor and through being what he was and writing what he did. I wish I knew how to say everything that should be said; I got what I could into this article.

Sincerely yours,
Joy Davidman   *Source: Yale*

To Harold Harwell Lewis[80]

[*New Masses*
461 Fourth Avenue
New York, N.Y.]
June 7, 1943

Dear H. H. Lewis,

I've been looking over some of your poems, and I've been impressed with the broadening scope of your work. More and more you are bringing current issues into your poetry, and consequently developing deeper meaning and deeper emotion. You are certainly growing as a poet.

There are, however, a number of "growing pains" that always annoy poets as they develop, and you seem to have a few of these. As the political and social content of your poetry becomes more complex, the poems and their language tend to become obscure. You must remember that only a working class audience can create or respond to great poetry nowadays, and that working class audience will rightly reject involved, obscure, and fancy language in poetry. In fact, the best working rule for all poetry is "Keep it simple."

Perhaps I'd better split this criticism into three parts, and begin with stanza form. Song writing, especially when you have no tune already on hand, is a tricky business; the temptation is to compose a sort of tune in your head, and try to get it into the words. As a result, one often makes the

---

80. Harold Harwell Lewis (1901-1985) was a Communist poet who wrote for a number of publications, including the *New Masses* and the *Daily Worker*. In addition, for a time he published his own magazine, *The Outlander*. His volumes of poetry include *Red Renaissance* (Holt, MN: B. C. Hagglund Publisher, 1930), and *Road to Utterly* (Holt, MN: B. C. Hagglund Publisher, 1935). For more on Lewis see Douglas Wixson, "In Search of the Low-Down Americano: H. H. Lewis, William Carlos Williams, and the Politics of Literary Reception, 1930-1950," *William Carlos Williams Review* 26, no. 1 (2006): 75-100.

words too strongly rhythmical, and I think you have done this. When one reads the poems aloud they have a tendency to singsong.

In the Middle Ages, and in the time of Queen Elizabeth, poetry was written by young gentlemen who used it to impress the ladies and to help in the careers at court — just as they used ribbons on their shoes, satin coats, and elaborately curled hair. Naturally they went to great trouble to show off their skill in verse, and they used the fanciest and most involved stanzas and language they could think of.[81] The more unnatural their poems were, the better; for they didn't really have anything to say; they were just putting on an act. Today, of course, our social system has outgrown these airs and graces, and this very elaborate poetry looks just as grotesque and affected as a man with long curled hair would. But this old poetry still has some influence on present day writers which they have to outgrow. And I notice that you use very fancy stanzas, full of double rhyme and internal rhyme. Nowadays such stanzas are useful only in light verse, where you want the reader to admire your cleverness and to laugh all the way through. But the minute you have a serious idea or emotion, the complicated stanza gets in your way. It is hard on the English language, which cannot be poured into such a mold; and it is hard on the ideas, which you have to distort for the sake of rhyming — though no rhyme is ever worth it. And if you *do* succeed in writing these fancy stanzas smoothly, they will still draw attention *to* your mere technical skill *away from* your thought and emotion; and so they will destroy the sincerity of the poem.

While the courtiers were showing off their tricks, the people were writing a very different kind of poetry — the old ballads, which express genuine emotion on social as well as private issues. There are some very great revolutionary ballads like the Robin Hood ones which are nearly five hundred years old. And the stanza form of the ballad is still the best song form in English — a simple four line stanza, rhyming *abcb*, with sometimes an internal rhyme in the first or third line. Like these:

O I have dreamed a dreary dream
Beyond the Isle of Skye,
For I saw a dead man win a fight,
And I think that man was I (700 years old).[82]

81. Davidman was very knowledgeable about these matters. See her "My Lord of Orrery," MA thesis, Columbia University, 1935.
82. From the Northumbrian "The Ballad of Otterburn."

and

> It was mirk, mirk night, there was no starlight,
> They waded through red blood to the knee;
> For all the blood that's shed on earth
> Runs through the springs of the countrie.[83]

"Joe Hill's" a good modern example of this form, and blues songs are closely related to it.[84] While apparently simple, it has so many possibilities for variety in the length and rhythm of the lines that it need never get monotonous. And it's easy to sing and to listen to. You must remember that poetry must be designed chiefly for the *listener* who has to get everything quickly, not for the *reader* who can go back and take another look. The minute one starts directing poetry chiefly to the reader, that poetry loses its vitality and its music.

Another way in which your work is getting above the heads of the audience is in its diction. Perhaps because those unnaturally rigid stanzas cramp you, you are using a literary English which is very different from the natural spoken English of the people you want to reach. You have a tendency to use out-of-the-way phrases and allusions, odd words, bits of strange knowledge, and inversions of the normal word order. This sort of thing has been the curse of modern poetry, leading the people to set it down as highbrow and pretentious art not worth bothering with. Our task is to bring poetry back to spoken English; a good rule is to use no expression in poetry that you can't imagine yourself using in conversation.

You may know that historically, when a ruling class becomes remote from the people and continues so for a long period of time, it is likely to develop first a distinct dialect, then a distinct language, which the ruling class scholars preserve in a mummified state while the language of the people continues to change and grow. For instance, in feudal days the upper class scholars talked a stiff and mummified Latin, despising the popular tongues — ancestors of modern French, English, Italian, etc. — as "jargon." But the popular tongue had a future, and the monks' Latin did not. Similarly the Chinese have through the centuries developed a gulf be-

83. From the traditional seventeenth-century ballad "Thomas the Rhymer."
84. Joe Hill (1879-1915) was a labor activist who was executed by firing squad; he had been convicted of murder after a controversial trial. Alfred Hayes later paid tribute to Hill in his poem "I Dreamed I Saw Joe Hill Last Night" (c. 1930); the poem was often referred to simply as "Joe Hill."

tween "literary" Chinese and the spoken tongue. In English we can see the beginnings of this tendency in the spoken language, in the difference between cockney and farmer English and the English spoken by the upper classes, who are always very alert to condemn anything "common" in speech. And in writing we can see it in the difference between the scholarly, "literary" or "poetic" English of so much verse, a language so unnatural that no one ever could speak it, and the genuine, strong language of the people.

Now, when in the "Song of the Split Second" you speak of "Cathay" for China, and use such phrases as "Top mortal of Hindustan," you are writing this dead "literary" snob language. Other words which you should avoid are: myriads, chattel, blackamoor, armageddon, phoenix, and the obsolete second person singular "falleth." These are known as clichés, language which has lost all poetic vitality through being worked to death. No more disfiguring affectation can be found in poetry than the outworn "Thou dost" and its kind.

Then you use unusual words like stocah, and unusual bits of history like Asoka and Yu. This is bound to impress the average man as mere showing off, especially in a song — and it's just the sort of thing that Ezra Pound, Mussolini's kept poet, does with his quotations from Greek and Sanskrit and Chinese. When you show that you know more than your audience, it should only be something that your audience really needs and wants to learn. You have another trick of inventing words, using hyphens to create what are known as neologisms — horrible things; and using a jawbreaker where a simple one-syllabled word will do. This results in unsingable lines. For instance, there's no such word as "historized" and no such word "reigner" and no good reason for inventing either. Chattalprised, up-hastening, worry-pelted, and the like, are hyphenated abortions, and this is a peculiarly awkward way of making things hard for your reader, still more for your listener, who will not be able to disentangle your meaning. Mass-career is about the worst and vaguest of these. Salience, fortitudeless, cartelhood are all clumsy and unnecessary inventions; there are simpler words already in existence, like *cowardly*. Not only do big words look grotesque; they are also limp and colorless, because they have no associations. A reader will get a mental image when you say tulip tree, but if you call it Liriodendron tulipifera you will leave him blank. Or imagine using "maternal progenitor" for mother.

These defects are thrown in sharp relief in your work by your habit of mixing styles. You will use the funniest, the least dignified of slang phrases in the same line with some of this pompous old stuff; and consequently the slang looks cruder and the fancy language sissier than ever. Once you pick a style, stick to it. It's like the tone of your voice; it adds a great deal of meaning to the words themselves, and if you changed tones five times in speaking a sentence you'd confuse everybody.

When you combine words you sometimes combine them in the wrong order, as in beginning "Song" with "Than Yu" and only getting to the main clause, which should precede it, some six lines later. "Property private" for "private property" is a very funny example of a common poetic defect, the inversion — that is, adjectives after nouns, sentences upside down. This is another of the fancy old-fashioned tricks, producing a pretentious and stilted effect. Moreover, in choosing words you should avoid both violent ones and stale ones. Abusive epithets have no place in poetry; they belong on the back fence. Instead of *calling* Hitler a so-and-so, the poet must *show* Hitler doing something which at once makes it clear to everybody that he *is* a so-and-so; then you must have proved your case without even needing to state it. The language of the newspaper must particularly be avoided, for a newspaper writer uses the most familiar language possible, so as to get his meaning across quickly; whereas a poet, while he should work with fairly familiar *words* and natural *word order*, must nevertheless *combine* his words in a vivid and unfamiliar way, so that new ideas arise. The task is to take everyday *words* and make new *images* out of them. For instance, "the sun shone on her golden hair" is trite and weak. But if you say, "the sun glinted golden on her fingernails" you have taken commonplace words and made an unfamiliar use of them.

Another trick you have, which is foreign to the English language, is that of suppressing *a* or *the* for the sake of rhythm. This is bad usage — "I would rather be as coolie" or "Truth is bayonet" or "Yankee brunt for Second Front." Almost pidgin-English. Where rhyme or rhythm conflict with grammar and good sense, you must sacrifice rhyme and rhythm. But, actually, this trick is also bad versification. For the beauty of English verse depends upon its ebb and flow, its freedom, the variety within the metrical pattern; and if you suppress unimportant words like *a* and *the*, which are unaccented syllables and fit easily into any line, you make your verse stiff and mechanical.

My last criticism concerns content. Poetry must appeal to the imagination and the emotions; correct political statement is not enough. Otherwise, why not write an editorial and the hell with verse? And to appeal to imagination and emotion, the poet must use both himself; he must work through the five senses, not through the power of argument. It is no good to talk about a million dead men in general terms; it presents no image. But take just one of those men — describe his eyes and his voice and the way he brushed his hair back with a grin, tell what he had in his pockets, mention his private jokes and his favorite amusement and his first love affair — and you have created a person. Now, when you kill him, the reader will feel that someone real has died. Or, if you want a mass approach, really *see* a battlefield with a million corpses on it. Take a good look at each one, touch it, examine its wounds, smell it, figure how it died, scare away the flies and the crows and try to arrange the corpses decently, gather up the shattered pieces and bury them in a great trench. When you have done all that in your mind you will be able to write about it and make it real.

But if you do not take the trouble to imagine your subject completely, how can you expect the reader to do it for you? Your unexplained "coolie" and "ryot" and "moujik" are not people whom you know; they are lifeless ideas.

So far you are at your best in satirical verse, which obeys other rules than the ones I have outlined for serious poetry. But you are beginning to find your way towards serious questions, and you will master them just as soon as you get rid of the miseducation about poetry which they give all of us in school and the textbooks. Poetry is the people's art and must talk their language. And it must not scream; violent punctuation and italics, like dirty words, just make poetry silly by over-emphasis. What the words do not contain, you cannot add with punctuation. And poetry must not argue; once you argue with your reader you have thrown away the chance of rousing his sympathetic emotions. Don't generalize about "underlings" and "parturient earth" — more fancy language. Just stop reining in your imagination; let it go and take a look at the real lives and sufferings of real people on this earth. Then come back and tell simply what you have seen. I'm pretty sure you can do it; and that will be poetry.

Yours sincerely,
Joy Davidman
[Associate Editor of *New Masses*]   *Source: Newberry*

39

To V. J. and Alice Jerome[85]

173 N. Highland Ave.
Ossining, N.Y.
January 19, 1945

Dear Alice and Jerry,

Sorry to take so long to answer your letter and Christmas card, but I wanted to make it a good thoughtful intelligent answer, and I've not had much time for getting thoughts on paper lately. Life up here is simpler and sweeter than in the city, yet somehow, when a day is over, I do not burst into deathless prose. My young man is now almost ten months old and beginning to walk around and yell for attention; at the moment I've got him fastened into his crib, but who knows how long this peace will last.[86]

Thanks lots for the Australian paper; it struck me as a very good job, especially for what seems to be a minor section of the country — or am I wrong? I'm feeling very cheerful these days, what with the news from the East, except for the limited opportunities for writing. In the grimmer moments of floor scrubbing I meditate between my teeth articles on male chauvinism. Why, why, why, is it always the Joys and Alices that stop writing to mind infants, and never the Bills and Jerrys? Men is WORMS.

Not that I really think it's the men's fault. Bill will always spell me at taking care of Davy or doing dishes, even though he's writing a novel in his spare time and has a contract date to meet — did I tell you he's sold his novel to Harcourt Brace?[87] But I myself wouldn't dream of reversing the usual procedure and compelling Bill to stay home while I go out and work on *Theatre Arts* — his present job. I wouldn't because with his training and the world in general watching, staying home would really make him suffer and feel inferior, whereas it only mildly incommodes me. What I'm mad about is the prevailing notion — even Bill falls into it at times — that, because I'm a woman, it's quite correct for me to be living this vegeta-

85. V. J. Jerome (1896-1965) immigrated from Poland in 1915 and joined the Communist Party of the United States of America in 1924. In 1935 he became editor of *The Communist,* publishing many essays in support of Communism and related causes. Alice Hamburger was his third wife.

86. David Gresham, the ten-month-old referred to here, was born March 27, 1944; Douglas Gresham was born November 10, 1945.

87. William L. Gresham, *Nightmare Alley* (New York: Rinehart & Co., 1946).

ble, parasitic life. I'm not suffering from overwork, but from a species of enforced mental and physical idleness; housework fills your time, but damn it, it doesn't make any really satisfactory demands either of your muscles or of your mind. You just get tired in a nasty, irritable sort of way. And you don't have the reward which gives productive work point, for when you have finished your housework there is nothing of any value to show for it and you start right over. In short, as Sherman did not say, socially unproductive labor is Hell. And I resent the contemptuous fashion in which the world demands no more of me — because I'm female.

The real trouble is not with the men, but with the women. Nobody ever tells them inertia is dishonorable; they're brought up to think home-making (what a word) the crown of life, the greatest bliss, etc. Even in wartime, even in this America; take a look at the movies and the women's magazines. A gal who gets out and takes a war job is actually supposed to be making a sacrifice, instead of getting out of a prison. Now the real attraction of housework is that it is the most easy, irresponsible form of work in the world, but you don't catch any of the parasite-class of women admitting that. They do their damndest to escape from the real world into the dreamworld of housekeeping-with-soap-operas; not having been taught the truth that only productive work can ever fill an adult's life satisfactorily, they are then bored and miserable without knowing why; and they whine endless complaints lest their husband suspect wifie is gypping him.

A couple of years back I mentioned, merely in passing in an article on films, that keeping house and having a baby were not adequate lifetime jobs for an able bodied female.[88] I got two indignant nine-page letters from women who wanted to convince me that they were doing their share in the world. Sure enough, both of them had maids. Their notion of an adult contribution was occasionally playing with the kids or playing golf with the husband, making sure the curtains hung straight, and reading the latest books so they could make like an intelligent wife. And these were tovarishi, if you please.[89]

Of course there's always an opportunity for the housework-frustrated mamma. She can devour the children's lives to make up for the one she hasn't got. Haven't you seen that horribly often? Or she can multiply the

88. See her "Women: Hollywood Style," *New Masses* 44 (July 14, 1942): 28-31. I discuss this article in "Joy Davidman and the *New Masses:* Communist Poet and Reviewer."
89. *Tovarishi* is Russian for comrades.

housework an unnecessary hundredfold by way of convincing herself and others that she is doing her share when she knows damn well she's not. She drapes her windows in fancy curtains to give her lotsa extra washing, she carefully selects furniture full of nooks and crannies hard to clean, she burrows into corners of the apartment that nobody knows are there — eventually this insanely magnified task becomes so important to her that her family can't breathe or smoke or relax in a home which is no longer a home, but Momma's Substitute for Productive Work. Nerts.

All this, though, doesn't get me any forwarder with the dishes in the sink. I'm not, thank God, the permanent-adolescent sort of female wither — that's our commonest type, the gal who will shrivel and die when separated from the movies and the juke joint for two weeks. We had a forty-year-old adolescent upstairs who moved to Yonkers because Ossining has only one movie house. I can sit in a house looking out at the lovely icicles and be perfectly happy; but I can't stop writing and be perfectly happy, and I do like to see my friends. For the next few years I am not likely to do much of either, unless Bill hits a best seller. Oh hell, I didn't mean to write the article in this letter.

Meant to ask Jerry; what about Canada Lee doing Caliban in the *Tempest*?[90] Interview I read says he's going to portray him as a slave filled with the desire for freedom, etc. but after all Caliban is not written that way. However sensitively interpreted, he remains a clown, though at times a tragic clown. I don't like the part for a Negro. There's all sorts of repetition in it about Caliban's sub-humanity, regular Southern Bourbon stuff. Has Lee asked anyone's advice? Of course it's a break for him and a good precedent to have Negroes in Shakespeare on an equal footing with white actors; but Caliban's no Othello. The only way they could take the curse off it, seems to me, is by making Ariel a Negro too, and they aren't.

I've been fooling with psychologic theory in my spare time; one of these days — or years — I shall be doing an article, I hope, on the death-fear as the primary human impulse, underlying libido and everything else; also on the cultural and class reasons why Freud and his disciples talk round it. A dying class always denies or evades the death-fear, till it spreads out and swallows up their whole lives. I'm getting a Marxist the-

90. Canada Lee (1907-1952), born Lionel Cornelius Canegata, pioneered stage roles for African Americans in the first half of the twentieth century. William Shakespeare's *The Tempest* is one of his most frequently staged plays. Caliban is half-man, half-monster, and is living in forced servitude to Prospero, a powerful magician and the ruler of the island where they both live.

ory of the unconscious into shape, slowly, with lots of reference to Karen Horney — she's done better than most.[91] No professional analyst will admit the death-fear as primary motive if he can help it, though; for of course the death-fear is the one thing analysis cannot remove; it's real.

Goodbye. Please write.

Joy   *Source: Yale*

Davidman's last review to appear in NM *was "Life with Mother" (book review of* The Ballad and the Source *by Rosamund Lehman), 56 (July 10, 1945): 26-27. Davidman's last poem to appear in* NM *was "Quisling at Twilight," 56 (July 31, 1945): 4. The last time Davidman's name appeared on the masthead of* NM *as a "contributing editor" was April 16, 1946. In effect, by the middle of 1946 Davidman was no longer active in the CPUSA.*

To Aaron Kramer

173 N. Highland Ave.
Ossining, N.Y.
August 18, 1946

Dear Aaron Kramer,

I'm very glad Louise brought along your latest book and gave me a chance to read it.[92] When I reviewed you some years ago I felt you had a lyric grace and a love of life that are very rare in our poets, and the latest book has developed these enormously. You've developed a style that's quite sharp and clear and unmistakably your own. I remember telling you that you needed more variety in your verse-patterns; that is no longer true, you seem to have mastered nearly all the possible rhythms and tunes — I particularly like the cadences of your blank verse, and that's a damned hard thing to write as well as you write it. Some of the poems I did not care for, but even so there's none that would not do you credit as a technician and a master of imagery.

---

91. Karen Horney (1885-1952) was a pioneering theorist in personality, psychoanalysis, and "feminine psychology."
92. Aaron Kramer, *The Glass Mountain* (New York: Beechhurst Press, 1946).

I think the Glass Mountain group is first-rate; builds from a beginning that at first I found rather slow and obscure to magnificent intensity
and a dramatic quality that's something new in your work — have you
thought of trying drama, prose or verse?[93] You've got a sense of character
that can use a broader medium than that of lyric poetry. The last pages,
and particularly the last lines, are inspired.[94] The other poems in the book
don't seem quite as powerful, though some — like On Fiftieth Street,
Dirge, and a couple of others — are as good as the big one ["The Glass
Mountain"].[95] You're rapidly reaching a point where there is little or
nothing in your work that anyone could tell you how to improve, for you
no longer need to be anyone's pupil no matter how talented the teacher. If
I may venture to mention my own reactions, though, I felt that one or two
of the political poems were rather too topical — Torgau, for instance.[96]
Events in newspapers are not the same thing as events in one's own emotions; it usually takes time for the topics of the day to sink into your unconscious and start really personal tumults in it; and if you try to write of
things too soon after they happen in the external world you are in danger
of becoming shallow and trite. On the technical side, there are a couple of
points I'd like to make. You have certain favorite words and images, as
what poet has not? And you, like the rest of us, ought to be on guard
against using those words and symbols too often. Birds, wings, sunlight,
flowers, gold, and rainbows — your vocabulary has more beauty than that
of almost all modern poets except [Walter] de la Mare[97] but you will have
to discipline it if you wish to avoid the lush exuberance of romanticism,
the sort of thing from which even Keats was not exempt — too much

93. The poems that make up the "Glass Mountain" section of the volume are: "The
Blackness," p. 9; "The Wise-Woman," pp. 9-11; "Goodbye," p. 11; "Three Sirens," p. 12;
"The Hand-Wringing Women," p. 13; "Song of the Death Bird," pp. 13-14; "Two Eagles,"
pp. 14-15; "Storm," pp. 15-19; and "Dawn," pp. 19-20.
94. Davidman is referring to the concluding lines of the last poem in the volume,
"Marching Song: Music by Charles Wakefield Cadman" (p. 35):

> How long is the road I have chosen? Let it be long as the lands,
> that the mingling blood of martyrs may flow through my heart and hands;
> and wherever their dream of a New World, of a griefless city, is spilled,
> I will take it up and sing it, until men listen and build.

95. "On Fiftieth Street," p. 22, and "Dirge," p. 23.
96. "Torgau," p. 29.
97. Walter de la Mare (1873-1956) was a popular poet and novelist who celebrated the
romantic imagination.

honey.[98] A slight tendency to faintly archaic words and phrases also contributes to this effect, though you don't indulge it much. And, to get really petty: could you do with less rhetorical punctuation, fewer questions and exclamation points? The effect is one of overstatement. Likewise the weak and sentimental exclamation, "Oh!" You keep using it to fill out the meter. It has no meaning at all except as an invocation in some ultimate intensity of emotion, and should never be used except in those rare moments when the poet is practically summoning God to take on flesh — when the poem becomes almost an incantation. And *then* it should be spelled plain O, to distinguish it from the flabby use of everyday speech. These are tiny points, and I mention them only because they seem to me out of tune with the general distinction of your style.

The only poems I felt didn't come off were the Mayflower ones, and that, I think, was because you were forcing the political parallel too far — always a dangerous thing to do, aesthetically.[99] One has the feeling that you weren't really interested in what the Puritans were in themselves, that you are merely using them to point a modern moral. You would have to feel the whole meaning of the Puritans' religion before you could in honesty write hymns for them.

Thanks again for a lovely book. You are one of the very few nowadays who can write social poetry that is poetic as well as political. And, God bless you, there isn't an atom of intellectual snobbery in your work — not once do you feel you have to be incomprehensible.

Yours,
Joy Davidman   *Source: UM*

98. John Keats's (1795-1821) brilliance as an English Romantic poet was cut short by his early and untimely death. His "Ode on a Grecian Urn," "Ode to a Nightingale," and "Ode to Psyche" are among his most powerful and enduring poems.
99. "The Mayflower: Three Hymns," consists of "Parting," pp. 30-31; "Storm," pp. 31-32; and "The Green Land," pp. 33-34.

To Aaron Kramer

173 N. Highland Ave.
Ossining, N.Y.
Sept. 9, 1946

Dear Aaron Kramer,

Your book just arrived this weekend, or I'd have written this before. I'm awfully glad you liked my letter; I meant every word of it.

What bothered me in the Puritan piece was a certain anachronism of mood rather than of fact. The humility and wistfulness of your Puritans is characteristic of our own people, of landless refugees. But the real Puritans were anything but humble; in fact spiritual pride was their great sin; and most of them were not city people at all, but dispossessed farmers. They were a part of the great revolution of the seventeenth century, which was only incidentally a religious revolution. Their reasoning went about as follows: We are being expropriated, taxed, and tortured, by an alliance of the king, the great landholders, and the Church of England. The Church cloaks these abuses and commits new ones of its own in the name of God. We are called godless if we protest. Yet the Church is utterly corrupt; we are far more godly than its bishops and prelates. We speak for God, not they. In every phase of life we shall show our superior virtue.

You see the point? Ostentatious godliness, piety, "purity" of religion, became the political answer to the political activities of the Church. Therefore the Puritans developed a grim and rather humorless pride in their own virtue. They were also anything but gentle; it was they who taught the Indians the trick of scalping. They were heroic, iron men, with all of the harder virtues and practically none of the softer ones. Milton's "Lycidas," in the famous "blind mouths" passage, expresses very well their attitude to the Church of England.[100] Your Green Land section is rather

---

100. Below is the passage from John Milton's "Lycidas" that Davidman alludes to (ll. 108-31):

> Last came, and last did go
> The Pilot of the *Galilean* lake;
> Two massy keys he bore of metals twain
> (The golden opes, the iron shuts amain).
> He [Camus] shook his mitered locks, and stern bespake:
> "How well could I have spared for thee, young swain,
> Enow of such as for their bellies' sake

out of character, since although they professed humility they had none. I don't think you can write a convincing Puritan hymn unless you give it an iron ring and get some hatred into it.

The Torgau sonnet seems to me over-elaborate technically; too much alliteration, for one thing, and that "world" echo, and all that playing with the caesura; a little goes a long way. The sonnet is always a temptation. Oh, blast this typewriter. I'll finish in longhand. The sonnet is always a temptation to a good technician to be too clever.

If my agent can sell it, I'll have another book of verse.[101] Look, why don't you and your wife come up to see us, say weekend of Sept. 28th? Bring the kids if possible. Let me know.

Yours,
Joy

Source: UM

Creep and intrude and climb into the fold!
Of other care they little reckoning make,
Than how to scramble at the shearers' feast,
And shove away the worthy bidden guest.
Blind mouths! that scarce themselves know how to hold
A sheep-hook, or have learned aught else the least
That to the faithful herdman's art belongs!
What recks it them? What need they? They are sped;
And when they list, their lean and flashy songs
Grate on their scrannel pipes of wretched straw.
The hungry sheep look up, and are not fed,
But swoln with wind, and the rank mist they draw,
Rot inwardly, and foul contagion spread,
Besides what the grim wolf with privy paw
Daily devours apace, and nothing said.
But that two-handed engine at the door
Stands ready to smite once, and smite no more."

101. This manuscript has not survived.

Eyes Opened

Letters 1948

To V. J. and Alice Jerome

Endekill Road
Staatsburg, N.Y.
January 21, 1948

Dear Jerry and Alice,

Thanks lots for your tripartite, or is it trinitarian, letter. I too miss you and hope you will come back soon. Our car has been out of order for two weeks; we're going broke paying for the repairs and God knows when we'll get into New York. But when we do I shall let you know. We're hoping to see Harold when we do, too.[1]

I hope Jerry's deadline is soon over; I've so much to discuss. I was afraid I'd have to write a book on philosophy, and my worst fears are being realized; I've already batted out several thousand words.

Eureka, also Hooray! I am right, I've been right all along. Ipse dixit, Engels himself has said it. See p. 35 in the Marxist Library edition of *Ludwig Feuerbach*, also and even more p. 59.[2] He declares that "irreligion" and "rationalism" are the "appropriate religion" of the industrial bourgeoisie.

Atheism is the characteristic philosophy of *industrial capitalism*. *Atheism* was developed, and exists, to suit the needs of the bourgeoisie.

---

1. Possibly Harold Harwell Lewis.
2. See Friedrich Engels, *Ludwig Feuerbach and the Outcome of Classical German Philosophy* (New York: International Publishers, 1941).

For
he himself has said it
and it's greatly to his credit . . .

But then, by God, what does he do? He forgets the negation of the negation! He applies dialectics, and the view of truth as an emergent factor, to all subjects but religion. On *this* subject, if you please, a final truth has been reached. And by whom? By the bourgeoisie!

Christianity is "incapable for the future of serving any progressive class as the ideological garb of its aspirations."[3] Why? Because the *bourgeoisie* is anti-Christian!

Yet as students of dialectics we *ought* to expect something quite different. If atheism suits the needs of industrial capital, it ought to be obvious that it cannot suit ours. If there is to be a negation of bourgeois thought in all departments of knowledge, if our ethics emerges as a negation of bourgeois ethics, then by heaven our religion must be a negation of bourgeois religion. (I am using religion here in the sense of a theory of the meaning, nature, and direction of the universe; in this sense atheism is very much a religion, and indeed its adherents fight for it with fanatical religious passion rather than with reason.)

Of course we cannot go back to feudal Christianity, which was itself a corruption of the original doctrine of revolutionary Christianity which substituted idolatrous worship of Christ the God for the political and economic doctrine of Christ the man. It is *this* return that the Catholic church is trying to foist on us, and unless we take Christ away from them they have some chance of making headway. By the way, medieval Christianity cannot be understood without tracing the tremendous influence of *Hindu* thought; Judaeo-Christianity is quite different from Indo-Christianity.

But what, then, is the real form of the negation-of-the-negation? I think it may very well be the *rediscovery* of the principles of Christ, the reemergence of *revolutionary* religion. For indeed *we*, for the first time in history, have given Christ's ideas the scientific and practical extension which alone can translate them into action.

How have we made the mistake of slavishly copying bourgeois atheism? I think it's easy enough to trace. *Engels* was, after all, the originator of our dialectic materialism (I am leaving Marx out only for convenience).

3. Engels, *Ludwig Feuerbach*, p. 59.

Hence the influences working on him were bound to be those of bourgeois society only; the science on which he based his work was the materialist and atheist science developed, as he says, to suit the needs of the bourgeoisie; more specifically, developed to justify man's inhumanity to man. (Was not "evolution" taken by Spencer to justify capitalism?)[4] Consequently Engels could not anticipate the future negation; all he could see was the negation which supplied him all his data, the *bourgeois* negation of feudal religion. On this subject he thinks like a bourgeois, simply because there is nothing else to think like in his time.

How was he to know that twentieth-century science would undermine his precious "matter in motion" by showing that matter was itself "motion" and that consequently we appear to have a universe composed of the constant motion of *nothing?* How was he to anticipate that the "conservation of energy" and its corollary, the eternal universe, were going to get blown to hell and gone by the discovery of entropy? How could he tell that the completely knowable, infinite-straight-line space and time of nineteenth century physics would give way to the relative bubble-universe of Einstein, in which space and time themselves are relative, curved, modifiable by mass and speed; and the universe is finite after all?

Make no mistake; these changes in science are not superficial; they are changes in the basic philosophy of science, from an absolute to a relative materialism. Modern physics is very Kantian. Engels might have realized, it is true, that he himself was eclectically combining the materialist cause-and-effect universe with the idealist conception of free will. But as it happened he hated eclectics with a violent hate; they are the only antagonists with whom he is really ill-mannered and sometimes almost unprintable. God knows why; I suspect a touch of Prussian authoritarianism.

For *Lenin's* Materialism there is less rational excuse. But there is much emotional excuse.

After all, Lenin grew up in a Greek Catholic world. To him, Christ meant the filthy popes. To him, religion meant the Czar's pet church. He could not see that the bourgeoisie was essentially atheistic and used religion as a pretense, a weapon; for the Russia of his childhood was not bourgeois at all; it was basically feudal. Thus *his* anti-clerical stand was itself the *bourgeois* attack on a feudal church. Only late in his life did capitalism

4. Herbert Spencer (1820-1903) was a political economist who adapted several of Charles Darwin's ideas and applied them to social philosophy. His writings include *Principles of Biology* (1864) and *Principles of Sociology* (1874).

begin to develop in Russia to an appreciable extent, and even then the bourgeois revolution — Kerensky's — preceded the proletarian one almost imperceptibly![5]

It was, of course, entirely necessary to break the Greek Catholic church, and Lenin's position was demonstrably *correct for his Russia.* But the trouble was that he was, essentially, a good Catholic!

You will have noticed a peculiarity of rebellious Catholics; they almost always become atheists. They practically never think of becoming Protestants. Their psychology is very simple; the Catholic Church speaks for God; therefore if the Church is corrupt there is no God. It never occurs to them that perhaps God doesn't agree with the official church.

Lenin was no exception. He regards all speculation about the mere possibility of God's existence as leading straight into the arms of the Czar's church-spies. The basic principle of his Materialism is not: Believe materialism because it is true, but Believe materialism because anything else may let God in! Thus he thinks that if he can show his enemies are idealists, and that *some* idealists become deists, he has sufficiently proved them wrong!

So he is betrayed into an extreme dogmatic absolutism which is undialectic and unscientific. He actually says: Truth is indefinite enough so that science can never be sure it's right; but truth is definite enough for science to know that religion is wrong!

You see he was thinking of Adam-and-Eve, the Bible myths, the Virgin Birth and all the rest of it; what *he* had been brought up to consider religion. But deism is something else again. By the way, I got an awful shock when I read *Materialism and Empirio-Criticism.*[6] What possesses us to offer *this* as a statement of our philosophy? No wonder we can never get anywhere with educated bourgeois thinkers! The book is pathetic; merely from the standpoint of construction it is rambling, repetitious to idiocy, irrelevant; its language, probably further corrupted by the translator, is of an

5. Alexander Fedorovitch Kerensky (1881-1970) was a revolutionary who served as prime minister of a provisional government in Russia from July to October 1917; eventually there was a Bolshevik takeover, and he was forced into exile when Vladimir Ilyich Lenin assumed power.

6. First published in 1909, V. I. Lenin's *Materialism and Empirio-Criticism: Critical Comments on a Reactionary Philosophy* was a foundational text of Communism. Davidman would have read the version printed in New York by International Publishers in 1927 (although it is a translation, the translator's name is not listed).

almost hysterical violence and bad manners.[7] Even the jokes ain't funny, they're just insults. As for its logic, it is unbelievable; the premises are wrong, the conclusions are wrong, and they're all non sequiturs anyway. He does not seem even to have understood the point under discussion, the question of whether sensory reality can be taken as the only or the whole reality; for his whole argument *depends* on the assumption of the absoluteness of sensory reality, and that is just the thing he is supposed to prove.

The joke is, of course, that it is just as possible for a materialist to believe in God as it is for an idealist! Most Christians are materialists in the sense that they consider the sensory appearance is really there and really works by cause and effect; they merely posit something *outside* the bubbleuniverse. Lewis is certainly a materialist; I was quite wrong to call him an idealist. He describes the universe as "a vast interlocking material event" and *insists* that matter in all its forms influences man's thinking.[8]

There are only two *really* atheistic philosophies: mechanical materialism and solipsism, and *both* are characteristic of the bourgeoisie. Lewis has personified them very neatly in *That Hideous Strength*, as the diabolists Wither and Frost.[9] Wither holds that *only* his consciousness exists, there-

---

7. Here is an example of the text:

The standpoint of life, of practice, should be first and fundamental in the theory of knowledge. And it invariably leads to materialism, brushing aside the endless fabrications of professorial scholasticism. Of course, we must not forget that the criterion of practice can never, in the nature of things, either confirm or refute any human idea *completely*. This criterion also is sufficiently "indefinite" not to allow human knowledge to become "absolute," but at the same time it is sufficiently definite to wage a ruthless fight on all varieties of idealism and agnosticism. If what our practice confirms is the sole, ultimate and objective truth, then from this must follow the recognition that the only path to this truth is the path of science, which holds the materialist point of view. . . . The sole conclusion to be drawn from the opinion of the Marxists that Marx's theory is an objective truth is that by following the *path* of Marxian theory we shall draw closer and closer to objective truth (without ever exhausting it); but by following *any other path* we shall arrive at nothing but confusion and lies. (p. 142; emphasis Lenin's)

8. C. S. Lewis (1898-1963) was an Oxford don at the time of this letter. He was a prolific writer in many genres, including poetry, literary criticism, fiction, essays, children's stories, and Christian apologetics; in addition, by one account he wrote over 10,000 letters to various correspondents. Davidman was profoundly influenced by his ideas, particularly by his books such as *The Screwtape Letters* (London: Geoffrey Bles, 1942). Davidman began corresponding with him in 1950.

9. These references are to characters in C. S. Lewis's *That Hideous Strength: A Modern Fairy-tale for Grown-ups* (London: Bodley Head, 1945).

fore he has no social responsibility; Frost holds that only matter exists, and consciousness and free will are illusions (like Diderot, on whom Lenin has to fall back when he explains what materialism really means to *him*) and therefore Frost too has no social responsibility.[10]

I said that Lenin's position was emotionally understandable. For he really *had* to destroy the Greek Catholic Church, nor could he anticipate that it would be reborn as it has been; and since that Church was infinitely corrupt we may pardon him the emotional intensity which dominates his discussion to the exclusion of reason. It is no good saying that he *ought* to have studied the problems of other countries, for his energies had to be directed to Russia, and what he knew of other countries added knowledge but did not change the emotional set of his youth.

But intellectually his position is not defensible; for he knew something about twentieth-century physics, and his chapters on space and time are real evasions of the whole issue, viz.: we don't know what space and time are, but we know that they must be exactly as they seem! Whereas the whole point of modern physics is that they are *only* seeming.

And what is still less defensible, by God, is the mediaevalism of our present approach; the endless reprinting, with superstitious reverence, of books like Lenin's *Materialism,* without the slightest attempt to develop Marxism, to use it as a science instead of a revelation from Heaven! Marx-idolatry is not one whit better than Bible-idolatry. It is true that there are tremendous truths in Marx. But so are there in the Bible. The point is not to parrot them, but to *apply* them.

I am not afraid of the epithet "revisionism." We have half killed the party with our divisive epithets, and proved nothing except our own superstitious misunderstanding of Marx. Of course any attempt to *apply* Marxism to a new situation involves a kind of revision, the addition of ideas which are not in the sacred writings, the incorporation of new knowledge, sometimes a categorical disagreement with some of Marx's own statements. Is anyone going to claim that Marx predicted the course of events in Germany exactly as they have happened, for instance? And do you think Marx *wanted* to be treated as an end instead of a means?

One new thing has certainly been added which Marx could not have prophesied. *He* could reasonably say that socialism was *bound* to come

---

10. Denis Diderot (1713-1784) was a thinker and writer of the French Enlightenment. His most important work was *Encyclopédie, ou dictionnaire raisonné des sciences, des arts et des métiers,* ed. D. Diderot and Jean le Rond d'Alembert, 17 vols. (Paris, 1751-66).

sooner or later; it was inevitable, it was a sure thing, and consequently in betting on it self-interest could at times be a sufficient motive. But make no mistake; *we* cannot say the same. The atom bomb and its little friends have introduced other possibilities — that civilization may be destroyed entirely, that all life may be destroyed. I am not an alarmist, Jerry; this *can* be done. I shouldn't like to calculate the odds on whether American capital will not, in the last analysis, prefer to smash the world rather than to lose hold of it. So we need to get a better basis for ethics than self-interest, now. It is time for the new negation-of-the-negation.

Love,
Joy

Source: Yale

To Aaron Kramer

Endekill Road
Staatsburg, N.Y.
January 26, 1948

Dear Aaron Kramer,

I appreciate very much the compliment you have paid me in asking my opinion on your pamphlet.[11] It seems to me that the best return I can make is to tell you the complete truth as I see it. I don't think you'd want me to flatter you against my judgment; nor would my opinion be of any conceivable use to you if I did. In consequence, this letter is going to be not only a stringent criticism but something of a treatise on aesthetics. If your real desire is not to do the best possible work but only to get personal self-satisfaction out of whatever work you do, then you had better not read past this paragraph, which I shall close by inviting you and your family up here to visit us. We have an enormous old house, and we go in for weekend guests. You might come up any Friday night or Saturday morning, talk poetry all weekend, and stagger exhausted back to New York! We're way out in the country, with a brook and a farm, and even buried under snow this part of the world is dazzlingly beautiful. To get here you take the train to Poughkeepsie, where we meet you with the car. Let me know when you can come, and I'll suggest trains, etc.

11. Aaron Kramer, *The Thunder of the Grass* (New York: International Publishers, 1948).

Now to our muttons. I remain, as I have always been, convinced of your talent. But I have never thought that you were making the best possible use of it; and it seems to me that in this latest collection you are not only failing to develop but in some places losing ground. I do not think that any intrinsic weakness in you is to blame; I think the trouble lies in an unquestioning acceptance of your environment, a refusal to see how much there is to learn.

In the old days, on *New Masses,* you may have noticed that the published review I did of your work was much more favorable than my private criticism.[12] This was partly because the published review was of course not meant to teach you but to inform the public of your achievements.[13] But it was also because I was yielding to the prevailing expediency of our criticism, to the opportunism which has been a serious disease among us for years — the sad notion that you gotta give a comrade an extra break. How many bad films I was ordered to praise because their authors had contributed money to the cause, out in Hollywood![14]

Now the trouble with this attitude in criticism is that it is suicidal. We do not fool the bourgeoisie, who can see perfectly well that we are calling a bad work (like *Jake Home*) good not for aesthetic but for political reasons; in consequence we lead middle-class progressives of real culture to despise us, when if we were aesthetically honest they might join us, since aesthetics is the main business of life to them.[15] But we *do* fool our own people. We have, by our dishonest criticism, and I use the word advisedly, led a whole generation of young left-wingers to believe that technique does not matter, characterization and psychology and the sense of beauty and even

12. For more on this, see my "Joy Davidman and the *New Masses:* Communist Poet and Reviewer," *The Chronicle of the Oxford C. S. Lewis Society* 4, no. 1 (February 2007): 18-44.

13. See, for example, her book review "Let the People Sing" of Kramer's *Till the Grass Is Ripe for Dancing, New Masses* 47 (June 1, 1943): 26-27. There she writes: "[This] is a collection of poems of the boyhood and early manhood of its author; inevitably, the verse is frequently uneven and experimental, sometimes a shade naïve. None the less its defects, at their worst, are only signs that the author has not yet realized all his potentialities. His work is already remarkable not only for rhythmic fluency, the united simplicity and distinction of its language, but also for genuine originality and emotional power. . . . Mr. Kramer is one more proof of the unconquerable and innate poetry of a people starved for poetry" (p. 27).

14. Davidman writes extensively about how she compromised her artistic and critical perspective in service of the *New Masses* in her autobiographical essay, "The Longest Way Round," which appears in this book, pp. 83-97.

15. Davidman is referring to *Jake Home* (New York: Harcourt, Brace and Company, 1943) by Ruth McKenney (1911-1972).

the ability to write good clear English do not matter; as long as your book is politically sound it's a book. We have destroyed not only Marxist criticism but Marxist creative writing for the time being. What has happened to the upsurge of the early thirties? Many competent writers have been forcibly *driven* away by the insistence of dishonest and half-literate critics on censoring their work. To tell you the truth, the alienation of our best minds has been so systematic that I suspect the fine hand of the FBI.

In this connection I refer you to V. J. Jerome's admirable recent pamphlet called "Culture in a Changing World."[16] We all ought to memorize its sections on self-criticism. The point Jerome makes, and which I have been trying to make for years without getting anybody to listen, is that you don't have to convince Marxists that art should be a weapon; they know that already. What you *do* have to convince them of is the fact that, in order to be a weapon, it first has to be art.[17] All the good political intentions in the world gather no readers, as *New Masses* has finally found out to its sorrow. God knows plenty of us tried to tell the magazine that for years; but they hadda learn it the hard way.

To understand what has gone wrong with our aesthetics, and consequently with your poetry, one has to start very far back. You know I suppose that Marx and Engels, who wrote so much on so many subjects, wrote neither an Ethics nor an Aesthetics; and this lack has never been filled, although both subjects are essential to our movement. There is a good reason why these two points were neglected. They both stem from the human consciousness itself; they are implicit in human psychology; you cannot derive them *entirely* from sensory experience. Example; the snow-covered hill outside my window is not beautiful in itself, it is only

16. V. J. Jerome, *Culture in a Changing World* (New York: New Century Publishers, 1947).

17. Jerome writes: "The artist, like every other individual, and even more than most, is socially active in his functioning. The issue therefore is not whether he should produce things that have social meaning; he cannot help doing so. The issue really is whether his social product reflects truth or distorts it, and thereby serves progress or reaction. The artist, sooner or later, must make his choice" (pp. 10-11). Later he adds: "It is our responsibility as Marxists to do better than we have done in imparting Marxist theory to broad sections of artists and professional people to spur and facilitate their recognition of the writer's, or artist's, social responsibility, without which he will fall prey to reaction. We Marxists must recognize that to win people to the fight for democratic culture means more than hanging the shingle of Marxism over our shop in the hope that someone will wander in; it means *struggle* to win them, with Marxist understanding, program, and methods of work" (p. 79; emphasis Jerome's).

beautiful to my mind, and if I were not a human being with an aesthetic faculty implicit in my nature, if I were a slug for instance, it would not be beautiful to me at all. To a Martian, though he might be quite as conscious and intelligent as I, it would not be beautiful — presumably. I labor this point because we are too easily swept into the mechanical and actually un-Marxist position that *everything* in a man's mind is created by external events.

Now there is a vague idea among Marxists that dialectical materialism is in some way the opposite of mechanical materialism. But if you compare Engels' *Ludwig Feuerbach* with Lenin's *Materialism* you will find that Lenin actually adopts the mechanical materialism of Diderot's view of consciousness, merely *implementing* it with the dialectical tool, at one point; whereas Engels makes it perfectly clear that all materialism is mechanical in the sense that it regards the universe as pure machine, and dialectics is merely the observation of how the machine *works*. The *real* thing that makes our materialism *unmechanical* is not the addition of dialectics but the admission by both Marx and Engels (and consequently Lenin in most of his work) of the concept of *man's free will,* i.e. freedom within the limits of necessity. The genuinely mechanical materialists like Diderot think that consciousness and free will are mere illusions; we don't.

I don't know whether you are interested in philosophy, so I will not chase down the implications of *free will,* fascinating though they are. The point I am driving at is that, although Marx and Engels accepted free will, it was not the point at issue; in that they agreed with almost everybody else in their time and ours, except the mechanicals. What they were trying to do was to convince men that their will was not entirely free, that they could not think in a vacuum; that external events and particularly productive relations *did,* in practice, condition what went on inside a man's head. Therefore they did not stress the independent part of consciousness, which everybody admitted already; they stressed the *influences from without.*

But ethics and aesthetics *do* depend to a certain extent upon the intrinsic nature of consciousness. It is not possible to arrive at a utilitarian or economic-determinist explanation of the sense of beauty; if you saw the unholy mess Sid Finkelstein made of his attempt at Marxist aesthetics recently you will have realized this.[18] Actually no real Marxist should try; it is the economic-determinist mechanical error. I think, therefore, that

---

18. Sidney Finkelstein (1909-1974) was a music critic; Davidman is referring to his *Art and Society* (New York: International Publishers, 1947).

Marx and Engels did not get round to these subjects simply because they did not involve the point at issue, which was the influence of the *external* world. Eventually, of course, they would have done so; but there was not time.

In practice, however, we have found that we need clear views of these subjects, and we have almost invariably, for lack of guidance from Marx, made the economic-determinist error, thus: *from* Ethics is what serves the working class *to* Ethics is what comes in handy at the moment. Also: *from* Aesthetics is the study of man's innate sense of beauty *to* Aesthetics is the study of man's recognition of his true self-interest.

I am not exaggerating; this has happened to my knowledge to a very grievous extent. Not once, but dozens of times, Marxist would-be writers have told me in one way or another that nothing is beautiful except as it is useful. Applied to writing, this comes out as: I need *only* to follow the party line and I will have created a masterpiece. It would be nice if it were true; unfortunately it ain't.

Can you see what I am driving at? I have compressed this discussion enormously, of course; it ought to be a book; but I think you can follow it. How does it apply to you?

Brace yourself, boy; here it comes. The trouble with your poetry is sheer unwillingness to get an education.

It is not your fault that you did not get an education from our schools; nobody can. They're supposed to keep the workers ignorant and to make them incapable of ever learning for themselves; not to *teach* them. But it *is* your fault if you do not, now, educate yourself. And I *don't* mean by reading and rereading Marxist literature and the Marxist press, which, little as we like it, is written by people who are nearly illiterate from the standpoint of English literature. It is not the task of a Marxist to smash everything that the aristocracy and the bourgeoisie have contributed to culture, any more than it is his task to smash the machines. And yet we find our people, who would shudder at the thought of refusing to use the industrial plant created by capitalism, constantly refusing to learn the literary and artistic *techniques* developed by capitalism. These too must be our tools. There is nothing revolutionary about ignorance.

I am going presently to discuss your work in detail; but first I want to make some general appraisals. You seem to have little power of self-criticism. There are some fine things in the pamphlet, but they are side by side with work which no one should be willing to have printed.

Worse yet, you have not developed your powers of observation. You seem to regard the visible world merely as a means of making a political point; a primrose by the river's brim a yellow primrose was *not* to him, nor an aesthetic experience either, it is merely a jumping-off place for a remark that the poor don't get enough primroses. This is incontrovertibly true; they don't; the trouble is that you yourself have not looked at or valued a primrose for itself, and in consequence your political point becomes phony; why should the poor want primroses *unless* primroses are valuable in themselves?

Do you follow me? I am saying that you know nothing of flowers and care less, and that therefore "flowers" in your poetry are both vague and phony; the oftener you mention them, the less meaning they have. Before a poet can mention flowers honestly, he ought at least to have looked at them and learned to tell them apart. You remind me of a story which I often tell to illustrate the horribly corrupt standard of values of capitalist culture.

A while back the *Daily News* inquiring photographer, in an issue which I happened to see, asked five or six New Yorkers to name their favorite flower and give their reasons for preference. The goddamn male and female jerks chose nothing but roses and orchids; and the reason, in every case, and very slightly disguised, was that roses and orchids cost lots of money!

You see they *had* no favorite flower. They were incapable of valuing a flower. They were incapable even of *seeing* it; all they could either see or value was money.

Well, all you seem able to appreciate in *any* experience is its possible political implication. This is all very well, and it is possible to be a good human being on this basis; but it is not possible to be a good poet. Please believe me; the aesthetic meaning of any experience is *not* quite the same thing as its value to the working class. Please, please!

Of course you are a good enough poet by nature so that you do not live *down* to your idea of aesthetics; in many places you have a real feeling for beauty. But you are making yourself as bad a poet as you can. Look here; for God's sake, the next time you want to crown a girl with wild roses, suppose you get some wild roses and try it on yourself. You'll have a surprise. *That* is not a piece of knowledge you'll find in the *D[aily] W[orker]*, but it's something a poet ought to know.[19]

19. The *Daily Worker* began publication in 1924 as the official newspaper of the CPUSA; it ceased publication in 1957.

The third and most serious general point I want to make is that you simply do not know the English language well enough.

It is not that you can't write grammatically; you can. But grammar is only the bare bones of a language. Its flesh and blood are generations of association of ideas, so that a word has not only its dictionary meaning but a whole range of emotional values, from the comic to the tragic, the grotesque to the exquisite. Words also have *class* associations; a given word or idiom may stamp you at once as proletarian, middle class, or gentleman — as literate or illiterate; as city-bred or rural, modern-minded or old-fashioned. No doubt you know this in theory. What you have not realized is that your own use of words stamps you, to the eye, say, of an intelligent college senior with a turn for literature — stamps you as a boy trying to make bluff serve instead of education.

It is not because you write simply. You don't write simply. You write with an appalling variety of out-of-date bourgeois affectation; words that not even a college professor would use in speech, let alone a worker, come tumbling off your typewriter in all their mid-Victorian lushness. You are wearing the cast-off rags of bourgeois language, and you don't even know it.

Now a real folk poet is saved by illiteracy from the use of cliché and fancy phrases; his speech is vigorous and original because it has never been corrupted, his ballads are spoken English instead of written English. A really educated poet, on the other hand, achieves an equal simplicity and directness as the end result of years of laborious study of literature and of words themselves. But you fall between two stools; you are still in the transitional stage of "poetic diction," Gawdelpus. Have you ever heard of what the English call "Babu English"? An educated Bengali, that is a Babu, usually talks the goddamndest fancy language you ever heard, a long string of involved, ten-syllable, florid words, mostly misused. "Poetic diction" as you use it is a sort of Babu-English, the showing-off of a boy who *thinks* he knows a language because he can use it elaborately; and its effect is no less grotesque and pathetic than a zoot-suiter's idea of what the well-dressed man will wear.

These are harsh words. I use them only because I *want* to shock you; I want to jolt you out of any complacent idea you may have that because your English looks good to a New York Jewish group it will look good to America. That idea is the curse of our movement; we are self-imprisoned in the ghetto of our smugness.

I would not say these things, believe me, if I did not feel the waste of your great talent such a tragic waste; if I did not know that you *can* rise above the limitations of your environment and learn how to write. For God's sake, don't suspect me of anti-Semitism because I make the very obvious but all-too-often forgotten point that there *is* a certain difference between the culture of first- and second-generation Jewish immigrants living together in New York and the culture of the American hinterland. It's not that either culture is better than the other intrinsically; but we are committed to America and not America to us. It is for us to learn; especially as it is we who are trying to convince *them* of something.

Well, what I am driving at is that I think you ought to embark on a systematic course of self-education; and that you should not write for at least a year while you are learning, or the old habits will be too strong to break. And I think, too, that you should take leave of political activity, courses, schools and what-not, unless you have some financial commitments, on an official leave for purposes of education if possible — at any rate get yourself an ivory tower, strictly temporary, and start working on *yourself.* You don't need to know any more about politics; you do need to know almost everything else.

I think I once suggested some reading to you. I'm going to add a reading list to the end of this letter.

Another piece of advice; for God's sake, learn to write prose. Even if you make yourself the finest poet in America, it still won't be a living. At present poetry is the refuge of the incompetent; the competent *sell* their work.

Now for chapter and verse.

1. The Death of Roosevelt.[20] This is what I mean by the politics-is-art error. What in God's name possessed you to imagine that an arrangement of newspaper remarks could be a poem? Would you mistake one of those silly collage pieces, where an avant-garde artist pastes postage stamps and old hairpins and bits of fluff on a canvas, for a painting? You have made the point that Roosevelt's death was definitely a misfortune. This we didn't know already yet, maybe? If you had any emotions of your own, you should have expressed them in your own language; then we might have had something. A scissors is no substitute for inspiration.

2. The Astoria sonnets. The first two are beauties.[21] It is work like this

---

20. *The Thunder of the Grass,* pp. 7-10; the poem has this postscript: "Every word of this report was taken from the New York newspapers of April 13 and 14, 1945."
21. "Waterfront" and "Massacre," p. 11.

which makes me so furious at you when you take the easy way. You've really observed what you're looking at here, and the language is straight English. I wish you did not use "flower" and "dream" so often, but they are not clichés here. In My Neighbors you begin to slip. "Toil upon the morrow" is corn of the oldest. Would you ask a neighbor, "Are you going to toil upon the morrow?" Can you imagine his reaction?[22]

The wonderful lines beginning "only the wail of tugboats . . ." are poetry of the ultimate loveliness which stands one's hair on end — four lines of that; and then, for God's sake, you had to drag in that "cute idea," as Hollywood would call it, of the moon's cynical speech. Couldn't you see that you were completely breaking the mood — and a mood worthy of Keats? What were you trying to be, Ogden Nash?[23] After *that* even the fine concluding couplet cannot reestablish the tragic effect.

Pregnant Women strikes me as terrible, but then I've been pregnant myself and I know what it really feels like; you sentimentalize it excessively.[24] It is a cheerful, earthy, rather animal and fierce state, usually accompanied by bad temper and greed (though few women will admit it). As for technique, such lines as "Not them can clouds appal" et seq. me do appal. "The gloomy winding-sheets of evening" would have seemed very tasteful to a Victorian young lady in a female academy; but I shudder to think of its effect on the *New Yorker,* which of all publications most sets the taste of the intellectual middle-class. Also it is not a good idea to write a sonnet in conventional meter and then toss in something like "a new heart — in them a new hope is made." By you if it's got ten syllables it's iambic pentameter, hey?

Prothalamium is better, but terribly trite in the Spring-bridegroom image, and the flowers and dreams are in again, not to mention the birds.[25] Would you know an English sparrow from a hermit thrush, let alone from a song-sparrow? Would you care? And if not, why not? The meter is erratic, too, in an obviously unintentional way.

Phrases like "bower for love" and words like "aquiver" are not now in good usage. To an educated person their effect is not only archaic but comic — try to imagine anyone *saying* them. One of your troubles is that you do not write sufficiently for the ear.

22. "My Neighbors," p. 12.
23. Ogden Nash (1902-1971) was a popular humorist, poet, and playwright.
24. "Pregnant Women," p. 12.
25. "Prothalamium," p. 13.

3. Isaac Woodard simply does not come off.[26] Indignation does not cover triteness, and the blind-Justice business at the end is so trite that it's comical, again. I pulled a similar stunt myself, once, ending a poem with the symbol of the clenched fist. I shall never forget Bertolt Brecht's sour comment when I showed it to him "Always the clenched fists! Geballte Faust mit Sauerbraten!"[27] Served me right.

4. *Heine* has the same weaknesses your translations had — by the way, whatever happened with them?[28] — florid phrases and rather clumsy meter. "Poor, painwracked thing!" is simply gush. It is perhaps not entirely a virtue that the tradition of English letters insists that emotion must be expressed with restrained intensity, i.e., understated; but that's how it is, and there is nothing we can do about it right now. You are neither a fluttery spinster nor a pansy, and you should not talk like them. Your use of "sigh . . ." also mars the poem, which otherwise is very lovely. But again: why just "blossoms"? Why just "birds"? Why not chestnut-bloom, lilac, apple-blossom, anemone, or even a geranium in a flowerpot, the sad springtime of the windowsill? Why not swallow, lark, finch, some bird really seen and listened to? Are they only words to you, only poetic conveniences?

5. Train Song.[29] Well, boy, that time you did it. That's a poem. That's a young masterpiece. *That* is also English as she is spoke. Here you are dealing with a real emotion simply and genuinely expressed; you are talking. The contrast between this and the conventional prettiness, like a lace-paper valentine, that you work for in most of your verse is amazing. How can anyone capable of work like Train Song print some of those other poems? It is this question which leads me to conclude that you have simply not read and studied enough to develop sound critical standards.

6. The New Year, Spring Song.[30] Conventional though graceful at times. Why *must* you stick so grimly to the tritest and emptiest subjects in poetry? And just where have you seen a "carpet of lily"? The only lily that grows wild in the spring here is the adder's tongue, which certainly neither burns nor carpets meadows. No doubt you think that this sort of conventional vagueness and inaccuracy is "poetic license." Poetic license is some-

---

26. "Isaac Woodard," p. 14.

27. Bertolt Brecht (1898-1956) was one of the most important playwrights of the first half of the twentieth century.

28. "Heine," p. 15. Kramer had recently published *The Poetry and Prose of Heinrich Heine,* trans. with F. Ewen (New York: Citadel, 1948).

29. "Train Song," p. 16.

30. "The New Year" and "Spring Song," pp. 17-18.

thing claimed not by good poets but by bad versifiers; good poets use their eyes. Take a look at the flower-passages in "Lycidas," [and] in Keats' "[Ode to a] Nightingale." The men who wrote them were just as much city-dwellers as you.

7. Advertisements.[31] You are neither savage enough nor crisp enough, as yet, for satire; it demands inspired phrasemakers. Treatment[32] is very good, with its delayed point; the others are shapeless, marred by your *determination* to make a Marxist point or bust. Please never again speak in public of France's fairest belles, not even to be funny; it's too stale even for that. The Encyclopedia poem seems peculiarly mechanical in philosophy.[33] Are you trying to say that because an encyclopedia is not the *Communist Manifesto* it isn't worth having? Or that it is bad or un-Marxist to acquire a fund of general knowledge? Or that one cannot learn anything political from an encyclopedia, because there is no knowledge but Marx and Lenin is his prophet? I am afraid your unconscious attitude to writing has a little of this in it.

8. "Help Wanted" is entirely prosaic, without avoiding the cliché.[34] One point; self-worship is not what it's cracked up to be and the Worship of Man has an awful way of degenerating into the Worship of Oneself. If we spent less time in admiring the nobility of our own political sentiments, and more in humbly trying to learn the psychology of our potential audience, we'd get a lot further with our job. At present the general tone of self-praise and self righteousness in our press is as far as possible from true Marxist *self-criticisms* and certainly does not endear us to the American people.

9. The Central Park poems are fairly good, I think, especially the first — except for things like "Love's majesty" and "rebel hordes of sorrow."[35] I shall repeat until the end of eternity that these "conceits" have long since ceased to be acceptable written English — they were never good spoken English. What on earth have you been reading — [Henry Wadsworth] Longfellow?[36] I didn't know anyone still *knew* such phrases, let alone *using*

---

31. "Advertisements," pp. 19-22.
32. "Treatment," p. 21.
33. "Encyclopedia," p. 21.
34. "Help Wanted!" p. 22.
35. These are phrases from "The Lovers," p. 23.
36. Henry Wadsworth Longfellow (1802-1882) was a popular poet of the American Romantic period. His most famous narrative poems include *Evangeline* (1847), *Hiawatha* (1855), and *The Courtship of Miles Standish* (1858).

them. "Snapshot" and "Picnic" seem to insist rather hard on the gloomy view of life — you can't let the poor workers enjoy life at all without rubbing it into them that they'll be miserable in a few minutes.[37] Is it a Marxist's duty to be miserable? You sound more like a dour Scottish Calvinist here than like one of us. The Burns-statue poem is a good instance of a subject *not* to write on — cute past bearing.[38]

10. I regret to say that your title poem were better named The Thunder of the Corn.[39]

a. Getting raped is no longer considered "a fate Worse than death." I doubt that it ever was, except by Victorian spinsters. The modern motto is, "When rape is inevitable, relax and enjoy it." Women have, very rarely, been known to kill themselves *afterward* but almost never before. And all Shakespeare's genius can barely make "The Rape of Lucrece" credible, there being no real reason for the poor wench's suicide. How then do you expect a modern reader to swallow *ninety-four* suicides? Why didn't you have them try to kill a few Nazis, if they had to get themselves killed! The general effect of this mass-suicide pact, with the amazed Nazis bouncing up off the corpses, is the reverse of tragic.

b. Hmm, a materialist yet. Anything connected with the Jewish religion seems sacred to you; would you treat a *Catholic* school with the same hushed reverence? I'm afraid a great many of us are only materialists where the *other* guy's religion is concerned.

c. What in God's name did they kill themselves *with?* The climax of the story, and he leaves it out!

d. The style and rhythm sound as if you'd been reading Shelley.[40] But if Shelley were alive now, you think he'd still write like that? It's a good idea to practice writing in the old styles; but not to print the practice pieces. And the mixture of high-flown fancy language with the crudest and most prosaic modern talk is something to bring out the worst of both styles. For instance: "a gang of wheeling birds!" Nu, so how about a Kafee Klatch of eagles? In case you don't know, the word *gang* has a humorous, contemptuous, slangy effect that precludes its use here. Oh, those roses! It

37. "Snapshot," p. 23, and "Picnic," p. 25.
38. "A Statue of Burns," p. 24.
39. "The Thunder of the Grass," pp. 27-35.
40. Percy Bysshe Shelley (1792-1822) was the most mercurial of the English Romantic poets; his poems reveal in different places both his deft lyricism and his passionate intensity. His most famous poems include "Ode to the West Wind," "Hymn to Intellectual Beauty," and "Mont Blanc."

was roses, roses, all the way. What, no orchids? A good instance of "cute-
ness" is in the tendrils of ivy "that greenly blushed their pride." [John]
Ruskin used to call this the *pathetic fallacy*.[41] It lies in ascribing human
emotions to the subhuman or even the inanimate, and its effect is ludi-
crous. Are you by any chance under the impression that the ivy would
have been less green if there had been Goyim inside instead of Jews?
What is nonsense in fact remains nonsense in poetry!

11. I hesitate to comment on anything so obviously sincere as your poems for your father; but I must tell you that so extreme an expression of
emotion, though it might be quite orthodox in Yiddish, is not accepted in
English *except* in love-poetry.[42] In consequence, the poems *read* like love-
poems to an Anglo-Saxon eye or even to mine, and the effect is not what
you intended.

In conclusion, you must not forget that I am deliberately, in this letter,
assuming the viewpoint of an educated middle-class critic; which after all
is the viewpoint which dominates the publishing world. As myself, I
should be inclined to give more weight to your political good intentions
and to the warmth and gentleness which come through even your poorest
work. But it is just such partiality which has weakened our criticism. You
may say that your work impresses proletarians — I think it would — and
that you do not wish to write for the middle class. But you must not forget
that it is the middle class that buys books; the working class cares even less
for poetry than the middle class, and in addition the working class has yet
to form its cultural standards; at present what speaks is the corruption of
values, the ignorance, foisted upon it by the rulers. If you please workers
with poetry it is not because of their knowledge of the subject.

The pleasure of seeing one's work in print is not, I think, enough to
offset the disadvantages of publishing in such a format, with so little self-
criticism, and with such complete certainty of remaining practically unread. It broke Sol Funaroff's heart, and he was a more completely developed poet than you.[43] You had much better learn to meet the standards of
commercial publishing.

Yours, with the hope you will not be too angry,
Joy

41. John Ruskin (1819-1900) was the foremost art critic of Victorian England.
42. "Songs in Memory of My Father," pp. 36-40.
43. Sol Funaroff (1911-1942) was for a time poetry editor at the *New Masses*.

EDUCATION OF A POET * means indispensable

1. **Classical antiquity**
   Iliad and Odyssey, at least one*
   Eschylus, Agamemnon
   Euripides, Trojan Women (at least)
   Sophocles, Oedipus
   Plato, Dialogues, Symposium, Apology*
   Marcus Aurelius
   Plutarch's Lives
   Odes of Horace (F.P.A.'s translation, say)
   Virgil and Theocritus, if you can make it
   Sappho*
   Bulfinch's Mythology**** (English literature is incomprehensible without some classical and mythological knowledge. This is a quick way to get it.)

2. **The Bible, King James Version*********
   You can skip the begats; but no one can really write English well unless he has been through the Bible a couple of times.

3. **Middle Ages, Renaissance**
   Boccaccio
   Chaucer, Canterbury Tales, preferably in the original*
   The Oxford Book of Ballads* *That's* what a people's poetry is like.
   François Villon**** Preferably in French. The greatest people's poet of history, not excepting Whitman

4. **English poets and prose writers, all indispensable**
   Shakespeare, every word
   Marlowe
   Herrick, in unlimited quantities
   Donne (as much as you can take)
   Milton, esp. shorter pieces
   Bacon's Essays

Sir Thomas Browne

Bunyan's Pilgrim's Progress (the only work on this list I have not read, but I should have)

Ben Jonson, some

Restoration comedy — Congreve, Wycherly, or what you will

William Blake**** *That* is how to do proletarian poetry of revolt

Jane Austen* (A liberal education in herself)

Coleridge, Shelley, Keats, in moderation only (you incline to over-romanticism already)

Emily Bronte, Wuthering Heights

Charles Dickens, in toto

Robert Browning

William Morris, short poems

Charles Lamb

Walter Savage Lander, Imaginary Conversations

Walter Pater

George Meredith

George Moore, Aphrodite in Aulis; The Book Kerith, etc.

Shaw, in entirety

Fowler's Modern English Usage***

5. **Americans**

Whitman, of course, but in moderation.

Melville, Moby Dick

Sidney Lanier, poems

Thoreau, Walden******

You had better avoid Poe.

6. **Europeans**

Goethe's Faust; but only in German

Heine, of course, you have read

Ibsen

Strindberg

Hauptmann, The Weavers

Turgeniev

Chekhov (lay off the other Russians; you're gloomy enough
  already)

Moliere, Tartuffe, etc.

Voltaire, stories

Victor Hugo, novels only

Verlaine, Rimbaud, the Symbolists as a group, Mallarme, etc; but
  only if you can read French. Without knowing at least these
  three you can claim no standing in the more snobbish circles of
  modern poetry

Flaubert*

Balzac*

Maupassant

Stendhal, Rouge et Noir

Anatole France**** every scrap you can get.

7. **Moderns, roughly speaking . . . go easy.**

Edwin Arlington Robinson

Stephen Vincent Benet

Robert Frost

T. S. Eliot (these four *are* modern American)

Elinor Wylie, some poetry

Galsworthy, Fraternity, etc.

Wells, in great moderation

Kipling, short stories; Kim. Yes, I *know* he was an imperialist. He
  still could write circles around anybody else.

Mark Twain, esp. Huckleberry Finn

Lion Feuchtwanger, novels, esp. the Josephus trilogy

Dunsany, everything you can get

James Stephens, ditto

Walter De La Mare, poetry

A. E. Housman

Avoid most American writing and all best-sellers, except as
  sedatives.

8. Science

The Collected Works of Charles Fort******* An essential for the questioning mind.

Menninger, The Human Mind

Clendenning, The Human Body

Any good popular books on botany and zoology; also any other sciences you've a mind to. Psychology is a must. Try:

Freud: Introduction to Psychoanalysis, etc. Karen Horney, The Neurotic Personality of Our Time, etc.

Naturalists like W. H. Hudson, Ernest Thompson-Seton, etc. It is a misfortune, not a distinction, to know only the city.

Do not read any nineteenth-century science, especially in physics and biology. It is surprising how little of it is still accepted.

9. Light Reading

Better stick to good English detective *stories:* Chesterton, Dorothy Sayers, Nicholas Blake, H. O. Bailey, etc.

This list is chosen for a specific purpose; to establish a background of culture and a foreground of good style. Many great authors have been omitted because they wrote badly from the standpoint of style.

Much of this you may already have read. When you have read it all, you will not of course be really educated; but you will be able to meet an Oxford don or a Harvard Professor of English and follow, more or less, what he is talking about; and you will certainly be better able to criticize your own work. Most important, you will know how much you still have to learn and where to find it. Well, I'd better stop before I collapse.

Yours,

J.

Source: UM

To Aaron Kramer

Endekill Road
Staatsburg, N.Y.
February 7, 1948

Dear Aaron,

Your letter relieved me inexpressibly; I'd been jittering ever since I sent mine as to how you'd take it. To be able to take criticism such as that in the spirit you've shown is itself a sign of tremendous ability; a person of little talent couldn't have done it. By all means let's wrestle on the points you don't agree with; on many things I *was* probably over-severe, and I'm starved up here for intelligent discussion anyway, so you'll certainly not be taking too much of my time.

Perish the thought that I wanted you to be *like* an Oxford don. I didn't express myself well; what I meant was that, to be a real Marxist, one must know all the enemy knows and all one's own stuff besides. By refusing to acquire the cultural knowledge of the middle class, the party has made itself ridiculous, to that middle class even when, as in *N[ew] M[asses]*, trying to win it. Also it has sterilized the principles of Marx and made their correct application difficult. For instance; how can you take a Marxist view of history if you don't know history? And you can't know it if you only study the few periods covered by the few Marxist historians.

As for commercial publishing, of course there isn't any where poetry is concerned; there are commercial publishers who issue poetry for reasons of *prestige*, and for prestige they have to have poetry of a high technical, linguistic, and cultural level. It is often sterile in content, of course, but not always. My own War poems anthology, which was printed by Dial, was certainly not written *down* to any commercial standards;[44] and it did much better and reached many more people than it would have under International [Publisher]'s auspices in a badly printed paper-covered edition. It is one of our grievous mistakes to limit ourselves to readers who *already* agree with us. This limitation wouldn't matter if the number of such readers was constantly increasing; unfortunately it's dwindling at the moment.

It is a favorite rationalization of left-wing writers to claim that they're too good for the commercial press, that it is their nobility and their uncompromising principle which keep them from regular publishing. But very of-

---

44. *War Poems of the United Nations*, ed. Joy Davidman (New York: Dial Press, 1943).

ten it is really their amateurishness, and when they do learn to write well they promptly embrace the commercial field with loud cries of joy and depart from us — perhaps in the direction of Hollywood. No professional writer who *can* have a good imprint would dream of turning it down.

My own work is progressing like mad; I'm working on the Canadian novel, for which I have a tentative contract, and doing occasional short stories;[45] also laying the groundwork for a study of Marxist philosophy, as you may have guessed from things in my last letter. Our philosophy has been left to vegetate too long, and Howard Selsam's work on the subject is more of a liability than an asset, I fear.[46] We have not as yet made any effort to bring Marxism into harmony with Einsteinian and quantum physics, probably because most of us don't know it's necessary, yet Engels based materialism entirely on the implications of the dogmatic and bourgeois Newtonian physics which prevailed during the nineteenth century. Indeed, he states in *Ludwig Feuerbach* that atheism was developed by the industrial bourgeoisie to meet its needs. Of course if what you want is to grow rich by exploiting your fellow men then it's very convenient to be an atheist, it frees you from the fear of judgment by a moral Deity. Engels showed that the bourgeoisie valued religion not for themselves but as a means of terrifying and controlling the workers, and therefore soon seized control of almost all the churches and soft-pedaled the revolutionary implications of the New Testament. In our time there is a growing underground movement in many churches, even in the Catholic church, with the object of driving the money-changers out of the temple. I have met some of these rebels; many of them are already with us, and many more would be if a harmony of philosophies could be achieved between us — in short, if we would give up imagining that we have *proved* the non-existence of God, which we have not. You remember the group of clergymen that went to Yugoslavia recently and brought back such a splendid report? That's the sort of thing we need.

Of course the atom bomb has made a certain reworking of our position absolutely necessary too, though again many of us have yet to realize the implications. You see, all along we have felt justified in saying that the triumph of the proletariat was inevitable. The working class *was* the future; on this statement we based our ethics. How could Marx have anticipated a weapon which would make it possible that there wasn't going to *be*

45. The Canadian novel eventually appeared as *Weeping Bay* (New York: Macmillan, 1950).

46. Howard Selsam, *Socialism and Ethics* (New York: International Publishers, 1943).

any future (this is entirely possible) or that there was going to be another Dark Ages? We now have to say not that the triumph of the proletariat is *evitable* but that the alternative is utter destruction; in short, we can say Repent, for the end of the world *may be* at hand. I think it strengthens our position a good deal, once we appreciate it.

I'll be looking forward to seeing you in the spring. It really is the best time here, with everything coming to life, hepaticas and anemones and columbines and apple-blossoms, scarlet tanagers and orioles and gold-finches, and ducks among the marsh-marigolds in our brook. Love to all.

Yours,
Joy

Source: UM

To Aaron Kramer

Endekill Road
Staatsburg, N.Y.
February 13, 1948

Dear Aaron,

Okay, okay I take it back about the publishers. If you're doing that well, you're quite right to be satisfied where you are, and more power to your elbow.

I'm afraid, you know, that it's not possible to *argue* anyone into liking a work of art. One's reaction to poetry is mostly a matter of emotion, and be the arguments never so convincing the emotion is likely to remain the same. What I try to do as a critic is to know *why* I feel as I do on reading a work, and there are so many intangible and unconscious factors involved that no doubt I *sometimes* come up with the wrong explanations. But no matter how much one knows about art, the point is still to know what you like, and I do.

So think I ought to answer your specific points.

1. Noo, so you come from a Jewish home? So maybe *I* come from the O'Davidmans and the McSpivacks of Blarney? Listen, landsman, I'm talking from bitter experience yet. It's a swell thing to be a Jewish writer, if a Jewish writer is what you want to be. It's also swell to add the flavor of Jewish culture to the great mixture of America. Nor is it really difficult for a Jew to master the other elements in American culture; as you say, we do a damn sight better with it than Irish or Italian Catholics, for instance.

The danger is not to know that there's anything to master. I know one Jewish Marxist gal, a teacher in the Jeffschool too,[47] who said to me recently when I talked of the need to master American culture — "Show me anything American that isn't hideous!" You would certainly not say the same; but your whole orientation on this subject, as a movement, is Jewish first and Marxist second — and to be first a Jew and second a Marxist is not to be a Marxist at all. Can you be unaware of how the party press looks to comrades who are *not* Jews? I was unaware of it once. My parents are in the New York school system, terribly proud of their Americanization; we spoke no Yiddish at home (might have been better if we had) and they taught me very pedantic English. But all the same I was Jewish in all my habits of thought and speech, and quite unable to see anything from a non-Jewish point of view, until I married a Goy. Boy, did I learn things then! I'm only beginning, still, to master America; but I know it's there.

2. I'd a suspicion you got that mass suicide out of the headlines; it's much too improbable to have been invented. It is just those things which are taken directly from life which are always hard to make convincing in art. Life is often improbable. Wild coincidences are always happening, long-lost children being identified by strawberry marks on the right shoulder, etc. But — I know you won't believe me, but it's true — it's the amateur writer who justifies his use of an improbability by proving that it really happened. The true is not always the believable; for instance, it's true that there are sea serpents, but who believes it? As for *how* they killed themselves, it was your one chance to make the thing believable at all — psychologically very important, for after all convenient instruments for suicide are not part of the equipment of a girl's school! The whole story would have seemed more plausible to me if the teacher, without saying a word, had simply poisoned the tea for all of them.

Tell Schappes to take that tallith off, I know him.[48] If that poem had been any *more* Jewish I'd have to address you as Rabbi Our Teacher. It was the *religious* Judaism of the poem I pointed out, not reverence for Jews as

47. The Jefferson School of Social Science (1943-56) was a Marxist adult education institute in New York City associated with the CPUSA. The faculty included leftist academics dismissed from the City University of New York — among them the school's director, Howard Selsam.

48. Morris U. Schappes (1907-2004) wrote for the *Daily Worker,* was a university professor, and actively promoted Jewish studies throughout his life, including serving as editor of *A Documentary History of the Jews in the U.S.A.: 1654-1875* (New York: Citadel, 1950). A *tallith* is a fringed Jewish prayer shawl.

people but reverence for their religion. Either one is an atheist, a materialist, or one is not. It is not philosophically permissible to make a mental reservation in favor of one's own ancestral creed. What I asked you was whether you'd speak in the same hushed tone of Catholic relics as you do of the Torah? Nor were our rabbis, in the old country, always so much better than the priests; do you know some of them used to turn Jewish radicals in to the Tsar's Okhrana?[49]

I was pretty shy of saying anything about the poems to your father, because, frankly, I thought they were bad poems. Not because you loved him, God knows, but because you chose what seemed to me alternately prosaic and over sentimental phrases to express your love. There are plenty of great grief-poems in English. All subjects are possible to poetry; but not all styles, and most of my criticisms of your work have to do with its style. Even the "Thunder of the Grass" seems bad to me primarily because of its lush and ornate treatment.

3. Quite so. [Robert] Herrick often doesn't specify.[50] If I use a melodramatic and absurd plot, can I justify it by pointing out what silly plots Shakespeare used for [*King*] *Lear* and *Othello*? The delicate and precise grace of Herrick's fairyland Devon is neither to be imitated nor to be equaled by either you or me. He is entitled to his style; it does not justify an absence of style in us.

Mechanical method, eh? Conceit for the ear of his love, eh? Read up on Herrick in a history of lit.

But, good God, my whole purpose was not to get you to imitate anybody but to encourage you to develop a reliable taste of your *own*. Taste's an intangible thing; quite easy to see where someone lacks it but terribly hard to explain his lack to him. All I can say is that much of your diction seems to me in bad taste, and unnecessarily so since you can often write with distinction.

Well, I'll plant primroses for you.

Yours,
Joy   *Source: UM*

---

49. The name of the greatly feared secret police of imperialist Russia; they held greatest power from 1881 until the Revolution of October 1917.

50. Robert Herrick (1591-1674) was a parson by vocation and a poet by inclination. His *Hesperides; or, The Works both Humane and Divine of Robert Herrick, Esq* (1648) is comprised of over 1,400 poems.

To V. J. Jerome

Endekill Road
Staatsburg, N.Y.
February 27, 1948

Dear Jerry,

Last night was swell [and] started my mind working so actively it hasn't slowed down yet, in spite of a tedious trip home and wrestling with the kids this morning. I've thought of a new way to make the point I've been struggling with. Thus: blind adherence to the letter, the acceptance of Marxism as a literal revelation, has killed the spirit and made it impossible to use Marxism properly as a technique for analyzing new situations. We have unconsciously been reduced to acting as if there *are* no new situations.

This literalism has blinded us to the fact that a great new negation of the negation has taken place in science and philosophy. The thesis — mediaeval assertion of the soul — and the antithesis, bourgeois atheism's assertion of the material, are being resolved before our eyes into a synthesis, a universe and a human being in which the material and the spiritual are, as it were, aspects of each other; in which neither is primary because both are essentially the same thing — i.e. concrete and specialized matter is reducible to abstract and unspecialized (and yet real) energy. We were theoretically prepared for this change, but in practice we have ignored it, and I fear that we have done so because the atheistic aspect of our philosophy was enormously attractive to us *emotionally* — because what we were doing was hating the Church instead of constructing a philosophy which could dispose of the Church by going beyond it.

Now it is not an academic question, any longer, whether we should take cognizance of this new development — for the educated portion of the bourgeoisie, and such comrades as Haldane have already had to accept it and are consequently keenly aware of the archaism of *our* scientific position, which does us no good.[51] As for the uneducated, bourgeois and worker alike, they have had the thing proved to them by the atom bomb, which has demonstrated both that the future is *not* predictable and that

51. Davidman is referring to one of the works of evolutionary biologist J. B. S. Haldane (1892-1964), probably either *Marxist Philosophy and the Sciences* (New York: Random House, 1939) or the pamphlet "Why Professional Workers Should Be Communists" (London: The Communist Party of Great Britain, 1945). Interestingly, some of Haldane's ideas were attacked by C. S. Lewis in *Perelandra* (London: Bodley Head, 1943) and *That Hideous Strength*.

matter is not the ultimate and self-existent reality. People know this even if they cannot express it. Nor does it help us to take refuge in ambiguity as we sometimes do and use "matter" to mean "everything that exists"; for by such a definition matter could also include God, the soul, or what have you.

We have all noticed the spontaneous revival of religious interest of all sorts, among all classes of people. Only such an unspeakable idiot as Dave Platt (who recently ascribed movies favoring spiritualist mediums to the influence of the Catholic Church!) could think that this is entirely due to a Catholic conspiracy, though of course Rome is trying to cash in on it.[52] I am inclined to the opinion that this religious revival, which is as yet a half-formed wish rather than a concrete movement, is itself a fact of the dialectical synthesis which is taking place; and I am very much concerned that *we* should supply its leadership, its aims and ethics, and its concrete form, instead of standing by as paralyzed spectators to watch it being perverted by the enemy. What has paralyzed us so far, of course, has nothing to do with Marxism; it is an uncontrolled emotional reaction against religion, masquerading as Marxism. I heard that demonstrated very graphically recently by a fairly prominent woman Marxist with whom I was discussing philosophy, and whom I was able to show that she could not even state the materialist philosophy which she thought that she believed. Unable to give any rational materialist statement, she finally cried out, "But I *hate* the word God!" This same woman has also said to me that one can't find anything American which isn't hideous — this, mind you, in a discussion of culture. And yet she is a devoted and intelligent comrade and teaches in a Marxist school.

Well, I don't want to burden you with any more of this — I know how much time they leave you for private life of any kind! But I do hope you will decide to open one of our publications for a free discussion of these questions. I may very well be wrong, but it seems to me that we have lost the spirit, which is also called the Zeitgeist, by closing our minds on this subject; and that we must repair the error if we are ever again to embody the spirit of the times.

Love to all,

Yours,

Joy

Source: Yale

---

52. David Platt (1903-1992) was a film and music critic; from 1933 to 1957 he wrote film reviews for the *Daily Worker*.

To William Rose Benét

Endekill Road
Staatsburg, N.Y.
October 31, 1948

Dear William Rose Benét,

I can't help writing to thank you for "To a Communist."[53] You've got it all said, all that I've been working out for myself — very painfully, very much against the grain — for the last few years. It's quite true, I'm afraid, that Marxism is just another of man's hopeless attempts to foresee and control the future, and a crystal ball would have done nearly as well. It's always the unforeseen that happens, as it happened with a bang at Hiroshima.

I wish there were others like you, who know enough to condemn Communism on the *real* ground, that it is false. The press and the politicians resort so freely to abuse, bullying, and plain lying that it almost seems they fear in their hearts that Communism may be true! At any rate, they seem to attack Marxism not so much for having achieved evil as for having intended good. So it was quite natural for all of us, conscious of our good intentions (and, I may add, of our innocence of spy plots, at least in my circles) but quite unconscious of our bad reasoning, to assume that if men persecuted us it must be for His Name's sake.

As for me, I had to have a direct and shattering experience of God, and then to plow my way through Lenin's *Materialism,* surely the world's most unreadable book (not to mention side excursions into light literature like the *Critique of Pure Reason,* God help me)[54] — in order to find out that Marxism was philosophically nonsensical, logically unsound, historically arbitrary, and scientifically half false from the start and the other half overthrown by Einstein's first work. So perhaps I oughtn't to blame the press and the politicians too much for taking the easy way!

All the more reason to be grateful to you for having pointed out the real fallacies. And thank you, too, for giving us credit for our good intentions, no matter what road they paved. For almost all of us had them. I've met a few definitely paranoid Communists, and a few embittered failures, but Lord knows the majority of us were just well-meaning half-educated

---

53. See W. R. Benét, "To a Communist," *The Saturday Review of Literature* 31 (October 23, 1948): 39.
54. Immanuel Kant's *Critique of Pure Reason* first appeared in 1781.

schlemiels, and none a bigger schlemiel than I. We knew something was wrong with the world, and knew so little else that we were ready to fall for any glib way of putting it right. Some of us had to take the Sacred Writings of Marx and Engels on superstitious trust because we couldn't understand a word of them. Others, like me, were simply too lazy to read them — until we began to wonder if they really proved the case.

I use the past tense because in truth the CPUSA is nearly dead — membership somewhere under twenty thousand, and much of that in splinter groups cutting each others' throats; three or four splinters are attacking the official Party for not being pro-Russian *enough!* Some of the Party's decline is no doubt due to fear, and some to the good look at Soviet foreign policy we have been getting; whatever they've got there, it doesn't seem to be the New Jerusalem. But mostly, I think, the failure is the Marxist failure in ethics. What brought us to the Party, whether we knew it or not, was the ethic of Christ: Love your neighbor as yourself. The Party's first act was to teach us that Marx recognized only the ethic of self-interest! If we ever convinced anybody of *that,* of course, self-interest took him straight to the Thomas Committee, to our rather naive surprise.[55] But the more usual result was moral confusion — the end justifying the means, as you have pointed out, with its inevitable coarsening and corrupting effect on our characters. Our desire to teach others led to contempt of them, our sense of justice to self-righteousness, our love to hate. Most of us were absurdly gentle people physically, and yet I do not think any of us were fit to trust with power. The alternatives at last were: stay and be corrupted, or get out and repent.

Perhaps you will help me a little further. I've been debating whether to send this letter to the editor, or privately to you. I don't mind confessing in public that I've made a damn fool of myself, and besides I can hardly pass as a Marxist writer in future; my literary reputation is almost non-existent, but what there is of it I don't want to enjoy under false colors. All the same; I knew the comrades and worked with them, and for all their unreasoning fanaticism they were good people in most ways; very good people, if you compare them to the advertising man, the Hollywood executive, the machine politician — all our Pharisees. I didn't

55. In 1947 New Jersey congressman John Parnell Thomas was appointed chairman of the House of Representatives Committee on Un-American Activities; the committee was sometimes referred to as the Thomas Committee. The committee was fiercely anti-Communist and was often abusive in its prosecution and persecution of suspected Communists in and out of the American government.

leave them in order to run to safety, and I don't like kicking them when they're down.

I'll leave it up to you. If you think this letter would have any point in print, pass it on.[56] If not, burn it. And thanks again for your poem. There's no more uncomfortable status than that of ex-Communist, but I think you will understand that it's possible to stop being a Communist without becoming something worse.

Yours sincerely,
Joy Davidman

P.S. Dear Bill Benét:

It was easier to keep the main letter formal. Less formally: that was a damn fine poem, true enough to make me writhe here and there and to exhilarate me tremendously at the end. I too have come to the old doctrine of death and resurrection by the roundabout road first of the atheist hedonism which, whether we like it or not, is the working philosophy of our culture, and second of the atheist future-of-man superstition of Marxism. Oh well, as long as one gets there!

I hope all the Benéts and their kinfolk are well. Give my good wishes to all of them, won't you please. My husband — Bill Gresham — particularly asks to be remembered to Laura,[57] and so do I. The Greshams are striking roots in Dutchess County and raising children, cabbages, and novels — which may have something to do with our return to sanity.

Yours,
Joy

Source: Yale

---

56. Key excerpts from the letter appeared in "The Phoenix Nest," *The Saturday Review of Literature* 32 (January 29, 1949): 42-43.
    57. Bill Benét's sister.

To the Editor of the *The Saturday Review of Literature*[58]

Letter to the Editor
The Saturday Review of Literature
December 25, 1948

Sir:

Denis de Rougemont has described the failure of modern marriage brilliantly.[59] The merely literary tradition he assigns as its cause, however, seems far too polite and superficial an explanation. A man's attitude toward love is not, after all, purely the result of what he has been taught about love; it is part and parcel of his basic attitude toward the whole of life. If we see in our marriages only a source of thrills-without-responsibility, it is not Tristan's fault nor even the fault of movies and magazines, which, though they aggravate our disease, are essentially only its symptoms. It is the fault of a materialist philosophy which sees nothing else in the universe. So the materialist — and, whether nominally Christian or not, a large majority are materialists — *must* translate the pursuit of happiness into the pursuit of pleasure. More gadgets, more liquor, more women, more thrills. In the end, of course, he not only fails to find happiness but destroys *even* his capacity for pleasure — which is why we are a country of sick minds, broken homes, and dyspeptic stomachs.

Joy Davidman
Staatsburg, N.Y.

---

58. This letter appeared in *The Saturday Review of Literature* 31 (December 25, 1948): 23.

59. See Denis de Rougemont, "The Romantic Route to Divorce," *The Saturday Review of Literature* 31 (November 13, 1948): 9-10, 59.

The Longest Way Round

When I was fourteen I went walking in the park on a Sunday afternoon, in clean, cold, luminous air. The trees tinkled with sleet; the city noises were muffled by the snow. Winter sunset, with a line of young maples sheathed in ice between me and the sun — as I looked up they burned unimaginably golden — burned and were not consumed.

I heard the voice in the burning tree; the meaning of all things was revealed and the sacrament at the heart of all beauty lay bare; time and space fell away, and for a moment the world was only a door swinging ajar. Then the light faded, the cold stung my toes, and I went home, reflecting that I had had another aesthetic experience. I had them fairly often. That was what beautiful things did to you, I recognized, probably because of some visceral or glandular reaction that hadn't been fully explored by science just yet. For I was a well-brought-up, right-thinking child of materialism. Beauty, I knew, existed; but God, of course, did not.

By now there is a whole generation like me in the cities of America. I was an atheist and the daughter of an atheist; I assumed that science had disproved God, just as I assumed that science had proved that matter was

---

This essay first appeared as the lead piece in *These Found the Way: Thirteen Converts to Protestant Christianity*, ed. David Wesley Soper (Philadelphia: The Westminster Press, 1951), pp. 13-26. When C. S. Lewis later read the book, he wrote a friend: "I happen to have 2 copies of this ugly book in wh. you may find some of the articles worth reading. Joy Davidman's is the best, I think" (*The Collected Letters of C. S. Lewis, Volume 3: Narnia, Cambridge, and Joy, 1950-1963*, ed. Walter Hooper [London: HarperCollins, 2006], March 25, 1954, p. 447).

indestructible. A religious conviction was something "nice people" didn't have, something not to be mentioned in polite society. Before my time an atheist had been essentially a *religious* man, one who had thought about God and thought hard, if not well. But my generation sucked in atheism with its canned milk. We hardly thought about it at all, and most of us were no less religious than many churchgoers.

A young poet like myself could be seized and shaken by spiritual powers a dozen times a day, and still take it for granted *that* there was no such thing as spirit. What happened to me was easily explained away; it was "only nerves" or "only glands." As soon as I discovered Freud, it became "only sex." And yet if ever a human life was haunted, Christ haunted me.

The country boy who comes to the big city often leaves his religion behind. My own parents were Jews, but their story differs only in degree from that of many Christians. They came to America as children, from small villages of eastern Europe where for a thousand years the Jews had held desperately to their faith against fire and terror and murder. Cut off, hemmed in, embittered, the Judaism of such villages resembled the taboo systems of savages more than it resembled the prophetic Judaism of the Old Testament or the philosophic and scholarly Judaism of medieval western Europe. Six hundred and more ritual taboos governed daily conduct; striking a match or stacking the dishes carelessly could be an offense against a very jealous God. This religion of the letter rather than the spirit heartened the Jews to endure their isolation. But it was kept going by persecution, as a dead man in a crowd may be kept on his feet by the pressure of those around him. In America, with the persecution removed, the corpse collapsed. Boys like my father, growing up in the polyglot world of New York, looked at their small-town religion and found it absurd.

Many Jews got rid of the traditional forms of Judaism, but kept a vague and well-meaning belief in a vaguely well-meaning God — a sort of Unitarianism. Such halfway measures, however, were not for my parents or me. My father declared proudly that he had retained the ethics of Judaism, the only "real" part of it, and got rid of the theology — rather as if he had kept the top floor of our house but torn down first floor and foundation. When I came along, I noticed that there was nothing supporting the ethics; down it crashed.

It's not true that an atheist cannot have any morality; what he cannot have is a *rational* morality. Unless we have a turn for philosophy, nine tenths of our moral code will be habit and sentiment, coaxed into us by Mamma, knocked into us by Papa. And ceasing to believe in God does not destroy a lifelong habit of telling the truth and holding the door politely for old ladies. My father persisted in justice, temperance, fortitude, and prudence. He was used to them. It never occurred to him that, in the meaningless and purposeless universe of the atheist, moral ideas could only be something men had put together for their own convenience, like the horse and buggy; something you could scrap as soon as an automobile morality came along. And he tried his level best to pass his virtues on to me.

Atheist virtues, however, don't keep very well.

My parents had never been taught that faith and hope and charity were virtues at all. With no revealed law, no conviction of sin, no weekly reminder of shortcomings, no humility before God, no wonder at mystery, no hope of heaven, no help of grace — what can the best atheist do but turn Pharisee? Since he himself is the only standard of value he recognizes, why shouldn't he be proud? Lacking God, the good man has a way of turning "unco guid."[1] If he checks up on his own virtues, he can only do it by measuring himself against his neighbor; and that way lies damnation. For there are two ways of desiring virtue, and the whole gulf of hell lies fixed between them — between wanting to be *good*, and wanting to be better than your neighbor.

I declared my own atheism at the age of eight, after reading [H. G.] Wells's *Outline of History* (allured thereto by enchanting pictures of dinosaurs).[2] In a few years I had rejected all morality as a pipe dream. If life had no meaning, what was there to live for except pleasure? Luckily for me, my preferred pleasure happened to be reading, or I shouldn't have been able to stay out of hot water so well as I did. The only lasting damage my philosophy caused me was nearsightedness.

If America had replaced my ancestral Judaism with other spiritual values, I might have been something better than a pleasure seeker. Let's face it, though; what America stressed in the twenties, and stresses far too much even today, is physical satisfaction. Every day, in every way, the world was getting more comfortable. True patriots love their country because they serve her; but our schools and newspapers taught us to love her because she enriched us. Our love of country, the upshot proved, was often

1. The phrase *unco guid* is used to describe those who are excessively self-righteous and narrow-minded. It derives from Robert Burns's "Address to the Unco Guid," a poem attacking rigidly self-righteous persons.

2. H. G. Wells, *The Outline of History: Being a Plain History of Life and Mankind* (London: Macmillan, 1920).

no deeper than any other kind of cupboard love. In 1929 I believed in nothing but American prosperity; in 1930 I believed in nothing.

Men, I said, are only apes. Virtue is only custom. Life is only an electrochemical reaction. Mind is only a set of conditioned reflexes, and anyway most people aren't rational like ME. Love, art, and altruism are only sex. The universe is only matter. Matter is only energy. I forget what I said energy was only.

Portrait of the happy materialist; and yet it is no more than half the picture, for, like most adolescents, I was really two people. The hard, cocksure young atheist was largely what psychologists call a "persona," a mask, a surface personality for dealing with the world. In the greedy, grabbing, big-city, middle-class world I knew, this seemed the sort of person that was wanted. But underneath the surface my own real personality stirred, stretched its wings, discovered its own tastes. It was a girl with vague eyes, who scribbled verses — scribbled them in a blind fury, not knowing what she wrote or why, and read them afterward with wonder. We call that fury "poetic inspiration" nowadays; we might be wiser to call it "prophecy."

This inner personality was deeply interested in Christ, and didn't know it. As a Jew, I had been led to feel cold chills at the mention of his name. Is this strange? For a thousand years Jews have lived among people who interpreted Christ's will to mean floggings and burnings, "gentleman's agreements," and closed universities. If nominal Christians so confuse their Master's teaching, surely a poor Jew may be pardoned a little confusion. Nevertheless I had read the Bible (for its literary beauty, of course!) and I quoted Jesus unconsciously in everything I did, from writing verse to fighting my parents. My first published poem *was* called "Resurrection" — a sort of private argument with Jesus, attempting to convince him (and myself) that he had never risen.[3] I wrote it at Easter, of all possible seasons, and never guessed why.

The cross recurs through most of my early poems, and I seem to remember explaining that Jesus was "a valuable literary convention."[4] Those

---

3. Joy Davidman, "Resurrection," *Poetry* 47 (January 1936): 193-94.

4. Here is another poem where Davidman focused upon the cross (*Letter to a Comrade*, pp. 81-82):

> **Againrising**
> The stroke of six
> my soul betrayed;
> as the clock ticks
> I am unmade;

verses were mainly the desperate question: Is life really only a matter of satisfying one's appetites, or is there more? They make gloomy reading. An *adult* as consistently atheist as I was, of course, would be a gloomy cuss, obsessed by the futility of all things. But it was only in my prophetic moments that I asked such questions. My other self — the "persona" of daily life — was quite content to get its appetites satisfied and no questions asked. I suppose the very young carry a kind of insurance against atheist despair; though they believe in nothing else, they will believe firmly in the importance of their own emotions and desires.

Yet it's strange how completely I failed to see where my emotions and desires were leading. For what I read, eagerly and untiringly, was fantasy. Ghost stories and superscience stories; George MacDonald in my

---

the clock struck nine;
my life ran down
on gears of time
with a sickened sound.

The noonday struck
a note of pride:
spread on the clock
I was crucified.

The clock struck one,
whose spear, whose dart
transfixed by bone
and narrow heart.

The sound of seven
filled me with bells;
I left great heaven
for little hells;

the midnight let
my blood run out
fierce and red
from my opened mouth.

Great chaos came
to murder me
when the clock named
the hour of three.

The dawn grew wide;
the clock struck five,
and all inside
I was alive.

childhood, Dunsany in my teens.[5] I believed the three-dimensional material world was the only thing that existed, but in literature it bored me. I didn't believe in the supernatural, but it interested me above all else. Only it had to be written as fiction; the supernatural presented as fact outraged my convictions. By disguising heaven as fairyland I was enabled to love heaven.

There is a myth that has always haunted mankind, the legend of the Way Out. "A stone, a leaf, an unfound door," wrote Thomas Wolfe — the door leading out of time and space into Somewhere Else.[6] We all go out of that door eventually, calling it death. But the tale persists that for a few lucky ones the door has swung open *before* death, letting them through, perhaps for the week of fairy time which is seven long years on earth; or at least granting them a glimpse of the land on the other side. The symbol varies with different men; for some, the door itself is important; for others, the undiscovered country beyond it — the never-never land, Saint Brendan's Island, the Land of Heart's Desire. C. S. Lewis, whose *Pilgrim's Regress* taught me its meaning, calls it simply the Island.[7] Whatever we call it, it is more our home than any earthly country. And for me the myth took a specific form.

As a child I had a recurring dream: I would walk down a familiar street which suddenly grew unfamiliar and opened onto a strange, golden, immeasurable plain, where far away there rose the towers of Fairyland. If I remembered the way carefully, the dream told me, I should be able to find it when I woke up. To conventional psychologists, I know, such visions are merely "wishful thinking." But why should all human beings be born wanting something like that, unless it exists?

The last time I had that dream I was grown up, and so I put it in rhymes, which I should like to quote here, not for any intrinsic excellence, but as proof of the hope of heaven, making itself known even to one so willfully blind as I.

5. George MacDonald (1824-1905) wrote fantasies, fairy-tales, romantic novels, and poetry; his work also profoundly influenced C. S. Lewis. Lord Dunsany (1878-1957), born Edward John Moreton Drax Plunkett, was one of the earliest writers of modern fantasy literature.

6. This line appears in the opening paragraph of Thomas Wolfe's first novel, *Look Homeward, Angel: A Story of the Buried Life* (New York: Charles Scribner's Sons, 1929).

7. C. S. Lewis, *The Pilgrim's Regress: An Allegorical Apology for Christianity, Reason and Romanticism* (London: J. M. Dent, 1933).

Fairytale
At night, when we dreamed,
we went down a street,
and turned a corner;
we went down the street
and turned the corner,
and there, it seemed,
there was the castle.

Always, if you knew,
if you knew how to go,
you could walk down a street
(the daylight street)
that twisted about
and ended in grass;
there it was
always, the castle.

Remote, unshadowed,
childish, immortal,
with two calm giants
guarding the portal,
stiff in the sunset,
strong to defend,
stood castle safety
at the world's end.

O castle safety,
Love without crying,
honey without cloying,
death without dying!

Hate and heartbreak
all were forgot there;
we always woke,
we never got there.[8]

---

8. "Fairytale" first appeared in *War Poems of the United Nations,* ed. Joy Davidman
(New York: Dial Press, 1943).

A rather odd poem, perhaps, for the convinced atheist and Communist who wrote it in 1940!

During the depression my spiritual insurance had lapsed. For one thing, I was getting a little old for the flitting-butterfly stuff; at twenty-two a girl begins to want a serious purpose. For another though I myself was prosperous and secure, my friends were not. To live entirely for my own pleasures, with hungry men selling apples on every street corner, demanded a callousness of which I seemed incapable. Maybe no rational person would worry about the rest of the world; I found myself worrying, all the same. And I wanted to *do* something, so I joined the Communist Party.

My motives were a mixed lot. Youthful rebelliousness, youthful vanity, youthful contempt of the "stupid people" who seemed to be running society, all these played a part. The world was out of joint, and, goody, goody, who so fit as I to set it right? Art had something to do with my decision, for those were the years in which great films and books and music were coming out of the Soviet Union. The war in Spain had much to do with it. Most of all, however, I think I was moved by the same unseen power that had directed my reading and my dreaming — I became a Communist because, later on, I was going to become a Christian.

I am not trying to excuse myself. I did something quite inexcusable; I entered the Party in a burst of emotion, without making the slightest effort to study Marxist theory. All I knew was that capitalism wasn't working very well, war was imminent — and socialism promised to change all that. And for the first time in my life I was willing to be my brother's keeper. So I rushed round to a Party acquaintance and said I wanted to join.

"Wait a minute," said she, listening suspiciously to my bubblings. "You mean you want to join for the sake of *other* people?"

Then and there I told my first lie for the Party. Her tone warned me that I was in danger of rejection. "To hell with other people!" I declared. "I want to join the Communists for my own sake, because I know I can't have a decent future without socialism!"

My friend relaxed and smiled. My Marxist education, the process of getting rid of my "bourgeois values," had begun.

I went to the meetings in Madison Square Garden, I and twenty thousand like me, and there we felt ourselves linked by that surge of spiritual power which unites all meetings of genuine worshipers, whatever they worship. "A feeling of solidarity!" we called it in our horrible jargon, and never remembered the text that runs: "Where two or three are gathered together in my name, there am I in the midst of them."[9]

Later, however, the dry rot began. Like the fabulous snake that swallowed its own tail and vanished, the corrupt philosophy of Marxism devoured the very motives that made Marxists of us. Self-interest is the law, I was taught; the ultimate victory of the Party was my victory. My visionary fairyland, transferred from Somewhere-Out-of-Space to Somewhere-Ahead-in-Time, began to seem at last a possible, even a probable goal; the never-never land turned into the Comes-the-Revolution Country.

I was working for heaven on earth, in short, and that end justified all means. And so the means I used began to corrupt me.

I had no idea what was happening to me, of course. Most American Communists are anything but scholars; as their leaders ruefully admit, they are unwilling to master Marxist theory, though it is true that the Party makes every effort to teach them. In consequence, Communist philosophy works on them by stealth. They do not see the deadly change from losing *self* in *class* to losing *class* in *self;* they never guess that they will end by justifying as "the future good of the working class" every imaginable indulgence of their own pride.

With my few scraps of knowledge, I was accepted almost at once as a journalist and critic on the Party's semiofficial magazine *New Masses.* And I began to learn. I learned that "love of the people" made it all right for us to lie to the rank and file of the Party; still worse, that in practice our vague "love of the people" turned into quite specific hatred of the people's enemies, and that the enemies of the people were all those of every class and opinion who happened to disagree with the Party. Hatred, to us, was a virtue, and, much as we hated Fascism, we hated even more bitterly the anti-Fascist liberals who were our rivals for the support of labor. I can remember a *New Masses* editor, while the war against Hitler was at its hottest, saying solemnly, "We can see now that the *real* enemies are the Social Democrats!"

I learned too that my judgment of a book or movie must depend not on its artistic merit, but on its Marxist orthodoxy, or even on whether its author was a liberal contributor to the Party's needy treasury; and that, at the sight of a hero, a martyr, or a genius, I must say, not, "How wonderful!" but, "How can we *use* him?"

I resisted all this somewhat, but mostly I gave in to it even before

9. Matthew 18:20.

pressure was applied, and then persuaded myself that it wasn't there. By nature I am the sort of woman who nurses sick kittens and hates to spank her bad little boys; yet as a Marxist I would have been willing to shoot people without trial. In practice I willingly gave my spare time, my spare cash, my love of truth, and my artistic conscience. Fortunately for me, I was never asked to do anything more dangerous than that.

There were, however, some signs of health in me. I made jokes at the Party's expense; I continued, in the teeth of the Party's contempt, to read fantasy; and I utterly failed to read the dreary books we called "proletarian novels."[10] Though I reproached myself bitterly for it, moreover, I was bored at meetings.

Presently I married a veteran of the Spanish War — the writer William Lindsay Gresham. Together we made a startling discovery: marriage had ended, overnight, all our lingering interest in going to Party social gatherings! I realized then a hitherto unsuspected attraction for the young which the Communist Party shares with the church social — it is a great matchmaker.

My husband had lost his enthusiasm for Communist speeches in Spain. What war did for him childbirth did for me. My little son was a real thing and so was my obligation to him; by comparison, my duty to that imaginary entity the working class seemed the most doubtful of abstractions. I began to notice what neglected, neurotic waifs the children of so many Communists were, and to question the genuineness of a love of mankind that didn't begin at home.

Meanwhile the Party itself was changing. During the depression, an honest anger at injustice and misery had brought many able and generous men into it. Now a renewed faith in America, and dismay at the antics of the Soviet Union, took them out of it again. The few who remained were chiefly embittered failures, more interested in revenge on the existing society than in building a better one; what had been the leading cultural force of the '30's dwindled, in the '40's, to a circle of amateur Russian agents. Far from being the sinister and efficient conspirators of newspaper imagination, however, the present Communists are so clumsy that they antagonize American workers every time they open their mouths.

By 1946 I had two babies; I had no time for Party activity, and was glad of it; I hardly mentioned the Party except with impatience. And yet,

---

10. For more on this, see my "Joy Davidman and the *New Masses:* Communist Poet and Reviewer," *The Chronicle of the Oxford C. S. Lewis Society* 4, no. 1 (February 2007): 18-44.

out of sheer habit, I went on believing that Marxism was true. Habit, and something more. For I had no knowledge of divine help, and all the world had lost faith in gradual progress; if now, in the day of the atomic bomb, I were to lose my trust in violent means of creating heaven on earth, what earthly hope was there?

A year or so before this, my interest in fantasy had led me to C. S. Lewis — *The Screwtape Letters* and *The Great Divorce*.[11] These books stirred an unused part of my brain to momentary sluggish life. Of course, I thought, atheism was *true;* but I hadn't given quite enough attention to developing the proof of it. Someday, when the children were older, I'd work it out. Then I forgot the whole matter. That was all, on the surface. And yet, that was a beginning.

Francis Thompson symbolized God as the "Hound of Heaven," pursuing on relentless feet.[12] With me, God was more like a cat. He had been stalking me for a very long time, waiting for his moment; he crept nearer so silently that I never knew he was there. Then, all at once, he sprang.

My husband had been overworking. One day he telephoned me from his New York office — I was at home in Westchester with the children — to tell me that he was having a nervous breakdown. He felt his mind going; he couldn't stay where he was and he couldn't bring himself to come home. . . . Then he rang off.

---

11. C. S. Lewis, *The Screwtape Letters* (London: Geoffrey Bles, 1942), and *The Great Divorce: A Dream* (London: Geoffrey Bles, 1945).

12. Davidman has in mind these lines from Thompson's poem, "The Hound of Heaven" (1893; ll. 1-15):

> I fled Him, down the nights and down the days;
>   I fled Him, down the arches of the years;
> I fled Him, down the labyrinthine ways
>   Of my own mind; and in the mist of tears
> I hid from Him, and under running laughter.
>   Up vistaed hopes I sped;
>   And shot, precipitated,
> Adown Titanic glooms of chasmed fears,
>   From those strong Feet that followed, followed after.
>   But with unhurrying chase,
>   And unperturbéd pace,
>   Deliberate speed, majestic instancy,
>   They beat — and a Voice beat
>   More instant than the Feet —
>   "All things betray thee, who betrayest Me."

There followed a day of frantic and vain telephoning. By nightfall there was nothing left to do but wait and see if he turned up, alive or dead. I put the babies to sleep and waited. For the first time in my life I felt helpless; for the first time my pride was forced to admit that I was not, after all, "the master of my fate" and "the captain of my soul."[13] All my defenses — the walls of arrogance and cocksureness and self-love behind which I had hid from God — went down momentarily. And God came in.

How can one describe the direct perception of God? It is infinite, unique; there are no words, there are no comparisons. Can one scoop up the sea in a teacup? Those who have known God will understand me; the others, I find, can neither listen nor understand. There was a Person with me in the room, directly present to my consciousness — a Person so real that all my previous life was by comparison mere shadow play. And I myself was more alive than I had ever been; it was like waking from sleep. So intense a life cannot be endured for long by flesh and blood; we must ordinarily take our life watered down, diluted as it were, by time and space and matter. My perception of God lasted perhaps half a minute.

In that time, however, many things happened. I forgave some of my enemies. I understood that God had always been there, and that, since childhood, I had been pouring half my energy into the task of keeping him out. I saw myself as I really was, with dismay and repentance; and, seeing, I changed. I have been turning into a different person since that half minute, everyone tells me.

When it was over I found myself on my knees, praying. I think I must have been the world's most astonished atheist.[14] My surprise was so great that for a moment it distracted me from my fear; only for a moment, however. My awareness of God was no comforting illusion, conjured up to reassure me about my husband's safety. I was just as worried afterward as before. No; it was terror and ecstasy, repentance and rebirth.

---

13. These phrases refer to the concluding lines of William E. Henley's "Invictus" (1888): "I am the master of my fate;/I am the captain of my soul."

14. Compare this to the way C. S. Lewis describes his own movement from atheism to theism: "You must picture me alone in that room in Magdalen [College], night after night, feeling, whenever my mind lifted even for a second from my work, the steady, unrelenting approach of Him whom I so earnestly desired not to meet. That which I greatly feared had at last come upon me. In the Trinity Term of 1929 I gave in, and admitted that God was God, and knelt and prayed: perhaps, that night, the most dejected and reluctant convert in all England" (*Surprised by Joy: The Shape of My Early Life* [London: Geoffrey Bles, 1955], pp. 228-29).

When my husband came home, he accepted my experience without question; he was himself on the way to something of the kind.[15] Together, in spite of illness and anxiety, we set about remaking our minds. For obviously they needed it. If my knowledge of God was true, the thinking of my whole life had been false.

I could not doubt the truth of my experience. It was so much the *realest* thing that had ever happened to me! And, in a gentler, less overwhelming form, it went right on happening. So my previous reasoning was at fault, and I must somehow find the error. I snatched at books I had despised before; reread *The Hound of Heaven*, which I had ridiculed as a piece of phony rhetoric — and, understanding it suddenly, burst into tears. (Also a new thing; I had seldom previously cried except with rage.) I went back to C. S. Lewis and learned from him, slowly, how I had gone wrong. Without his works, I wonder if I and many others might not still be infants "crying in the night."

One of my first acts of faith was a renewed interest in the Communist Party. Logical enough; for though materialism had proved false, I still thought Marxist economic theory was sound. While I remained an atheist, Party work had been a matter of inclination, but once I recognized God I recognized moral responsibility, and it seemed I had a duty to do Party work whether I wanted to be a Communist or not. If I had found, as I thought, a mistake in Marxist philosophy, my job was to show that the Party didn't need atheism — couldn't socialism be built upon the Golden Rule? (It can be; but not the Marxist, revolutionary, hate-obsessed kind of socialism.) And so I did, at long last, what I should have done in the first place: I studied Marxist theory.

It was a difficult and painful study. Inch by inch I retreated from my revolutionary position; fallacy after fallacy, contradiction upon contradiction, absurdity upon absurdity turned up in Lenin's *Materialism and Empirio-Criticism,* one of the basic textbooks of Marxist philosophers. This is not the place for taking dialectical materialism apart; enough to say that it was unsound as philosophy to begin with, and that its "scientific

15. Gresham outlines his own conversion to Christianity in three articles that appeared in *Presbyterian Life* magazine: "From Communist to Christian, Part 1," *Presbyterian Life* 3 (February 18, 1950): 20-22 and 35-36; "From Communist to Christian, Part 2," *Presbyterian Life* 3 (March 4, 1950): 22-23, 46; and "From Communist to Christian, Part 3," *Presbyterian Life* 3 (March 18, 1950): 21-24. The articles were later combined as "From Communist to Christian" and appeared in *These Found the Way: Thirteen Converts to Protestant Christianity.*

foundation" had been swept away by Einstein's early work even before Lenin wrote.[16]

Even yet I did not quite give up. I tried to cling to Marxist economics, at least — then I realized that this economics assumed an infinitely increasing food supply, and that any farmer knew better. I reminded myself of the wonderful achievements of Soviet Russia — and realized that I had taken them all on faith; I had no idea *what* went on in Russia. Gradually my Communism shriveled up and blew away like a withered tumbleweed; I cannot tell exactly when it went, but I looked and found it gone.

And something else had come in its place. I was by no means a Christian at first; all my atheist life I had regarded the "apostate" with traditional Jewish horror.[17] What I wanted was to become a good Jew, of the comfortable "Reformed" persuasion. I had the usual delusion that "all religions mean the same thing." Fortunately I had learned my lesson, and this time I looked before I leaped; I *studied* religions, and found them anything but the same thing. Some of them had wisdom up to a point, some of them had good ethical intentions, some of them had flashes of spiritual insight; but only one of them had complete understanding of the grace and repentance and charity that had come to me from God. And the Redeemer who had made himself known, whose personality I would have recognized among ten thousand — well, when I read the New Testament, I recognized him. He was Jesus.

The rest was fairly simple. I could not doubt the divinity of Jesus, and, step by step, orthodox Christian theology followed logically from it. My modernist objections to the miraculous proved to be mere superstition, unsupported by logic. I am a writer of fiction; I have made up stories myself, and I think I can tell a made-up story from a true one. The men who told of the resurrection told of something they had *seen*. Not Shakespeare himself could have invented the Synoptic Gospels. My beliefs took shape; I accepted the sacraments as meaningful but not magical; I recognized the duty of going to church, while I rejected the claim of any church to infallibility and an absolute monopoly on divine authority. So what I was, it appeared, was a Protestant Christian, of the orthodox Trinitarian kind.

I believed that one should worship along with one's neighbors, not go

16. However, elsewhere Davidman does "take it apart"; see her letters to William Rose Benét of October 31, 1948; February 1, 1949; July 24, 1949; and August 19, 1949.

17. Her early story "Apostate" appeared in the *Hunter College Echo*, November 1934, pp. 17-26. The story was the winner of the Bernard Cohen Prize Story.

far afield in search of "kindred spirits." The church nearest my present home in Dutchess County, New York, happened to be Presbyterian; I visited it and found that its theology suited me well. Perhaps I should be equally at home with Methodists and Episcopalians and some others — I look forward to the coming union of all Protestants in one Church. But it was in the Presbyterian church of Pleasant Plains that I was baptized in 1948, and saw my children baptized; and there, if I may, I will remain.

My present hope is twofold. I want to go deeper into the mystical knowledge of God, and I want that knowledge to govern my daily life. I had a good deal of pride and anger to overcome, and at times my progress is heartbreakingly slow — yet I think that I am going somewhere, by God's grace, according to plan. My present tasks are to look after my children and my husband and my garden and my house — and, perhaps, to serve God in books and letters as best I can. And my reward is a happiness such as I never dreamed possible. "In His will is our peace."

Growing in Belief

Letters 1949–1951

To William Rose Benét

Endekill Road
Staatsburg, N.Y.
February 1, 1949

Dear Bill:

The Saturday Review [of Literature] came last night and I read your complete article with great appreciation.[1] The golden mean is the trickiest of all tightropes; but I think you have stayed on it without teetering once. I'm trying to teach myself to do the same thing, but it's hard going for someone whose youth was spent in the passionate conviction that only the extremes made sense.

I had only a nodding acquaintance with Dick Boyer, but respected him and his ability; he wrote better, I think, than anyone else on the defunct *New Masses*.[2] (What killed that, incidentally was simply the entire incompetence of its editors; they didn't know there was such a thing as a technique of editing, and refused to consider the possibility of learning it. They didn't know anything about their readers and did nothing to find

1. See W. R. Benét's "The Phoenix Nest," *The Saturday Review of Literature* 32 (January 29, 1949): 42-43.

2. Communist journalist Richard O. Boyer (1903-1973) contributed numerous articles to *New Masses*. He was a prolific writer, and his writings included books and articles for other magazines such as the *New Yorker*. Benét had referred in his article to Boyer's pro-Communist pamphlet, *If This Be Treason* (New York: New Century Publishers, 1948).

out; their position was that reading *New Masses* was a moral duty, so it didn't have to be interesting. They existed only by begging money from soft-hearted Party groups and members.)

Since my conversion — I am now, believe it or not, a deaconess of the Presbyterian Church, and it feels odd to say the least. Oy! — since becoming a Christian, I am reveling in my new-found ability to admit my ignorance. In my old world, you just *had* to have an opinion on every conceivable subject that came up; an open mind was a moral offense. You can't imagine what a luxury it is to have no opinions where I have no evidence!

I have read so many books on the Soviet Union, and spoken to so many people who've been there that it's all cancelled out; I know nothing definite about the place and I never did, though the abuses you mention are certainly real. There are a few *good* things that are equally real, that I've been able to check up on; but none of it adds up to a coherent picture. Travel reports from the USSR always remind me of [Charles] Dickens' American Notes and the American section of *Martin Chuzzlewit* — the emphasis is on a newness and rawness. But that doesn't mean that Russia's necessarily going to develop in our direction.

I do, however know something about the [Communist] doctrines which are in question at the current trial. (As to the article I suggested, I'd forgotten about the trial at the time; I have no intention of heaping fuel on that fire. In England, I believe, a case which is sub judice cannot be discussed in the press, and a damn good thing too.)

You are quite right about the double-talk; the revolutionary elements in the doctrine are always kept so ambiguous in this country that even in the Party we used to argue passionately about just how revolutionary we were. My more ladylike friends had an unconscious reservation about the revolution — not in our time, please Marx! I was on the violent side myself, poor silly. But I really cannot make up my mind whether the prosecution is justified or not.

The theory runs like this; no revolution against the *present* government of the United States is either desirable or possible. Legal means of exerting pressure, and those only, are to be used. When and if, however, the legal government is replaced by a Fascist tyranny, it will be the duty of the Communists to organize and lead a revolution against it.

So far so good; I imagine any halfway liberal American might say the same, and the Party always makes a great deal of what Jefferson and Lincoln said along similar lines. The catch is that according to Marxist-Leninist-Stalinist-whatsist theory at present, the US is going to be a Fascist state, inevitably. During the war, under Browder, the Party considered that a progressive capitalism is on the march here, and Varga in Moscow was saying much the same thing; but since they've both been bounced the line is more orthodox.[3]

Indeed, they consider that the US is partly Fascist already, and that the revolution, though it will be provoked by capitalist violence, is inevitable. In consequence they have to work now for the future revolution. The $64 question is; *when* will the CP decide that the end stage of Fascism has been reached, and call for the revolution?

I fear there is only one answer. The CP will so decide just as soon as it figures it's strong enough to win that revolution.

That, of course, is an infinite distance in the future. But whether, on that ground, the present prosecution is justified would take a legal mind to settle. I have no opinion.

Privately, I haven't any doubt that the Party serves as a voluntary and unpaid Russian agency, and there may very well be actual Soviet spies in it, though I never knew of any and can hardly believe that the people I knew would be trusted by any intelligent secret service. I realized belatedly that simple Russian patriotism of a rather odd kind inspired most New York Communists. My own people came from Europe in their early childhood; neither they nor I had any more personal feelings about Russia than about Austria-Hungary under the empire of my father's place of origin. But a great many New York Jews from the Ukraine and thereabouts apparently *do* love the Russian land with all the sentimentality of the exile — little reason though they had to love it in the old days! I came to understand this when I learned that many Negroes actually love the South deeply, love the land. In the same way the Russian Jew was only waiting until Russia gave him a break, to give it his heart.

The Jewish factor in American Communism is something that no Gentile of good will ever wants to mention.[4] You are all, to your credit,

---

3. Earl R. Browder (1891–1973) was executive secretary of the CPUSA and was its party's candidate for the presidency of the United States in 1936 and 1940. Eugene Varga (1879–1964) was for a time a major Soviet expert on capitalism and world economies until he fell out of favor for publishing anti-Stalinist views.

4. For more on this, see Barbara Foley, "Women and the Left in the 1930s," *American Literary History* 2 (Spring 1990): 150–69; Vivian Gornick, *The Romance of American Communism* (New York: Basic Books, 1977); Dorothy Healey and Maurice Isserman, *Dorothy Healey Remembers: A Life in the American Communist Party* (Oxford: Oxford University Press, 1990); Maurice Isserman, *Which Side Were You On? The American Communist Party*

leaning over backward. Yet the fact remains that there *is* a Jewish culture, a Jewish way of thinking; that the Ashkenazim (including myself) are different in certain important respects from the people around them, partly no doubt as a result of persecution but partly also because the Old Testament, taken alone, is bitterly unlike the New. (Protestant sects who concentrate on the Old Testament often get very Hebraic in their emotional attitudes, without any persecution.) And the real question asked by most Communists in this country remains, "Is it good or bad for the Jews?" The rise of Israel, I hope, will distract their attention!

As a Christian Jew, I have had to analyze in myself and my background all the peculiarly Jewish attitudes toward the Christian. I think very few Gentiles realize that even the most Americanized Jew usually shudders when he sees a church, a cross, or even the name of Christ in print. It is, of course, a shudder of fear; but it gives rise to hate immediately. I have never had any personal experience of anti-Semitism, barring an aged and drunken Irishman on a trolley-car who told me that I was nicer than some noisy Jews in the next seat. But I have almost never met a Jew who wasn't anti-Christian. I have had parties of Jews, at my dinner-table, pour out contempt of Christians while my Christian husband smiled and passed the roast. If the situation had been reversed?

The American [Communist] party, in the large cities at least, has an almost entirely Jewish character, though it tries desperately to shove its few Anglo-Saxons and the like into the foreground. Its atheism is the Jews' atheism, based not on reason but on a combination of disillusion with dead Judaism and hatred of live Christianity. Its ethos is the ethos of the ghetto Jew, surrounded by jeering moujiks,[5] trying to lie himself out of trouble — hence the curious reluctance to stand up and avow themselves Communists, which annoys you and was one of the first things to alienate me. A thousand years of fear and helplessness go to the making of this sort of double tongue. And it is very hard for anyone with a background of freedom to understand it, I know; it seems merely cowardly and deceitful to you; but in the Jew's world you were a coward and a liar or you died.

Hence too the CP regards American law as an instrument of oppression to be evaded by superior cunning. What do they know of Magna Charta?

During the Second World War (Middletown, CT: Wesleyan University Press, 1982); and Harvey Klehr, *The Heyday of American Communism: The Depression Decade* (New York: Basic Books, 1984).

5. Russian peasants.

Marx himself, I think, functioned primarily as a Jewish atheist rationalizing the emotions that came out of the ghetto; at his desk in the British Museum he was not so unlike the Yeshiva-bocher poring over the Talmud in the synagogue!

But I don't want to burden you with the whole substance of my unwritten article. There was more to it than this — the laws of dialectics and the kitchen sink. Of course the *SRL* could get a real philosopher to handle the question, though, far better than I could; though I don't know if any American philosopher has given it serious study — all the sources I have are English, and very good. J. M. Cameron's *Scrutiny of Marxism*, published by Viewpoints, taught me a lot, and so did a Macmillan book called *The Christian Significance of Karl Marx*, about two years back.[6] I've forgotten the author. I picked this book up at *New Masses* and asked to review it. The editors looked at the title and said in horror, "What do you want to bother with that for!"

Hmm, I said, if it were the *Jewish* significance of Marx you'd be fighting for it! They blushed.

But that book occasioned my first definite split with the Marxists. For in my review I said that we didn't mind anyone thinking Christ was God as long as they thought Christ knew what He was talking about — and obeyed Him. This provoked charges of heresy, and *NM* asked for the book back to give another reviewer. (They never reviewed it.)

Three pages are more than enough!

Regards
Joy Davidman

Source: Yale

Benét replied, in part, on March 5, 1949:

> *I'm glad you think I kept my balance. . . . Of course we know no few gentiles who are anti-Semitic, and we hate that ourselves. I suppose it is natural enough, in a way, that Jews should feel bitterly against Christians, because they have suffered a good deal from them. Which certainly has nothing whatever to do with a person named Jesus Christ who was a Jew. One day I realized, being brought up an Episcopalian, that the concept in*

6. J. M. Cameron, *Scrutiny of Marxism* (London: SCM, 1948); and Alexander Miller, *The Christian Significance of Karl Marx* (London: SCM, 1947).

most paintings of Christ was either that he was an Italian or a German! I used to think of Christ with a blonde beard. He may well have had one, as there is a distinctly rufous strain among the Jews. But he looked, Teutonic. I never inclined much toward the swarthier Italian interpretation. . . . As for your being inclined to extremes, the best young people (I think) are inclined to extremes. But now I have reached the age of 63 with a good deal of scepticism for quick panaceas or for cut-and-dried remedies. Also I don't believe (much as good laws are needed) that you can reform men and women by good laws. Every law is constantly being broken by crooked minds and wills. Law can do just so much, but until you really touch the spirit of the people, that will not wholly avail. Once socialism was an ideal that could do so. For many years it has made me think from time to time that perhaps it had the solution. The Soviet Union has had a great chance. The chance didn't lie in making herself necessarily a great industrial country. It lay in the realm of the spirit. I am sorry to say that I think that there *it has miserably failed, though the Russian people (who really have an intensely devout side, or seem to) have followed devotedly what they were told.* Source: Yale

To Chad Walsh[7]

Endekill Road
Staatsburg, N.Y.
June 21, 1949

Dear Dr. Walsh,

No — we're buried under two small sons and can't get very far afield yet, or I'd certainly take you up on your invitation. We more than share your feeling for [C. S.] Lewis; with us it was not the last step but the first that came from reading his books, for we were raised atheists and took the truth of atheism for granted, and like most Marxists were so busy acting that we never stopped to think. If I hadn't picked up *The Great Di-*

---

7. Chad Walsh (1914-1991), longtime professor of English at Beloit College, wrote the first critical work on C. S. Lewis, *C. S. Lewis: Apostle to the Skeptics* (New York: Macmillan, 1949). After making acquaintance with Walsh, Davidman eventually began corresponding with Lewis, as she suggests later in this letter.

vorce one day — brr, I suppose I'd still be running madly around with leaflets, showing as much intelligent purpose as a headless chicken. But I wouldn't have picked up *The Great Divorce* if I hadn't loved fantasy, and I wouldn't have loved fantasy if I hadn't, as a twelve-year-old moping in the school library, found *Phantastes.*[8] It had exactly the effect on me that Lewis describes only more blurred around the edges and with less positive consequence; anyway I forgot the author's name. My taste for fantasy was something I was once ashamed of; got rebuked sternly by Marxist authorities for bringing "Astounding Stories" into the *New Masses* office. Tee hee.

What I am working round to is, yes we would dearly love to talk about Lewis' work, particularly (of course) about what it is doing to our *own* novels. Do you and your wife ever come east? We live in a fourteen-story (oops) -room barn of a farmhouse, surrounded by chickens and apple trees and we love having guests. How about staying here for a while on your vacation?

I'll be watching for your new books. My husband Bill (otherwise William Lindsay Gresham) wrote one called *Nightmare Alley* a couple of years back and has just published another called *Limbo Tower;*[9] the two make up a picture of Gresham before and after Lewis. I used to be a poet myself, but I'm afraid my inspiration gave out when I discovered that people would *pay* for prose. Macmillan has a novel of mine *Weeping Bay* — it's about the Gaspé peninsula — scheduled for next spring.

I have Williams' novels, all except *The Greater Trumps;*[10] they're extraordinarily illuminating, though I have to read them three times before I begin to understand them. We have studied occultism a bit; but with Wil-

8. George MacDonald, *Phantastes: A Faerie Romance for Men and Women* (London: Arthur C. Fifield, 1905).

9. William L. Gresham, *Limbo Tower* (New York: Rinehart & Co., 1949).

10. Charles Williams, *The Greater Trumps* (London: Victor Gollancz, 1932). Williams's other novels include *War in Heaven* (1930), *Many Dimensions* (1931), *The Place of the Lion* (1931), *Shadows of Ecstasy* (1933), *Descent into Hell* (1937), and *All Hallow's Eve* (1945). Williams, who was also a poet, dramatist, essayist, and lecturer, became a close friend to Lewis during World War II, in part because his job with the Oxford University Press was moved from London to Oxford. The two admired each other as writers and soon were meeting regularly; Williams became a frequent face at meetings of the Inklings. Although it was a relatively short friendship because of Williams's unexpected death during a routine operation, Lewis felt his loss keenly. Davidman later gave a lecture on Williams to Oxford undergraduates on February 26, 1956 (see her letters of November 11, 1955; February 14, 1956; and February 29, 1956).

liams you get a queer impression that it didn't all come out of books, that the man *saw* things differently. By the way, your remark that Lewis answered even asinine letters gave us courage to write to him — so we sent the unfortunate man five single-spaced pages of personal history and what not.[11]

Let us know if you can come this way. We have *lots* of fantasy books high up on a shelf, where the kids can't get them — do you know *The Worm Ouroboros?*[12]

Joy Davidman   *Source: Wade*

Walsh replied, in part, on June 24, 1949:

> *You don't know what you're inviting. I think in my other letter I neglected to mention that I have four (4) daughters, aged nine months to ten years. So here's your opportunity to withdraw your invitation gracefully, with no hurt feelings. . . . We do want a chance to know you and Mr. Gresham, not to speak of the two boys. . . . I haven't kept up with recent poetry and fiction as I should, but I'm tormented by the feeling that I've come on both of your names frequently — probably read about you rather than read you. Did you have a volume of poetry published by the Yale Series of Younger Poets? I'm planning to work on a short novel this summer — fantasy rather in the manner of Macdonald and Williams combined, though I started on it before I have read either of them. I've started a couple of other novels, but never finished them. Like you, I feel that the possibility of making a little money from fiction is a strong inducement. I'm sorry that I've never read "The Worm Ouroboros." In high school I eagerly devoured the interplanetary thrillers in pulp magazines, but only recently have I started on Wells, Williams, etc. Have you ever read David Lindsay's "Voyage to Arcturus"? It's a loathsome book in many ways, but memorable. . . . Do you prefer to be called Miss Davidman or Mrs. Gresham? I feel a bit odd addressing the mother of two children as* Miss!   *Source: Wade*

11. This letter has not survived.
12. Edward R. Eddison, *The Worm Ouroboros* (London: Jonathan Cape, 1922).

To William Rose Benét

Endekill Road
Staatsburg, N.Y.
July 24, 1949

Dear Bill:

Congratulations, you've done it: again. Your piece on Pound is the first really Christian comment I've seen since the whole blasted controversy started.[13] Also the first one that showed any interest in poetry itself, other than as a means of political expression.

Since becoming a Christian I've been slowly teaching myself *not* to form opinions on matters of which I know nothing; a new experience for me. I've no idea whether Pound ought to have got the award, or whether the committee acted honestly in making it, or even whether in the present position of poetry as an occult science it matters a damn that its practitioners live by taking in each other's washing. To me *The Pisan Cantos* do seem the work of a noble mind o'erthrown, but then most of what the bright young men write today in presumable sanity doesn't look any different.

But I do feel very strongly that there's been a horrible lack of charity in almost everything the *Saturday Review* has printed on both sides, and a kind of vicious irrelevance; however justified [Robert] Hillyer's attack may have been, he certainly descended both to politics and to personalities, and the letters of comment have been written in the spirit of a lynch mob.[14] After all; so much vindictiveness for a sick man whose only offense has been that he talked! François Villon was a worse man; he killed, yet if you felt he deserved an award you'd have to give it to him though you might well hang him the day after.[15] To anyone who's been struggling painfully free of Communist habits of thought, like myself, it's a great shock to find identical habits calling themselves democracy.

I regret particularly the red herring of anti-Semitism. I think, having

13. In 1948 Ezra Pound was awarded the Bollingen Award for his controversial volume of poetry, *The Pisan Cantos*. Davidman is referring to Benét's commentary on the poetry of Pound in "The Phoenix Nest," *The Saturday Review of Literature* 32 (July 23, 1949): 28-29.

14. Robert Hillyer (1895-1961) was a critic, novelist, and poet; his *Collected Verses* (1933) won him a Pulitzer Prize. See Robert Hillyer, "Treason's Strange Fruit: The Case of Ezra Pound and the Bollingen Award," *The Saturday Review of Literature* 32 (June 11, 1949): 9-11, 28.

15. Artist-outlaw François Villon (1431-1463), the greatest writer of fifteenth-century France, was its first notable creative poet of lyrical verse.

been born a Jew, I have the right to say that a man ought to be free to criticize the Jews honestly. The present tendency of so many Jewish groups to scream for special immunity is easy enough to understand, but disastrous all the same; it can only end by creating the very resentment it fears. If we want everybody to love us, we'd better devote ourselves to learning to be lovable.

So it was a tremendous relief to me to read your column, and see all the necessary things being said at last, with charity and humility. Everyone else has been so pontifical. And good too to have someone remember that the purpose of poetry is not the same as that of the Voice of America broadcasts. I used to think of poetry as the Voice of the People, myself, but now I suspect that at its best it is the Voice of God. Thank you for the reminder.

Are you at the [MacDowell] Colony now? If so, give everyone my love won't you? We're hoping to pay a visit there in September.

Yours,
Joy

P.S. Forgive the pencil. My husband has gone to North Carolina with the only pen in the house. *Source: Yale*

Benét replied to Davidman, in part, on July 29, 1949:

> *I am glad you liked what I said about Pound. Ben Ray Redman has also written a very good piece about him in his regular column, "New Editions," in the July 30 number. I recommend that too. I don't think that Pound should have got the award, and just between you and me, I don't know how the Committee got themselves to thinking that he should. Nevertheless, there are some good things in "The Pisan Cantos," and I thought it fair to mention them. It's either the heat or the cold war or natural human cussedness, but whenever anybody starts an argument now, people seem to pitch in with lack of charity, as you say. I agree with about everything you do say. I don't believe that poetry should either be pontifical or propagandist.* *Source: Yale*

To William Rose Benét

Endekill Road
Staatsburg, N.Y.
August 19, 1949

Dear Bill,

Thanks for "Assumption," which I appreciated with a wry grin, having until so lately been one of the solemn band of determinist jackasses myself.[16] What cleared my head was largely the writings of C. S. Lewis. I seem to remember that you like fantasy; have you read his? Wonderful stuff. I'm beginning to think "dialectic essence" is something very like damnation.

> I'd rather eat a poisoned bagel
> than get involved again with Hegel
> but for each sucker that his pen gulls
> ten thousand more are gulled by Engels.

I could keep this up longer, but I'm feeling rather shaken. I wrote a letter to the *SRL* which you may have seen; thought it was about time I went on record against *both* the idea that the CP is a band of efficient archangels and the idea that it's a band of efficient devils, since in my experience it was never anything but a collection of confused and quite inefficient human beings.[17] Perhaps I was a little uncharitable myself, but I named no names and know everything I said to be demonstrably true. So far so good; but I wasn't prepared for the *Daily News* to quote me in an editorial, which is what has happened. I can't quite decide whether to laugh or to hide under the bed.

I rather expect, though, to be hearing strange things about my past in the next weeks. One of the nastiest things about Marxist theory is that it actually *forbids* you to believe in an honest change of opinion; anyone who ceases to be a Communist must, by definition, be corrupt. Thus when a man who'd known my husband for years heard that he'd become a Presbyterian elder, the comrade remarked, appalled, "Good God, he musta been an FBI spy all along!"

---

16. See "Assumption" in Benét's "The Phoenix Nest," *The Saturday Review of Literature* 30 (May 10, 1947): 35.

17. I have been unable to find this letter in *The Saturday Review of Literature*.

One angle on determinist thinking can be found in the works of that great mind Lysenko, whose pamphlets my scientist brother-in-law keeps showing me with smothered curses.[18] That plant-breeder is almost as inarticulate as his vegetables, it would appear, yet it's possible to extract from his doubletalk the definition of science as a prediction and control of the future; if you consider anything unpredictable you are not a scientist. But of course your prediction must match revealed truth as expressed in the holy book of Marxism-Leninism-Stalinism. Isn't this where we came in, Galileo?

I suppose what really underlies all this is the old story of the Appointment in Samarra — you know, the man who met Death in the bazaar in Damascus and fled at once to Samarra in order to outwit him, only to find — well, the Russians seem in an awful hurry to get to Samarra. They aren't the only ones, though.

Cape Ann sounds lovely. We'd love to drop in — if we ever get loose from the children long enough to travel; it looks unlikely.

Regards all round,
Joy   *Source: Yale*

According to Warren Lewis, his brother received his first letter from Davidman on January 10, 1950: "Until 10th January 1950 neither of us had ever heard of her; then she appeared in the mail as just another American fan, Mrs. W. L. Gresham from the neighbourhood of New York. With however the difference that she stood out from the ruck by her amusing and well-written letters, and soon J and she had become 'pen-friends.'"[19]

Near the same time, Davidman's second novel, Weeping Bay, *was published by Macmillan.[20]*

18. Davidman is referring to her brother-in-law, Henry (nicknamed Hank) Gresham. Trofim Lysenko (1898-1976) was a Soviet agronomist.

19. Warren Lewis, *Brothers and Friends: The Diaries of Major Warren Hamilton Lewis,* ed. Clyde S. Kilby and Marjorie Lamp Mead (San Francisco: Harper & Row, 1982), p. 244.

20. For reviews of *Weeping Bay,* see R. P. Breaden, Review of Joy Davidman's *Weeping Bay, Library Journal* 75 (February 1, 1950): 171; August Derleth, Review of Joy Davidman's *Weeping Bay, Sunday Chicago Tribune,* March 12, 1950, p. 4; Granville Hicks, Review of Joy Davidman's *Weeping Bay, New York Times,* March 5, 1950, p. 30; James Hilton, Review of Joy Davidman's *Weeping Bay, New York Herald Tribune Book Review,* March 12, 1950, p. 6; J. H. Jackson, Review of Joy Davidman's *Weeping Bay, San Francisco Chronicle,* March 7, 1950,

To Chad Walsh

Endekill Road
Staatsburg, N.Y.
January 27, 1950

Dear Chad,

Been trying to answer your letter all afternoon, without much success; my wits are addled with Anahist[21] and anyhow it's hard to explain just *how* one tells a report of fact from a piece of fiction. Reporters and cops develop a sixth sense for recognizing a liar in the flesh; professional writers can sometimes tell one in print. It's partly one's knowledge of psychology — for instance, if the Apostles had been romancing they would never have told so many stories which made them look silly. Nor would their immediate followers. They would have said, "*We* knew Him when, *we* were the extra-special faithful who understood Him perfectly, *we* were the ones appointed to govern the rest of you!" If they had lied, they would have been lying for their own advantage, surely? Instead of which — continual rebukes, and "He that would be first among you, let him be last!"[22]

And, similarly — and in addition to Lewis' reasoning on this point — anyone who thinks Jesus could have been a paranoid with delusions of grandeur has only to read up on *real* paranoids, in the asylum and out, and see what they sound like.[23] History is full of self-appointed Messiahs, and

---

p. 18; Review of Joy Davidman's *Weeping Bay*, *Kirkus* 18 (January 1, 1950), p. 8; Review of Joy Davidman's *Weeping Bay*, *New Yorker* 26 (March 11, 1950): 103; Review of Joy Davidman's *Weeping Bay*, *United States Quarterly Booklist* 6 (June 1950): 156; Mary Sandrock, Review of Joy Davidman's *Weeping Bay*, *Catholic World* 171 (June 1950): 171; Chad Walsh, "First Things First: How Does One Come to Know God?" *Presbyterian Life* 3 (May 27, 1950): 36-38; and A. F. Wolfe, Review of Joy Davidman's *Weeping Bay*, *Saturday Review of Literature* 33 (March 18, 1950): 16.

21. Anahist was probably an allergy medicine.

22. Mark 9:35.

23. C. S. Lewis had given a series of radio broadcasts for the BBC during World War II that were later published in America as *The Case for Christianity* (New York: Macmillan, 1943). The passage Davidman has in mind here is the following:

I'm trying here to prevent anyone saying the really silly thing that people often say about Him [Christ]: "I'm ready to accept Jesus as a great moral teacher, but I don't accept His claim to be God." That's the one thing we mustn't say. A man who was merely man and said the sort of things Jesus said wouldn't be a great moral teacher. He'd either be a lunatic — on a level with the man who says he's a poached egg — or

they all sound the same, mad with pride. The humor and commonsense of Jesus never came from a disturbed mind.

But mostly, I think, what convinced us was our sense of the difference between fiction and life. Fiction is always congruous, life usually incongruous. In fiction there is a unity of effect, of style; the people all say exactly what they should say to be in character and in the mood. And all the effects are heightened, arranged. If there *is* an incongruous reaction, that too is obviously arranged — either for humor or for some plot reason; and it looks as blatant as a movie double-take.

Lies, being planned, have that same congruousness and extra effectiveness — they're all of a piece. But in real life one has no time to plan, one merely reacts; and the reaction is likely to be ever so slightly off key, inapposite. Like Lady Macbeth when they tell her Duncan's been murdered: "What, in our house?"[24]

Hardly anyone but Shakespeare could have brought that off and even so perhaps he was using something he'd heard. For the remark is that of an innocent woman. A guilty one, with time for preparation, would have launched into three yards of high-grade fustian.

Well, the Gospels are full of these little incongruities — like the cut-off ear of the high priest's servant.[25] That's a thing that happened; no one could have invented it. The account of the Virgin Birth, not being eyewitness, seems on the other hand an invented and composed story, without a single false note. Everyone strikes exactly the right attitude, from Mary's first words to the Angel on through that beautifully composed artistic climax.[26] How artistically the contrast between the Prince of Peace and the Manger is worked out!

Whatever actually happened (and, frankly, I consider the Virgin Birth not unbelievable but merely irrelevant) that story as we have it is a work of art. But the eyewitness accounts are quite otherwise. Details an inventor would fill in are lacking; details a faker would suppress are there. That touch about all the scraps picked up after the loaves and fishes mir-

---

else he'd be the Devil of Hell. You must make your choice. Either this man was, and is, the Son of God: or else a madman or something worse. (p. 45)

24. The allusion is to Shakespeare's Lady Macbeth, who, knowing perfectly well that Macbeth has murdered Duncan in the bed she had provided for him, feigns surprise when the slain king is discovered: "Woe, alas!/What, in our house?" (*Macbeth*, Act II, scene iii, ll. 83-84).

25. John 18:10.

26. Luke 1:26-38.

acle![27] A faker in the grand manner would have loftily ignored the scraps as undignified; couldn't the miracle worker always make more? It's just the sort of illogical thing that *really* happens. You can see them saying, "We musta dreamed it. But, golly, looka all them scraps!" A writer clever enough to understand the force of such a corroborative detail, I think, would have written the rest of the story with more drama.

And the little dead girl who was resurrected: a faker would have had Jesus tell her to pray and, like as not, the story would have been rounded off with a touching household thanksgiving service. But Jesus simply tells the family to give her something to eat.[28] That *happened*. The man who could have invented it would have been greater than Shakespeare. And the blind man who sees people after the miracle like trees walking.[29]

And, most of all, the Resurrection. The women who mistake Jesus for the gardener![30] The general slowness to recognize him, and Thomas' insistence on a material demonstration;[31] in fact, the Apostles are always remarkably materialist. People talk as if they were credulous men in a primitive and credulous age. But the age was anything but primitive — decadent rather, wasn't it, and very like ours? Its excrescent cults of phallic-worship and divination and astrology were exactly what we've got today, and, as today, the great majority of people were hard-headed materialists; if they listened to fortune-telling, it was not for the wonder's sake but in hope of getting a business advantage. And the Apostles always seem to come from Missouri.

I could mention other things — for instance, there's just the *right* amount of discrepancy in the eyewitness stories. And the intangible of style; the personality of Jesus is luminous in everything he says. I've met oafs who contend that Jesus escaped somehow from the cross, retired to Patmos, and grew up to be St. John! I find it incredible that anyone should be so unaware that the style's the man. To mistake the bitter, humorless, florid and fanciful poet of Revelations for Jesus, but then, there are serious scholars who work hard at proving that Bacon wasn't Shakespeare, without ever noticing the one conclusive fact that, simply by the kind of man that comes through Bacon's writing, he couldn't have been Shakespeare.

But mostly it's just that I know the sort of thing that people make up,

27. Matthew 14:13-21.
28. Mark 5:21-43.
29. Mark 8:24.
30. John 20:11-18.
31. John 20:24-29.

and this ain't it. I suppose that's what Lewis feels too, when he says we couldn't have invented it, and also what Tertullian meant when he said *Credo quia impossibile.*[32]

Got the magazine with your remarks on modern poetry. We almost agree; but I still think you surrender too easily. It would be agonizingly hard to work out a direct idiom, much harder than to write a good obscure one. But worth trying; and who knows? Then, too, I think the intellectual style may be rooted mainly in the modern distrust of emotion; poets are all Prufrocks afraid of seeming ridiculous.[33] *That* may very well come of lack of faith, as you suggest, for a Christian (and indeed most other believers) doesn't much mind, looking like a fool. I found that out when I was looking back at the arrogant, brash kid I used to be, and writhing with regret over the impression I must have made on people — when suddenly I asked: Who am I, that I shouldn't look like a fool? Felt much better at once.

Don't you think there is a defensive quality, a fear of people, behind the elaborations of the bright young men? And then, I think their amateur standing has something to do with it. In countries where poetry still has an audience and admirers, this obscurity hasn't shown up; when I did my anthology of War Poems I found that it was confined to England and France and the United States and, to a lesser extent, Germany. But elsewhere poetry was reverenced. As a professional, I feel one needs an audience to keep one's standards up; more than that, a market. Why was the Elizabethan theatre so much better than Elizabethan closet verse? Surely because the talent went where the public demand was while Harvey and his circle, despising the vulgar, fooled around with distorting English to fit Greek meters. No more alien to the tongue than what we're doing now. But men who write only to please themselves have a complaisant audience!

Sometimes, of course, the verse *will* come out esoteric, and then had better be left that way. But why not go on with your experiments? The derivative quality will vanish if you keep at it long enough. I was well on the way to a simple style myself, I think, when I turned completely professional and concentrated on prose. And I do think that the poetry audience, in this country, is not dead but only sleeping. There's been plenty of evidence of that.

32. Latin for "I believe it because it is impossible."
33. This refers to T. S. Eliot's poem "The Love Song of J. Alfred Prufrock."

Two days later: I'm in my usual pickle; so much that I want to say that this letter is in danger of developing into a *Ladies Home Journal* serial. Wanted to thank you for the piece on Bill; every word of it delighted me. (I'll admit that the adjective "gentle" startled me a little, but that was due to recollections of the old, pre-Christian Bill Gresham, whom I have heard yell loud enough to scare a whole Greenwich Village apartment house.)

The Essays for Williams is a delight, specially Lewis and Dorothy Sayers, who sent me tearing off to read Dante.[34] Alas, I had two translations and both were very stale, flat, and unprofitable; I can never read that sort of thing without itching to try it myself. But of course any poet good enough to do Dante or Goethe justice is too good to devote his life to other men's work. I shall have to read Dante the way I read Greek — from an interlinear pony. Lewis's writing in this book is not as full-dress as the other stuff of his I've read, and therefore much warmer; I didn't think I could like him better, but this made me. I think the other book I asked for was one of his on literature?[35]

Your prayers may have taken partial effect on my parents. My mother called up and announced a forthcoming visit. This, however, is one of the cases where half a loaf is *not* better than no bread, for it's the same old mamma; her theme was how sharper than a serpent's tooth it is to have a child who mentions you in the newspapers in terms this side idolatry.[36] (Of course I can see her point. I tried to protect my parents in every possible way, stressing their anti-Communism and fervent patriotism and so on — but it was necessary to show some of the factors that had made me a rebel by temperament. I described my parents as "well-meaning but strict," which is certainly damning by faint praise. But since the truth would have called for loud damns, I don't know how I could have put it any milder.)

But, now I come to think of it, something *has* changed. My parents,

---

34. *Essays Presented to Charles Williams*, ed. C. S. Lewis (Oxford: Oxford University Press, 1947). Lewis's essay was "On Stories" and Dorothy L. Sayers's essay was "'. . . And Telling You a Story': A Note on the *Divine Comedy*."

35. This is a reference to C. S. Lewis, *The Allegory of Love: A Study in Medieval Tradition* (Oxford: Clarendon Press, 1936).

36. See Oliver Pilat's "Girl Communist [Joy Davidman]: An Intimate Story of Eight Years in the Party," *The New York Post*, October 31; November 1-4, 6-11, and 13, 1949. The allusion is to Shakespeare's King Lear, who rails at his daughter, Goneril: "How sharper than a serpent's tooth it is/To have a thankless child" (*King Lear*, Act I, scene iv, ll. 279-80).

since my first discovery of (or by) God, had lost their old power to hurt me; but they were still able to rattle me a bit — though I knew better by experience, I almost found myself falling back into an attitude of my childhood, in which my parents represented the World, and the World's judgments were entirely on their side. (That's what makes the adolescent rebel; that calm assumption by parents that their views represent all authority and the known universe.) Yet now that seems gone. For the first time I was able to laugh whole-heartedly and feel whole-hearted pity. . . . Keep up the prayer, please please!

Just got a letter from Lewis in the mail.[37] I think I told you I'd raised an argument or two on some points? Lord, he knocked my props out from under me unerringly; one shot to a pigeon. I haven't a scrap of my case left. And, what's more, I've seldom enjoyed anything more. Being disposed of so neatly by a master of debate, all fair and square — it seems to be one of the great pleasures of life, though I'd never have suspected it in my arrogant youth. I suppose it's *unfair* tricks of argument that leave wounds. But after the sort of thing that Lewis does, what I feel is a craftsman's joy at the sight of a superior performance.

As usual, four pages; and this was going to be a short letter. The one lasting thing the CP gave me was an ability to think on the typewriter. But I'm not sure it's a blessing, for typing is so much swifter and easier than writing that it encourages my natural gabble. Love and blessings to all of you. We're over the worst of our fatigue and feel very happy.

Yours,
Joy

P.S. Bill asks if you know Alan Watts, who gave a lecture on Zen Buddhism at Beloit in 1945.[38]   *Source: Wade*

---

37. This letter has not survived.
38. The letter also has this postscript in the handwriting of Bill Gresham: "Do you know anything about a weird and wonderful world-view called 'Zen'? Started in China (called *Ch'an*), from Buddhism, developed in Japan. Fascinating stuff. Will tell more later if you are interested. And I want to write to Lewis about it. It may have something we can use" (source: Wade).

To Kenneth W. Porter

Endekill Road
Staatsburg, N.Y.
May 29, 1951

Dear Kenneth Porter,

Good to hear from you again, and so pleasantly! I enjoyed our brief correspondence in my *New Masses* days though I'm afraid I spoiled it with Marxist propaganda. Looked for you at Vassar after we moved here, but found you'd flitted.

You're right, I was never a typical or trusted communist. I *would* make the wrong joke at the wrong time — I actually found the Party funny! Got into hot water, once, by defending the Soviet purges on the ground that, judging by the American CP, any revolutionary government would have to kill off the old Bolsheviks if it ever wanted to get any real work done. I think they put up with me merely because I could write English fairly fast and fairly correctly; most of 'em couldn't.

And, as you say, I'm not a typical ex-comrade either. I'm sorry I made such a blithering ass of myself, but I don't feel that it was anyone's fault but my own; the other comrades were mostly bigger and honester fools than I. Looking back, I find the Party not so much sinister as comic. I suppose all that spying and conspiring did go on, but I certainly never saw any of it; what I *did* see was almost unbelievable muddle-headedness, inefficiency, and buck-passing. I distrust very much the accurate recollections of the characters who testify before committees — "On June 10, 1937, I met so-and-so at a meeting in X's house" — for my own memory is just a featureless blur of endless dull meetings. I suspect *that* sort of ex-comrade has just exchanged one kind of lying for another.

What puzzles me most is that no one on either side ever seems to ask what, to me, is the only relevant question: is Marxism *true?* They join the Party because they like the people in it; they leave because they get disillusioned about the people they oppose because they hate the people. As for me, I left because I finally got round to working my way through Lenin's *Materialism and Empirio-Criticism,* and a few other of the basic textbooks, and found to my horror that they were nonsense.

I don't think I knew you were a Christian socialist in my *New Masses* days, or even that such a thing existed.[39] But later my last act as a commu-

---

39. In an April 2, 1981, letter to Walsh, Porter writes: "I was brought up as a Calvinist

nist was to review a book called *The Christian Significance of Karl Marx* and remark that a communist needn't quarrel with people who believed in the divinity of Christ if only they *also* believed that He knew what He was talking about. *New Masses* bounced the review and accused me of heresy, thus speeding me a little faster on my journey.

Right now I'm teaching myself *not* to have views — to recognize that I'm not entitled to an opinion where I don't know the facts. I know something about English literature, cookery, gardening, and botany — but on social, political, and economic questions I'm capable only of an ignorant guess. Living on a farm has at least suggested to me that the problem is far harder than I supposed in my youth, that our real difficulty has to do with the relation of population to land; but whether or not there is *any* way of making an industrial system work for long, I daren't try to judge.

This is not despair but a basic shift in values. I gather I'm a more traditional sort of Christian than you, for I'm Presbyterian merely because the local church is officially Presbyterian (actually, alas, practically nothing definite except Prohibitionist). I really belong with the Anglicans, and not Broad Church either — C. S. Lewis and Charles Williams are the teachers I follow. That is, I believe in the divinity of Christ and in the resurrection of the dead; the world around us seems to me, now, a process of growth rather than an end in itself. So of course material disasters don't seem as terrifying as they once did.

But certainly, for Bill and me, getting rid of communism hasn't meant accepting capitalism; to us they seem less like opposites than like different phases of the same sin. This country seems a great deal better to us now than it did in our depression-haunted and embittered youth (why not? it *is* better than it was then) but still no earthly paradise! Makes a difference, though, when one really comes to understand original sin — one stops expecting perfection and flying into a fury edged with bullets when one finds imperfection instead. And it's possible, at last, to work rationally and effectively *toward* perfection — by working on oneself.

Are you still writing poetry? I hardly either write or read it any more, and I don't follow the critics, so I wouldn't know. Bill and I, being freelance writers with two kids, have become severely professional — we write for money, damn it. What you say about *Anya* delights me; one of my

---

and of course believed in 'once in grace, always in grace,' even though the predestinate saint might fall into grievous sin" (source: Wade).

main problems these days is explaining Jews to Gentiles and Gentiles to Jews. I find the Gentile much the better listener; the Jews are too busy hating. As for the anthology, *that* was a rush job and shows it — originally planned as a League of American Writers production, it was left on my shoulders when the League folded up. I did the whole thing — collection, translation, and what-not — in four months, and am not particularly proud of the result.

I hope you like *Weeping Bay* — if you can find a copy. The book was quietly suppressed at Macmillan's home office by an ardently Catholic sales manager, for reasons you'll understand when you read it. They've since fired the guy and sent me an implied apology, but too late to do me any good. Oh, well, here's a chance for me to practice Christian forgiveness, if I can stop gnashing my teeth long enough.

Thanks for writing — and how are things in Texas? Warmer than here, I hope; we're having endless cold rains. Yours for the communion of saints.

Joy Davidman   *Source: Wade*

To Kenneth W. Porter

Endekill Road
Staatsburg, N.Y.
August 16, 1951

Dear Kenneth,

Been away on vacation, fleeing the weather into the (comparatively) clear and pleasant climate of New England, so couldn't answer you before. I hear Texas is unspeakable! People dropping dead all over, steers melting away into a puddle, etc. It's just as bad here but in a different style — incredibly damp and steaming, rain most of the time and warm clammy fog the rest of it; weeds growing like mad, tomatoes refusing to ripen, corn all leaf and no ear, and the handsomest thunderstorms you ever saw. People are saying it's all the fault of the atom bomb, and here and there I catch dark mutters that the end of the world is at hand.

Don't know anyone at Vassar, though I used to have a nodding acquaintance with Ruth Lechlitner. Dick Rovere of the *New Yorker* lives almost around the corner; Connie Seabrook (Bill Seabrook's widow) up the road a piece;[40] sundry journalists, artists, and what not here and there. It's a very arty countryside — but, as usual the old native families, Dutch farmers and so on, have a natural talent for eccentricity and Bohemianism which beats anything the literary refugees from the big city can dream up. In my experience farmers are much more individual and less conventional than city people; for sheer narrow-minded parochialism give me the Bronx every time. Another literary importation, whom I do not intend to cultivate, is one of the latest pansy novelists — Gore Vidal I think — who has bought an octagon house just one jump away from the Bard College campus — wow! all those beautiful young men within reach![41] Don't know anything sillier than the present literary fashion of treating homosexual writers as if they were serious adult workers instead of sick and exhibitionist children.

What *was* the row in the Vassar philosophy department? I don't read the papers much. Yes, I can't find anything very sinister about *my* CP recollections either, though they'd make a wonderful humorous book. If I ever get time I may write some satirical reminiscences in fiction form — but Lord! will they hate me then! They don't mind being called sinister much, it's quite flattering; but how they loathe being laughed at!

The temptation of the party, though, seems to me to have very little to do with class — much more to do with one's basic philosophy. Plenty of lads with rich uncles have joined it — so have some of the uncles! One of Marxism's worst errors is the materialist assumption that all men's ideas are determined mostly by their "relation to the forces of production" — i.e. their pocketbooks. It's the usual wallowing in "undistributed middles" characteristic of people who have never mastered logic — about the first thing I've taught my boys is how to distinguish between "all" and "some." The thesis ought to be "*Some* men's ideas are *somewhat* determined by their economic position" — and unless your man is notably dishonest and corrupt, it'll never be more than somewhat. I myself had prosperous parents and plenty of security while I was in the Party; but a wildly insecure and often dead-broke married life has given me wisdom and taken me out of it!

I think the *real* basis for joining the Party is simply materialism. One

40. Richard H. Rovere (1915-1979) was a political journalist. William B. Seabrook (1886-1945) was a writer of bizarre stories and supernatural tales.

41. Gore Vidal (1925-) is a popular writer of short stories, novels, plays, television scripts, and movie scripts.

must believe that physical realities are the only realities, and that therefore you can make people happy by making them rich — i.e. physically comfortable. Further, one must believe that there is no God and consequently no absolute right and wrong; that men are entirely the product of the physical forces working on them and consequently have no appreciable free will, and that therefore history is "governed by scientific laws" which men can know, and by knowing which men can predict the future.

Well now, of course all of this is great nonsense. But in fact many people do believe it. Primarily, the "enlightened" Jews, who are left spiritually bankrupt by the degeneracy of orthodox Judaism into a mixture of insane ritualism and insane nationalist pride. It is not an accident that Communism had a Jewish origin and that almost all of its members in this country are Jews. (The few Gentiles are deliberately shoved into positions of prominence to conceal this fact.)

Secondarily, the progress-worshippers, science-worshippers, etc. of modern capitalism. I wish there were space in this letter to trace the inexorable evolution of Lutheran and Calvinist Protestantism, through the Presbyterian worship of respectability and riches, into the modern industrial system and the worship of material goods whose inevitable outcome we are now enduring. In a sense Communism is only capitalism that has lost patience. Since you've read *Weeping Bay,* you are not likely to think me pro-Catholic; but I fear Catholics are quite right in pointing out that Calvin was the ancestor of capital!

Pretty hard for me to define exactly *what* I am, as you can see; I don't fall into any of the current categories. Politically, I have come to suspect that forms and organizations of government and class don't really matter a damn, that they are not causes but products, that any society will create them out of its own traditions and needs as a tree grows leaves, and that therefore any attempt to invent and impose a new system is as pathetically futile as the attempts to impose new languages like Esperanto. As a believer in original sin, though, I could hardly find anarchism either possible or desirable.

Am I radical or conservative? I think of all the squabbles about reorganizing the economic system as mere superficial tinkering; as far as I can see, there is no possible way of making an overpopulated industrial system work *at all.* "Too many people, not enough land!" to quote my own book. Even in America, it is rapidly becoming uneconomical to produce meat for eating. The only really thriving country would seem to be Ireland, of all places — poorest in the world until it began to keep its birthrate low!

An English acquaintance of mine writes that he's off to Ireland for steak with onions and cheap whisky.

It would be equally misleading for me to define myself crisply as High Anglican. The Anglo-Catholics would reject me with horror; I regard ritual as useful but not indispensable (and easily decaying into mere magic) and I don't believe for a moment that the Old Testament is anything but an excellent compendium of a nation's literature, with amazing flashes of prophecy and insight and divine inspiration shooting through it now and then like lightning! I do, however, believe unshakably in the incarnation, the Atonement, and the Resurrection (though as for the Virgin Birth, I can take it or let it alone). Since I am one of C. S. Lewis' converts I tend to follow him fairly closely, and nobody has yet been able to define *him!* I'm not quite as traditional as my teacher though on several points, particularly things like birth control, on which I've been having a running argument with him on and off for a couple of years.

Lord, yes, I know just how you feel about the Fundamentalists; essentially they are, I think, more responsible for the spread of atheism than any *directly* atheist teaching could ever be. Have you ever studied the *historical* Scottish Covenanters, say about 1650? I've been reading about them recently in the course of research on Charles II. They were indescribably awful people and their "Christianity" was really a kind of devil-worship; they used to murder the women and children of defeated enemies in the name of Christ. Calvin was rigid enough himself but essentially a civilized man, and what the Lowland Scots made of his doctrine would have given him the collywobbles. You'll find studying them a good offset to your own Presbyterian background, and you may come to think better of the comparative good manners and good humor of the Church of England.

Yes — the usual Jewish view of "what Christians believe about Jews" is pure paranoia. It comes as a great shock, and rather a disappointment, to most Jews, to discover how little most Christians bother their heads about us! My husband once said profoundly, "Anti-Semitism is the Jews' religion," and I have seen printed arguments by Jewish rabbis to the effect that it's very bad for the Jews *not* to be persecuted — allows them to forget their racial superiority! One of them, a little while back, accused the Soviet Union of "asemitism," the crime of being indifferent to the Jews. Phooey.

Well, we *did* crucify Christ; the Romans wouldn't have given a damn, and what's worse we did, as a people, reject Him — though of course throughout history innumerable Jews have accepted Him and ceased to exist as Jews. But then, as you say, everyone is always crucifying Christ.

For their rejection the Jews have paid and are continuing to pay in the spiritual heartbreak of basing their culture on false premises. The persecutions — horrible enough, though not so unremitting as Jews imagine — are only the result of the Jews' willful self-isolation.

The whiskey-drinking preacher of *Weeping Bay* is my Southern husband's contribution — he's known plenty of them. You are probably thinking of the wrong church. On the share-cropper level, the "Holiness" and Pentecostal groups are often quite hard-drinking; I'll never forget one such I saw in action. And of course the Puritan tradition was originally hard-drinking too.

I've had the same experience as yours with poetry. It's almost impossible to find a satisfactory style; like you, I can't stand the current fashion — it's fit only for pansies and incompetents. But so far I've had no luck in finding a medium of my own. I've tried folk-style, like that of some of the pieces you enclose, but not as successfully; I think your "Grandfather" is quite good but somewhat hampered by self-consciousness about its homespun idiom. How can we help it? We are simply too literate to write ballads perfectly at our ease. "Winter Solstice" is as effective as a poem of indignation can ever be, I think. Somehow anger and the poetic emotion don't usually mix well; the only *completely* successful mixture I know is *Lycidas,* and that's because the indignation is kept down to one brief passage. I feel much as you do about this question of "war criminals" — some of them had to be shot, no doubt, but much better to shoot 'em out of hand, in hot blood, than by this mockery of legality.

I think you've put your finger on the difficulty — nowadays poetry has become an art for special occasions. We have either the cold-blooded finicking with words of the cliques or the bursts of "topical" verse — love or politics. I, too, have based most of my verse on one or the other! But we don't sing naturally, as an everyday matter. Prose is our real and spontaneous speech. The last spontaneous American poets to my taste were [Robert] Frost and Stephen Benét and Ridgely Torrence — and two of them are dead and one is very old.[42]

About being "overwhelmed with world problems" — aren't you forgetting your Christianity a trifle if you let them bother you *that* much? Of course it's rather a horrid world; but then, it always has been — there's never been an age that didn't expect the end of the world in its own time

---

42. Robert Frost (1874-1963) was the most critically acclaimed American poet of the twentieth century. Ridgely Torrence (1874-1950) was a poet and dramatist.

because "things can't possibly get any worse!" And of course atom bombs murder a great many people — but then, weren't they all going to die someday anyhow? The great error of our time is a sort of pseudo-social thinking that doesn't really improve anybody's life but on the contrary makes a lot of good people needlessly worried and unhappy; we forget to think in terms of the individual, we assume (along with the materialists) that the important thing is the physical survival, as long as possible, of a mysterious abstract monster called "culture" or "civilization" or "the human species." As if it mattered whether or not the species were wiped out tomorrow! What matters is the salvation of each individual soul — whether or not you, and I, and Joe Doakes have achieved union with God. That, and nothing else. The just society (which is *not* necessarily the comfortable or the long-lived society) is desirable as a means to individual salvation — i.e. the unjust and unloving man cannot know God. But it is not an end in itself, except to materialists.

(The great weakness of Protestantism, of course, is that under its lip-service to Christ it unthinkingly accepts the values of *this* world, the assumption that the church exists in order to build a universally comfortable society here and now, and that the goal of life is to live as long as possible as comfortably as possible! I once said ruefully that the Catholics are strong because, in spite of everything, they really *do* believe in Christ; whereas the Protestants are weak because, in spite of everything, they don't.)

Well this is a lot of serious discussion for August weather! I meant to add, one possible spot for poetry is the *Beloit Poetry Journal,* edited by Chad Walsh at Beloit College, Beloit, Wisconsin. A good place for Christian liberals, though to my taste far too much in the Eliot tradition — but then, they've recently bounced some of my stuff, so I may be prejudiced!

Yours,
Joy

Source: Wade

To Kenneth W. Porter

Endekill Rd.
Staatsburg, N.Y.
August 18, 1951

Dear Kenneth,

Your booklet just came, so I'll add this to my last letter.[43] I like most of these poems, particularly "The All-Sufficient Wonder," "The Faithful," and "The Wrath of the Lamb" — the last is magnificent.[44] You approach, here, the intense vision of [William] Blake.[45] Most of the rest are fairly good; they would be more than that, I think, except for two faults — they lack compression and they lack conviction.[46] In many of them you are explaining and sympathizing with Jesus, rather than accepting him — you are, indeed, not following Jesus but trying to get him to follow you; using him as an agency of your own special revolutionary theory. I did this myself in the early days of my conversion; explained away what I didn't like in the Gospel, valued Jesus not as the gateway to my own salvation, but as a *means* which I could use to support my own ideas — until it dawned on me that unless Jesus was God he was nothing, just another man with a handful of random ideas, and that all I valued such a man for was the accidental support his ideas gave my own position. You see, I was still being my own God!

To take an instance which is useful because it isn't as controversial as the others — the Mary-Martha poem.[47] What Jesus told Martha, explicitly, was that she was making a fuss about nothing and that Mary was perfectly right. Martha, no doubt, was the very common type of woman who wants to be admired for her indispensable housewifely virtues — *she* keeps

43. Porter had sent her his volume of poetry, *Pilate before Jesus and Other Biblical and Legendary Poems* (North Montpelier, VT: The Driftwood Press, 1936). Each poem is glossed to biblical passages.

44. "The All-Sufficient Wonder" is glossed to John 18:10 and Luke 22:51; "The Faithful" to Matthew 10:29; and "The Wrath of the Lamb" to Revelation 14:1; 5:5; 6:15-16; Numbers 23:24; and Genesis 49:9.

45. William Blake (1757-1827) was an artist and poet; his work often had mystical or religious themes.

46. In Porter's April 2, 1981, letter to Chad Walsh, he writes: "I . . . think that her comments on my *Pilate before Jesus* poems are too generous, from a literary viewpoint, although the ones she selected for such favorable comment are, or would be, of interest" (source: Wade).

47. "'That Good Part'"; it is glossed to Luke 10:38-42.

everything running, the world couldn't run without her! So she puts on a terrific act; and can't resist trying to capture the men's admiration and attention by pointing out how much better *she* is than her lazy good-for-nothing sister Mary! (Being a housewife myself, I know a lot about female pretenses!) Jesus was not fooled. But what do you do with the incident? Being yourself the product of a feminist culture and a culture which values constant physical activity above quiet contemplation, you refuse to accept Jesus' opinion — you reverse his judgment completely, declaring that Martha was really the better and wiser of the two and poor Mary was only good for sitting still and listening, so Jesus was merely being kind!

A small example, but significant. You are not trying here to understand and believe in Jesus. You are trying to turn Jesus into a modern Socialist; much what Bruce Barton did in that awful book when he tried to turn Jesus into a modern business executive.[48]

I gather you still hold the ideas expressed in these poems, or I wouldn't analyze them in such detail. I feel that you take an equivocal position about the divinity of Jesus; now, really, was he God or wasn't he? That's the $64 question. No amount of talk about Jesus' saintly ideas will help if we don't think he's God; for if he was just another human, then he could be mistaken like the rest of us and his ideas are just his private whims, as ours are. By whose authority, then, can we call his ideas saintly? By God's? But how do *we* know what God thinks (except through what Jesus told us, and unless Jesus was God he was just guessing)? All the talk about Jesus as "a good man" really means only that we like him because he agrees with *us* — and the minute he doesn't agree with us we will toss him overboard, as you toss overboard all the Gospel speeches which counsel acceptance of existing government.

It's very hard to explain why I feel the "social gospel" is on the wrong track, without giving the wrong impression that I'm against social reform. I suppose you and I would both agree that it's our job to build the Kingdom of Heaven on earth, and we wouldn't disagree much on what the Kingdom of Heaven ought to be like, though perhaps I'd want more danger and less comfort than you would, my experience being that comfort rots the soul far more than pain ever does. Still — no slums, no profit system, no exploitation, no hunger, no injustice. Right?

But, you see, I believe in some kind of life after death (without being

---

48. Bruce F. Barton (1886-1967) was an American businessman. Davidman is referring to Barton's *The Man Nobody Knows: A Discovery of Jesus* (Indianapolis: Bobbs-Merrill, 1925).

specific as to its nature) and I cannot tell from your poems whether you do; that is, whether you are a Christian at all. For unless you believe what Jesus said about these things you are not a Christian, any more than an admiration of Mohammed as a good man and a wise social thinker would be sufficient to make you a Mohammedan. And one's whole approach to life, one's whole philosophy turns on this point. If this life is all, then our goal is simple — to enjoy it as much as possible and make it last as long as possible and any talk of "social duty" is mere irrational sentimentality. But if there's something yet in store, then our goal is to make ourselves into beings *capable* of Heaven — to produce, inside ourselves, a divine nature. Therefore we practice virtues, sacrifices, self-denials, and undergo suffering in *this* life — because we must, in order to become the sort of creature that is wanted. Not, God help us, because we *like* suffering, or because it's a good thing in itself! Of course it isn't; whereas pleasure *is*. But because we must become beings of perfect love and selflessness; because the walls of the Self are walls shutting out God.

St. Paul faced this issue squarely; when asked, "What if you Christians are wrong about the afterlife?" he said, "Then we Christians are of all men the most miserable."[49] Because then, you see, the only real good would be the good things of this world — which Christians must often give up.

But the modern "social-minded Christian" does assume that the only real good is the good of this world; that our actions count and not our intentions (in flat denial of what Jesus said on the subject) and that therefore slum dwellers etc. are "destroyed" by their environment — i.e. that poverty damns the poor. By no means; it damns the rich.

Yes, injustice is wrong. But in whom is it wrong? In the victim of injustice, or in the unjust man? The victim of injustice may actually emerge a better man inside though his outward actions may be "antisocial." If there is no recompense for being a victim, then this world is truly hell and ruled by a devil; for all our scurrying round in hope of building a better *future* will not undo or repay one moment of pain suffered by one individual in past or present. You say "Christ is crucified with all who suffer want or know abuse."[50] And that is true — but, more important, he is crucified in the heart of every man who causes want or commits abuse.

I think it of little use to urge people to set the social house in order, without first setting their private spiritual house in order! Revolutions al-

49. 1 Corinthians 15:12-19.
50. See "Crucifer"; it is glossed to Matthew 27:32 and Luke 23:26.

ways make that mistake; they look without rather than within, they are all for putting the world right without first reforming the reformers — and the result has invariably been a worse tyranny than the one they overthrew. From the social reforms of the self-righteous, Good Lord deliver us!

All this has to be thrashed out afresh in every generation. There are always plenty of people who judge by actions, who argue "He can't be wrong whose life is in the right,"[51] and who conclude, therefore, that the goal is to give everyone a respectable, comfortable life in which he is not tempted to perform antisocial actions. And there are the rest of us, who argue that no life is in the right, however outwardly sweet and virtuous, if the heart is wrong; and who think a man may more readily be damned (i.e. corrupt and horrible and ultimately miserable inwardly) simply for approving his own virtues than for being a thief and a murderer. (Not that I'm advising driving people to theft and murder, or committing them yourself! It is simply that it's often easier to repent of theft and murder than of spiritual pride; the Pharisee is the most stubborn of all sinners.) We make a mistake in telling the prosperous, "Reform the economic system, because it's making the poor wicked!" We should say, "Reform it, because it's making *you* wicked!"

Ah, well, Blake said, "The vision of Christ that thou dost see/Is my vision's greatest enemy." And that's how we weaken our own good intentions — by setting 'em against each other. I don't think it really matters much how we *think,* either, if we have the charity and the grace. God forbid men should have to be saved by their wisdom! There'd be an awful lot of damn fools like me in hell![52]

Yours,
Joy

P.S. And thanks for the book; reading it has been both pleasant and exciting.

Source: Wade

51. The precise quotation is "His can't be wrong whose life is in the right." From *An Essay on Man,* Epistle 3, line 303, by Alexander Pope (1688-1744).

52. In Porter's April 2, 1981, letter to Walsh he adds: "I must admit . . . that I sometimes found her somewhat exasperating when she began to lay down the law on theological problems. But her general good sense, high spirits, and sometimes rather malicious wit left them far on the credit side. I have often wondered why she was willing to spend so much time and energy writing to me and regret that our correspondence terminated — probably my fault" (source: Wade).

To Norman V. Donaldson

Endekill Road
Staatsburg, N.Y.
October 12, 1951

Mr. Norman V. Donaldson
Director, Yale University Press
New Haven, Conn.

Dear Mr. Donaldson:

I'm returning your letter to me, signed. The arrangement seems eminently fair — thirteen years is quite long enough to keep a volume of verse in stock. By this time I'm beginning to regard it as a juvenile indiscretion.

I've a minor question or two. (1) Am I right in assuming I get my copies of *Letter to a Comrade* for nothing? Even to me, 'tisn't worth paying for. (2) In the unlikely event of anyone's ever wishing to reprint a poem from the book, am I entitled to grant permission or do I refer them to the Yale Press?

And (3) may I ask the brand of typewriter, and the typeface, used in your letter to me? It's much the most beautiful type-face I've ever seen.

Yours truly,
Joy Davidman   *Source: Yale UP*

Crisis and Hope

Letters 1952-1953

In August 1952, Davidman left her sons and Bill in the care of her cousin, Renée, and set sail for England in order to fulfill a lifelong dream. In order to escape from her own bad marriage to Claude Pierce, Renée and her two children, Bob and Rosemary, came to stay with Bill, David, and Douglas while Joy went to England.[1] Renée was to act as housekeeper and attend to the needs of the children while Joy was gone; however, things became greatly complicated when Bill and Renée fell in love during Joy's absence.

Apparently none of Joy's letters from that period survive. C. S. Lewis's letter of September 12, 1952, refers to her as an "old and valued pen-friend."[2] Davidman had written Lewis and asked if she could meet him for lunch when she visited Oxford. In fact, Lewis and George Sayer met Davidman and her friend Phyllis Haring for lunch at the Eastgate Hotel in Oxford on September 24, 1952.[3] According-ing to Sayer, Lewis "was delighted by her bluntness and her anti-American views."[4] Warren Lewis recalls his first meeting her during this same time period:

1. Renée Rodriguez was Joy's first cousin; according to Douglas Gresham, Renée "was a stunningly beautiful girl"; see Douglas Gresham, *Lenten Lands: My Childhood with Joy Davidman and C. S. Lewis* (New York: Macmillan, 1988), p. 13.

2. *The Collected Letters of C. S. Lewis, Volume 3: Narnia, Cambridge, and Joy, 1950-1963,* ed. Walter Hooper (London: HarperCollins, 2006), p. 222; hereafter CL, 3. Lewis also refers to Davidman in his letter of August 26, 1952, p. 230.

3. Phyllis Haring was a writer who lived in London; Davidman had first met her through correspondence. She is identified as Phyllis Williams in George Sayer, *Jack: C. S. Lewis and His Times* (London: Macmillan, 1988), p. 214, and in Lyle Dorsett, *And God Came In: The Extraordinary Story of Joy Davidman* (New York: Macmillan, 1983), pp. 85-86, 102, 106. Douglas Gresham recalls her name as Haring.

4. See Sayer, *Jack*, pp. 214-15.

In the winter of 1952 she visited Oxford. I was some time in making up my mind about her; she proved to be a Jewess, or rather a Christian convert of Jewish race, medium height, good figure, horn rimmed spec., quite extraordinarily uninhibited. Our first meeting was at a lunch in Magdalen [College], where she turned to me in the presence of three or four men, and asked in the most natural tone in the world, "Is there anywhere in this monastic establishment where a lady can relieve herself?" But her visit was a great success and a rapid friendship developed; she liked walking, and she liked beer, and we had many merry days together; and when she left for home in January 1953, it was with common regrets, and a sincere hope that we would meet again.[5]

On October 8, 1952, Renée wrote Joy with newsy information:

I believe Bill has told you that Grace [the housekeeper] has not been coming to clean for about three or four weeks and that we have even stopped taking the clothes to Mrs. Millroy due to being broke. What with kids, meals, dishes, housecleaning, washing, and ironing of the clothes etc. I've been kept on the go. Bill has been worrying about sending you your money and has been trying like mad to get it to you, but honestly we are as broke as can be. If he has a buck in change in his jeans, it's more than I have, for I don't have the proverbial sou. We've long since used what little I had in the bank. . . . I'm not trying to paint a black picture, but I do think you should know just how things are here. Nor am I trying to alarm you in any way, but if you have a clearer view of the situation you will see that it has been impossible for Bill to send you any money. The guy just ain't got it.

Renée adds that she has been mending clothes for David and Doug to wear to school and recounts struggles Bill is having trying to get stories published, adding:

Bill has also exhausted every source for credit or loans, but things have got to change sometime, and at this rate, it can only be for the better. I know this sounds like making "a poor mouth," but it is just the gosh awful

---

5. Warren Lewis (1895-1973) was Lewis's beloved elder brother. After a career in the army, Warren served as his brother's secretary and devoted himself to writing books on seventeenth-century France. This passage comes from his *Brothers and Friends: The Diaries of Major Warren Hamilton Lewis,* ed. Clyde S. Kilby and Marjorie Lamp Mead (San Francisco: Harper & Row, 1982), pp. 244-45.

truth. In the meantime, you try to make the most of your trip [to England] and enjoy it to the fullest, for it is one of those "once in a lifetime" things. Don't worry about us, for I am sure we will manage to get out of this hole. (Source: Wade)

Just before her return to the U.S. in early January 1953, Joy received the following letter from Bill.

Late winter 1952 or early January 1953

Dear Joy:

You have written several times that you can't understand the cool tone of my letters and have wondered what makes. I didn't think the letters were unusually cool but if I understand you right, you have wanted me to say definitely what was going to happen when you come home. I wanted things to get clear in my own mind and also felt letters can do just so much and they are no substitute for personal discussion. Also I didn't want to cloud your holiday with things which would upset you.

Renée and I are in love and have been since about the middle of August. If it had not been for our love I could not have come through this summer with as little anguish as I have for things have been rugged financially. I hate making a poor mouth and didn't want to darken your trip with too much complaining about finances but the main problem we have had over here has been seeing that we all had enough to eat. I wanted you to have your England trip and just before you left I tried to do everything I could to expedite it. But this left us with lots of unpaid bills and most of them are still unpaid. I found out another thing: the Dutchess Countyniks were most friendly when we first came up here and were obviously not worried about money. But when word gets around that we are broke they seem to react as if they have been somehow betrayed; here were people who promised a jot of business and suddenly they have to watch pennies like ordinary mortals. It seems a bitter pill for the gorgio to swallow. So far we have always eaten and most miraculous of all I have plowed away, working like blazes right through it, with Renée's love and care to help me. I couldn't have done it without her.

The four kids have been a pretty explosive force, the Pierce kids puzzled and upset, missing their Daddy, and our own kids missing you more than they usually admit. But all the kids have been surprisingly good considering the strain in the household. Renée gets more and more able to

133

compute on her own case as we get lock chains scanned off and engrams reduced.[6]

I can understand, I believe, what resolutions you have made about coming home and trying to make a go of our marriage. But I feel that all such decisions are sacrifices of human life on the altar of Will Power, with the women's magazine hacks serving as high priests. I have never yet know[n] will power and determination to "make a go of marriage," to take the place of love in its complete sense. I have tremendous affection for you and have certainly missed you, although I was glad that you were having fun and adventures and seeing all the things you wanted to see. But affection and intellectual camaraderie are not marriage. People who are fond of each other and respect each other and set out to "make a go of the marriage" for the sake of the children are setting up a situation of constant affinity enforcers and reality deniers. I have so many units available to the analyzer now that great sections of my life show up as self-deception — usually with pretty good motives, since my engrams and my family training just didn't contain the nastiest kind of behavior. I can't take any credit for this, natch.

I don't think we can realistically expect you, even with the firmest determination in the world, to be anything but a writer. Renée has a different orientation; her only interest is in taking care of her husband and children and making a home for them. And it is unrealistic for us to count on my being able to make enough money to hire a stall of servants to handle the cooking, the cleaning, and the child care so that you and I can both have careers as writers.

If you set your teeth grimly and determined to make yourself over into a housewife you'd blow your cork sooner or later. I know something about writers.

I am not trying to minimize the difficulties of our situation in the least. The optimum solution, as I can visualize it now, would be for you to be married happily to some really swell guy, Renée and I to be married, both families to live in easy calling distance so that the Gresham kids could have Mommy and Daddy on hand; and the Pierce children to get dianetic processing as soon as possible, certainly before the locks hook on to such a degree that they have a hard time of it.

Obviously there is the question of your cooperation in this ideal solution. If you are not in love with anyone whom you could marry, it's a ques-

6. This is a reference to psychoanalytical techniques Bill was practicing at the time, including dianetics.

tion of having to wait until you meet such a person. But I don't see how Renée and I can manage any solution at all without your help.

The typical gossipy neighbor, viewing our problem from the outside, might comment that what Bill Gresham wants is to have his cake and eat it too. We might point out that the optimum solution of all human problems is just this: homo sapiens have progressed precisely in the ratio of having his cake and eating it too: a man, forcing himself into a dress shirt sixty years ago, undoubtedly moaned to his wife about wishing he could hear the opera and be comfortable in dressing gown and slippers at the same time. The result of this wanting to have his cake and eat it too is the phonograph record industry.

In our own case I cannot see anything sinful in wanting to figure out a method of handling our problem so that the kids have the maximum security and we — all three of us grown folks — have a maximum of love. This may seem to leave you out on a limb but if you look at your own responses, your own spontaneous responses, not authoritarian judgments, I think you will agree that we can work out a better arrangement for the kids than one founded on the frustration and eventual despair of their parents.

When physical attraction is gone from a relationship between a man and a woman, all the comradeship in the world will not bring it back, and between you and me it is gone and has been gone for years. I am more than willing to take full responsibility for this if it is a question of responsibility. But people cannot fall in love by will power and they certainly cannot fall back in love by it.

What Renée and I have found together came as an earth-shaking surprise for both of us. We never knew any such happiness nor thought there was such a thing. All of my awkward fumbling around down the years taught me nothing about such a thing. We discussed it at great length, tried on for size all possible conclusions about it, and decided that it is not a rebound business, is not a hasty infatuation and is nothing that either of us can either control or deny without damage to ourselves and everyone around us. It's here. We are more married than either of us ever knew people could be. We feel that unless we set out to make this marriage as secure as we can, that we are doing violence to the Tao.

I know how you used to react when anything threatened your happiness and I have audited you for so many hundreds of hours that I think I understand better than anyone all the forces which went into creating this reaction and the need for it in the early years. Don't hesitate to speak your mind about anything. I think you should. But I am confident that when you come home we can talk it over with our analyzers turned full on and work out the best solution for everyone.

The Macmillan check for $70 arrived in the same mail as your letter mentioning it. I shall cable you the money as soon as I can. I had to use this $70 for groceries, Frank Battenfield having grown exceedingly caustic about an unpaid bill of $9.20 for November. However, "What Are We Scared Of?", the carnival story which the slicks nixed, has landed at the Bluebook *for $500.* Esquire *is reprinting "Load of Respect" in an anthology of the best of* Esquire *during its 20 years of publishing, and paying me $75 which they don't have to pay but are paying for good-will purposes. I have a circus book to review for the* New York Times *which should bring in another $50. None of this dough is in hand but it's all going to come and I am only in debt to Brandt and Brandt for $200. So it looks like Santa Claus rides again.*

If I could sell one short story to Colliers *it would wipe out all the bills outstanding, including the school tax on the property which I have not been able to pay yet. But I am not counting on this, just plowing away at turning the stuff out.*

Henry Wheeler came over yesterday morning and with Renée washing the storm windows, Henry on the ladder and me boosting them up to him, we got them up in about an hour. Also I turned to and made Davy a snake stick with a broom handle and an angle iron which he practically takes to bed with him. Great feeling of accomplishment all around.

My own personal goal, for the immediate future, is to get a professional auditor's course and get my own service facsimiles run off by experts. My asthma is better but not gone, my facial itch likewise, and I lock-scanned off so many "tired," "exhausted," and similar decisions that my work energy has risen rapidly. My sleep pattern is still screwy and I have had to sleep in the mornings and work during the afternoons and evenings. Renée cooks two dinners — one for the kids early and one for me later.

Renée has had to do all the washing herself without a washing machine and we have had Grace in only on Fridays to clean and help with the ironing. If I could only feel that you were not too unhappy about all this I would not face the future with any qualms at all. The income tax debt is piling up interest at such an appalling rate that I can really see no solution except to give the government the house eventually — if they'd take it. I haven't spoken to Charlie Butts about this but I do know that in similar cases they sometimes make a settlement. Where this would leave us seems very terrifying until I stop to think that it leaves us right where we were before the [Nightmare] Alley *was published, except that you and I are to-tally changed people, able to think and feel in a healthy manner, we're rid of the damned Communist party, alcoholism, a bunch of screwy acquaintances who pulled us down in tone, and have had several years of very comfortable living while working our way back to sanity. The best is yet to be, Poogle. The red-headed sea captain, God rest his tormented soul, has really saved our lives, and we can't take that away from him, no matter how many thetans he chases with a butterfly net. All the prayer, meditation and good works in the world could not do for badly aberrated homo sapiens what dianetics can do, for it puts in repairs the praying, meditating and good-works performing mechanism. In further processing is our hope. We cannot expect God to help us until we have done everything we can to help our-selves and to me this means more dianetic technique, more processing and better computation all along the line.*

If you feel lost, forsaken and unloved, Poogle, just try to remember that there are a vast horde of lock chains that remain to be scanned off your case, including that year-long engram of your illness with Jenine [Davidman's mother] lying always underfoot like a krait in the dust.

I don't think it will be practical to take the boys down to meet the boat. I talked it over with Davy and described the pier and how cold it is and how long we would have to wait and he agreed that it would be better for me to drive down alone and get Mommy and her baggage. You will find Davy very much of a man, a startlingly beautiful and sensible man, too. Doug is his usual Rotarian, Masonic, volunteer fire department, adorable self. Bobby is a sweet kid who drops into a very complaining, growly va-lence occasionally. Rosemary is better about the chronic weeps and is getting to be quite a person and is much prettier than she was when she arrived. Davy's latest exploit is taking a rabbit skin away from the dogs and stuff-ing it with cotton and sewing it up. I knew taxidermy would come but didn't know it was imminent.

Love,
[Bill]

Source: Wade

To Chad Walsh

Endekill Road
Staatsburg, N.Y.
January 25, 1953

Dear Chad,

First chance I've had to write to you — so much has been happening. I stayed with Jack and Warnie over a fortnight just before I sailed for home, and had a marvelous time; by the way, they both send their love.[7] Quite an experience it was, Christmas with the Lewises![8] (An enormous turkey, and burgundy from the Magdalen [College, Oxford] cellars to go with it; I stole a wineglassful to put in the gravy, and they thought it was practically lese majeste — till they tasted the gravy.) Being on vacation, Jack was taking life easy — he was merely writing his book on prayer (it's going to be a wonder, I've read part of it), correcting OHEL proofs, setting scholarship and fellowship exam papers, doing a college edition of Spenser for an American publisher, and finishing the *seventh* Narnia book.[9] Also, of course, answering the endless letters. This left him time to go over my own Decalogue book with me (about 50,000 words of it) and tell me how to fix it; he liked it quite well, thank heaven.[10] Also there was a lot of walking and talking. One day the three of us were over Shotover to Horspath and then to Garsington, coming back by way of Wheatley (do you remember all those places?) and getting caught in a savage rain — I blistered my feet, and Jack and Warnie

7. Jack was the name C. S. Lewis gave himself as a young child; Warnie was Warren Lewis's nickname.

8. See Lewis's less than rosy comments on this visit in his letter of December 19, 1952, to his godson, Laurence Harwood, in CL, 3, p. 268; for more about this visit, see also his letters of December 18 (p. 267), December 19 (pp. 268-69), December 20 (p. 269), December 22 (p. 270), December 23 (p. 271), January 24, 1953 (p. 284), and January 26 (p. 285). From this time forward scattered references to Davidman appear increasingly in Lewis's letters.

9. Lewis eventually did publish a book on prayer, although it did not appear until after his death; see C. S. Lewis, *Letters to Malcolm: Chiefly on Prayer* (London: Geoffrey Bles, 1964). OHEL was Lewis's ironic acronym for his *English Literature in the Sixteenth Century Excluding Drama*, The Oxford History of English Literature, vol. 3 (Oxford: Clarendon Press, 1954). The seventh Narnia book was *The Last Battle: A Story for Children* (London: Bodley Head, 1956).

10. This refers to Davidman's *Smoke on the Mountain: An Interpretation of the Ten Commandments* (Philadelphia: Westminster Press, 1954).

practically had to pull me up Shotover on the last stretch. But it was great fun.

I even got taken to a Christmas pantomime, where we all roared enthusiastically at the oldest jokes and joined in the choruses of the songs. I'll never forget Jack coming in loudly on something that went like this:

Am I going to be a bad boy? No, no, no!
Am I going to be awful? No, no, no!
I promise not to put some crumbs in Auntie Fanny's bed,
I promise not to pour the gravy over baby's head . . . etc.

I wish the critic of *Presbyterian Life* who objected to my quoting Yeats' "Fiddler of Dooney" ("The good are always the merry") could have heard that!

And, of course, the pubs — Eastgate and Bird and Baby and the Ampleforth (up in Headington) and lots of others. Some day *I'm* going to open a pub in Oxford. I've become a complete Anglomaniac anyhow, can't wait to transplant; I've never felt at home anywhere as I do in London or Oxford. And after the magical gold light of the English landscape, ours looks strangely flat and dull to me.

— The OHEL volume is going to make people sizzle; it's full of controversial stuff and reversals of conventional judgments. I am the *first* person to see those galleys, and I feel very honored. By the way, I also read a lot of Jack's poetry and I think you're wrong about it. It's quite new and strange and unfashionable, a complete break with the modern conventions of intellectual and bloodless verse, and for that reason rather difficult to appraise; but I thought a lot of it was damn good. Technically it's amazing. He's used very old forms and given them an entirely new twist. (He liked *my* poetry too — so there!) But you and I will never see eye to eye on verse.

I'm in fine shape now and all set to do lots of writing. Let me know if there's something I can do for Episcopal Churchnews, huh? Love to Eva and the four Graces. I hope *your* English trip comes off all right.

Love,
Joy

Source: Wade

In February 1953 Davidman became a member of the Episcopal Church and was confirmed in the Cathedral of St. John the Divine, New York.

To Chad Walsh

Endekill Road
Staatsburg, N.Y.
February 27, 1953

Dear Chad,

Where are you — New Mexico, New England, or old England? Do break down and write a girl, huh? I could stand some comforting just now; Bill and I are on the point of divorce, more or less by mutual agreement. I can't pretend I'm sorry; I've been pretty wretched for years, and my conscience wouldn't let me quit — I had hoped that my vacation in England would soothe my shattered nerves and give me strength to go on. It *did* do that; but in the meantime Bill decided he wanted to marry the cousin I'd left keeping house for me. I was rather shattered at first, but have now decided it will be a blessed release.

I don't know how you feel about divorce. I always took it that divorce was only the last possible resort, and felt I ought to put up with anything I could bear for the children's sake. And I hoped that Bill's adulteries, irresponsibilities, etc. would end if he ever recovered from his various neuroses; also that his becoming a Christian would make a difference. Unfortunately I've been disappointed on both counts. Bill gave up being a Christian as soon as he found out it meant living by a moral code and admitting and repenting one's sins. And now that he is reasonably stable, cheerful, and energetic as a result of dianetics, he feels ready to go out and paint the town red. In a way I can see how he feels — for so long he was unable to enjoy life at all, what with anxiety and psychosomatic ailments, that now he's like a man just out of prison and off on a bender.

I never felt I could talk to anybody about my married life, in the past. But when this new situation developed I asked Lewis for advice and told him a good deal of the story — an expurgated version, at that. Some of it I simply can't put into words. Anyhow Lewis strongly advised me to divorce Bill; and has repeated it even more strongly since I've been home — Bill greeted me by knocking me about a bit, and I wrote Lewis about that.[11] So now I'm rid of the feeling that it's my duty to go on!

There's one thing I must say in Bill's defense — my love for him died very suddenly and completely two years ago, as a result of something he did when I was seriously ill. And he knows that; and in his philosophy a marriage is over when the sexual excitement passes. Besides, he's very dependent on admiration, and it must be agonizing for him to live in the same house with a woman who neither loves nor respects him.

At the moment we can't *afford* a divorce — Bill earned almost no money while I was away and there's a mountain of debts. Things are improving, however, and I hope to get away within a year at the most. I hope to take the children to England and bring them up there — not so much because I'm completely in love with England, though that's part of it, as because living is so much cheaper there and I'll be able to live decently on what Bill can pay. Knowing him, I'm very doubtful whether he will pay for long; but perhaps I can sell enough stuff myself through my American agent to keep me going no matter what.

Well, it's a dreary business! My cousin has left now for Florida, to divorce her own husband, a violent drunken Alabama man whom she left a year or so ago. But for more than a month she and Bill and I were all here together, and she was tortured by guilt and embarrassment and worry, and would take to her bed with crying fits — whereupon Bill lectured me for my lack of Christian charity in not enabling her to enjoy her love affair more. I *did* tell her that I felt it would be a blessing for me in the end, was not jealous, and didn't — knowing my Bill — blame her for what had happened between them. And we parted very good friends. But one of Bill's queer traits is his refusal to admit that *his* actions could ever be wrong or could ever hurt anybody. Two days after he'd half choked me, he asked in all seriousness, "Have you ever known me to do a brutal or unkind thing?" And he has often told me that the only reason his unfaithfulness, alcoholism, temper tantrums etc. upset me is that I am so neurotic. Thank Heavens, I'm finally growing able to laugh at him.

My boy Davy has proved a wonderful comfort. He knew what was going on, and he's never liked Bill much — though in all fairness I must say Bill has always been kind to the children. And Davy's quite eager for me to divorce his father — talked to me like a Dutch uncle: "There is a

11. Lewis's letters to Davidman advising her to divorce Gresham have not survived. On occasion he wrote correspondents about divorce; see his letter of March 2, 1955, CL, 3, p. 575.

point at which patience stops being a virtue!" says he. And lots more, all very adult and shrewd — uncanny in a child not yet nine. I'm a little worried about the other boy — he *is* fond of Bill and will miss him. But I think the adventure of going to England will carry them both over the transition period.

Enough of this doleful stuff now. How are *you* doing, and what? By the way, on the *Franconia* coming over there were a lot of English families emigrating to Canada or the States, and they had a church-service hookup by which, through their church at home, they arranged to be met and shepherded around a bit by people from the Episcopal church wherever they were going. Have you ever done an article about that? Strikes me it would make a wonderful story; either for Churchnews or for one of the big slicks, the *S[aturday] E[vening] P[ost]* for instance.

Do write me. And — well, you might pray for me a bit, I need it. Love to Eva and the Four.

Yours,
Joy

Source: Wade

Walsh replies on March 6, 1953:

> *Your letter of the 27th was not an utter surprise to Eva and me, but it was still a considerable jolt. I suppose one always hates to see a marriage break up, and especially when one loves both of the people involved. But neither of us can find it in our hearts to argue with you and urge a different course of action. I think we had sensed a little of the situation, though we had not realized that things had actually come to the breaking point. About the whole question of divorce — there is actually nothing in Christianity to prevent a divorce per se. The complications and theological deep waters come with the question of remarriage — but that's a bridge you must cross, when and if. From everything you tell in your letter — and it seemed a very restrained and objective letter to me — you seem amply justified.*
>
> *You are very dear to us, Joy; perhaps dearer than you realize. Eva confesses that when we first met you and Bill, Bill interested her the more. But by last summer she had come to have the deeper feeling for you. Is there any chance next summer that you could slip away by yourself for a few days, and come and visit us at the lake? We'll be there — at the same cottage from late June to about 25 Aug. If you can come, we promise we won't make it a tear*

fest. We'll have fun, just being together. Think about it, won't you, Joy? It would mean very much to us.

I got a warm letter the other day from Jack — that's how he now signs his letters to me — your influence? And he spoke with affection of you. I envy you the prolonged time you had with him and the chance to see his new books.

Speaking of books, are you planning to publish the Decalogue in book form? I imagine Macmillan would snap it up for publication after it appears in Presbyterian Life.

Are you definitely decided that you will settle in England? I hate to think of your being so far away. Though if you settle there by the summer of 1954, maybe we will see you. We hope to go abroad that summer.

I'll be writing more later. But I want to get this letter off right now. You are very much in our hearts — and will be in our prayers.

Source: Wade

To Renée Rodriguez

Endekill Road
Staatsburg, N.Y.
March 10, 1953

Dear Renée,

Your last letter came yesterday and is sitting here patiently waiting; Bill's away again and may not be back for a week, so in case he doesn't have a chance to write I will so you won't worry. Things are going as well as can be expected here. The last I heard, your kids were well and happy; I can't get to see them, though, because of Bill's absence. We got the various checks and paid *all* the bills, which still leaves us eating money enough for a while. Life certainly looks brighter that way than it did two months ago!

Bill is in good shape and behaving well, except for his normal peevishness — but you wouldn't have seen as much of that as I have. He is being careful about money too. When he went down to Tennessee last week I suggested he journey a little *further* South, but he said it would cost too much. I don't know if I told you that I had got him to be a little more definite about divorce plans? I keep at it, gently, and make slight but visible progress. It isn't that he doesn't want it, but that his nature is to put off *any* decisive step as long as possible, just as he did about the house. He said cheerfully the other day that he was in no hurry, couldn't remarry quickly in any case; whereupon I said, but I was in a hurry — it being *my* nature to act, once I've decided. He looked appalled and objected that he'd be lonely if I left with the boys before his next marriage was ready. What a pathetic child it is, really. He can't see any reason why I shouldn't be willing to go on looking after him until he's good and ready to throw me out. I remember Douglas, at the age of three, getting angry at me one day and saying: "When I grow up I'm going burn down your house!" I asked, "Why wait till you grow up, Dougaboo; why not burn it now?" To which he answered with perfect logic, "Where I live?"

Well, Bill seems to me just like that — he wants to burn down *this* marriage, but not until he's got a new place to live all set up. And he no more expects me to take action of my own than Douglas expected me to throw him out of the house. But it is obvious to me that I will have to take the initiative — he will just drift from day to day in his usual fashion, otherwise. And the more I see of him the more impatient I become to get away; so I'll do something as soon as this book [*Smoke on the Mountain*] is out of the way.

Wrote Chad Walsh what was happening (censored version) and he and Eva said they were of course grieved but not surprised my marriage was breaking up; had suspected things were a mess long ago. So you see, recent events and people are *not* to blame.

Had a long talk with Bill about his own personality one day and got him to see, by putting it in dianetic language, that what *he* does really does affect other people and sometimes rather painfully; that he's a powerful personality and must realize his responsibility for his influence on others' lives. And that people's reaction to *his* behavior is not necessarily based on something Mamma did to them when they were unborn. His blind spot about his own behavior is really his greatest weakness; if he could get rid of *that*, all his good qualities would have a real chance. It's really very curious at times — as when you were so depressed over the future, etc. shortly before you left. I tried to tell him then what was upsetting you, and he insisted it was entirely worry about Claude.

The idea that what *he* does counts seems to come as a great surprise to him, whenever it comes up. I can only get it across by phrasing it in dianetic jargon and sweetening it with enormous flattery about what a terrific person he is.

— Got a nice letter from Warnie — Jack's brother, you know. Poor lambs, they've both had flu, but thank Heaven not badly. I had written

Warnie about Davy's snake pet shop project, etc. and he sent his complete fortune in American stamps — 79¢ — for their savings toward a trip to England. He *is* a darling.

O how I envy you those sunny beaches. There's sun enough here today — cold, glittery, murderous March sun, with a terrific gale blowing, and the temperature about ten degrees. It's been beastly cold all week, and I've been shoveling coal into the furnace at a great rate. I've got my last two revisions off to *Presbyterian Life*, thank God.[12] But *now* I'm getting the whole book in shape for Bernice,[13] and I find I've got to rewrite the first article! Bill did it, or most of it, in his best rhetorical style — and I think it stinks.

Take care of yourself, cookie-pie, and don't get bopped on the head by a beach ball.

Yours,
Joy

Source: Wade

To Renée Rodriguez

Endekill Road
Staatsburg, N.Y.
April 16, 1953

Dear Renée,

Glad to hear things are breaking so well for you! What a difference three months have made in everything; in January, remember how hopeless the situation looked? But hopelessness is catching, and when Bill gets into one of his defeatist spells everybody around him is likely to share his feeling that nothing can be done about anything except to go to bed. We're jogging along not too badly here, at least we've got money in the bank and I got him as far as the family lawyer the other day to discuss ways and means. But I can't make up my mind about his mental condition. He is certainly better than he used to be; healthier and more considerate,

---

12. Davidman's "Into the Full Light" appeared in *Presbyterian Life* 6 (April 4, 1953): 12-13, 26-29; it is Chapter XI, "Light of Light," the last chapter in *Smoke on the Mountain*. The second essay, "God Comes First," appeared in *Presbyterian Life* 6 (May 2, 1953): 12-14; it is the first chapter of *Smoke on the Mountain*. The book appeared the following year.

13. Bernice Baumgarten was Davidman's literary agent and on the staff of the literary agency Brandt & Brandt.

and his tantrums nowadays last only about ten minutes instead of three hours as they used to. And he is not drinking, at least not around the house. On the other hand, his heavy addiction to sleeping pills is worse than ever, and he's been sleeping till noon at least almost every day for the last month or two. He is trying to break loose from the sleeping pills, at my urging; for I see signs of cumulative barbiturate poisoning — the fits of temper and a fogginess of the mind.

Of course he will always be unpredictable — he's a temperamental man. Most of the time he is quite nice and reasonable, but I can never know when he'll have a spell — the other day he had a bad one while he was driving and scared hell out of me. Fortunately they pass off harmlessly at present, usually in a crying jag. He is quite taken up at the moment with his fire-eating act, talks of little else and is working out all the details, down to the costume. Perhaps I am wrong to consider this a childish reaction in a man nearly forty-five; it's possible that it's just a useful hobby and distraction for him in the present difficult situation. Yet I feel as if I were looking at a kid of fourteen planning what he'll do when he grows up.

I am adopting the tone of soothing flattery which seems the only one he can bear; for the slightest sign of coldness, even an attempt on my part to get away and do my own work, throws him into a tizzy. But don't worry, cookie, I haven't forgotten my promise. And promise or no, I wouldn't have him back for a million bucks. He gives me the creeps.

Don't know if he told you — I didn't get any phone call from Claude at any time. Easter Sunday I was out with the kids from 2 till 7, so no telling. I *did* get a phone call from your mamma the other day. She had herself announced as Mrs. Unterberg; they sound alike to me on the phone and I thought she was Frances for the first couple of minutes. She wanted to know if you had gone back to Claude, and I told her No in a hurry — figured you wouldn't want her writing to you at that address. Then she wanted to know if you were still here; I said No, nowhere near here, and that I knew where you were but had promised not to say. She accepted that without protest, and just asked if you and the kids were well. I said yes, and that you felt you needed to be on your own for a while. She said she could understand that! All very friendly and well-behaved. Did not tell Bill about the call, as any mention of our relatives seems to upset him.

Not much other news. I'm writing short stories, but no sales yet. My first article came out in *Pres. Life* at last! Actually they used the last one first; it looked pretty good and I've had a bit of fan mail. I got the stuff into book form and sent it off to Bernice — I hope she can sell it.

Lots of letters from Jack, full of encouragement and good advice, bless him.[14] One thing he doesn't understand, though, is that with a man like Bill you can't just announce your desires and expect to have them gratified! He doesn't realize I can't even get to a lawyer unless Bill consents, and that to oppose Bill on anything always means trouble, if only an unpleasant scene. Either the men in England (at least round Oxford) are amazingly gracious to their wives; or else Jack has heard too much about the Dominant American Woman. Gosh; I wish he could see your Claude in action, for instance.

Grace [the housekeeper] was off duty for a month, while her father died; but is now back on the job. The boys are fine, still crazy to get to England. Begins to look as if I might really do it; keep your fingers crossed for me! And give my regards to your father, when you see him.

Yours,

Joy

Source: Wade

To Renée Rodriguez

Endekill Road
Staatsburg, N.Y.
July 9, 1953

Dear Renée,

It is no satisfaction to me, honey, that you are suffering too! And I know very well what you are going through; after all, there was a time when *I* believed in Bill, and I tried desperately hard to keep the belief, against my own better judgment. Though I know you don't want to hear about him, I think there are some things I can say which might help. One of the things about being the victim of such a man is the self-contempt it brings — the woman despises herself for being a fool and a sucker. And I know you tend to undervalue yourself anyway. So remember this; I'm a fairly bright girl, and yet I was so much under Bill's influence that I had to run away from him physically and consult one of the clearest thinkers of our time for help, before I could see clearly what he was! So don't call yourself a stupid fool. People with honest emotions are always more or less

14. These letters have not survived.

at the mercy of the clever, conscienceless, heartless scoundrel with a talent for acting.

A day or two before I got your letter, Bill told me what he'd done and suggested we get back together again. I reminded him of his promises to you and me; his answer was, "That was when I was neurotic!" and he went on to say that a neurotic's promises oughtn't to be considered binding and that a "rapidly changing personality" like his couldn't be held to any promise. In short, he's entitled to be fickly because he's fickle. Needless to say, I turned him down and am going ahead with plans for divorce. The Virgin Islands, alas, are far too expensive — the newest fashion resort for these affairs. I shall do my damndest to keep your name out of it; my lawyer says it can be done, and anyhow it won't happen till your divorce is clear.

Bill has tried to bully me in every conceivable way; why he should think that bullying would get me back I don't know. After the agony of these last months, I cannot bear his presence. Part of the truth about him is that he *likes* to hurt people, likes the sadistic use of power, and is always subtly undermining one's self-confidence. Hence his constant insistence that he never, but never wants to hurt anyone! I've known for some time that he could teach your mother a thing or two about 1.1 tactics. You will notice also that he likes his women helpless, with no defenders; always picks victims like you and me who are on the outs with their relatives, and does his best to make the rift wider.

Apropos of that, your mother has told everybody that you are "completely under Joy's influence" and that's why you have suddenly turned against her, for you always loved her before far more than most girls love their mothers. Another story is that someone met you in Miami and you said you loved your mother very much! And this from my folks, who dropped in on their way to Maine, very indignant over the State-cop episode. Also, on the famous clothes expedition, Rose claims we forced our way into Bonwit Teller's and made a scene![15]

Hope you're out from under the sedative by now. And remember — you *are* well out of it; if you'd had the long torture I've been through on top of your first marriage it would have been far worse. Remember too that Bill is a rare bird indeed — most men in the world are not as bad as that!

Love,
Joy

Source: Wade

15. Rose was Renée's mother, the sister of Davidman's father.

To Chad Walsh

Endekill Road
Staatsburg, N.Y.
July 10, 1953

Dear Chad,

You *have* been skipping around — how you manage it with all those children, without going nuts, I don't know. Must be the assistance of the Holy Spirit! Meanwhile I sit here and stew in my own juice. Your letter did me good, coming as it did on top of a disheartening conference with lawyers that left me very depressed. Bill has suddenly broken with his mistress (she sent me a heart-breaking letter about it, poor girl),[16] and decided that he wants me back! I suppose it was to be expected; but it comes six months too late. I have spent all this time adjusting my mind and emotions to the idea of divorce; have come to see that it is the only solution, for Bill's behavior these last months has been worse than ever. Even if I could accept intellectually the idea of continuing a marriage to a violent neurotic relapsing into alcoholism — [and] my body and nerves would refuse to accept — he makes me physically ill. The children react almost the same way.

I'm afraid he's likely to turn very nasty indeed when he finds that he cannot bully me into giving in; opposition always makes him murderous. And the devil of it is, I still seem to have affection for him — at least, the nasty things he does and says afflict me with a sort of personal shame as well as hurt, as if I had done them myself. There's more to this one-flesh business than meets the eye.

And I can't help wondering, these days, whether all modern thinking about neurosis isn't hogwash! Certainly Bill has often behaved wildly, noisily, and terrifyingly. Yet he has always been able to appear normal at the drop of a hat, if any outsider came in. Sometimes lately I've thought him completely mad, and pitied him; and then, seeing how quickly he could control his behavior when he wanted to, I've wondered if "neurosis" is not merely his alibi. When he is reminded of past promises, he says that promises made by a neurotic oughtn't to be held against him and that a rapidly changing personality like his can't be bound by the past. It seems possible

16. On July 16, 1953, Renée writes Joy from Florida that she is heart-sick because Bill is trying to force Joy to come back to him. Renée feels betrayed and a "real sucker" and "wants to erase from my mind completely everyone" (source: Wade).

to me that he is merely a fickle, selfish, and undisciplined man who clings to belief in his "neurosis" as a defense against a guilty conscience and as an excuse for doing exactly as he likes. And I am coming to think that the easy diagnosis of "neurosis," whenever anybody behaves badly or irrationally, is an outgrowth of humanist and Utopian thinking about the nature of man. That is, most moderns feel man is naturally good; therefore, a "healthy" man, by their definition, is a perfectly good one, and all sins are illnesses which can be cured! Also they don't allow for individual differences at all; the word "normal" has been perverted into a synonym for "healthy." We who know there's such a thing as original sin must find it tragicomic to see so many people paying thousands of dollars to self-appointed experts of the mind, in order to be "cured" of being human.

But this is all old stuff to you, I suppose!

I think Macmillan merely meant that *Campus Gods* expressed the same views on the world that my book did; there's lots about modern society and its values in mine.[17] Thanks for the tip on Harper; if Westminster's no go, I'll tell my agent to try there.

Well, I must try to write some marketable fiction now! Love to Eva and the kids, and we *must* get together this summer.

Yours,
Joy

P.S. I meant to add an explanation of why I always feel my friends don't love me any more when they don't write! Of course intellectually I know it's nonsense. But, you see, Bill has been telling me for many years what a cross-grained, difficult, unlikeable woman I am — by which he meant that I sometimes criticized him, demanded things of him, or failed to admire him sufficiently. And there are times when my battered self-confidence sags and I believe him.   *Source: Wade*

---

17. Chad Walsh, *Campus Gods on Trial* (New York: Macmillan, 1953).

To Renée Rodriguez

Endekill Road
Staatsburg, N.Y.
July 20, 1953

Dear Renée,

Talk about poetic justice! This week I wrote Bill refusing his offer of reconciliation *again* and asking him not to come up here (on both lawyer's and doctor's instructions) till we got our affairs settled. But, knowing his disregard of anyone's wishes but his own, I felt sure he'd come anyway, and the boys and I hid out with the Wheelers. So he was alone here when your letter arrived — so I came home and found it ripped open and creased by an angry thumb! We might have known he protested too much about not reading other people's mail! Well, he certainly didn't read any good of himself. What you said served him right, and would have made him ashamed of himself, if he were capable of shame, which I doubt.

I honestly don't know whether, as Fritz suggested,[18] he is a psychopath, or whether he's just a louse. (Is there a difference?) A psychopath is one of those guys who live entirely in the moment, as Bill boasts he does, and are always at the mercy of their momentary impulses — promise anything, then walk out and forget all about it the moment temptation comes in sight. They're often very charming and convincing with the lovableness of a small child. But most of them get *themselves* in trouble, and Bill seems pretty shrewd about feathering his own nest at the expense of others — remember that quart of cream, while you were slaving over the wash. He could have got credit for the wash as easily as for the cream!

Look, honey — I'm just back from seeing my lawyer and signing divorce papers. He says it can be done without ever mentioning your last name, and without anything becoming public unless *Bill* chooses to make a stink. And much as I hate it, it's got to be done in New York, because only a New York court can have financial jurisdiction over a New York resident — i.e., a Florida award of support couldn't be enforced. As for trusting Bill's *promises* of support — well, he's rolling in money just now, what with his job and magazine sales, buying himself new clothes etc., and welshing already on the sum he promised to pay me!

My lawyer says that it would help a great deal if you would write me a

---

18. Dr. Fritz Cohen was the Greshams' family doctor.

letter specifically admitting adultery.[19] You needn't sign anything but your first name if you want to. But if you really feel you'd like to do something to help, here's your chance. I know it's a painful thing to ask, and I wouldn't if there were an easier way out. But I think that, by clinching matters, it would make for *less* publicity, not more — since I have to sue on that count anyway; and your divorce is final by now anyway, isn't it? My lawyer doesn't even know your last name and he swears to me that the whole thing can be managed safely. So — well, you do what you think is right.

I don't have your new home address, I find. If you'll send it, I can send you those last few packages — I don't suppose you'll want them sent to the office. (Isn't it typical of him to let *that* go unfinished!)

As to your emotional problems; don't, don't try to wall yourself off from the world. I know just how you feel, but, believe me, it never works — you'll just shut yourself up with your pain, and in the end the barrier will crash down just when you least want it to. For the moment you aren't going to want the deeper emotions, of course; but friendships can do a great deal to tide you over this bad spell. I'm having my own bad spells — there are frequent moments, with Bill at his abusive worse, when I am physically afraid — and I couldn't get through it at all without my friends. Chad and Eva Walsh dropped by the other day and were very comforting; it seems they had Bill pretty well sized up a long time ago. And Jack continues to build up my morale and help me think things out — I wish I could have asked his advice *before* I married! Here's what he said about Bill's latest behavior, over the separation agreement: "A rooted dislike of promises which *can* be enforced, coupled with a lavishness in making those that can't, fits in with the rest of the picture. Hence bluster or whimpering when the moment of real commitment arrives."[20] Believe me, you *will* get over it, for no sane person — and you're very sane or you couldn't have gone through all you've had to take — can go on loving someone she doesn't respect for long. And above all don't think that you've made a mess of your life. Why, look at you! You're only 33, is it? A mere chicken — and you've fought free of agonies and entanglements which were no choice of yours and which seemed impossible to break free of; and you're standing on your own feet. Life is *ahead*.

I wish I could say as much of myself! My life seems pretty thoroughly

19. On July 29, 1953, Renée writes Joy and says she simply cannot write a letter admitting adultery with Bill. She is mad that he read her letter to Joy, especially the part where she confesses she still loves him. She is still very angry with Bill: "I hope he rots in hell" (source: Wade).

20. The letter containing this quote has not survived.

tangled. But sometimes I think of you going off there and starting fresh; and it gives me courage. See! Do cry on my shoulder whenever you feel like it, honey; as fellow victims, we can understand each other's problems! Love to the kids.

Yours,

Joy

Davy wants me to send *his* love to the children. I'm the one who messed up this envelope, by the way, opened it again after sealing it.   *Source: Wade*

It has been four or five months since Bill and Joy have lived in the same house; they never again live together. While Joy has been moving ahead with her plans to move to England, where she thinks it will be cheaper to raise and educate her boys, Bill is struggling with serious financial problems, including huge back taxes and penalties owed to the IRS. In addition, his writing is not going well, so he has taken a temporary position with a traveling carnival; this experience inspired his next book, Monster Midway: A Book about Circus Life and Sideshows *(New York: Rinehart & Co., 1953). In the letter that follows, Joy asserts her determination to remain independent of Bill and insists that she has not done anything to turn their sons against him.*

To William Lindsay Gresham

Endekill Road
Staatsburg, N.Y.
July 28, 1953

Dear Bill,

I have just received your check for $50. As you will be living on your expense account while on the road, you will no doubt be able to do better from now on. In the meantime, I am enclosing your unpaid bills, which have been lying around the house for some time. You're about $100 behind on your payments to me; if you'd paid the sum we agreed on, I could have afforded to clear these up and I'd have been glad to do it.[21] As it is, I

---

21. Bill had agreed to pay Joy $60 a week.

can't — there are plenty of bills of my own, doctor and coal and what not, to take care of.

I keep feeling that I owe you an explanation of my refusal to take you back; and yet I despair of ever making my reasons clear to you. I was very near giving in, more than once — I still have far more affection for you than you realize. If only you had not tried to bully me into submission! If only you had not insisted on continuing to drink! If only you had kept your promises about the money! Words are not enough, Bill; actions have to match them. And your actions these last months seem to indicate that you are, as inflexibly as ever, determined on putting your own needs and desires and whims first, and the boys' necessities and mine (not to mention our feelings) a very bad second.

I think I succeeded in running off my resentment of the past; at least I no longer feel it, and I remember mainly the many good and delightful things about you. But I am convinced that survival, for them and me, demands separation.

Mr. Butts tells me that you think I have turned the boys against you. That is not so, Bill; though I can see it is a tempting rationalization. They have, after all, eyes and ears and very good brains; it is no longer possible to cover up, as I did when they were babies, with, "Daddy isn't feeling very well!" They find your temper just as wearing as I do, and as they approach adolescence and begin to assert their own very strong personalities there is bound to be increasing conflict.

And it is not that they have turned against you, but rather that there has never been anything positive to turn *to* — no relation warm enough to outweigh the surface friction. Think back to your own childhood, and you will remember that kindness and indulgence are not enough. When I went to England I thought that you and the boys might come closer to each other in my absence. But you were taken up with Renée instead. They were well aware of the situation — Davy was often awake at night — and they resented it very much; and in the friction between them and Renée, they felt that you backed her unjustly. I heard all about this my first afternoon at home.

I have told you very little of the children's attitude these last months, partly because I was afraid to, and partly because I knew it would hurt you a great deal and probably do no good — my occasional suggestions about your behavior to them have not been well received. But perhaps now, if your therapy is working well, the knowledge may be useful in your growth.

Meanwhile, I cannot lie to the boys about facts and I could not —

though at first I tried — conceal the storm and stress of the last few months from them. What I *can* do, and have done, is to soften the intolerant judgments of childhood and remind them constantly of all the good and kind things you have done for them. Perhaps with separation their resentments, which after all are not based on physical pain, will dissipate easily enough. The antagonism between you and Davy is an old story; you are too much alike to agree; well, it is pretty much you and Steve[22] over again except that Davy is not a terrified child. And I think I can keep him from becoming as inflexible and bitter as you were with Steve. As for Douglas, I think he has considerable affection for you; but, like me, he has practiced appeasement to keep the peace and has comforted himself with friendships outside the family.

I suppose it's no use asking you to return to AA? Well, have a good summer! I know that the carnival world is home to you, far more than any other, and if you can find serenity anywhere you'll find it there.

Yours,
Joy

Business notes: some nibbles on the house, but I'm afraid we'll never get more than $15,000. As far as I know, you have not yet paid this year's taxes. Have you done anything on "The Rootless Cosmopolitan"? If not, I can dig it out for you and send it along.   *Source: Wade*

To Chad and Eva Walsh

Endekill Road
Staatsburg, N.Y.
August 3, 1953

Dear Chad and Eva,
A belated note to tell you how much I appreciated your stopping off to see me! I needed new heart put into me very badly just then, and you did it. I hope my jittery state wasn't too alarming — I'm much better now. I haven't seen Bill since then, and in his absence I'm able to get control of my nerves and think things out.

22. Steve was Bill Gresham's father.

What terrified me so badly, these last months, was that he seemed nearly insane; his threats and rages and sudden reversals made no sense at all, on the supposition that he was in love with Renée and wanted to marry her. Yet he *did* insist that he loved her, he did ask for a divorce last year when I was still willing to forgive the adultery and take him back; so what was I to think? Now, of course, I can see that his fury was inspired by my giving him what he *said* he wanted. Not a nice reaction, but at least a sane one; so I can stop being terrified and begin to pity him.

Poor devil! All he really needed to say was, "I've been a fool; will you forgive me?" I'd have given in at once. But that was the one thing his pride would not let him say. I've never seen so clear an instance of the destructiveness of pride; it made Bill do all the things which were sure to drive me away instead of getting me back. I suppose he wanted *me* to ask for reconciliation. So he bullied me with threats of physical violence, threats of cutting off financial support for the children; he assured me that his conduct and character were exemplary and doubts of him were neurotic; he did his best to keep me penniless and helpless; he even tried blackmail of a peculiarly nasty kind, as I think I told you. The one thing that really turned the scales against him was the danger of relapse into alcoholism, and I told him so more than once; yet, though he insists that drink means nothing to him now, he would not even try to give it up.

All the same, I've been thinking and praying hard since I saw you, trying to be sure that I am doing the right thing. Jack wrote me a few days ago, saying what I thought myself; that I must disregard my own feelings and base my decision on what is best for the boys.[23] The boys, Davy particularly, beg me *not* to take Bill back — they say he makes them nervous and jumpy, and Lord knows I've seen it happen! Worse yet, I think, is what they learn from him — I've known both of them to try tantrums just like his on me. If only *his* mother had used the paddle as I do, how much better off he'd be!

What it comes down to is whether the greater chance of financial security for the boys, if I stay with Bill, offsets the unhappiness, nerve-strain, bad training, danger of neurosis, and most of all the probable relapse in alcoholism which would be dangerous physically as well as mentally. I don't think it does. And I'm not even sure that there *is* a greater chance of financial security; Bill has always insisted on blowing all his money on his own impulse, refused to save for the boys' education or carry insurance. Perhaps

23. This letter has not survived.

the judgment of a court, and the action of a lawyer, will do better for it than I have ever been able to do for myself. What do you think at this stage?

Meanwhile, we're doing not too badly; it's clear and cool here now and I'm even getting a tiny bit of writing on paper. Hope Lake Iroquois is as lovely as usual! I'm afraid I won't be able to get up and see you, alas! Too much to do here; I've got to be near my lawyer and I'm trying to sell the house. Prospective buyers wander through daily, but no luck so far. Selling furniture too! The piano, which I've had for twenty years, went back to Steinway the other day, and I cried bitterly. One shouldn't have that sort of attachment to possessions, but there's something almost alive about a piano. What the hell, though — I scarcely touched the thing in recent years!

Perhaps you can stop by on your way home? I'm pretty certain to be here till cold weather starts, I think. Love to the Four. Tell Madeline to catch a sunfish for me! By the way, I can't remember if E[piscopal] Churchnews ever prints poetry; if it does I've got three sonnets I'd like to send in. (Though you didn't like them, you brute!)

Love,
Joy

Source: Wade

To Renée Rodriguez

Endekill Road
Staatsburg, N.Y.
August 3, 1953

Dear Renée,

Yes, I see your point of view; and I hesitate to say what I'd do if I were in your shoes — I really don't know. Particularly as your divorce is not through; I thought it was, when I asked. What led me to ask was my fear lest Bill, as his lawyer said, "plays nasty" — tries to fight the divorce. Considering that he is pretty well known as a writer, this might lead to newspaper publicity, which is just what both you and I most want to avoid. And the better the evidence against him, the less chance of his making a row. But who knows? Things may go more smoothly than I expect.

Damn funny about that card from Ruth. I don't know how she could have got the address from anyone but Bill — the one I gave the State cops was an old one. And he never mentioned her at all. By the way, I got a card or something addressed to Rosemary from your mother, which I forwarded to the old address, couldn't find the Airlines one at that moment. So it would seem Ruth hasn't passed on the information.

I should have thought reading your letter would make him feel like a louse. What surprised me was that, having ripped it open, he actually left it for me to find! But try not to hate him too much, for that kind of hatred is only reversed love and will hurt you terribly — I know! In the end, he'll be unhappier than you, for he's got to go on living with himself and his self-created loneliness. I was forced to tell him recently that the boys do not want him back, since he appealed to me to take him back on the presumption that they needed and wanted him. And I'm sure that this hurt him a good deal; if he has any genuine affection at all, it's for them, though it doesn't carry him far enough to treat them with real consideration or give any thought to their future. It doesn't seem to dawn on him that you can't wipe out the effect of peevishness, disregard, and tantrums in your children's minds just by a few presents or a few minutes of petting. Even Douglas, the imperturbable, complains that Bill strains his nerves.

Anyhow, Bill's away now on his summer tour and I'm getting my own nerves unjangled — they were pretty bad. The boys are home from school, of course, and we're isolated here and can't get anywhere, which makes things rough; I have to hitch-hike when I want to get to Poughkeepsie. But at least there's peace and quiet. Our love to the kids.

Yours,
Joy

Source: Wade

To William Lindsay Gresham

2 Harbor Lane
New Rochelle, N.Y.
October 29, 1953

Dear Bill,

Here's your latest mail. There was a mix-up over my change-of-address card and your mail is following me here; I'll try to get it redirected to Hamid.[24]

---

24. This is a reference to the Hamid Circus where Bill was temporarily living and working.

Haven't had your check yet for this week. It would be as well if you sent this one soon, as I am sailing next week. Future checks can be sent c/o Haring, 65 Belsize Park Gardens, London N.W.3.

Incidentally, I purposely delayed my sailing until November to give you a chance to come and see the boys before we left; but it's up to you. They are in fine spirits and enjoying themselves hugely after the long dull isolation at Staatsburg; they have caught their first real fish, which I cleaned and cooked for their dinner, and have been taken for motorboat and sailboat excursions by some of the men here — we have several Coast Guard lads, and the boys are great favorites.

I note that *Monster Midway* is being very well advertised.[25] Good luck with it!

Yours,
Joy

Hadn't you better give Rinehart & Brandt & Brandt your current address?

[The following in Joy's handwriting notes where she plans to stay in London]: Avoca House Private Hotel, 10 Belsize Park, London N.W.3.

Source: Wade

To William Lindsay Gresham

Avoca House
43 Belsize Park
London, N.W.3
November 14, 1953

Dear Bill,

Safely arrived and without seasickness. The boys had a fine time on the way over and made friends with all sorts of people, from the ship's clerk to a Sikh princeling. This last, impressively bearded and turbaned, turned out to be a 24 year old student from UCLA. The Chamber of Commerce had bit him, and when you wanted to hear about India, all he would talk about is the agricultural future of Southern California.

25. William L. Gresham, *Monster Midway: A Book about Circus Life and Sideshows* (New York: Rinehart & Co., 1953).

We're in a very pleasant hotel, but frightfully expensive, and I must start looking for a flat at once. I'm disheartened not to find your check awaiting me at Phyl's [Phyllis Haring]; I was sure it would be here by now. Please, Bill, do send something. You're now nearly a month behind, and at the very least you're able to send the usual part of your salary.

When we left you were so friendly and sweet that I found myself beginning to trust you again; I should be sorry to have still another letdown. And you know I can't possibly support the children by myself here — I can't even get a job at first.

How did the battle with Hamid turn out? I hope all's serene again. London's very warm and full of flowers — after lunch we're off to the zoo.

Yours,
Joy

Source: Wade

To William Lindsay Gresham

14, Belsize Park
London, N.W.3
November 19, 1953

Dear Bill,

Your $60 arrived by wire yesterday afternoon; thanks for sending it through — my first days here have been very expensive and I was getting more than nervous. Sorry the Libidinous Lebanese is still uncooperative; by the way, have you got a home address now? If so, I can write you there instead of the office. Meanwhile, I've had one of those strokes of amazing luck that seem to happen to me only in England. I was dreading the job of finding a flat in a hurry, being near the end of my strength; and very few people will rent a furnished flat to tenants with children, while an unfurnished place demands an enormous premium to begin with, and then all the business of furniture and housework . . . ooh. But it turned out that the hotel here rented furnished rooms — *and* the owner made a point of taking children, because she arrived in London thirty years ago with three of her own and couldn't find a place! So here I am with two enormous rooms, each about the size of our living room at Staatsburg only better proportioned (obviously a lady's drawing room 100 years ago, with moulded plaster ceilings and built-in mirrors and all). Beautifully furnished, too — there's even

a grand piano nestling in one corner. Bright and sunny and heated by powerful gas heaters (no work) and opening on a garden where the boys can
play. Complete housekeeping service — daily bedmaking and cleaning.
Linens and laundry and light all supplied; a gas ring I can do bits of cooking on; and breakfast and dinner, both large and good, at the hotel! All this
for the grand total of 12 gn. [guineas] a week ($36) which is unusual even
for London. The Lord really *is* my shepherd, by gum!

Of course this will not do as a permanent arrangement; I'll need
something cheaper. But I can manage on it for the time being, until I've
got my strength back and can look around and take my pick. I don't know
yet whether the boys will be happy in London — they miss the country.
For the last two days we've had a depressing smog, which they didn't like.
It's sunny again now, though, and they're out playing in the garden.

School fees here, I learn, run about 35 gn. a term for a very good school,
the sort that prepares students for the public schools. That would be about
$400 a year, of which 17 weeks are holiday. This seems very expensive to the
English! The boys are clamoring for a boarding school in the country
rather than a London day school. I shall go to an educational agent in a day
or two and find out what there is available. We are nearly on the winter vacation now, and I won't want them to start before the February term, so
there's plenty of time. I'll let you know how things work out.

From now on, it would be easier and more practical for you simply to
send my weekly, or fortnightly, cheque to this address. (Lamp the spelling;
I'm training myself to English ways as fast as I can.) I find I can have an
"American account" in the bank, into which I can pay dollars and draw either dollars or sterling; the only restriction is that I can't pay sterling *in*, and
I'm not likely to want that. So just put the dough in an air mail envelope and
send it along; it'll be in plenty of time, and much less bother than having to
tear down to American Express in Haymarket and fill out umpteen forms.

Also, would you send me a copy of *Monster Midway*? Phyl and Sel are
very anxious to see it. How's it doing? Phyl, by the way, is much *much*
better; her analysis may be partly nonsense — for instance, her thyroid
trouble is interpreted thus: there is a brain-Phyl and a body-Phyl, the neck
is the meeting place of head and body, consequently trouble in the neck!
Nevertheless it seems to be doing a world of good; she looks ten years
younger than she did last year and is much more cheerful and active.
Robin [their son] seems pretty good and gets along well with the boys.

Warnie's book is out; he has just sent me a copy. Lord, the way they
publish here. It's a whopping big volume, beautifully printed, with fifteen

black-and-white plates and handsome end papers; price, 25 s. [shillings] or
$3.50! Would be at least $6 with us. Haven't had a chance to read it yet,
but it looks good and Jack says it's getting terrific reviews. Title, *The
Splendid Century.*[26]

We've been through the Abbey, past Buckingham Palace, through St.
James's Park, round Trafalgar Square. Pigeons sat on our heads and we
talked to coots, terns, moorhens, mallards, wood ducks, pelicans and some
others I don't know. Favorite experience; watching the guards at the Palace walk their beats and turn with that wonderful toy-soldier click and
kick at the end.

I think I'm going to spend a couple of weeks just resting — until last
night I've been sharing a room with the boys for two weeks and getting
very little sleep — and then to work! Let me know how you're doing.
Goodbye for now —

Yours,
Joy   *Source: Wade*

To William Lindsay Gresham

14, Belsize Park
London, N.W.3
December 10, 1953

Dear Bill,

Your $70 check has arrived, delivered by the faithful Phyl on motor-
bike as usual. Thanks for the extra bit, which was much appreciated by the
boys, as it will make the difference between a modest Christmas and practically none at all. Davy has changed his mind and *now* wants a vivarium,
having saved his allowance and bought himself a book on Reptiles as Pets
which describes some beauties. Pet store ahoy! We are getting quite well
known at the Zoo, the keepers reminisce about animals with us. Last time
we saw an enormous Emperor penguin chick being fed — they are bigger
than adults, with a sort of chocolate-colored teddy-bear down all over. He
was offered a fish, turned up his beak at it and brushed it away with his

---

26. Warren H. Lewis, *The Splendid Century: Some Aspects of French Life in the Reign of
Louis XIV* (London: Eyre & Spottiswoode, 1953).

flipper in a disdainful gesture of rejection — then suddenly changed his mind and gobbled it down with the funniest gulping motions. Also two monitor lizards disputing a white rat; nasty things to watch, but the boys loved 'em.

Mostly we have been visiting schools; I've now seen four. I watch particularly for the character of the headmaster and his wife, and the emotional state of the boys. The first, Dane Court, is my choice: gracious, well-established, comfortable without being luxurious and modern without being faddist. I've consulted a couple of their references — one of Mrs. Travers who wrote the Mary Poppins books, very successful children's books — and they're all enthusiastic; so am I.[27] It's the most expensive of the lot, 61 guineas a term (slight reduction for brothers) but I think well worth it. Also, it's only a half hour's journey away and there are lots of opportunities for parents to visit and take the boys out.

The others were all cheaper and newer; one quite good, I think, but rather unfinished and undeveloped, with an energetic young headmaster knocking new classrooms together in the holidays. One I thought very bad, with a vague dreamy headmaster, John Graves, who turned out to be Robert Graves' brother.[28] School very neglected looking, cold, and uncomfortable, with the boys doing such upkeep work as was done. Poor devil had a much younger wife who snapped at him mildly in my presence — if she'll do that in front of a prospective customer, I can imagine. He told me one interesting story; Robert Graves, in the first World War, was wounded and left for dead, then evacuated in a train that jolted him agonizingly all night while other wounded men screamed; and now he cannot ride in a train at all, will only travel by air or sea or car. He lives in Majorca, which ought to take care of the problem.

The last and cheapest school was miraculously comfortable and well run on the physical side; lovely grounds and buildings, etc. Only catch, it was run by the elderly widow of the last headmaster and a personable young German Jew with a strong accent, neither having any academic qualifications they cared to list in the prospectus — anyone can open a private school in England. And the boys seemed drilled to a Prussian perfection of discipline; *he* said he didn't go in for games much and believed in hard work. . . . Ulp. If I'm to have the boys learn the ways of

27. Pamela L. Travers (1899-1996), nom de plume of Helen Lyndon Goff, was the author of the series of Mary Poppins books.

28. Robert Graves (1895-1985) was a poet, novelist, and translator.

English life, I'd think they'd better learn them from the English. Dane Court it is.

It'll mean living on short commons myself — either I get this room at 5 gn. a week or find a cheaper one — but it's worth it. Of course even this has drawbacks; bath upstairs in the hall, like yours, and hot water erratic; lunches cooked kneeling at a single gas ring. But the boys and I have the knack of turning such difficulties into picnics, and are having a fine time. They've been to Hampstead Heath with a new friend, the lady upstairs, and brought back great wads of clay they're making into pots and statues, after instructions on Children's TV.

Have you received my previous letters? I wish you'd acknowledge them; also, as I said before, stop sending my letters to Phyl. And an ordinary check will do; my bank is very understanding. We've just been to the eye-doctor; Davy needs glasses, but only -1 correction, which isn't bad at all; *mine* is -5. Hooray for National Health Service. I've seen two doctors and not had to pay a farthing. The glasses will probably cost me something though.

Saw Arthur Clarke and the others at the pub.[29] Arthur astonished and appalled the lot by coming home married to a sexy Florida night club hostess whom he'd wooed and won in 48 hours; they thought him an incurable bachelor.

Joy

Please make out checks to Joy Gresham. Letter from Davy on the way!

Source: Wade

To William Lindsay Gresham

14, Belsize Park
London, N.W.3
December 22, 1953

Dear Bill,

We got back from our first visit to the Lewises yesterday to find your very pleasant letter awaiting us; the first *really* nice letter you've sent me

---

29. Arthur C. Clarke (1917-2008) was one of the most popular science fiction writers of the twentieth century. Perhaps his most famous book is *2001: A Space Odyssey* (1968).

these last two years, somehow — I think it's because it's the first one that has been a genuine communication, asking questions and answering them, acknowledging the things I've said in *my* letters. Until now you've always written what were, however bright and amusing, no more than impersonal news-letters. (Kiplinger Billy they calls him.) It's a very welcome change; sumpin [sic] must be integrating.

Yes, Arthur Clarke *is* in the chips, and how — selling in the hundreds of thousands. Seems quite unspoiled; mellowed, if anything. No news of Hubbard — I'm scared to ask.[30] I expect he's dropped from view. I'm more and more convinced that, though the technique is certainly useful as counter suggestion to psychogenic ailments, it is otherwise nothing but sound and phooey (see Hyman Kaplan).[31] We wuz had. Oh well, it takes a conman to catch a conman!

Dane Court is the one I'm taking. Ordinary schools here are a trifle better, perhaps, than ours, but not much, and have the added disadvantage of being socially inferior. What I want most for the boys is the coherent view of life which makes England tick — the tradition we recognized, for instance, in Burke's conservatism. I believe a great deal of the mental disturbance in America, and certainly much of the aimlessness and restlessness, comes from our lack of it. You and I had no stability to give the boys and they were beginning to suffer from its absence; but Dane Court people have it, all right.

I think I can say this now — never could talk about the boys' future before, you always got mad at me, but I've a feeling your views have changed — I do really feel that giving them the right education, particularly the right moral and social education, ought to be the chief aim of both our lives, and that it's worth any sacrifice. As I grow older and untangle my own emotional tizzies, I get a good deal more conservative about all these things; no doubt you do too. We had no right to live so much in the present that we made no provision for the boys' future.

As to what their careers will be, that's up to them; I only want them to have the kind of character training, and the kind of general background, that will fit them for what they choose. I am hoping that Davy may win a scholarship; that would be a big help.

30. This is a reference to L. Ron Hubbard (1911-1986), who founded the Church of Scientology.
31. Hyman Kaplan is a fictional character appearing in a series of comic stories in the 1930s by Leo Rosten. Kaplan is always very earnest and enthusiastic, but he is completely incapable of learning.

Incidentally, both boys were a big success with the Lewises.[32] We had a very relaxed and friendly visit, though physically strenuous enough; long walks through the hills, during which Jack reverted completely to schoolboy tactics and went charging ahead with the boys through all the thorniest, muddiest, steepest places; Warnie and I meanwhile toiling behind and feeling very old. Also we climbed Magdalen Tower to the top, up a twisty spiral mediaeval staircase barely wide enough, and a steep ladder; and the boys were let into the deer park and spent half an hour stalking the deer. Also Jack and Warnie taught Davy chess; he astonished them by learning it instantly and doing very well. Douglas, meanwhile, enjoyed himself sawing huge armfuls of firewood, which was *very* well received. Jack gave them the typescript of the *next* Narnia book, *The Horse and His Boy*, which is dedicated to them; it's very good.[33] I shouldn't dream of visiting Jack often — we're much too exhausting an experience for that quiet bachelor household; but a little of it's probably good for them, judging by their reactions.

Belle wrote that she'd seen you, said you seemed in fine shape but were missing the boys.[34] I'm glad you're having such an active grown-up life, at any rate. Mine, for the most part, is mere routine of shopping and mothering — barring an occasional hour in the near-by pub. Told a woman there it was one of the only *two* places my children couldn't follow me; she said she envied me, *hers* was a girl and the pub was the only *one!* Just now they have stopped an extremely noisy wrestling match around my feet to send Daddy their love; your letter to Davy was greatly appreciated.

Yours,
Joy

Source: Wade

---

32. Apparently Lewis and his brother enjoyed but were exhausted by this visit. See Lewis's reflections on the visit in CL, 3, letters of December 18, 1953 (p. 388), two on December 21 (pp. 389-90), December 23 (pp. 394-95), and December 26 (p. 395). Lewis wrote Joy shortly after the visit as well; see his letter of December 22, 1953 (pp. 390-92).

33. C. S. Lewis, *The Horse and His Boy* (London: Geoffrey Bles, 1954).

34. Belle Kaufman (1911-) was Davidman's classmate at Hunter College; she later wrote the award-winning novel *Up the Down Staircase* (New York: Prentice-Hall, 1965).

Anglophile

Letters 1954

In late January 1954 Bill, now living in Miami, writes Joy and explains that his publicity job for the Hamid Circus gradually "petered out." He wasn't making much money there anyway and hated the work. He tells her he thinks he has sold a short story based on circus tightrope acts and has moved to Miami hoping the warmer weather might improve his health. He recounts that he is bone poor and taking his meals at Renée's to save money. He offers this about Miami: "Miami has a magic all its own. The New York Jewish folks who settle down here develop in time a soft, easy-going manner and their faces relax and their voices lower in pitch and they putter around in their yards growing hibiscus blooms. It is a lovely tropical city, as lush and jungly as Los Angeles is dry and moth-eaten. Down here the palms really bust into bloom and one of the perils of walking down the street is being conked in the head by falling coconuts."

Source: Wade

To William Lindsay Gresham

14, Belsize Park
London, N.W.3
January 4, 1954

Dear Bill,

Golly, how'd it happen? I thought you were really set at Hamid's, from the way you spoke and wrote about it. And at Christmas time too! Did the Christmas spirit get out of hand, or what?

Anglophile

Couldn't come at a worse time, drat it; I've just depleted my savings by paying the boys' school fees and buying the necessary outfits, which came to £75. Not that the school requirements are so expensive, but they'd no clothes at all; I was letting them wear out the last of their American ones. You should see them now, you'd hardly know them; they've grown chubby and rosy-cheeked as children are here (I suspect the American fad for lots of green vegetables, etc. isn't really *good* for people. Lots of starch and meat, the way they do it here, seems to agree with us all much better.) And the boys have mackintoshes, grey flannel suits with short pants, school caps and ties; they look delightful. Davy has his glasses now, and is very happy with them; thank Heaven they didn't cost me a penny.

Well, send me as much as you can — after all, *we* gotta eat and pay rent too. I do hope you have luck with the stuff you're writing. But my advice, for what it's worth, would be to get a job — I imagine you feel the same way. The roller-coaster ride of the last few years has left me with a holy horror of free-lancing; even if one *can* make a go of it, the wear and tear on one's nerves and temper is too great. With all your contacts, I'm sure you can land something less nerve-racking — if not publicity, how about newspapers, magazines, television, publishing, whatnot?

As soon as the boys are in school, I hope to get at some writing myself; at the moment it's impossible to keep them off my neck for more than ten minutes at a time, London being far more confining than the wilds of Staatsburg. I've just thrown Douglas out for the third time during the writing of this letter.

They're very enthusiastic about Dane Court, and no wonder; it's an ideal place, I've checked on it carefully. Had tea with Mrs. Travers, who wrote the Mary Poppins books (enormously successful children's books, they've sold about a million copies) — her boy went to Dane Court and they were both devoted to the school. Did I tell you that, unlike most English schools, Dane Court doesn't whack the children?

No more news — except that Mickey, the lady upstairs, is going to take the boys to their first pantomime today. Me, I take 'em to nice free places like the British Museum. Davy is crazy about it, Doug is not — on coming out, he grabbed one of the enormous pillars and said, "Lookit, Ma! Samson!"

Hope Christmas with the aunts wasn't too wearing; I know Ripley and Grace must have been fun.

Yours,
Joy

Source: Wade

168

To William Lindsay Gresham

14, Belsize Park
London, N.W.3
January 8, 1954

Dear Bill,

Your check for $35 came today. From what you tell me I can see that you're doing everything you can — I'm particularly glad you thought of Jim Putnam; he ought to have *some* ideas — and I wouldn't really know what to suggest in addition, except perhaps Jack Danby and those lads we met at Carl Carmer's.[1] (By the way, you still haven't sent me my copy of *Monster Midway*.) We are tightening our belts as well as we can — peanut-butter sandwiches for lunch — and making up for it at our other meals, which are provided by the house. I've got the school to let me off some of the things called for in its inventory, such as overcoats, which I hadn't bought yet. If it gets no colder than it is now the boys will be all right.

Our Christmas wasn't bad at all; the hotel really went to town with decorations and a bang-up Christmas dinner — the works. Umpteen courses, turkey and ham and sausages and two kinds of stuffing and three kinds of potatoes and cranberries, the inevitable Brussels sprouts, plum pudding and trifle — also sherry and claret and port, whee! All this for a mere ten bob extra. Mickey (the lady upstairs, who lost her only baby some years ago and adores children) bought the boys books; I got 'em Davy's coveted chess set, vivarium, and lizard, and Doug an assortment of toys culminating in a snazzy tool set. Fortunately Jack had tipped them each a pound (what a nice old English custom *that* is, tipping schoolboys) so we could spread ourselves a bit. The lizard is a brown, green wall lizard with a long tail, named Bill — not after you but after Bill the Lizard in *Alice*. I feed him mealworms, but I haven't seen him eat any.

Last night at the pub Arthur Clarke turned up with Dr. Marie Stopes the birth-control lady — gosh, I thought she was dead, and she more or less looked it; a weird old girl nearing seventy with dyed straggly hair and strong opinions.[2] He was trying to lure her into his Interplanetary Soci-

---

1. Jack Danby (1905-1983) was an editor at the magazine *Redbook*. Carl Carmer (1893-1976) was a popular New York regional writer of poetry, folklore, history, and stories. Jim Putnam was a publisher for whom Gresham worked in the past.

2. Marie C. Stopes (1880-1958) was one of the first persons in England to promote the use of birth control.

ety. The new project — sounds quite imminent — is a radar or radio-controlled unmanned rocket to make a swoop round the moon. Arthur is now off on a diving expedition in the English Channel — seems he shares your passion for diving. He'll be in America again in a month; you might meet him at the Hydra Club and talk about it.

I got talking with Bill Temple and another guy, and what do you suppose they were gnashing their teeth about? The awfulness of being a married writer with wives and kids who don't understand that Daddy's writing is important! They work in offices during the week and do their writing on weekends; it's the passion of their lives — but apparently the wives just think it a waste of time and effort. Yet Bill Temple has had considerable success at it; did the book *Four-Sided Triangle*, which has been made into a film over here.[3] It's about two scientists in love with the same girl; she loves and marries one of them, then they have the bright idea of duplicating her by a gimmick they've invented so each of them can have one — only to find that the duplicate, of course, is in love with the same one the original is! Anyhow, Bill T. was showing in considerable bewilderment an American ad for the film which ran: "He created this beautiful woman to gratify his strange lust for passion!" What, he inquired plaintively, did Americans mean by a lust for passion? I told him it didn't have to mean anything; *lust* and *passion* are both exciting words, and by adding "strange" they touched it up with a spicy hint of perversion — there'll always be an ad man.

I like that pub — never have to buy myself a drink. There's a nice one right near too, very much Greenwich Village — Hampstead would seem familiar to you, except that where the village has the tough Italian boys *we* just have nice quiet Bengalis, and an occasional Sikh. The boys have got quite blasé already about the pretty creatures in saris who live all up and down the street and keep rushing out after their toddlers. Funny, the men all wear completely Western outfits, except for the Sikh turbans; but none of the women will. Ah well, time to get back to sewing name-tapes on boy clothes. Good luck. I hope the book picks up; it might be a slow-but-steady seller, after all.

Yours,

Joy

Source: Wade

---

3. William F. Temple (1914-1989) was a science fiction writer; his novel *Four-Sided Triangle* (London: Long, 1949) explores the relationship between cloning and love.

In early January 1954, Bill writes Joy that, due to Fawcett's finally paying off on a writing assignment (in a later letter he says he received $1,600), he has sent her some money. He is planning some articles and working "on the plot of my pain-drug-hypnosis novel. I still think this theme has as much shocker value as the geek, have thought so ever since [L. Ron] Hubbard advanced the theory. I am having trouble finding a pivotal character for the hypnotism story and have been doing research on hypnotism like crazy. Not thorough enough, however, to let anybody hypnotize me, natch." He also says he has been listening to the Mc-Carthy hearings on the radio and thinks the "Commie hysteria" is everywhere and foolish. Perhaps most important, he notes that he has met a lawyer who says he can arrange a relatively easy divorce for the two of them: "It would certainly be the least expensive way of getting us untangled."

He goes on to say he has recently been put through a battery of psychological tests for intelligence, personality, interests, and aptitudes. According to the doctor who conducted the tests on over 1500 people in the previous three years, "I turned out the smartest. This surprised me no end. Interesting observations: I have no deep anxiety left — the tests show a mentally yuman bean [sic]. Also I am good at math, although not as good as at verbal things. General conclusions: I should be in some line of work dealing with the written and spoken word!" He adds the doctor said all his talents suggested he should have been a trial lawyer. "Will probably be giving a talk soon to the forum run by the local Unitarians on 'The Advantages of Being an Ex-Communist.' It should be fun. Fireworks too, maybe, for the commrades are infiltrating the Unitarian Church as cover, what I hear tell." He ends by saying that he has pretty much had it with dianetics.

Source: Wade

To William Lindsay Gresham

14, Belsize Park
London, N.W.3
January 25, 1954

Dear Bill,

Glad to hear everything is under control and you've made a sale; your last letters were so inscrutable I couldn't unscrew 'em. Miami sounds like a dream city, but I'll still take London, though at the moment it's a trifle wintry for once. But I think the tropics ought to suit you much better than

New York, which is hardly a city at all any more but a combination prison-and-madhouse.

The boys got off to school at last, a week ago; I took them to Waterloo station and handed them over to the assistant headmaster, about six feet four of Greek-god-with-brains, who had little boys in school caps swarming all over him but controlled them effortlessly. They waved merrily and started off with a lot of other perfectly happy schoolboys, leaving a line of rather forlorn parents on the platform; no doubt about which side feels the separation most! Since then I've had a card from Douglas to say he's having a fine time, and the headmaster phoned to let me know how they're doing — very well, apparently, with no homesickness or upsets.[4] After all, they've had more experience of the world than the average small boy, and are more independent.

I hope you will soon be able to send the correct allowance, instead of what you're sending now! I can manage to live on it for the moment if I do nothing, go nowhere, spend nothing; but by the second week of April I shall need $350 for next term's fees, and I can't possibly save that, or a tenth of it, on this sort of money. I *could* have saved it on the agreed $60 [per week] and was planning to. I can understand the uncertainties of your position, but I must be able to educate the boys decently; they can't be shifted and dragged around. I've always felt that one really rock-like and stable part of your personality is your love for the boys, and surely you can see that it's not enough to love them like pets, to amuse and entertain them in the present; we must love them as people, creatures with a future. Sorry if this sounds like a sermon. But I keep remembering the sort of irresponsible treatment *you* got as a child, and what it did to you, and wanting something better for the boys. I'm letting you know this early about the fees so you'll have time to do something about it.

Meanwhile I'm getting back to the typewriter myself. On rereading my Britannia story, I realize that it's far too compressed, ought to be a novelette; so I'm reworking it as a three-part serial, fifteen to twenty thousand [words] or so, and trying to remember all I've learned about construction.[5]

The presents from Hank [Bill's brother] arrived and I sent them off unopened in the boys' trunk. (Note the comparative expenses: that trunk cost nearly eight bucks to send from New Rochelle to the ship. *Here* it cost four shillings [56 cents] to send a much longer distance into Surrey.)

4. Douglas Gresham recalls being miserable and homesick at this time.
5. This story has not survived.

Shall also forward your letter to Douglas. Glad to hear Renée and the children are doing so well; do give them my regards.

England, my England; t'other night the Lord Mayor, in a public speech, amused himself by translating the Latin tag Nemo mortalium omnibus horis sapit (no mortal is wise at all hours) thus: "No man is safe in the omnibus because of the ladies." I love 'em.

Yours,
Joy

P. S. Bob and Jackie Jackson (remember them at Chad's?) are studying at Oxford and have just had a baby.[6]

P. P. S. A. M. Heath and Company is the English connection of Brandt and Brandt, and a very good agency indeed. I dropped in to see them the other day and they were very enthusiastic about your work. Certain magazines here are wide open for fiction, I'm told, rather like American stuff, and don't pay at all badly. Would it be worth your while to send over some of the turkeys Brandt and Brandt couldn't sell in the States? Heath's address is 91 Regent Street, London, W.1.   *Source: Wade*

To William Lindsay Gresham

14, Belsize Park
London, N.W.3
February 4, 1954

Dear Bill,

Well, I suppose I ought to be glad you're managing to send anything, in the circumstances! I do hope the mail brings in some telegrams from Heaven and checks, signed, presently; when we talked about free-lancing being either a feast or a famine, I never expected the famine to get as literal as this. My lunch it is a leek, which I eat it every week or, at any rate, a sixpenny loaf and can of luncheon meat or soup (one bob, you can get it in

---

6. Jacqueline Jackson (1928-) is a writer of children's stories; she first met Joy during a visit to Chad Walsh's summer cottage at Lake Iroquois in 1950 or 1951. She married Robert S. Jackson on June 17, 1950.

Woolworth's here), which I stretch. Maybe you can get Bernice to advance the Gollancz money.[7]

You're breaking my heart with all them palms and hibiscus. Right now my love of England is being put to the acid test; after a mild winter we've suddenly got an unprecedented cold spell. All the papers have head-lines about the Deep Freeze, Kent is buried under ten-foot drifts, and Phyl [Haring] has gotten into bed for the duration. Hardier characters like my-self (who except you can *type* in bed?) wear eighteen layers of jersey and cower over the gas-fire all day. Not that it's so cold by Staatsburg stan-dards — 23 degrees, which the press headlined as Nine Degrees of Frost! has been the lowest. But the vast unheated Victorian houses can't take it. All the pipes have burst and the washstands are stopped up, and I've got chilblains on my right hand so badly that I can hardly use it. If I could af-ford it I would get the enormous fur gloves and fleece-lined boots that Londoners go in for, but no can do. Anyway, I got reckless and blew five bob on a hot-water bottle; you can't imagine what a comfort it is.

I've been worrying whether the boys were warm enough at school, but it's a well-run place and their letters say nothing about cold at all. They're getting extraordinarily literate already (how *do* the English do it?) and Davy's latest ran, "Dear Mother, I have seen a heath. It is not like Hamp-stead. It is a place with few trees, no grass, and all heather. Respondez s'il vous plait! Your son." On Saturday I'm allowed to visit them for the first time, after that can come every week. Their address is: Dane Court, Pyrford, Woking, Surrey. And I address them as "Master" but I don't sup-pose you *have* to.

My Britannia story progresses as well as the cold will let it. I've done about four thousand words so far and am just reaching the point where the original story began; you're quite right about milking the scenes — I keep remembering what you taught me about that as I go, and boy am I squeez-ing both emotion and suspense out of it now. By the way, among the mag-azines here are *John Bull*, which [is] rather like the *S[aturday] E[vening] P[ost]* and prints some of the same authors — I'm told they're wide open for adventure fiction. And *Argosy* (not a relative of ours), which prints mostly reprints, rather masculine adventure stuff. Nu? I keep thinking the "Drinking Gourd" *would* sell, over here.

I met a Canadian writer with a completely commercial slant who gave me various tips on all these things; he had the bright idea we might col-

7. Bernice Baumgarten was Davidman's literary agent.

laborate and I did half of one woman's magazine story with him and plotted another; but alas, he had the wrong idea of collaboration and I hadda discourage him but good, since when he hasn't been back. He promised on his honor as a waiting-list AA to introduce me to editors and film people and such, but I've long since got cynical about that approach.

No more news except that I am going to the dentist (for free natch). The guy turned pale when he looked into my mouth and at once began worrying how much he dared stick the National Health Board for. It seems that to do me properly would cost about £45 even here ($150 with us) and daren't risk it for fear of questions in Parliament, or whatever; so he has applied for permission to do crowns and inlays, we'll wait till they call me up for examination, then they'll argue with him and grudgingly permit about half of what he asks, then he'll do the work, and then they'll probably reexamine me and object in triplicate. All of which no doubt will cost nearly as much as the work on the teeth. Socialism yet! When it's all over I plan an article called "My Two Front Teeth" about it; maybe Bernice can sell it.

Hope your allergy is better. Don't go biting any cobras.

Yours,
Joy

Source: Wade

To William Lindsay Gresham

14, Belsize Park
London, N.W.3
February 8, 1954

Dear Bill,

This week's check arrived very opportunely — I'd used up the last one over the weekend visiting the boys. You'll be glad to know that the school is a success with them beyond my wildest expectations — I knew they'd like it and it would teach them well, but was hardly prepared for the paean of enthusiasm I got both from them and from the headmaster. Everything pleases them — the food, the work, the games, the walks on the heath, the masters, etc. Davy used to be very discontented with his classes in Staatsburg; now he's just the other way: memorizing bits of Shakespeare, learning Latin and French with enthusiasm (even Doug is already learning French) and, he tells me, having no trouble with arithmetic, which used to throw him. They both like football and have learned a lot of English birds and plants already. They didn't even notice the Big Freeze! Of course the school is centrally heated and the matron takes very good care to keep them warm; she told me their health was remarkable; many boys were down with sniffles and quite a few had chilblains but ours never turned a hair.[8]

It's amazing what you get for your money here; in addition to all the formal subjects, taught by people bristling with Oxford degrees, they get Hobbies, carpentry, Scripture (Davy's reading Joshua and enjoying himself sinfully), swimming (the school's got its own pool), and riding if you pay a bit extra; but that can wait, of course. Mr. Pooley, the headmaster, talked to me about the boys; he says they have a great deal of general knowledge, Davy in particular, but almost no formal education — so much for three years of Ken Stewart's school! Of course I knew this already. He finds them so alert, intelligent, and eager to learn, however, that he thinks they'll catch up very quickly. Davy impressed them all very much by an achievement of his in geography (which he was not taught in America at all, but has been working on a little by himself with maps and a globe.) The first day, the geography master reviewed last term's work. The second day, he questioned them on the review and of course on the whole previous term; and Davy, who had not been there, got the best marks in the class! When asked how he knew so much, he said he had thought he needed to, so he'd read the relevant chapters in the textbook between sessions! *He'll* be all right. As for Doug, his personality is having its usual effect — rather a contrast to the much shyer English boys of his age, I gather! It seems he treated the masters to a dissertation on flying saucers, the other night at dinner.

They are both getting on well with the other boys too, they tell me, and Davy, to my delight, is making friends like mad. One of their classmates is a French boy, rather looked down on because he kicks, bites and scratches, not like us; another is a lad named Atiyah from India, whose father is an army officer (very haikara, to mix my Orientals a bit) and who tells 'em how awful India is; but adds lovely tall stories of tiger-shooting.

8. Douglas Gresham notes that he and David often had a harder time at school than his mother reported in her letters to Bill. She may have painted rosy pictures because she was so determined to get the boys a good education that she may have wanted to believe the rosy picture herself; on the other hand, she may have done this because if she had told Bill it was not going as well as she hoped, he might have insisted that the boys should go somewhere else that was cheaper.

So it's cosmopolitan enough to suit any taste. Physically, too, they're in fine shape, pinker and plumper than ever. Their accents are already changing; you should hear Doug clip his words and broaden his A's!

I think cobra-skin belts might be very welcome, though not quite regulation — the school isn't *too* strict about uniform.

I do wish you'd send that copy of *Monster Midway;* Phyl was asking for it again. She's doing fairly well these days; that is she's talking vaguely about doing some work instead of talking meaningly about suicide. *I* do nothing but sit at my typewriter, trying to grind words out. Britannia progresses pretty well, but it's a new length for me and a lot of trial and error involved. I think it'll come out somewhere about 20,000 [words], but I may want to expand still further.

I suppose a lot of women would be particularly angry at you just now, but for some reason I find myself thinking of you with considerable affection and sympathy — perhaps because you're obviously trying as hard as you can, perhaps because I've had time to get over my fear of you. It was more psychological than physical, anyhow; not so much that I thought you dangerous, but being bewildered about your motives and all tensed up wondering what the hell you were going to spring on me next. At any rate, I seem able to talk to you more freely in letters, in the old way; for so long I had the feeling I was talking to a blank wall.

I think you're right about Miami suiting you; a city with a future is a better place for a writer than one like New York, which I suspect has passed its peak. It may go on getting richer and larger, but never more livable. Regards to Renée, and good luck!

Yours,
Joy

Source: Wade

To William Lindsay Gresham

14, Belsize Park
London, N.W.3
Feb. 19, 1954

Dear Bill,

I'm so glad things seem to be picking up; you sounded cheerful, but I know you must have been worried. And thanks for the Bodenheim story;[9] it wasn't reported here, but my parents, who met him with me at my very first public speech (when he embraced me on the stage in front of 500 people, ooh!) sent me the first account. I'm glad they got the poor nut. Max is well out of it, God knows; but it's so seldom anyone bothers to murder a poet, even a bad one! There oughta be a story in this somewhere — especially the bit about his begging on the street as a fake blind man.

Crime is so different over here! The three big stories since I came have been a) Lord Mantagu of Beaulieu, whom they cracked down on for buggering Boy Scouts — with complete, *but* complete details in the press; b) the rape murder of a little girl by a Chelsea artist, who was picked up over in Iran in *36 hours;* c) the murder of wife and mother-in-law by a shady character who killed himself in Germany when Scotland Yard caught up with him, a mere two days after the discovery of the crime. Of course there are the usual passion-bashings and muggings, but real murder is quite rare and almost instantly published. I learned that Scotland Yard gets its men on the Continent through Interpol, the international police organization to which practically every important nation belongs *except* Russia and the U.S. We used to be in, but dropped out alleging that it cost more than it's worth. As the cost to Britain is only £1000 a year, this smells funny — perhaps our police departments couldn't afford to throw open their files to critical foreign scrutiny.

The boys continue to enjoy themselves and their letter-writing is improving remarkably. I'll go down to see them again on Sunday. Dane Court has the reputation of being a free-and-easy school, but what *they* call free discipline over here is far from being our sort of "progressive" neglect; they are trained to discipline themselves — make their own decisions, etc. I met one of its graduates down at Heath's and he spoke very highly of it; Jack has heard good reports of it from someone too. I agree that the boys should have shorthand and typing, but that will be when they're a lot older. The great criticism people here make of American education is that it doesn't even teach *English,* let alone the humanities; the other night I attended a National Book League meeting on science fiction, addressed by Arthur Clarke and others, at which the head of one of the big London libraries protested violently against the Americanization of

9. Maxwell Bodenheim (1892-1954) was a poet, novelist, and playwright. Davidman is alluding to the murder of Bodenheim and his wife, Ruth, who were gunned down by a former mental patient.

style that English science-fiction writers are forced to go in for. It's amazing how literate all these lads are, compared to the pulp writers we knew.

By the way, Arthur Clarke is flying over today and will turn up in Miami presently. Arthur has the gift of success and personal publicity more than any writer I know; it's wonderful to watch him in action. Awhile ago I suggested he send *Childhood's End* to Jack, who then wrote me an enthusiastic letter about it which I passed on to Arthur.[10] Next thing I knew, Arthur wrote Jack asking if his publishers could quote the letter in publicity! Jack, though slightly startled, agreed cheerfully and invited Arthur to come round and have a pint or two if he was ever in Oxford. Needless to say, Arthur found occasion to be in Oxford and had lunch at the Eastgate with Jack, Warnie, Humphrey Havard, Tolkien, etc.[11] What Jack chiefly noticed about him was that he's a teetotaler. But Arthur used his ears to good advantage, and in his speech at the NBL [National Book League] meeting made great play with "As C. S. Lewis recently remarked to me. . . ." What makes it amusing rather than annoying is that he's quite unselfconscious about it and seems genuinely thrilled about all this rather than calculating or conceited.

As soon as I get Britannia off my neck (it's growing longer and longer, drat it) I must see if I can do some science fiction; why waste my opportunities? The field is prospering so madly, both here and in the States, that it's a pity not to cash in on it. Meanwhile, Heath thinks they might sell *Smoke on the Mountain* for me here, if I make a few changes of its Americanisms. And Warnie keeps suggesting that I collaborate with him on a life of Mm. de Maintenon, Louis XIV's morganatic wife.[12] She's never been done, and she's fascinating — a noblewoman born in the workhouse, spending a mysterious girlhood in the West Indies, coming back and marrying a paralyzed poet and wit, later becoming the governess of the king's

---

10. Arthur C. Clarke, *Childhood's End* (New York: Ballantine, 1953). Lewis writes Joy at great length about *Childhood's End* in his letter of December 22, 1953, *The Collected Letters of C. S. Lewis, Volume 3: Narnia, Cambridge, and Joy, 1950-1963,* ed. Walter Hooper (London: HarperCollins, 2006), pp. 390-92; hereafter CL, 3.

11. Robert Emlyn Havard (1901-1985), known to his friends as Humphrey, was Lewis's medical doctor, friend, and fellow Inkling. John Ronald Reuel Tolkien (1892-1973) was Lewis's close friend, university colleague, fellow Inkling, and author of *The Hobbit* (1937) and *The Lord of the Rings* (1954-55).

12. Davidman worked on this book on and off for several years, but it was never completed. However, Warren Lewis writes at some length about Mm. de Maintenon in his *Louis XIV: An Informal Portrait* (London: Deutsch, 1959).

illegitimate children and catching the king! She was interested in education for women, founded a girls' school, and used to pop out of the king's
bed at dawn to go and get the little ones up and take a few classes herself.
Wow! If we can get a publisher interested at the start, I think it should be
worth doing; and he's done practically all the research already.

Thank God it's warmer here now, though dank and gray. Snowdrops
and crocuses are in bloom too. But I go nowhere (except the science fiction pub) and sit at my typewriter all day with no company but Sambo, my
kitten, a very terrific cat. Regards all round.

Joy   *Source: Wade*

To William Lindsay Gresham

14, Belsize Park
London, N.W.3
February 26, 1954

Dear Bill,

Goody, goody, now at least I can buy today's cream buns for my tea instead of yesterday's reduced to tuppence ha'penny each — one of the latter
made me violently sick last night. I oughta had more sense, but I somehow
thought Salmonella didn't thrive in the English climate. And I can go and
see the boys a bit more; it costs nearly a quid every time I go down, even
though I walk to and from the school to save taxi fare, and daren't do it often. But I *did* see them last weekend. They're in fine shape and enjoying
themselves thoroughly, except for mathematics, in which they seem to
have inherited your perplexities! The only catch is that I'd like to take
them on an occasional outing to London, and I can't because the school
doesn't allow train travel during term time for fear of their bringing back
infections. I wish I knew someone who has a car!

The Houdini piece sounds great; before you're done you'll probably
have a book on him. I thought you found the Staatsburg office hard to
work in; you always used to say you could work much better in a hall bedroom. But alas, I'm afraid the only way a writer can "condition himself" to
work at all (watch the gobbledygook, son, you've been down the alley with
too many psychoanalysts) is by firmly shoving out of his mind, his room,
and his life every possible excuse for *not* working. At least that's how it is

with me. I keep writing like grim death, and I can't afford to go out! Though I did get reckless after receiving your latest check; went round to the pub and played six rounds on the pinball machine — which costs a penny here, not a nickel.

My Britannia story has grown into a young novel; 18,000 words on paper already, and about 5,000 to go. Boy, I'm pulling out all the stops on this one. I've even got a group of American prisoners, penned in the local church and told ironically to sing hymns, defiantly breaking into Yankee Doodle! (By the way, can you remember the chorus? I can't.) Corn, but marketable corn, I hope. And Leland, which thank Heaven I had the sense to bring along, is being invaluable.[13] Incidentally, *Monster Midway* has arrived (Forever Gresham; imagine waiting here three months to send it and then shipping it airmail at a cost of a quid!) and I find it fun to reread; was amused to notice what good use you made of Leland in the Romany passages, but you sure played hokkani-pakni with the hokkani-pakni!

If you get a *large* chunk of dough, 'twould be nice if you sent me a big piece of it so I could stash it away against next term's fees. April can't be far away now, judging by the weather! The last week has been like a pleasant April in Staatsburg, with spring flowers coming up and birds tweeting. And I saw a palm tree in Surrey last week, large as life, standing quite sleek and healthy in somebody's front garden.

I expect Renée has probably thought of this already, but just in case she hasn't, why not get her to go over your income tax for this year and see if she can wangle some money back out of the deductions on the Hamid job? Also, you might possibly be able to claim capital loss on the sale of the house, since you always considered about $10,000 of its valuation was used for business premises and they accepted that. I don't know if capital loss can be spread over successive years, but it might be; in which case you can probably fix it so that you won't pay *any* income tax for quite a while. Your losses ought to be deductible like any other business man's. Are the State income tax boys still on your neck? I don't suppose they could really do anything now you're in Florida.

I bet *one* thing that could be sold over here is the series on Tom Coryat.[14] Did I tell you that English magazines don't mind in the least re-

13. This is a reference to Waldo G. Leland and Newton D. Mereness, *Introduction to American Official Sources for the Economic and Social History of the War* (1926).
14. Thomas Coryat (1577-1617) was an English travel writer of the late Elizabethan and early Jacobean age. Gresham had written a series of articles on him.

printing stuff from American magazines, since *those* don't get into the country much? The new Sherlock Holmes stories that were in *Colliers* are now turning up in a newspaper here. I've got an appointment with the short story specialist at Heath this coming Monday and will find out what I can about the field.

I'm a little troubled about what to do on the boys' holidays — hate to have nothing better to offer them than a London boarding house. Perhaps by the summer I'll be able to take them to Scotland or the Lakes — or at least Cornwall. Eventually, I hope, things will break well enough so I can get out of London altogether and find a country cottage.

Well, back to hokkani-pakni. By the way, English currency is singularly well adapted to rolling over the backs of your fingers; *I* can almost do it. Kushto bak te kushto divvus [Good luck and good day].

Been chorin a gry lately?

Joy   *Source: Wade*

To William Lindsay Gresham

14, Belsize Park
London, N.W.3
March 8, 1954

Dear Bill,

Check for $25 arrived. How long is Valley Forge going to last? I am barely able to cover my expenses at this rate, and what I'm going to do about the boys' holiday I don't know. Surely you can get somewhere if you are really working and not just planning to work. It would be a good idea for you to write the boys; perhaps you can explain to them why there is not money to take *them* on trips to anything better than a tenpenny busride and a tea-shop. I'm finding it rather difficult to make them understand.

They are, however, thriving on the school life; they've picked up a whole new vocabulary and set of interests. I've never seen them in such good physical condition. And their manners, which were always fair, are now beautiful; they seem to have matured a good deal, Davy in particular. The only sour note is their arithmetic — neither of them has any number sense at all; these things must be hereditary and innate. I shall have to work with them in the holiday. Doug has had to be put back in the First

Form, a great blow to his pride. In every other subject, however, they are doing quite well.

It's spring here now indeed; all round the school there were fruit trees popping into bloom. The birds are singing like mad, I've got my windows wide open, and no fire on. (Thank heaven; that's one expense less.) We had some snow at the beginning of the month, but it obligingly fell at night, treated us to exquisitely feathered trees for a morning delight, and melted in the sun almost at once.

I'd thought of expanding Britannia still further for a paperback novel, but first I'll see if Carl can sell her at her present length, 25,000 [words]. I'm just finishing typing her on white paper and shall send her off in a day or two. After that I'll have a crack at short stories.

Allegate me no alligators! Ain't I got enough troubles? Davy is planning to catch me a hedgehog and bring it here for me to raise along with the kitten. All I'll need to do is dig it a plentiful supply of earthworms in the back yard.

I'll be interested to know what made with Saga. *That* looks really screwy, but with all the fly-by-night reprint and digest magazines I shouldn't be surprised if one or two of them just went in for unblushing swipes.

Don't know anything about Arthur Clarke's wife except that she's a night club hostess, lush brunette, been married before, and is not generally expected to stay married long this time. Her name is Marilyn.

Well, it's lunch time, so I'll go demolish a can of baked beans. Good luck with Houdini; if he could get himself out of underwater boxes, he oughta be able to do a little thing like getting Gresham out of the red.

Yours,
Joy

Source: Wade

To William Lindsay Gresham

14, Belsize Park
London, N.W.3
March 16, 1954

Dear Bill,

Gosh; I feel like the showers-of-blessings song. "Mercy drops round us are falling, but O for the moola we need!" 'Twould be nice if you could work out something on the daredevils, and a thousand isn't to be sneezed at with the depression just round the corner. Perhaps you could make it pay by doing some of it as magazine articles first. Lookit what's come of my *Smoke on the Mountain* stuff; Heath has just sold the English rights to a publisher here. They won't pay much; I'm lucky if I clear £50 on it for an advance, but considering everything I haven't done badly on a book that has yet to see print. And the bit of money will at least buy me a few nylons; I've sunk to lisle.

I've been rereading the *Monster* and I think I see pretty clearly why it didn't sell. It's a specialist's book. When you did the *[Nightmare] Alley* you were not yet a carnival expert; you saw from the outside with a sucker's eye view. But now you are really in, and you can't help seeing from a viewpoint too remote from that of the dear little woman reader who buys books. I find the stuff fascinating (particularly the bits of it I wrote myself) but Phyl, for instance, can't make head or tail of it. It's as difficult for the average read as those science-fiction tales that bristle with equations and molecular physics; and unfortunately there are more s-f aficionados than carny buffs. Or, at least, more literate ones. Most of the characters who would really appreciate the *Monster* probably can't read without moving their lips.

Have you got a good idea for a movie script laid in England but involving one American character? That's what they want over here; I went to see a film agent, in a terrific office on Park Lane overlooking Hyde Park, and he said there are no jobs but there *is* something of a market for that kind of original. What they do is to get an American star to come over and work for a share of the take.

Re paperbacks; the people who are going to do *Smoke on the Mountain* here broached the subject with fear and trembling; they wanted to do a cheap paper edition along with a cloth-bound one, and were afraid it would hurt my sensitive feelings that I don't got! They showed me as an example a little number by the Rt. Rev. etc. etc. Cyril Garbett; so I said sweetly that if the Archbishop of York didn't mind, I didn't see why I should!

Publishers are really wonderful over here; they make you feel that you are doing *them* a favor by letting them publish you. They even apologize for interrupting your work by asking for an appointment.

Had a nice note from Doug this morning — he can write script now — saying, among other things, "Are you happy? I am happy. Please send me a nice water pistol." I've got to go down on Davy's birthday, which is also school sports day, and watch 'em in action. Ordinarily, when I visit, it's always the same; Doug is out on the playing field kicking balls around with boys three times his size, and Davy is in the library reading.

The weather's turned nasty here again, all gray and cold. Not that it bothers me; I just sit by the fire and try to dream up a good plot about an unwed mother.

Yours,
Joy

P.S. What in the hell makes with McCarthy?[15] He's in all the headlines here, and adds a good deal to the three-ring circus look which America has to British eyes. I don't mind the ordinary criticisms of things American, most of which are justified. But I find I get no thrill at all out of seeing my country look *that* ridiculous!   *Source: Wade*

To William Lindsay Gresham

14, Belsize Park
London, N.W.3
March 25, 1954

Dear Bill,

Why, no, all is not well with me and the boys. How do you expect it to be, on five-dollar checks? This weekend is Davy's birthday, too; I had hoped you'd do something about that.

I'm doing the best I can, and working as hard as I can. But I'm pretty near the end of my tether, Bill, and I can't stand much more of this. So far this year you've sent me about $300, or very little more. I doubt whether you've lived on as little as that. And I certainly can't support myself, let alone two children, on it.

If you really love them as much as you say, you won't want them to end in an orphan's home somewhere. But that's the way it's going to go, if this keeps up. I'm not going to reproach you — if you can do these things, you will be impervious to anything said about them. But I wish you would get a

15. Joseph R. McCarthy (1908-1957), Republican senator from Wisconsin, became the chair of the Permanent Investigations Subcommittee of the Senate Committee on Governmental Operations in 1952; he led what some have called a witch hunt against alleged Communists.

job and stick to it. Perhaps you can take this hand-to-mouth existence without suffering appreciably. I never could, though; and the children can't.

I will get £45 for my book when the contract comes through. I had hoped to apply that on next term's school fees, but at this rate I suppose it will have to keep us for the month of our vacation. After that God knows what we'll do. I'm about ready to call quits.

Yours,

Joy

Source: Wade

To William Lindsay Gresham

14, Belsize Park
London, N.W.3
April 2, 1954

Dear Bill,

I know stinginess is not one of your faults; quite the contrary. The trouble has always been improvidence, the principle of "living in the moment" which kept you from ever building up savings to tide us over times like these. And I went along with you too easily, because you would tolerate no resistance or contradiction and I hadn't the courage to argue. What a pair of idiot children we were! I wish I had played the sly game so many wives play, taking all the money I could get from you and secretly stashing it away. Instead I played the "self-effacing" role, took as little as I could and tried to make up for your extravagance by spending almost nothing on myself — and lookit.

I hope the Houdini story is almost done — I had no idea it was to be 20,000 words! They certainly ought to give an advance on *that*. Are you quite determined on not looking for a job? I would take one myself, here, if it weren't that one needs a special work permit, and the Home Office won't issue them unless you can show the job couldn't be done by a British subject. I keep my eyes open for possible jobs for Americans — even applied for one — but there aren't many.

In the last two and a half months I've written a 25,000 word novelette and three short stories, which isn't bad for me — I hope to God some of it sells![16] But I've just about used my last strength to do it — had to blast

---

16. None of these works were published.

most of it out with Dexedrine, and now I feel about half alive. I had hoped for a chance to rest in England and recover; but it doesn't look likely. I shall go and have a medical check-up next week and see if they can do anything for me.

I've also got six teeth that have to come out, according to the National Health Board's X-rays. Perhaps they're abscessed or something — that would explain my wretched health and weakness. All the dental work, including upper and lower dentures, will cost four pound five, or about $12. Not bad — though it looks like a hell of a lot at the moment.

The boys came home from school yesterday. They are in wonderful shape and extraordinarily grown-up — that's the one bright spot in all this. I certainly made no mistake in sending them to an English school, if only I can keep them there! They've never been so happy and well-adjusted in their lives — or so well taught; they seem to have learned more in these few weeks than in all their years at Staatsburg. Davy has been getting private instruction in arithmetic from the headmaster's wife to bring him up to the level of his form, and she tells me that he *can* grasp arithmetic; it's just his knowledge that [is] defective. I shall be drilling him in the multiplication table, which I gather our "progressive education" regards as too old fashioned to worry about. He's very good in everything else — so's Doug. You should hear them chatter French!

Last Saturday they had School Sports, and I went down to watch. Doug was in four of the finals — very good for his first term, and he's one of the smallest there; the English boys grow big, at least in the upper classes! He managed to take third in the Long Jump for under 9 years; never was a white ribbon worn with more pride. You should have seen him fling himself nine-feet odd through space. Incidentally, small boys here seem far more athletic on the whole than ours do, and he doesn't stand out as he did at home. Perhaps it's the training they get. Whatever the intellectuals think of the English emphasis on school sports, all one has to do is to compare the sort of boy I saw in those races and leaps with *our* product, and you see what they're after; a beautiful coordination and discipline. Doug is mad about cricket, by the way — says it's much better than baseball.

What delights me most is the enormous improvement in their manners. All that is annoying in the small child seems to have vanished overnight, along with their American accents! They're both beside me now, playing rummy in a very well-bred fashion and disturbing me no more than adults would.

Well, I've got to phone the dentist; one of those teeth has an exposed nerve and is giving me hell. Chosen for what? Chosen for tsouris![17] Oh, by the way, Phyl's analysis is going beautifully; she's started to write fiction, under my instruction, and is doing amazingly well.

Yours,
Joy

Source: Wade

To William Lindsay Gresham

14, Belsize Park
London, N.W.3
April 15, 1954

Dear Bill,

Your check for $10 arrived today. It seems a pity you are reduced to borrowing; at the risk of being a nag, I can't help asking if it is really impossible for you to find some temporary work, no matter what kind? After all, this situation is hardly fair to Renée, as well as unfair to me and children. Doesn't she think you should find work? I know she is an extremely self-effacing girl, even more than I was, and no doubt she feels glad that she is able to make sacrifices for you and tells you that she doesn't mind. I've been there myself; I know the feeling. But even in the "self-effacing type," Nature has its limits; in the end we just can't take it any more. And can you really square it with your own conscience to spend your life using up one self-effacing woman after another?

Your check, together with a $10 check from my parents for Davy's birthday, will get us through this week. My advance has been slow in coming, but we got through one penniless week by spending it as Jack's guests, a much needed holiday.[18] During it we were taken on a trip to Whipsnade, a gigantic country branch of the London Zoo, where the animals wander about almost loose — in fact, some of them *are* loose, includ-

17. Yiddish for trouble or distress.
18. Lewis writes George and Moria Sayer about this visit in his letter of April 2, 1954: "By bad luck Mrs. Gresham (our queer, Jewish, ex-Communist, American convert) and her two boys will be here all next week. So we can't come and dine. . . . She's a queer fish and I'm not at all sure that she is either yours or Moria's cup of tea (she is, at any rate, *not* a Bore)" (CL, 3, p. 450).

ing a wallaby with a baby in her pouch who almost let us stroke her. It's a fabulous place, perched on top of the Chiltern Hills; from the edge of it one gets a view for miles across the chalk country of Buckinghamshire, and the lions and bears and so on live in huge pits or bowls scooped out of the chalk. There was a whole pack of wolves, and a temperamental lioness with a cub, and a rhino, heavily doped and out cold without even a twitch, getting his toenails manicured. And the best was two mother Kodiak bears with three cubs, who nursed indiscriminately on both of them. We walked all round the place twice — I thought Jack and Warnie deserved medals for valor. But a good time was had by all, except that on the way home Davy suddenly hadda Go. We stopped the car for him; he dived into a convenient ditch — and sat down plop on a patch of nettles. Poor lamb, his sensitivity to all skin irritants (sound familiar?) and the results were startling; he had to soak in a hot bicarbonate bath all evening.

You can't conceive the beauty of the English countryside in spring. By the first week of April the trees are all misted with green already, pink almond and white cherry and flowering rose-colored currant bushes are all in bloom, daffodils and blue primroses and a million flowers I don't know run almost wild; yellow primroses and bluebells *are* wild, so are anemone and violet and kingcup and tiny daisies like innumerable stars in the grass. At Studley Priory last Sunday, the four of us (Humphrey Havard was along) took our beer into the woods and drank it among the violets, while pretty birds flew round about.

A joke of Jack's I can't resist passing on; Warnie mentioned the custom, among Viennese officers before the war, of taking as mistress or semi-official wife a girl of respectable family in a quite recognized way; dining with *her* people on Sundays and introducing her to his own wife and family, etc. We wondered how such an introduction could be made, and Jack suggested: "Meet meine Wiener schnitzel!"

The boys' school reports have come and are very good indeed. But what am I to do about next term, in God's name? The bill has come too. Nearly £150, what with last term's extras, shoe repairs, etc. to pay for. And there is no alternative. I cannot take them out of there and send them to a County Council school without finding a flat and supporting them here in London; the actual saving might be about £70 for the twelve weeks of term if I did that, but it would do them great harm, and it would make any writing at all impossible for me. Since my only hope of augmenting my income is to sell something, I must stick to my last. So far I've had no luck; but Carl has only had my stuff a few weeks. And in spite of my holiday I am feeling very ill and exhausted, mainly, I suppose, with worry. Shall go to the doctor this week and see if he can do something for me; now that I don't have to pay for it, I find I can pay more attention to my health than I ever felt justified in doing in the States.

Well, I've got little boys' clothes to wash and mend.

Yours,

Joy

Source: Wade

To William Lindsay Gresham

14, Belsize Park
London, N.W.3
April 23, 1954

Dear Bill,

I'm keeping my fingers crossed for the story! Sounds as if it's a young book by this time — any possibilities for paper bound sales or whatever? I do hope *True* pays in proportion to its length; if they do we'll both be out of the woods for a bit and the boys can stay in school.

I can't write much today; I'm far from at my best. Had two of my bad teeth yanked on Thursday, lower jaw molars, and what a mess they were. It took ages, but I was full of injections and didn't mind. In fact, I went off in the afternoon to a Royal Literary Society meeting Jack gave me a card for, because Angela Thirkell was in the chair and I rather wanted to meet her.[19] Then, just as she was smiling at me over the teacups, the injections wore off quite suddenly — oops! I gave her a weak but brave smile (I hope that's what it was; it may have been a ghastly grimace) and fled. I've never felt anything like it, though I've had extractions before. Got home, broke down and yowled, then sent Doug to fetch Phyl and Sel and tell them to bring codeine, which got me through the night.

Now, two days later, my jaw is still sore as a boil. I hope there aren't going to be complications; couldn't stand any more trouble just now! One of those teeth was abscessed and had been aching for a couple of days quite badly; I suppose that's why the merry hell.

---

19. Angela M. Thirkell (1890-1961) was a short story writer and novelist; her most famous work was *Love among Ruins* (London: Hamish Hamilton, 1948).

Bill Gresham, 1941 *(Wade)*

Joy Davidman, 1941 *(Wade)*

Joy Davidman
*(The Lotte Jacobi Collection,
University of New Hampshire)*

The Gresham family, ca. 1950 *(Wade)*

The Greshams' farmhouse at Staatsburg, New York, 1949 *(Wade)*

Bill and Renée Gresham with Rosemary and Bob, late 1950s *(Wade)*

The Kilns property, ca. 1930 *(Wade)*

Jack and Warren Lewis, 1949 *(Wade)*

C. S. Lewis, ca. 1959
(Wade; photograph by Wolf Suschitzky)

Joy Davidman, ca. 1957 *(Wade)*

I've been out in my wheelchair for
walks, have no pain in the bad leg and
on the whole have a fairly good time
— except that at the moment I am suffering
agonies from having my rear rammed
into a chair arm by a clumsy orderly.
The rear is *not* protected by plaster
and I feel as if I'd been kicked by a
mule.

Drat those sons of yours — they rejoiced in the magic tricks, performed
with brilliant success among all

Part of a letter from Joy Davidman to Bill Gresham, February 28, 1957 *(Wade)*

10 Old High Street,
Headington, Oxford
(Wade)

Lewis with David
(left) and Douglas
Gresham, 1957
(Wade)

Joy and Jack Lewis, with Susie, 1958 *(Michael Peto; photograph courtesy of University of Dundee Archive Services)*

Joy and Jack Lewis, 1958 *(Michael Peto; photograph courtesy of University of Dundee Archive Services)*

Charles Williams *(Wade)*

J. R. R. Tolkien *(Douglas Gilbert)*

Chad Walsh
*(Beloit College Archives;
photograph by Ray Metzker)*

Roger Lancelyn Green
(Douglas Gilbert)

Joy at the Kilns around 1958, holding the air rifle that she used to discourage trespassers *(Walter Hooper; photographer unknown)*

The Eagle and Child *(Wade)*

Joy's memorial in Headington Crematorium *(Wade)*

The boys — though you never ask — are quite well and getting very grown up. They were extremely considerate and brought me some hot soup for dinner that first night. They're even reaching the point where they'll pick up their clothes without an argument; and I've been drilling them in the multiplication table all through the holiday, with quite good results.

I met a Mrs. William Empson — her husband's a don and a poet — who lives near here in a terrific big house.[20] She has two boys a little older than ours, and the four have been doing things together — the Empson kids treated Davy and Douglas to rides on the local Fun Fair (i.e. carny) up on Hampstead Heath. I took a look at it myself. They don't have a single traveling carny as we do; each showman with one ride or pitch or whatever rents space directly from the borough council. No posing shows, no motordromes, no ten-in-one, no glitter. Just a lot of rides, not very varied or streamlined, and a lot of rifle ranges, ball throws, darts, etc. And do they work strong! It's almost impossible to get the right change. The place was teeming with gypsies, too.

O hell, there goes my jaw again. Goodbye.

Joy   *Source: Wade*

To William Lindsay Gresham

14, Belsize Park
London, N.W.3
April 30, 1954

Dear Bill,

Your nice normal-size check came just in time to restore my morale. I couldn't have needed it more; needn't remind *you* what it's like to lie awake at three in the morning with no money, no hope, a couple of infected dry sockets throbbing away, and a large box of codeine tablets handy. You can get codeine over the counter here, and I've been badly in need of it. So far, my extracted teeth are following the exact course of yours. Dry sockets, due to low blood pressure and general debility; infection in the sockets;

---

20. William Empson (1906-1984) was an important twentieth-century poet and literary critic.

hell on earth. There's no danger of injury to the hinge of the jaw in this case, but it *feels* broken. All my sinuses have lit up and are throbbing in sympathy; and the sockets themselves act as if the Miner's Union had got back to work with enthusiasm after a long strike. My mouth won't open all the way, either, but I can still yell!

The only bit of silver lining is that, since infection and pain raise one's blood pressure, I've more energy otherwise than I've had for weeks! Even managed to take the boys rowing in the Serpentine and walking all about Kew. Between times I go back to the dentist, he puts packing in, he pulls packing out, etc. Also I've been to the doctor and got so many penicillin shots my rump feels like a pincushion. Hooray for National Health, at least I get all this misery for free; *you* hadda pay for yours.

The doctor thinks my thyroid is misbehaving again — seems it's to be expected at my time of life; and by great good luck he turns out to have specialized in thyroid for five years under the leading expert in England and Europe to whom he is referring me. Boy, will I be a delight with all my anomalous symptoms; here's where I make medical history!

Making literary history too; Jack has done a perfectly lovely preface for the English edition of *Smoke on the Mountain,* but I'm afraid it's just too late for the American edition. If only the blasted book sells!

Your new-trades-for-old-people man has the *rumba del canon* (hope I'm spelling it right?). Nowadays the old are beginning to have the same universal appeal, in fiction, once possessed by babies and dogs. If it doesn't go as an article (and I think it should) there's at least one good story in it.

One bright spot at the dentist's; yesterday I took both boys along to have *their* teeth checked (nothing much wrong). Doug had a toy catapult; the dentist promptly bought it from him, leaped to the window, and began potting at the blackbirds who were eating his flower seeds in the back garden! I suggested he use extracted teeth for ammunition.

Doug is in bed today, complaining of indigestion. I went out to get him an Alka-Seltzer; when I came back, I asked him if he wanted any lunch, to which he answered, "Oh, no, I just ate a pork pie!" I expect he'll live.

Pork pies, incidentally, are sevenpence or eightpence; a smoked herring ninepence; a pint of milk sixpence halfpenny; a cucumber a foot long ninepence. With those and a sixpenny loaf, we've managed to live! I even manage an evening of wild dissipation playing the pinball machine at the pub, sometimes — it costs a penny a shot. The other evening I played my friends for sixpence and (having become an expert) won enough to more than pay for my pint.

Well, enough for now; I've got kids' clothes to mend.

Yours,

Joy

Source: Wade

To William Lindsay Gresham

14, Belsize Park
London, N.W.3
May 10, 1954

Dear Bill,

I thank you, Davy thanks you, Doug thanks you; Sambo the cat, who was wondering where his next tin of fishgunk was coming from, thanks you likewise. Also, Jack's charity cases, who will now not have to move over and make room for the boys, thank you! He's put some of his royalties into a charitable trust fund for helping with education, etc. and offered to help with the boys from it.[21] But I hardly think you would like your sons educated by another man's charity. It might do for the Pierces, them low-down crackers, but hardly for the Greshams, huh?

I admit I was hoping for enough to cover the fees entirely — they came to £148. Still, if you send $60 a week from now on, can do. You don't say how much Fawcett's paid you, but it ought to be enough to carry you for a while, though I suppose you owed a lot to Renée and others that had to be paid off.

Jowitt's book was reissued in the States with certain changes; I haven't checked up, but the printed story and his own statement was that he had made certain errors of fact and only caught them at the last minute. Must get it and read it here. I never saw any evidence in the press, at the time of the case, worth a damn; but I've the impression that a mind like Chambers' is its own monkeywrench and needs no other.[22]

21. This refers to the "Agapony" (love + money) charitable trust that was created by Owen Barfield in 1942 at Lewis's request; most of Lewis's royalties went into the trust and were given to those in need. For more details, see *The Collected Letters of C. S. Lewis, Volume 2: Books, Broadcasts and the War, 1931-1949*, ed. Walter Hooper (London: HarperCollins, 2004), p. 483.

22. William A. Jowitt, *The Strange Case of Alger Hiss* (London: Hodder & Stoughton, 1953).

There's considerable interest here in McCarthy and our anti-Red hysteria; the English are regretfully concluding that America's not much better than Russia after all. I've a notion that part of the McCarthy business is only what always happens when a strong President is succeeded by a weak one. Under our peculiar and delightful system, the strong President has wrested a lot of power from Congress; when the weak one comes along, Congress gets to work and snatches it back! Cf. Lincoln-Johnson, Wilson-Harding, etc. I cannot believe the present ugly hysteria is as dangerous as it seems to the sane and law-abiding English, who seem to expect us to produce a Hitler any moment; I tell 'em that hysteria is merely the American Way of Life. But then, seen from here, the great "conflict of philosophies and moral issues" does look more like a simple conflict of empires.

As to a divorce, I think it would be a good idea, the polite Florida way. But I should like a written agreement continuing the present arrangement — i.e. $60 a week subject to change according to your income (would be nice if it changed *up* some day, for both of us) and sole custody of the boys for me; of course you can have unlimited visiting privileges etc. and I hope you'll be able to take advantage of them one of these days. It would be good if we could settle this by ourselves; otherwise, I suppose, I shall have to get a lawyer of my own, and I hate enriching the legal boys.

I'm not surprised the psychiatrist found you wuz smart. You're nearly the most intelligent guy *I* ever met, drat you — and one of the most original. Who ever doubted it? Glad your energy is fine; I wish mine was. My jaw seems to be healing fairly well now, though it's still tender, but my glands or something are misbehaving. Hey ho for the thyroid clinic!

The pain-drug hypnosis novel would be terrific; I'd like to see you do it — and have you thought of doing something political with it? Might as well cash in on the anti-Red excitement while it lasts.

The boys are fine. Just before school started they busted two windows across the street with catapults, egged on by Robin![23] Descent of irate tenants and landlord; confiscation of catapults; bill for one pound fifteen, to cleaning out and putting in new panes. I've got Robin, who probably did most of the damage, to pay one-third; the rest comes out of their school allowance, poor lambs.

Perhaps some day they'll get so they can write letters without me standing over them grinding my teeth, but the time is not yet. All *I* ever get — and I equip them with stamped addressed envelopes — is brief

23. Robin was the son of Phyllis and Sel Haring.

notes like this: "Are you happy I am happy, pleas [sic] send my penknife and 2 box Turkish Delight. Your son." It's amazing; they seem so literate until they start to write! But at least Doug has finally mastered script, and the new school list reveals that they've each gone up three places in the form — they started at the bottom, of course.

A beautiful morning today: brilliant sun and warmth, leaves and flowers and birds everywhere. I never saw such a flowery place as Hampstead; there are Japanese cherry trees covered with a cloud of double blossoms like small roses in all shades of pink and rose, and there are others with flowers like silver bells. Tulips are selling for ninepence a dozen on the street corners. By God, I'll be extravagant for once and buy some!

Regards to Renée and the children.

Yours,

Joy   *Source: Wade*

To William Lindsay Gresham

14, Belsize Park
London, N.W.3
May 19, 1954

Dear Bill,

Nothing was ever more welcome than the sight of that air-mail envelope in the box.[24] I've been cutting corners a bit; I didn't tell you before, because I figured you were doing the best you could and would only be panicked, but that book advance of mine hit a snag and I *still* haven't got all of it. First the publishers forgot to pay (they've a bad name for grinding the faces of the authors) and hadda be reminded. *Then* it turned out that Her Majesty's Exchequer charges American authors living in England nine shillings in the pound copyright tax (I can get it back from the income tax people, but I should live so long). My agent tried to pay me the

---

24. Bill writes to Joy on May 17, 1954, and tells her that in spite of Fawcett paying him $1,600, he has spent half of it paying off debts. He sends Joy $70. He has spent some money to purchase a new typewriter and is applying for unemployment benefits. He comments more on the "silliness" of the McCarthy hearings and shares about stories he is working on, including one titled "The Forsaken Earthman." Also, he is thinking of buying a motor bike and has applied for a public relations job.

lot but the Bank of England, which has to OK American accounts, bounced the check. So I went down there and looked miserable and they advanced me the tax money, private and secret-like, and were going to send the remainder; only it hasn't come through yet. I must needle the agents again, so you can imagine. Anyhow, gee, thanks. I eat lunch again!

My teeth, thank God, have healed now; it was rough while it lasted, but no complications remain. Was round to the thyroid clinic yesterday; it took five hours — conference with *eight* doctors, two of 'em as famous thyroid men as exist, all poking and prodding me in the eye and neck and elsewhere. Much edified by my original symptoms and the fact that the radium collar hadn't burned me; apparently they've quite given it up here and most people were scarred by it. General conclusion, I'm hypothyroid! This I didn't know? They're going to increase the dose and see what happens next. Part of my recent trouble may be that the British half-grain is much less than the American, and I've switched from the old to the new. But I've been singularly cold and woozy. One of the doctors, by the way, turned out to be Graham Greene's brother and we had lots of literary discussions on Dostoievsky and such. Over here it seems even medical men are literate. Had been reading Berdyaev too.[25]

Papers here have been discussing the American Recession very freely. Perhaps *that's* what happened to *Monster Midway*. England, by contrast, is at last prospering splendidly. The Queen, God bless her, came home last Saturday and were we thrilled! I watched it on Phyl's television. A nasty cold day it was, and that poor girl riding gallantly up the windy Thames in an open launch in her pretty spring outfit. Little Princess Anne's a born show stealer; she always does something to hog the camera.

Robin's tapeworm seems vanished; he's growing up a true Cockney sparrow, pert and lively. A pity they can't send him to a better school — his is rather tough and it's ruining his accent. He's being analyzed but it doesn't seem to be doing him any harm.

Warnie writes that his book got terrific reviews in the States; have you seen any of them? What got him mad, though, was a line in the *Texan Lone Star:* "Historian Lewis sometimes lets himself slip into admiration for monarchy." "Me, I ask you!" he wailed. "Me that believes in the divine

---

25. Graham Greene (1904-1991) was a novelist; perhaps his most famous novel was *The Power and the Glory* (1940). Russian novelist Fyodor Dostoyevsky (1821-1881) wrote several brilliant and provocative novels, including *Crime and Punishment* (1866) and *The Brothers Karamazov* (1880). Nikolai Berdyaev (1874-1948) was the central Russian philosopher whose work helped bridge religious thought between Russia and the West.

right of kings, God's anointed, and all that. *Damn* his impudence!" Even much less conservative Britons than Warnie would get mad at that one; but I told him not to mind Texas — we just keep it around for laughs.

I was thinking about "The Forsaken Earthman" only a week or so back and wishing you'd finish it; if it's up to the beginning, it's a humdinger. I've got a couple good story ideas cooking myself if I get strength to do them. I got a sob-filled story about an Unwed Mother off last week, but I loathed doing it — I just can't get my mind round the ladies' magazine gloop — and I haven't too much hope. Next ones will have action in 'em. I wish Carl could sell what I send him; all I get is a deafening silence.

If I could get one good sale I'd tackle the biography of Mme. De Maintenon; Warnie's sent me a full outline of the lady's life complete with book and page references all the way, and *what* a life; born in the workhouse, mysterious childhood visit to America, married as a girl to brilliant paralyzed poet, widowed, gets to be governess to the king's bastards and next thing you know she's reformed the king and married him! Her hobby was a girls' school she founded and she used to pop out of the royal bed at dawn, tear off to the school, help get the children up and teach a few classes herself. Do I hear a movie sale? But no, alas, she's in the public domain.

London gets more beautiful all the time; there are May trees, rose and red and white, flowering everywhere now. And of course lilac and laburnum, and all the front gardens full of millions of flowers. It's a cold spring this year, but a beautiful one. Note from Doug yesterday, his first since he went back — lovely handwriting at last: "Could you send me a parcel with some sweets in it please. I have learned how to play cricket. Love."

Yours,
Joy

Source: Wade

To William Lindsay Gresham

14, Belsize Park
London, N.W.3
May 31, 1954

Dear Bill,
Tickled to hear about the job! With your experience as a radio cowboy you should be right in your element. Florida being what it is, you'll get

into bigger and better publicity jobs soon, I'm sure — from cows to dinosaurs yet. From this he makes a living?

I'm enclosing Davy's latest letter to me, so you can get an idea of his progress. Handwriting, style, and neatness are coming along well, and don't you think he expresses himself like a grownup, bless him? Perhaps some day his spelling will catch up a bit. I took the boys out for the day last week, to a Disney film — *The Living Desert;* they were thrilled by all the animal stuff. Davy has read a book about India (about thirty years out of date at least, I gather) and has decided that when he grows up he wants to be an Indian Civil Service wallah and make a fortune! I undeceived him gently. He is now considering being a tea planter in Ceylon; he says snakes will be his hobby, but for his career he wants something that makes money!

Doug wrote me a very neat letter the other day, too — the only one so far this term. I keep reminding them to write to you; I expect the cobra-skin belts might do the trick.

I'm feeling much better — more thyroid — and working hard. Got a lovely idea — a woman's magazine story about Job's wife, she to be working silently to pull the wreckage of the place together while he's sitting on the ash heap yelling and scratching his boils. A natural. I'm going to take time to do it properly. Dunno what happened to the things I send to Carl; I never hear about them again. One exception: "Blue Nightmare" (the lady drunk). He sent it to *Manhunt,* of all places, and they commented that they'd read it several times but it wasn't their sort of thing at all!

Whatever Florida looks like in spring, it can't be as beautiful as things here. Rhododendrons and roses are coming out now, and elder-trees, and all the garden flowers. Lots of sunshine too! Sometimes I sit on Primrose Hill with a notebook to do my plotting.

Yours,

Joy

Source: Wade

To William Lindsay Gresham

14, Belsize Park
London, N.W.3
June 11, 1954

Dear Bill,

I've just been notified by the British consul that you've started a divorce action. It would have been more honorable of you to tell me yourself, but perhaps I expect too much. I am sorry you did not see fit to come to an agreement with me beforehand, as it has compelled me to take legal steps of my own. I don't want to interfere with your plans any more than I can help, but you will understand that my first responsibility is to the children; I must do whatever I can to see that their rights are protected. And I suppose I have some responsibility to myself. At all events, I no longer feel that I ought to make sacrifices for you.

The boys are home just now for the half-term holiday weekend. I'm glad to say that the news of your action doesn't seem to upset them at all. Douglas says he has sent you a letter, and both of them send their love. They are now extremely well trained and very literate. They got up early this morning, dressed and made their beds, all without disturbing me; and later, while I was having breakfast, they made mine. Davy is now fifth in his form and his French is quite good. On the way home from the station Davy remarked, "Let's see, was it Julius Caesar that invaded Britain in 43 A.D.?" to which Doug: "No, that was Claudius!"

Yours,
Joy

Source: Wade

On June 14, 1954, Bill writes Joy:

> *I thought you understood about the divorce action — I said in a letter that it could be put through quickly and easily down here with no trouble to anyone and you agreed. I certainly have no intention of not supporting the boys; you should know that by this time. We were married for ten years or so and not once did you ever have to complain about money. When I had it you had it. I never once came back from a trip without bringing the boys something. You remember. When you wanted some money for the house I*

would never even count how much you took out of the wallet. It was a fam-
ily joke. You must remember that. There is no question whatever about my
sending money, as long as I have any at all and I see no reason why over
any period of time I shouldn't make some. Certainly I shall try and keep
trying. When I have been broke and only sent you $5 at a time it was be-
cause I had less than $10 in the bank — I have sent you money when I
didn't know how I was going to raise my own rent money. For years the
boys were the only things that gave me any apparent reason for being and
the only thing I held on to when the going got rough. How you can imagine
that I won't do everything I can for them now even though I cannot be
with them to watch them grow up — how you can think that is more than I
can understand. For a long time after you and the boys sailed I was so
knocked out that I could only go through the motions of writing. It took me
a long time to get on my feet and I had to have Renée help me by using the
examiner to run some of the grief off or else I couldn't work at all.

He finishes by saying he is hopeful for a series of articles and other writing
projects.   Source: Wade

To William Lindsay Gresham

14, Belsize Park
London, N.W.3
June 17, 1954

Dear Bill,

Wish you could manage to send your cheque every week instead of
every week-and-a-half, or whatever; makes things very difficult, and God
knows they're difficult enough already.

The boys had their half-term holiday, but it rained the whole time
and was very disappointing; we couldn't have any outings. This has been
the wettest June in 49 years, and for the first time I see why people
loathe the English climate. It's been cold too! I'm still wearing woolens
most of the time. When we *do* have a bright day, however, it makes up
for everything. And the procession of the flowers continues — what
roses the English grow! The front gardens are full of them in all colors,
the sort of thing you see only in florist's shops with us. There are tall
spiky things called lupines everywhere, too, in all the shades of pink and

blue and lavender and white; general effect rather like a stand of delphinium, though the flower itself is not at all like that.

One thing we did manage was a birthday party the boys were invited to at the house of a classmate named Eric Coningsby. It was at a fairly posh address in Marylebone, and I rather expected to be overawed by the Anglo-Saxon Coningsbys — till I walked in and gave a look! So who should it be but the Galitzianer Coningsbys! Poppa a neurologist, small boy a bit of a piano prodigy, composing his own music — but when we gave him our present, a harmonica, he deserted the piano with loud whoops of joy and started tootling cacophonously all round the house.

Wish I could take the boys on a trip during the summer holidays, but I don't see how. A pity, with Cornwall and Devon and the Lakes all so near.

Sensation in the academic world; Jack is going to Cambridge. They've created a new chair specially for him — Professor of Mediaeval and Renaissance Literature.[26] Serves Oxford right; they should have done it long ago. It's a lot more prestige and I suppose more money; but what's really important is that it's far less work. The real work of a don in an English university is not lecturing, which is easy; not even the private tutoring, which is harder but not drudgery; but the endless setting of examination papers and then correcting them, which goes on for weeks. I've seen something of those examinations — you wouldn't believe what they expect of their students here! I'm pretty sure I couldn't pass.

Hope the measles and tonsillitis are all over, now. I'll have a glass of milk for lunch and think of you.

Yours,
Joy

Source: Wade

26. For more on Lewis's move from Magdalen College, Oxford, to Magdalene College, Cambridge, see Walter Hooper, *C. S. Lewis: A Companion and Guide* (London: HarperCollins, 1996), pp. 69-77.

To William Lindsay Gresham

14, Belsize Park
London, N.W.3
June 18, 1954

Dear Bill,

I suppose you are upset about my getting a lawyer; I am sorry, but I feel it is the only sane thing to do. I agreed that a divorce might be a good idea under certain circumstances; but you told me there would be no accusations of "moral turpitude" or whatever. I got a severe shock when I read your Bill of Complaint. If it was really necessary to tell all those lies about my character and my behaviour as wife and mother, you should have had the sense to warn me beforehand. As it was, I was not only deeply hurt but alarmed; I wondered if you were trying to pull a fast one. For if I were a judge I should think twice about awarding the custody of children to the sort of woman you describe. And I certainly cannot let you proceed with such an action without having someone on the spot to protect my rights and the boys'.

Yes, I know you were liberal with your money and lavish with presents. But that's quite irrelevant. The important thing with children is their education, their future — all the things you refused to think about. No doubt you think it very Jewish of me to look ahead and to provide for the morrow, but I notice that all the science-fiction boys here hold jobs all week and do their writing on weekends, just so they can provide security for their families.

And I know you love the boys in your way and have been trying hard to keep your end up. I have no doubt of the sincerity of your good intentions. But after all, you won't claim that your personality is as stable as rock; and I cannot forget how, when I reminded you of promises made to Renée and me, you said airily, "That was then!" and proceeded to explain that a rapidly changing personality like yours couldn't be bound by the past.

But this too is irrelevant. Even if you had the integrity of Abraham Lincoln, I should still insist on getting our financial relation legally defined; in fact, if you had that sort of integrity you would too. It is the sane way, the usual way, and the only way to end all the upset and uncertainty from which I suffer, just as much as you. After all, the strain of that bad period was no better for me — if you must know, I got through it by pounding a Varitype machine eight or nine hours a day in a filthy damp basement office, for a lousy six quid a week, and thought myself lucky.

If you are afraid that I will be too hard on you once there is a court award, you ought to know better. I should have far greater peace of mind and be much more disposed to charity. And I should like to see all of us well out of the present tangle — I keep thinking that Renée has the hardest time of us all. After all, her relatives are my relatives too, and the situation must be agonizing for her. All you have to do is to play fair with me, and you'll be able to work things out satisfactorily. But I must insist that you play fair. Even if I were disposed to give way on my own account, I'd be a rotten bad mother if I did not do everything possible for the boys' interests, and the time would come when they'd hate me for it.

In conclusion, I can only say that I'm sorry the situation upsets you, but I feel it's a situation of your own making. If you had played fair with me last year, it would all be happily over now. For Heaven's sake, man, get smart! All you've ever brought about with your shifts and evasions and con-games of the emotions is your own misery. Play it straight for once; you'll find it pays — and you'll feel better.

Yours,
Joy

Source: Wade

On June 24, 1954, Bill writes Joy:

I don't understand all the legal technicalities involved in this but apparently you engaged a lawyer by remote control to see that your allowance was set at $60 a week. This was not necessary since whenever possible I have sent you that much and have every intention of continuing to do so whenever I can. Furthermore, your lawyer over here insists on being paid in advance and I just don't have any money. I have to eat and send you money and I don't have it. If I am constantly in a froth of anxiety about money I won't be able to work and send you any money. It goes around in a circle. Where you ever got the idea that I would let you and the boys starve I have no idea but you seem to have it and you don't seem able to bring things into focus. There is no need for you to hire a lawyer down here — I have no intention of demanding custody of the boys — how could I take care of two little boys and work too? As much as I miss them and as much grief as I feel for their being so far away I agreed with you long ago that little boys belong *with their mother. And I have told you time and again I would send you all I could spare. I fully agree to put the figure of $60 a week into the divorce proceedings and have never had any intentions of doing otherwise. If you insist on bringing in this lawyer who has to be paid in advance I won't be able to do anything about paying him, and the divorce won't go through; I will be left up in the air and as uncertain as I have been all these months and consequently I won't be able to organize my work and if I can't write I can't sell anything and if I don't sell anything I can't send you anything. It's to your advantage to let this go through without bringing in another law-yer who has to be paid as much again as I paid my lawyer. You don't stand to gain by having a lawyer here because I have instructed my lawyer to give you custody of the boys and $60 a week. Please let me know about this right away. You are a writer and you should know how indecision para-lyzes the imagination and makes it impossible to write.* Source: Wade*

To William Lindsay Gresham

14, Belsize Park
London, N.W.3
June 26, 1954

Dear Bill,

I'm sorry, but, well, I'm afraid it *is* possible to knock a lop-eared mark. All through our marriage you used to argue that you must get your own way in everything or else a) you would kill yourself, b) you would get drunk, c) you would go on strike and not support the family. I have no doubt your anxiety was partly genuine, but the use you made of it was not. If I feel uncertain of your good intentions now, it is simply because of the record.

And you can't expect to ride roughshod over my wishes and get no kick back. If you were willing to put the financial arrangement in writing, and in the divorce decree, why the devil didn't you say so? Not you. You never said another word about divorce in any of your letters after I named my terms. The first *I* knew about it was a notification by the British Con-sul and the arrival of the divorce papers. If I hadn't got a lawyer at once I'd have been crazy. And it's too late to drop him now — he's taken on the job and done the work. As usual, you've brought it on yourself.

What I *can* do is write to him and see if I can arrange a delay in paying the fees for you. After all, in the last year you've been $600 or $700 short of what you agreed to pay me, and I'm not pressing for the collection of that. So you're getting off pretty easily by paying my fees instead. I can never understand that blind spot of yours — the mental quirk which says that if Bill Gresham *promises* to do something, and then for some reason fails to do it, nobody's got a right to hold his failure against him! If you *had* lived up to the agreement, I might have more trust in your future living up to it. I know you had a reasonably good excuse and I shall always be disposed to let you get away with quite a lot. But not with everything, cookie, not with everything!

It must be a great surprise to you that I now have such powers of resisting your commands and persuasions. Throughout our marriage you could always make me knuckle under one way or another, and I'm sure you find difficulty in understanding that them days are gone forever. You mistook my submissiveness for the weakness of a self-effacing neurotic. But, as I told you, it is not inherently part of my character, and I shall never practice it again. To your argument that unless you get your own way you can't write, I can only answer that there are other ways of making a living; and as your other letter (which I like very well) indicates, you are already exploring them.

Incidentally, I imagine that some of the trouble you're having in writing is the same as mine: the difficulty of breaking up a team. We were a good team; we each had what the other lacked, and I hated to dissolve it. A pity that your ego made you resent the collaboration so much. And then, as you say, the fiction market's bad; the boys here are complaining too, and I've just had a regretful note from Naome that Collier's has no room for Britannia.

Well, I must write to my lawyer and see what I can do for you. Glad the children are doing so well. The boys are thriving; Davy is now second top in his form — very good going for his second term! Doug is beginning to write beautiful neat letters, but they're very infrequent. You can't believe the difference a *real* school makes — and they're happier than they've ever been in their lives. They're great favourites.

Jack's previous job was that of Fellow of Magdalen — i.e. tutor, with the task of lecturing, seeing each Eng. Lit. student privately for hours and hours and going over his papers, setting exams, conducting exams, "invigilating" exams, correcting exams, oy! A Professorship is very different and much easier — no tutoring; I dunno about exams but I think much less of that too. The professorships in these universities are great plums and you have to be elected to them. All very complicated and I understand only a little of it.

Glad to hear about Aunt Ruth's engagement. Gosh, us Davidman girls must have something — age cannot wither us, nor custom stale, etc. I'm looking pretty good myself these days, what with a new hairdo and thoroughly repaired teeth. It's almost a rain-forest in London too; no palms but terrific jungles of flowering trees and bushes — roses all over everything these days in incredible profusion. I've got the balcony window open, and the wind in the back-garden trees sounds like the forest primeval and then some. Keep your chin up, fella — there's nothing to get panicky about. Just play it straight.

Joy   *Source: Wade*

To William Lindsay Gresham

14, Belsize Park
London, N.W.3
July 6, 1954

Dear Bill,

Glad to hear you're trying for newspaper work; it's certainly up your alley. I do hope you land something very soon; don't forget that the boys will be home for the long vac. in another three weeks, and then I'll have to pay for their keep at home till the end of September, when the next school fees fall due. Looks like a vacation trip will be impossible. Poor lambs; they keep wanting to go to Torquay or the New Forest or the Highlands. But at least they're having a lovely time at school.

I went down there last weekend and saw my first cricket match — between the assembled fathers and the first eleven of the school. To my astonishment, I found that I'd read so much about cricket over the years that I grasped the rudiments almost at once, though it's a very complicated game. An interesting game, too; I got quite excited. The boys won, and when I asked the headmaster's wife if they always did, she said No, sometimes they got a father who refused to go out! But these were most cooperative. Both our boys are mad about cricket and enjoy playing; this was inevitable with Doug, of course, but less so with Davy and I'm very pleased. He's far more sociable than he used to be. And Mrs. Pooley has succeeded in waking his mathematical sense; he's beginning to enjoy it.[27]

The last trace of American accent has now gone and they talk a completely English idiom, slang and all; sounds very charming. They're bigger, pinker, and hardier every time I see them. At six, with a chill wind blowing and storm clouds drifting past the sun, they got into their [swimming] trunks while I shivered in my woolen coat. (The weather has been abominable for the last month or so, cold and rainy.)

Canon Fox of Westminster Abbey, an old friend of Mr. Pooley (and a former colleague of Jack's; the educated classes in England all seem to know one another or at least have friends in common) came down to give us parents a talk on suitable public schools — he used to be the headmaster of one.[28] When they talk about Eton and Harrow, naturally, I don't even listen; barring a scholarship, we couldn't manage it, and anyhow I don't think I like these schools. Eton especially is an extravagant snob school. A very minor public school for us, I think; I'm going to make an appointment to discuss them with Mr. Pooley. It is advisable to enter the boys years ahead, hence this apparent hurry. And of course the right school, here, *can* make all the difference in a man's career. I hope I can find one that won't cost any more than I'm paying now!

Incidentally I've been reading Jack's autobiography in manuscript and I shan't send them to *his* old school, Malvern. Wow! He's as violent a satirist as Swift when he wants to be.[29]

Yes, you're right about the s[cience]-f[iction] writers. Most of them have graduated from the ranks of the fans, and make their living in unexpected ways. Bill Temple, poor bloke, did very well in his spare time while he was working for the Stock Exchange; sold a book to the movies, though only a small low-price English company. So, as he hated the Exchange, he decided to quit and free-lance — and fell flat on his face. For about a year he wrote 2,000 words a day and nothing sold. Now he's working for a motorcar company. I visited the Temples a week or so ago; they live up in Wembley, a very charming suburb, and we walked up to Harrow — it stands on a hill with a miraculous view in all directions. The build-

---

27. Mr. Pooley was the headmaster; his wife had been giving David private tutoring in mathematics.

28. Adam Fox (1883-1977) was Lewis's colleague at Magdalen College, Oxford.

29. C. S. Lewis, *Surprised by Joy: The Shape of My Early Life* (London: Geoffrey Bles, 1955). Jonathan Swift (1667-1745) was an Anglo-Irish clergyman and satiric writer, author of *Gulliver's Travels*.

ings are only Victorian, but not bad, and the gardens are fine. But the boys wear the goddamndest outfit you ever saw — black swallowtail coat and flat round straw hat! Heaven knows who designed it and when it dates from, but in this land, sir, tradition is tradition. Change it? Horrors!

I borrowed *An Adventure* (the Versailles garden book) from [Bill] Temple. I suppose you know Howard Browne finally printed your piece on that?[30]

The boys are wearing their cobra skin belts with great pride. They took me all over the school grounds and showed me the best bits — their garden patch, full of cress and radishes; the cook's Persian kitten; the nettle bed; and a pathetic dead hedgehog that drowned himself in the swimming bath that morning. Their reaction to Jack's Cambridge chair was typical small boy: "I suppose that means there'll be no more climbs up Magdalen Tower!"

Too bad about Nat Silver. I always liked him; he was a good egg. I didn't hear that; but I *do* hear that Rose is on good terms with Renée again and contributing money, or says she is. Did Nick Rodriguez ever turn up?[31] Regards to all.

Yours,
Joy

By the way, are we divorced?   *Source: Wade*

To William Lindsay Gresham

14, Belsize Park
London, N.W.3
July 25, 1954

Dear Bill,

Sorry things are at a low ebb with you. Would be nice if you *could* collect some of the dough people have taken off you in the past. But you've

---

30. Howard Browne (1907-1999) was a writer of mystery and private eye stories for several pulp fiction distributors. In the 1940s he was an editor for Ziff-Davis, popular pulp fiction publisher of magazines, including *Amazing Stories, Fantastic Adventures, Fantastic, Conflict,* and *Tales of the Sea.*

31. Rose was Renée's mother, Nick Rodriguez her estranged father.

always been able to find a job when you needed it, and I think you will again. Can't be too soon for me; the boys come home tomorrow.

Fortunately Jack, that perennial rescuer, has saved the situation as far as the first month of holidays are concerned; he is lending us his house for August, during which he and Warnie will be in Ireland as usual. And if the worst comes to the worst I suppose we can eat out of his garden, which is also at our disposal. Of course I'll need to pay a retaining fee on my room here, and there will be lots of other expenses; but it's a big help. If it's a choice between your paying my lawyer and paying me, I'd rather you paid me.

Our address, for Aug. 4th-31st, will be: c/o Lewis, The Kilns, Headington Quarry, Oxford.

Arthur Clarke is back in England; separated from his wife [and] making her a $5000 a year allowance; hasn't even had any kids, too. The trouble with me is I pick the wrong ex-husbands. Arthur is writing a science column for *Seventeen*, of all unlikely markets; stuff the teen-age girl wants to know about science. News to me that they wanted to know *anything* about it, except for the occasional s-f fan. After a bit he'll be off to Australia to write a book on the Great Barrier Reef — he goes in for underwater frogman photography. Had a couple of nice shots of himself being goosed by a barracuda.

I went down to the school yesterday: the big day, speeches and prize-giving and the school play. The play was "Saul and David," arranged from the Bible by the headmaster's wife and very well done; good costumes, quite good acting, and an open-air theatre. Davy was a slave-boy, poured out wine for the King and showed great presence of mind in retrieving his chair when he accidentally knocked it over while being possessed of an evil spirit. Doug was a singer, in a burnoose and so on. They looked delightful.

And, believe it or not, Davy won two prizes! One for Art — the whole school's prize — and a special one for getting top marks in his form, not counting math in which he isn't marked yet. He tied the boy who got top marks all round. This is an extraordinarily good show considering it's only his second term; Mr. Pooley thinks he may very well get a scholarship for a public school if his math improves. I was astonished at the Art prize; he's always drawing imaginatively, but no idea how well he could work in colour. He's turned out half a dozen terrific paintings — jungle scenes, Chinese landscapes, an End-of-the-World number, etc. Well, goodbye for now.

Joy

Source: Wade

To William Lindsay Gresham

14, Belsize Park
London, N.W.3
July 30, 1954

Dear Bill,

Your cheque for $20 just arrived and was a very great relief. I am glad you're writing full blast; wish I was, but with the boys home and the financial need I can't. I managed to earn 61.7s. this week by going back to the job-printing place — even the boys came along, bless 'em, and helped by folding and assembling copy. But it's a miserable business on its last legs; some of the lads are so much worse off than I that they lunch on dry bread or nothing unless I buy them ninepence worth of garlic sausage. A miserable damp basement too, and I don't like the boys being there for long. I worked like a Trojan for my six quid, combining the jobs of Varityper, editor, designer, and salesman — also soothing the creditors. The landlord came in one day suffering from mumps, yelling for his back rent — I scared him back to his bed by telling him he'd lose more than money if he wasn't careful. Amusingly enough, their best customer is the offshoot of Dianetics, Hubbard's screwy Scientology outfit; I've been printing up their bulletins, and I never saw such doubletalk in my life.

Thank Heavens we're off to Oxford on the 4th — don't forget to address us there. I need a rest rather badly, and the boys are getting over persistent coughs — Doug's is nothing, but Davy's got quite a bad one. I took him to the doctor the other day and was told it was nothing to worry about, only a mild catarrh. He's well and strong otherwise, and eats like a horse.

Had to go see my publisher this week too — he was afraid *Smoke on the Mountain* might be libelous! The English libel laws are really terrific. They took out the bit about Ingrid Bergman and Rita Hayworth,[32] and questioned several other things — though I think their solicitor was just having a little fun when he said that probably no one was in a position to bring a libel action over my description of the Black Mass at Louis XIV's court. Incidentally, I've been reading copy on Warnie's new book for him (mostly for spelling — the Lewises have a family failing of being unable to

32. Ingrid Bergman (1915-1982) was an iconic Swedish film star. Rita Hayworth (1918-1987) was the prototypical glamorous movie queen of many films in the 1940s.

remember when and where *i* comes before *e* or the reverse) and he's got quite a lot of stuff on the black-magic-and-poisoning business.[33]

Can't seem to think of anything coherent to say; I'm too tired. And after dinner I've got to pack our trunk. And Davy and Douglas, having been perfect Philip Sidneys of courtesy all week, have suddenly reverted to type and are wrestling madly for possession of a water pistol — oops, Davy has Doug in a scissors again. Excuse please while I go break it up.

Yours,
Joy

Source: Wade

Bill and Joy's divorce was finalized in Miami, Florida, on August 5, 1954; he married Renée the same day.

To William Lindsay Gresham

The Kilns
August 10, 1954

Dear Bill,

Well! I am glad for my own sake the suspense is over. I sincerely hope you'll be happy; you have my congratulations, and Renée my good wishes. She has had a hard life through no fault of hers, and she is certainly entitled to expect a little peace and security now. I drank a pint of the Bird and Baby's special cider today to your happiness;[34] as for Jack, he drank to the repentance and forgiveness of all sinners. After which we went out on top of Shotover Hill and helped the boys fly a kite, with fifty miles of England stretched out all round us. A beautiful bright windy day; *we* are having an unusually cool summer, all roses and rainbows.

But all this is besides the point which is financial. You cannot really expect the boys and me to go on eating air, promise-crammed. Of course there is a job in Miami for you, if work is what you want; Renée doesn't

33. Warren H. Lewis, *The Sunset of the Splendid Century: The Life and Times of Louis Auguste de Bourbon, Duc de Maine, 1670-1736* (London: Eyre & Spottiswoode, 1955).

34. The Bird and Baby was the nickname of The Eagle and Child, one of Lewis's favorite pubs in Oxford.

seem to have had any trouble finding one. I should be very glad to see the writing work out. But it seems harder and harder for all writers to live these days, and you and I prospered far better as a team than we are likely to prosper apart. It may very well be necessary for you to take the sort of job you can get, not the sort you dream of.

At any rate, please do something fairly soon. Promises are not legal tender in England, any more than in the States.

The boys are quite well, and enjoying their stay here very much. Yesterday we were taken to tea at Studley Priory, where they had (in addition to a fourteenth-century building) fourteen Dalmatian puppies, a lady badger in a pen, and umpteen hamsters all ages. Great fun. Also a heavenly tea, clotted cream and gooseberry jam, so we aren't starving for the moment, but I dread our return to London at the end of the month. Tomorrow, if it keeps fine, we're to go punting on the Cherwell.

I met Professor Tolkien yesterday (you know, *The Hobbit* and a terrific fantasy that's just come out here, *The Fellowship of the Ring*) when we came into the Eastgate. And the poor man was horribly embarrassed to meet an admirer; he'd just been to the dentist and was temporarily without his false teeth. Also there was a young R. C. priest with him who looked vaguely familiar to Jack, and when he was identified it was Jack's turn to be embarrassed; the lad, a Canadian, had just faced him in exams and been ploughed. I must say he was taking it very well. Tolkien was understandably shy at first, then very pleasant. And he came rushing after us this morning in the High, crying, "Now you can see what I look like with my teeth!"

Jack is leaving here in a blaze of glory, all his pupils this year having taken firsts or seconds. I think he's equally good at teaching small boys, judging by his effect on Davy and Doug. He sends thanks for your congrats on the Cambridge job.

Joy   *Source: Wade*

Letters 1954

To William Lindsay Gresham

14, Belsize Park
London, N.W.3
August 27, 1954

Dear Bill,

Never was money more heartily welcome; I had got to the point where I was going without lunch to save what I've got. Your account of activities is impressive and it seems to me the publicity and advertising fields ought to have something for you in Miami. I remember that my cousin Eddie was an advertising salesman on a newspaper and knew all the boys; have you thought of such a job as a way in? Your theory about the writing market seems probable, and of course there are always new lads coming up. But why be proud? If the field's played out, anyone as versatile as you can find another. I don't know anyone who's better qualified than you to be a super-salesman; you've got charm, ready wit, persistence, the gift of talking the hind leg off a donkey and the last sixpence frae a Scot — and you like meeting people. It might be a pleasant change from writing and its heartaches.

Point of information. I took my lawyer to task for charging you $200 in addition to what *I* paid him — I don't even know if it's ethical to charge both parties; you might ask *your* lawyer. Whereupon he writes huffily to insist that he only charged you $100, and says he has asked you to correct the statement. I should very much like to know the facts. *If* he is pulling a fast one, perhaps something can be done about it. What I feel about having to pay lawyers is better imagined than said.

Taxes, oy! The story is even worse here, but at least there are public services that are worth something. I think I told you that when I had a bit of thyroid trouble in May I was examined by seven doctors, including two world-famous authorities, for nothing; and I wouldn't have to pay for hospitalization either. But it does look as if all Western governments are headed for bankruptcy. One more war will certainly do it — *that* consideration may keep the peace a while. What is the reaction in the States to Congress' anti-Communist spree? Over here it has inspired universal disgust even in the diehard Tory press. The English *really* believe in liberty, and over here you *can* fight City Hall, or even Whitehall — there are constant cases in the Press of John Smith defying Government successfully. They think of the U.S. as a country trembling on the verge of Fascist totalitarianism. Not that they love Russia, either!

Weather here is beautiful again. I've been working in Jack's rooms in Magdalen on the book I hope to write on Mme. de M. It's so pleasant I can almost forget my troubles. On one side, windows give on the deer park, and the stags whinny (it's almost a whinny) all day. On the other side there's the quad, gay with flowers — and with tourists. They're really a menace, tiptoeing up and down stairs all day and poking into rooms, though they're not supposed to enter the Fellows' building. Yesterday two horrible German yentas tried furtively to enter Jack's rooms and froze when they saw me, their eyes roving from me to the lettered "Mr. C. S. Lewis" over the door. I guess I didn't look the part. I challenged them; they squeaked, "Ve chust vanted ve should see the house!" and fled.

Jack and Warnie are in Ireland now, far from all cares — Jack doesn't even leave his address at college. This morning the Master of Balliol phoned and asked ME for it. Gosh do I feel important — hmm, this and tuppence'll buy me a bus ride.

Whadda I do about the boys' school fees? Total, £140 payable next month. Bless 'em, they're very happy here and growing by leaps and bounds. Davy has been reading the French translation of one of Jack's Narnia books, his own idea, to improve his French. Doug has been practicing cricket on the lawn (with an old tennis racket for a bat) with Davy as the bowler. Susie, a six-month-old French poodle, shaggiest dog you ever saw, does the fielding. Wish I didn't have to take them back to London next week. You really ought to write them oftener. They still feel hurt at your not writing; but the day will come when they are merely indifferent whether you write or not. You don't want that to happen.

Regards to your new family.

Yours,
Joy

Source: Wade

To William Lindsay Gresham

14, Belsize Park
London, N.W.3
September 8, 1954

Dear Bill,

Money and letter received with great relief. I hope to God you can keep it up well enough to pay for this term's fees. We are scrimping ardently; the boys actually saved all their last term's spending money and gave it back to me for expenses, their own idea. Doug has been invited to spend a few days with a school friend, so yesterday when your cheque came I blew six bob on a trip to Kew [Gardens] for Davy — I thought he ought to have an outing too. He's become an ardent botanist and is particularly fond of tree-ferns and jungle stuff. He's also teaching himself to type, out of the *Book of Knowledge,* and has done a letter to you which I'll send by ordinary mail.

Incidentally, I shall enclose in it a bad cheque of yours which will speak for itself; I notice you have changed your bank, so there's no point in putting it through again. Knowing your arithmetic, I assume this was a pure accident, but don't do it again. Luckily, banks here are a damn sight more human than they are in the States; if they know you at all they'll give you an overdraft, and after I broke down and wept in the bank manager's office one day he was good for a small one. Warnie tells me *he's* got one for £150. "Living on your overdraft" is a favorite phrase here.

I notice you maintain an eloquent silence on the subject of my lawyer's fee. Tsk, tsk, o what a tangled web we weave, etc. Well well, we'll say no more about it.

We had lots of fun at Oxford; after Jack left, though, things were very quiet and we were housebound by rain for a week or so. There hasn't been a summer like this in England for more than a century; incredible storms — there was even a small tornado near Oxford. I saw a photo of it in the newspaper, and it was the real thing all right. But we got a bit of nice weather at the end. We walked, picked plums and pears and apples in the orchard, lived on broad beans and garden sass and hamburger (minced meat to you, American) and eggs and stuff. The boys embarked on a heroic project of clearing Jack's orchard of nettles and thistles and succeeded very well. I got started on my research for the Mme. de M. book; it'll take a long time, but ought to be a humdinger.

The boys have slight coughs, but are well and strong and growing tall. I'm rather ill myself — tore a muscle in my side coughing, and can't shake off the cough. Nothing serious, though.

It was too bad about Nat Silver. I'm glad Rose's operation went off all right; she's young enough to recover her sight perfectly. Mrs. MacDowell had one when she was about eighty-five, but it didn't help.

Writers here are saying that one can make more out of the paperbacks than out of hard-cover writing, and they're all writing directly for Ballantine and the others. I suppose dignified agents frown on it, but you ought to be able to do well at that game. I think Scott Meredith does much more of that trade than Brandt, though.

How did you make out with the Martian story?

Davy enjoyed your letter very much; Doug, who is not such a voracious reader, had a bit of trouble with it. Just a tip: at their age *long* letters are regarded as a nuisance; little and often is the idea. They both find their attention flags after a page or so.

Doug wants a bicycle the worst way — most of the boys in school have them, and he can now ride perfectly on his friends' bikes. I'd like to get him one for his birthday, if you can make it possible. A new one is ten or eleven quid, but I might be able to find a good secondhand one.

Monster Midway is getting a lot of advertising here; perhaps it is doing quite well. I do hope so! Did I tell you that hard-cover books here sell anywhere from 5s. to 12/6? 21s. — $3 — is a staggering price, asked only for great big impressive scholarly works.

Regards to your family.

Yours,
Joy

Source: Wade

On September 20, 1954, Bill explains how he paid the lawyers. Like Joy he is disgusted with the whole bunch of them: "Regarding Mr. Godfrey Newman: I gave my lawyer, Nat Williams, a check for $100 made out to Newman which I presume he passed along. I didn't have a second hundred so I gave Williams two checks, each for $50, made out to him and predated. He was to send Newman another hundred and then cash my checks when I had money to cover them — the dates that appeared on them. This was the only way I could work it, since Newman demanded $200 cash on the barrelhead. I don't see why he should pester you for the money unless Williams didn't pass it along. I don't want anything *more to do with [the] whole business and I don't see why you should be involved, either." He also updates Joy on the fallout from the McCarthy affairs, including that he is now under scrutiny by the IRS. Other routine matters (weather, needing eyeglasses, no news from his agent, and so on) are reported.* Source: Wade

To William Lindsay Gresham

14, Belsize Park
London, N.W.3
September 23, 1954

Dear Bill,

Gosh (as Hyman Kaplan would say) you certainly took a load off![35] They're pretty patient at the school, but I don't like to keep them waiting, as fees are supposed to be paid before school starts. It began on the 20th and the boys are already there; I saw them off at Waterloo Station Monday afternoon, and as soon as they were in the railway carriage with the other boys they forgot about me completely, which I consider a very healthy reaction. Start of term is always a doleful sight in an English railway station; train full of laughing chattering boys, platform full of droopy forlorn-looking parents. You can always spot the new boys, though; they are either frankly weeping or wearing pale unconvincing smiles.

I'm awfully glad about that article; it's about time you got a break. About the bounced check, which you probably have by now, since it was only for $5, it's hardly worth bothering about. I suppose the bank made some infernal charge or other, as they do when an account gets low, and didn't notify you.

One at least — more likely both — of our lawyers is a crook. Thus: a. Newman demanded an advance payment of $150 from *me*, which I made out of the money I'd earmarked for school fees, and how it hurt. b. My bank (it *would* happen to me) made a mistake and sent him $250 instead. (*That* was when I broke down and cried in the bank manager's office.) He profited by the occasion to insist that he was entitled to keep $50 of the error payment, as he was having a terrible wrangle with you and your lawyer to get yez [sic] to agree to terms, etc. This although he had at first said $150 would be his entire charge.

---

35. In the September 20, 1954, letter Bill sends a check based on an advance he received from *Sports Illustrated* for an article on carnival wrestling shows.

c. You informed me that you'd paid him $100. I wrote Newman and said that in that case he ought to refund $100 to me. No answer for a month or two.

d. You informed me that you'd paid him *another* $100. At the same time he finally sent me the divorce papers and declared that it was the usual practice for the husband to pay part of the fees and he'd taken that into consideration in charging me such a low one.

e. I wrote him implying in polite terms that he was a louse. He replied with a splutter about his high ethical standards (hmm, Honest Godfrey they call him in Miami) and insisted that he had charged you only $100 and that he had asked *your* lawyer to write me to that effect. Your lawyer (Honest Nat?) has not written me.

Between 'em, they've done pretty well out of it, and someone's got away with $100. I am not so spiritless about these matters as you and if I were on the spot I would make noises in the direction of the Bar Association. But there is not much I can do from a distance. I don't see why *you* should take it, though; you might justifiably stop payment on those checks you gave Williams.

Yes, you bet we kept the *Book of Knowledge;* shipped it, carefully insured, in ten packages to Jack. The boys read it constantly when we are there. So far there hasn't been any point in bringing it to London, as it would be in the way in my one room and the boys are so seldom here.

My parents are coming over next month on the start of an extensive trip through Southern Europe, Israel, etc. I warned 'em not to come to England in late autumn — they'll be just in time for the fog season — but they wanted to spend the summer in their usual place in Maine. So what did they get? Hurricanes!

I bet I can get a bicycle for Douglas out of them.

Did I tell you that the boys saved all their spending money last term and gave it back to me to help with the expenses? Nearly broke my heart. Of course I spent it on them — some of it went to buy a large disused aquarium from Phyl. Davy has planted it with assorted flora to produce a jungle effect — there is one small palm tree. He will certainly appreciate any jungly pictures you can send him. Doug is beginning to sing like an angel; he's got a good ear, too. Regards to the wife and kiddies.

Yours,
Joy

Source: Wade

To William Lindsay Gresham

14, Belsize Park
London, N.W.3
September 30, 1954

Dear Bill,

The enclosed letters will explain what *really* happened to your two cheques for $50 each.[36] I'm glad to have this cleared up, and it's nice to know that whoever was wrong, it wasn't Mr. Newman, who came to me very well recommended.

I dunno if Williams actually lied to you or if you misunderstood him. In any case, the matter is now entirely between the two of you, and I'm out of it, thank Heaven. I suspect the moral of *this* is, as the Duchess (or is it the Queen?)[37] would say, Never trust an amateur magician!

Haven't received anything from you yet this week, but I suppose it is waiting on the final pay from the magazine. More power to your typewriter! I am working simultaneously on an article on "The Pleasures of Repentance" (in the hope that when my book comes out I'll have openings in religious magazines) and a long ballad, just for my amusement (and Jack's, he being a passionate admirer of my poetry.) It's called "The Ballad of the Jew's Daughter" and begins like this:

> The tale of the Jew's daughter
> Who sat in a box of bone,
> Windowless, lightless, deaf and blind,
> Spinning the silk of her spider mind
> Into a net to catch the wind;
> Christ came to the Jew's daughter
> In her dark mind alone.[38]

36. In a letter from Williams to Joy, Williams explained that the two $50 checks went to him for the additional expenses involved in handling the divorce — he said it was because the divorce, which he thought initially was going to be uncontested, was contested by Joy. In a letter from Newman to Joy, Newman explained that he only received $100 — the fee he originally said he required. He stated emphatically that he never asked for $200, suggesting that Williams may have fabricated the request for $200 (source: Wade).

37. Davidman is alluding here to Lewis Carroll's *Alice in Wonderland*, chapter 9. It is in fact the Duchess who is so fond of finding morals in things.

38. The lines are published here for the first time.

There are about 75 lines of it already; if I can keep it up, it may be quite good.

Also: *The Observer,* a highly literary newspaper here, is offering £200 and twenty prizes of £20 each for a short story (fantasy probably better than s-f), set in the year 2500, not more than 3000 words. Entries by Nov. 8. I'll have a crack; and if you want to have one too, I'll put it in for you.

Regards to Renée.

Yours,
Joy

Source: Wade

To William Lindsay Gresham

14, Belsize Park
London, N.W.3
October 22, 1954

Dear Bill,

Your letter and cheque came very apropos indeed, not only for the money's sake, but because it enabled me to wave them both at my parents and prove to them that you *were* doing your part. It would appear the Davidman family has been fighting over our affairs far more violently than we ever fought over them ourselves, and with that sublime disregard for truth and justice that characterizes the lot of them. I, at least, am safely on this side of the Atlantic; I hope Renée hasn't been having trouble. When I can get a word in edgewise, I insist that at least a third of the responsibility for everything that happened is mine; you may tell anyone I said so, if there's any occasion to.

At any rate, my parents have bought me a winter coat and are going to get Doug a bike for his birthday — and believe me, I've earned it. Since they got here last Saturday I have made:

6 trips to laundries
5 visits to Woolworth's
3 expeditions to look at neighbourhood shops
1 expedition to look at neighbourhood shops after dark to see what they looked like shut
4 promenades down Regent Street to look at shops

1 visit to the hairdresser
2 visits to doctors for imaginary ailments
2 visits to cleaners
3 more visits to Woolworth's
7 assorted trips to chemists, banks, greengrocers, etc. etc.

They don't seem to have much interest in sightseeing. I did get them as far as the Abbey on Sunday (shops being shut) but Mother's feet hurt, so we didn't go in.

About the lawyers it seems fairly clear what happened; you thought you were giving Williams those two cheques for Newman, whereas you were really giving them to Williams for Williams. Whether he lied to you, or you merely misunderstood him, I wouldn't know.

The boys are well, as usual. Had a nice letter from Davy today, full of palm trees and castle pictures in crayon. They did enjoy your postcards a good deal, remarked on them to me with enthusiasm when I was last down. The more of those the merrier. And if you type a letter, better double space it; I notice they've less trouble that way. Did I tell you Davy found typing instructions in the *Book of Knowledge* and was teaching himself to type by the touch system?

I'm starting on my new book at last, having borrowed some essential source books from Warnie. Who knows, maybe I'll hit the jackpot?

Yours,
Joy

Source: Wade

To William Lindsay Gresham

14, Belsize Park
London, N.W.3
October 29, 1954

Dear Bill,

Glory hallelujah, hi ho jorum, school bills get paid and Mommy eats. Though, to tell you the truth, I am now eating lunch at my parents' expense, and after some months of salt-herring-and-a-crust-of-bread I find I can put away a three-course lunch with great appreciation. It's one compensation for the wear and tear. "Hands full" is an understatement. I find, however, that (what with continual prayer for grace) I am far better able to endure it and keep my temper than I was ten years ago. I've got so far away from that background now that what was once terrifying is now merely comic — or even pathetic. They do try to be amiable in their fashion; but what a fashion!

I succeeded after strong pressure in getting them to the Tower of London yesterday, since Mother wanted very much to see the Crown Jewels. (Fabulous things they are too, like the treasures of Aladdin's cave.) They complained because the English hadn't installed lifts in William the Conqueror's keep. And Mother, looking at the collar of the Garter: "You know, that could be cut into two very nice pieces of costume jewelry!"

Jack had to come to London the 27th to take part in a debate; and we took him to tea at the Piccadilly Hotel beforehand. (His suggestion; my organizing work; my parents' dough.) We had [Phyl and Sel] too; they are having a hard time, but had had *us* to tea and been very nice. Jack laid himself out to be charming to both my parents and succeeded admirably; when I complimented him on it privately he said pathetically, "I'm doing my best!" Poor lamb; there were moments, as when my father lectured him on the blessings of Prohibition, when I saw his smile grow slightly fixed. I told the story of how, at about twelve, I priggishly poured Dad's private bottle of apricot brandy down the drain after hearing him proclaim his belief in Prohibition — and got myself walloped. Dad hadn't the sense to let it alone, but insisted that *his* was a special case; *he* wasn't really a breaker of the law, etc. This was too much for Jack, who remarked, "I think there was more than one prig in the family. Of course, our *own* case is always different, isn't it?" But it went completely past Dad, whose perceptions are duller than ever.

At the meeting they heard Jack acclaimed as one of the leaders of a new trend in popular thinking, etc. etc. Afterward Dad said condescendingly that he was a nice chap — and gave the show away by enquiring anxiously, "What did he say about ME?" He also asked me if Professor Lewis hadn't told me what a handsome woman my mother was!

(She was wearing a fancy black suit with rhinestone buttons, a pearl bracelet, a pearl choker, dingle-dangle pearl earrings, a pink lace blouse and a shocking pink hat; I'll let you imagine Jack's reaction for yourself.) Mother's mania about her own beauty has grown worse than ever; she is continually imagining that men try to pick her up in the street. She was a few feet away from us one day and had a moment of dizziness and leaned against a shop window rather blue about the lips; a respectable elderly bloke asked solicitously if he could be of any assistance. She was convinced that his intentions were dishonourable. Interestingly enough, Dad believes implicitly in this myth and is very proud of her attractions.

Dorothy Sayers was at the debate too; she's enormously witty and a very eloquent speaker, a forthright old lady who wears rather mannish clothes and doesn't give a damn about her hairdo.[39] Mother said if brains made a woman look like that she was glad she wasn't intellectual. How they do run to form, the dears, don't they. But Jack must be aiming for a halo; he's invited us all to lunch at Magdalen next week.

Took my parents to Dane Court. They had to admit the boys looked amazingly well and happy and had exquisite manners and seemed much more grown up (you should have heard 'em exchanging the lightning-swift English schoolboy repartee, and Doug's impeccable Oxford vowels). But my father noticed that the desks were old and battered. He did mental arithmetic about how much money was coming into the school and complained all the way home and at dinner that they ought to invest it in new desks and not let the place "run to seed." (It's impeccably kept up.) Nothing I could do would make him understand the English preference for the traditional as against the new and slick, though my dining-room tablemate (Eton and Trinity and a very intelligent man) did his best to help me.[40]

About Arthur Clarke; he told me all about his wife, whom he's now shedding. (*She* gets $5000 a year although no kids; count your blessings.) She *was* a night club hostess; she is also a dipso.

One interesting thing from the folks, how bad American education has got; they are now giving remedial reading courses in *colleges*. New York schools are not even trying to teach reading till the *second* grade. (By the way, Davy is taking up reading French for fun!) Too bad about Kendrick; hope he pulls out of it. I thought he had done very well, what with films and so on.

Yours,
Joy

Source: Wade

39. Dorothy L. Sayers (1893-1957) was a mystery novelist, essayist, poet, Christian apologist, dramatist, and Dante scholar. She and Lewis exchanged dozens of letters.
40. The tablemate mentioned here was a Mr. Clayton.

To William Lindsay Gresham

14, Belsize Park
London, N.W.3
November 4, 1954

Dear Bill,

Goody goody grapenuts! I've just finished waving your latest cheque at my parents and saying Yah! By dint of pointing out your virtues to them over the last couple of weeks, I've talked myself into a quite admiring frame of mind about you and am glad to have it confirmed. You're quite the nicest ex-husband I have. Some of *this* cheque can be applied on *next* term's fees if all goes well. I think you are a bit ahead on your payments since the divorce; as for the arrears *before,* I shan't fuss about them.

The boys will be home this weekend for half-term holidays; please to remember the Fifth of November, whiz bang and sparkle and all that — I gotta go out and buy fireworks.[41] My parents leave for the Continent next week. Yesterday we had lunch with Jack at Magdalen. I'd brought them up to Oxford the day before, walked them in and out of Christ Church, Tom Quad, Magdalen Cloisters, up the High and down the Broad and round through Turl and by Longwall Street and Holywell Street, and I did think all those miracles of stone had made *some* impression. But when Jack asked Mother what had most impressed her in Oxford, she said, "The Market!" He reeled slightly, but carried on. Dad, meanwhile, was telling him all about a speech on Progressive Education, "Down With It!" he'd delivered to the St. Albans Civic Improvement Association of Queens, N.Y. What a speech, too — it's just taken me two days to type it for him. I must say Jack did nobly as a host; they sang his praises all the way back to London, which is not their usual way with my friends. And he's the first person I've ever seen kid Dad and get away with it.

I'm getting my teeth into *Queen Cinderella* — provisional title for my biography of Mme. de Maintenon; what do you think of it? Warnie's lent me some of his treasured books. There's miles of reading to do, but I think I ought to be able to sell it on an outline and a few specimen chapters; the

---

41. November 5 is Guy Fawkes Day. It commemorates the Gunpowder Plot, a conspiracy to blow up the English Parliament and King James I in 1605. The day was named after the most famous of the conspirators, and it is celebrated with fireworks and bonfires in which Fawkes is burned in effigy.

story's sure-fire. I don't hope much for *Smoke on the Mountain*, which is just out in the States (if you see any reviews, would you send them along?), but the biography smells to me like a money-maker if I can get it done.

No more news — and I gotta run now; I'm expected to assist the folks in a walk-up-Finchley-Road-to-look-at-the-shops.

Yours,

Joy

Source: Wade

To William Lindsay Gresham

14, Belsize Park
London, N.W.3
November 30, 1954

Dear Bill,

Glad to hear from you in any shape or form or cheque size![42] New York sounds its dear sweet lovable self, but I'm glad you came out of it with a couple of nibbles. Very mysterious about *Red Book*, but I suppose we'll never know; it certainly curdled overnight without a sign of trouble, and I suspect it may have been politics. Things over here are very tranquil, except that I'm recovering from a spell of intestinal flu (not very bad, but it played hell with my beer-drinking) and Davy wants to become a Mohammedan. Chip off the old block? Though that's *one* religion you seem to have missed. I suspect his influences are a small dark object named Zaffar Ali Khan, a minor princeling of sorts in his form; Rex Harrison's performance as Saladin in a film about the Crusades I took him to; and his general liking for Oriental costumes.[43] His intellectual precocity has made quite a stir at Dane Court and they were worrying for fear *I'd* worry about this; they were greatly relieved when I didn't turn a hair. I shall cope with it by buying him a Koran and, if possible, an account of the different Mohammedan sects — and seeing that he reads them. If the case proves

42. On November 26, 1954, Bill writes Joy a newsy letter updating her on happenings in his and Renée's lives. He has visited New York and met with agents and publishers, trying to understand better what now sells. He also reports that his IRS problem includes $3600 of interest — something he is hoping to get cancelled (source: Wade).

43. Rex Harrison (1908-1990) was a commanding actor of both film and stage from the 1930s through the 1970s.

stubborn, I might go so far as seeing that he memorized suitable passages from the Koran, as I believe you're supposed to, and said his prayers regularly in the direction of Mecca. That sort of cat is best killed by choking it with cream.

Went down to St. James' Park on a sunny day last week to look at the ducks and discovered the Mall lined with a crowd waiting to see the Queen Mother's homecoming, so I joined it. I'd got behind some short people and thought I'd have a view, but the damn things all waved their silly arms just as she passed so all I could spot was the coachmen etc. Anyway I seen [sic] the little carriage-lamp.

Yesterday I went up to Cambridge for Jack's inaugural address — there was damn near as much fuss about that as a Coronation.[44] I lurked modestly in the crowd and didn't go near him — he was walled about with caps and gowns and yards of recording apparatus. A great success; instead of, as usual with teachers of the humanities, talking about the continuity of culture and pleading for the traditional values, *he* tells 'em the "Old Western Culture" is quite dead, has been supplanted by a machine-culture, we are now living in "post-Christian Europe," and learning about literature from a representative of the older culture like himself is like learning about Neanderthal men *from* one or studying paleontology from a live dinosaur. He ended by telling them to study their dinosaur while they could; there wouldn't be any around much longer! He made a remarkably effective case (with which I do not much agree) for the *really* important historic break between cultures coming not with the fall of Rome or the Renaissance but with the rise of science as a power; I don't know how the dons liked it but the students ate it up. But I think, for once, he was sacrificing accuracy in the interests of a good show.

Afterward I oozed out with the mob and looked without much hope for a taxi. Miracle of miracles, there was one waiting in the rain. "Railway station!" says I. Right, says he, and off we go. When we got there, he says, "Glad I found you, didn't know who I was to meet!" Apparently I'd stolen someone's taxi. There was one minute to catch the *only* good London train — and realized I'd probably stolen Jack's cab; he usually has one waiting for a mad dash to the station, whenever he speaks away from home, and the best way from Cambridge to Oxford is by way of London. Let's hope it was some other sucker, not that he'd mind.

---

44. The address was later published as *"De Descriptione Temporum,"* in C. S. Lewis, *Selected Literary Essays* (Cambridge: Cambridge University Press, 1969).

Phyl and Sel are coming along pretty well; still very inert and not *doing* anything, and the infantile quality of Phyl's thinking is if anything increased by analysis. But she's writing a bit and is much calmer and happier. Sooner or later she will get it through her head that it is *not* horrible for human beings to have aggression in them, but it's taking a long while to penetrate. I must confess, though, that Freudian interpretations such as she and her analyst dream up together seem to me just so much jabberwocky. The fact that people gotta eat, first and foremost, has not yet dawned on the orthodox Freudians — why should it? Who ever saw a starving psychoanalyst?

Well, back to the seventeenth century. I'm working like blazes on the research for my Mme. de M. book, which ought to be a dilly. Good luck with your stories.

Yours,
Joy

Source: Wade

To Chad Walsh

14, Belsize Park
London, N.W.3
December 13, 1954

Dear Chad,

Bless you for them kind words. It's nice to know that *someone* has noticed the emergence of *Smoke on the Mountain* — so far I've received no letters, reviews, or comment of any kind. And still nicer when it's you who notice it. I hope you are right about its chances. I'll send you a copy of the English edition with Jack's preface when that emerges.

Yes, I *would* very much like your poetry book, thank you sir.[45] You'll find my present address (my permanent one) on the outside of this letter.

Jack is moving officially to Cambridge on New Year's Day — in fact, I shall be there to help, though I don't really know what is needed except for someone to stand by and look wise in Headington while he's doing the same in Cambridge. He is having Pickford's, the famous magical movers,

---

45. Chad Walsh, *Eden Two-Way* (New York: Harper, 1954).

do the trick — they do all the packing and sorting out etc. All the customer has to do is treat the men to drinks at suitable intervals.

He is keeping the Headington house and planning to come back to Oxford two or three days a week. But I shouldn't be surprised to see him strike roots in Cambridge and move there altogether after a couple of years; it would mean leaving a great many friends, but those weekly train trips will be a nuisance. And he's already quite at home in Cambridge. I attended his inaugural lecture on Nov. 29th; it was brilliant, intellectually exciting, unexpected, and funny as hell — as you can imagine. The hall was crowded, and there were so many capped and gowned dons in the front rows that they looked like a rookery. Instead of talking in the usual professorial way about the continuity of culture, the value of traditions, etc., he announced that "Old Western Culture," as he called it, was practically dead, leaving only a few scattered survivors like himself; that the change to the Age of Science was a more profound one than that from Medieval to Renaissance or even Classical to Dark Ages; and that learning about literature from him would be rather like having a Neanderthal man to lecture on the Neanderthal or studying paleontology from a live dinosaur! As I remember, he ended with, "Study your dinosaurs while you may; you won't have us around for long!" How that man loves being in a minority, even a lost-cause minority! Athanasius contra mundum, or Don Quixote against the windmills. He talked blandly of "post-Christian Europe," which I thought rather previous of him. I sometimes wonder what he would do if Christianity really did triumph everywhere; I suppose he would have to invent a new heresy.

My own affairs are quite humdrum. I think I wrote you that I've been divorced; Bill is erratic in sending money, but he sends it when he's got it — the rest of the time he lives on his new wife. Fortunately, my parents came to England to visit me not long ago, and in the excitement of reunion blurted out that in addition to their pensions (I thought that was all they had) they've got about $25,000 stashed away and can afford to help me out when I'm broke so the worst of my worries are over. In consequence, I've stopped trying to write commercial short stories, which I hate and am really no good at by myself, and have plunged into research for the life of Mme. de Maintenon which Warnie suggested to me and provided me with an outline for. So I'm living a very quiet life, deep in the seventeenth century.

The boys are progressing splendidly; they're extraordinarily grown up and self-reliant. Davy is less like Bill than he used to be, the discipline of school having had a good effect. But he startled me the other day by announcing that he wants to become a Mohammedan! The influence of a Pakistani classmate is responsible, I think; and he has always been susceptible to the romance of India. I bought him a copy of the Koran and shall leave matters to time and the effect of that very dull book.

Glad to hear you're all in such a whirl of pleasant activity — and how I envy your energy! I'm looking forward to next summer. Love to all.

Yours,
Joy
Source: Wade

To William Lindsay Gresham

14, Belsize Park
London, N.W.3
December 21, 1954

Dear Daddy,
    Thank you for the microscope. Nothing was broken. I have made slides containing hair, mouldy cheese, and blood. I'm making many others. I can see germs and bloodcapsules. Everything is allright. All best wishes.

Your son,
David

Dear Daddy,
    Thank you very much for our wonderful presents. We love them as much as possible. I have been using mine practically every time I can. I hung upside down. I did a somersault in mid air hanging on to them.
    I am getting on very well in school, and I am second top in my form. I was in four things in the play and I hope I did them well. I wish you had been there to see them. If you had it would have been very nice for you and for me. When do you think you can possibly come to England?
    That Easy Way gym bar you have sent me is very useful for chinning. I do boxing at school and I can box quite well. I like the sports book that you sent me as well. It is quite funny in some places.

Love from
Douglas (dictated to Mommy)

Dear Bill,

As you can see from the foregoing, the presents arrived in good shape. The boys were so impatient that I hadn't the heart to keep them waiting till Christmas, but let them open them as soon as they got home yesterday.[46] I had to pay thirty bob in customs and purchase tax on Doug's, which I consider a gyp — next time better wrap things yourself and mark them *used*. But for some reason Davy's came through free, so I suppose I'm lucky. He has been glued to it since he came home, and has already decided he wants to be a doctor!

The Christmas festivities at the school were delightful. An accident on the railway line unfortunately delayed me so that I missed the first part, in which Davy acted in a play; but I came in time to see both of them perform in song-and-dance and carol numbers. The high spot, I thought, was the Boar's Head carol. Old Mr. Pooley, the headmaster (seventy if he's a day, but he's got a rather good baritone) did himself up in a traditional cook's outfit, tall white cap and all, and marched in carrying an enormous imitation boar's head and singing, with four very small candle-bearers following him! Doug was one of them, and looked very sweet.

They are both amazingly civilized. Yesterday, just after Davy had finished making tea, I accidentally knocked over the teapot and spilled it all. Whereupon, without a word of fuss, Davy cleaned up the mess and Doug brewed a new pot of tea; and when I apologized, "Never mind, Mummy. Everyone has accidents now and then!"

We shall be going to Oxford on the 30th for a week — would be more, but it's the week Jack's moving finally (I'm to superintend the Oxford end) and he has to be in Cambridge most of the holiday and correct a Fellowship exam. I'm lucky there *is* somewhere I can go; finances being what they are, we'd have no chance to get out of London otherwise. I do hope you can send an appreciable sum of money soon! School begins again on Jan. 17th, and I simply *must* have more money by then. As it is, the boys are doing without winter coats again; fortunately it's been quite warm. Rainy, of course, but they have mackintoshes for that.

I shall pass your cards on to Phyl. I thought you had her address; for future reference, it's 175 — now wait a minute; I'm not sure myself whether the numbers are for Howitt Rd. or Haverstock Hill. Let it go. She and Sel are quite well, but have very little energy, and are rather worried about

46. On December 16, 1954, Bill writes and says: "My love to the boys. Wish I could be with them this Christmas and every Christmas" (source: Wade).

Robin; not surprisingly, he copies their inertia and has few friends or out-side interests. He seems rather undeveloped and infantile for half-past-fourteen; but this may be partly because Davy and Doug are so mature. Anyhow, they get on well with him.

Merry Christmas and all that.

Yours,
Joy

Source: Wade

Hard Times

Letters 1955

To William Lindsay Gresham

14, Belsize Park
London, N.W.3
January 14, 1955

Dear Bill,

I suppose I'm a fool to go on being patient; any other woman would go to court.[1] I've always hoped you wouldn't force me to do that, and I shall continue to hope as long as I can. I have some reason to know you are not always scrupulously truthful, but I believe your account of your present difficulties is the truth — it's so characteristic! It wouldn't occur to you that getting a job and working at it would solve all your problems? How about your carnival connections — is there nothing doing there?

Anyhow, *we* are lunching on bread, salted sprats, and Spanish tangerines (sevenpence a pound, thank God, and very sweet) and praying for a kindhearted editor. My book, I am told, has sold about 1425 copies, nowheres near enough to pay its advance. The boys have both been rather ill — there's a virus flu going around — but seem better now; they return to school on Monday, and what the hell am I supposed to do about paying

---

1. On January 6, 1955, Bill writes Joy about how hard a time he is having selling anything he has written and about how broke he and Renée are. He also says: "I got a nice note from Davy in which he said he is going to be a Mohammedan. Ah, youth! Better yet he should be a Mohammedan than a Church of Christ Saved and Sanctified Holiness of the Signs Following Congregation" (source: Wade).

their fees? It's a lucky thing English clothes are durable; the only things I've had to replace are a few pairs of socks and one sweater, and I knitted that.

They appreciate your postcards; but surely you realize they are old enough now to know that pretty picture[s] and fancy toys don't make up for unpaid bills. If you want them to go on being fond of you, give them some reason.

At the moment we've had one of our rare snowfalls — about four inches of soft, powdery snow, just enough to make everything radiantly beautiful in the sun. I've run into an Australian parson, here with wife and kids, who has taken us driving to Canterbury and Windsor — mainly, I think, because he's dying for an introduction to Jack. To hear him tell it, Australia is a paradise of high wages and jobs for all, the sort of coming country that ours was fifty or a hundred years ago; I wonder if he's right?

Regards to the family —

Joy

Source: Wade

To Robert and Jackie Jackson

14, Belsize Park
London, N.W.3
Jan. 19, 1955

Dear Bob and Jackie,

Good to hear from you and the whopping big girl child again; she looks plump and merry and more like a duckling than a gazelle. My affairs march not too badly. My book hasn't sold much in the States, but I never thought it would; it's not out here yet. The European Press magazine folded, not surprisingly, after five issues. I stayed there several weeks doing job printing, but it was a hopeless affair — made barely enough to pay two operators and the rent, nothing to pay off its debts. I left in August, when I went to stay in Oxford for a month, and when I came back *alles war kaput.*

Since then I've been doing research for the life of Mme. de Maintenon that Major Lewis started me on — I've got a pile of his most cherished books here to work my way through, and it's going very well. (Financially I'm keeping my head above water; Bill's not much use, but it turns out that my parents have thousands stashed away in banks and insurance accounts and are willing to hand over some of it. They came over to visit me in November and were very helpful.)

I started my Mme. de M. research in Lewis' rooms in Magdalen, where the books were then, in August, while he was in Ireland; much to the appalled surprise of two would-be gate-crashing female tourists, who sneaked into the place one day, no doubt hoping for a glimpse of the great man, and weren't too pleased to get me instead! I wish I could have photographed their faces as their eyes traveled from the "Mr. C. S. Lewis" over the door to me, and back again. Even in slacks I don't think I looked the part.

Lewis has now moved to Magdalene, Cambridge. I visited for a week over New Year's and helped a bit with the move; though aside from dusting books and buying sheets and so on, I wasn't allowed to do much. Poor lamb, he was suffering all the pangs and qualms of a new boy going to a formidable school — went around muttering, "Oh, what a fool I am! I had a good home and I left!" and turning his mouth down at the corners most pathetical. He always makes his distresses into a joke, but of course there's a genuine grief in leaving a place like Magdalen after thirty years; rather like a divorce, I imagine. Even *I* feel that I shall miss those cloisters, after a mere dozen visits! The Cambridge college is nothing like so beautiful, though pleasant enough; and Lewis has just written to say that they only get *one* glass of port after dinner, instead of Magdalen's three. Ichabod.[2]

In spite of the move, he keeps working as hard as usual; has finished his autobiography — I've got the last chapters here now and must set my wits to work on criticism. I think it a first-rate job, though it will disappoint those who are curious for personal details; it is really chiefly the story of his conversion.

We're all looking forward to the Walshes' visit. Love all round —

Joy   *Source: Bodleian*

2. This letter has not survived.

To William Lindsay Gresham

14, Belsize Park
London, N.W.3
January 24, 1955

Dear Bill,

I have been ill with flu, or would have acknowledged your cheque sooner. It was a great relief to get it; it arrived just as I came home from seeing the boys off to school. Had it been a little sooner, I'd have gotten them overcoats — as it is, they have only their mackintoshes, and though that's usually enough for an English winter the weather *this* year is something special. There's been quite a bit of snow, and there are floods everywhere now that it's thawing. But the weirdest thing was a ten-minute smog that darkened the sky to midnight black around noon on Sunday; it looked like the end of the world, and the boys yelled, "Atom bomb!"

Glad you've sold something; hope to God there's more to come, for this can't go on much longer. I ought to enter Davy for public school, but haven't been able to spare the money. I'm trying to work as fast as possible myself; my book looks like being a humdinger, and if I can grind out a few chapters and an outline I ought to be able to sell it. But the research takes forever.

As for news, heard from Chad Walsh the other day. He and Eva and the two oldest are planning to come to England next summer. He's been doing research for Adlai Stevenson's recent speeches and is terrifically impressed with Stevenson.[3] He's also sent me his latest volume of verse. I think it's better than the earlier ones, but I wish he wouldn't mix his styles with newspaper slang, arithmetic, and what have you, bursting into his serious moments.

Got the reviews of my own book, all very good, but only from small local papers and church magazines, damn it.[4] The English edition won't be out till next month.

3. Adlai E. Stevenson (1900-1965) was the Democratic nominee for president of the United States of America in 1952 and 1956; he lost both times to Dwight D. Eisenhower.

4. For a sample of the reviews of *Smoke on the Mountain*, see L. R. Miller, review of Joy Davidman's *Smoke on the Mountain*, *Library Journal* 79 (September 1, 1954): 1496; review of Joy Davidman's *Smoke on the Mountain*, *Christian Century* 72 (February 16, 1955): 72; review of Joy Davidman's *Smoke on the Mountain*, *Journal of Bible and Religion* 23 (April 1955): 157;

Phyl and Sel [Haring] are both at tricky stages in their analyses and shooting off sparks. I wish I could believe that analysis ever did any permanent good to anyone, but so far I've seen only the contrary. Any[one] who goes to a psychiatrist ought to have his head examined.

The boys had a bright idea just before they left here; wanted to see if you could really shoot the inside bolt of a door by standing outside and pulling a string. Result: locked-room mystery in our only john. It hadn't occurred to them that it would be a problem to *open* it again! Finally the housekeeper's husband busted the door down; no damage but a bolt pulled loose, much to our relief.

I've been told that Senator McCarthy has resigned his seat. Is that straight? We also hear much about the terrific prosperity of the U.S.; wish some of it would come our way.

Yours,
Joy

Source: Wade

To William Lindsay Gresham

14, Belsize Park
London, N.W.3
February 8, 1955

Dear Bill,

Thanks for the scratch, only I wish there were more.[5] Lookie, cookie, even if I could live myself on $100 a month (and I'm already on a lunchless, beerless diet) what am I supposed to do with the boys? Drown them? They got laws against that in this country! Besides, I've put a lot of

---

review of Joy Davidman's *Smoke on the Mountain, Kirkus* 22 (September 15, 1954): 661; review of Joy Davidman's *Smoke on the Mountain, Saturday Review of Literature* 38 (March 5, 1955): 31; review of Joy Davidman's *Smoke on the Mountain, Times Literary Supplement* [London], May 6, 1955, p. iii.

5. On February 3, 1955, Bill writes Joy and sends another check, telling her: "*Sports Il-lustrated* finally paid off for the piece I sold them in September." He adds that he is considering doing lectures, but doesn't like the contractual side of things. He describes a recent free lecture in Miami he gave where he demonstrated fire eating as the "Human Volcano — taking a sip of lighter fluid and spraying it at the torch with a satisfying 'Whoom!' Scared the pants off some of the old folks but they seemed to like it" (source: Wade).

effort into bringing them this far and I think they're quite nice boys; it would be a pity to give them back to the Indians now!

I went down to see them on Sunday and they took me for a walk. The day has finally come when they can walk the legs off Mommy, who comes toiling along behind. It was a brief stroll of three to four miles over Surrey hillsides, all green, with snowdrops coming up and the sun shining. We're having heavenly weather here now, and it looks like an early spring. Average temperature 50 to 60 degrees — and I see in the papers it's been 18 below zero at Poughkeepsie!

We went to see the church they attend; it's a tiny 12th century Saxon building, as Davy explained to me — but he pointed out that bits of it were Elizabethan. He's quite an architecture enthusiast. Both of them have a keen sense of landscape and keep showing me special good bits. England seems to have that effect on people; but of course they were trained to it even in the States.

Davy is the delight of his English master; his essays and stories are extraordinarily good. I've got one here I'm planning to type up; when I do, I'll send you a copy. What with reading for my own book, and earning a little extra dough by typing Jack's new book [*Surprised by Joy*] for him (he insists on paying) I haven't a moment just yet.

Went up to Cambridge, ostensibly to help Jack buy a hearthrug, which took five minutes; and really to spend the day, talk, walk, and drink. (Also eat like a horse.) He has now got over the awful moment of leaving his old college and is bubbling with delight in his new one — and why not? Three large rooms, a private bath, and (so far) two hours' work a week! The professors are the aristocracy of an English university; they don't even have to talk to students unless they want to!

Bernice [Baumgarten] tells me my book has been put on the Protestant Lenten Reading List; sounds like an ambiguous sort of honour — prescribed as a penance! I should worry; they should only buy it!

Hope you're over the virus by now and have some luck with the lecturing. Has Renée got another job?

Yours,
Joy

Source: Wade

To William Lindsay Gresham

14, Belsize Park
London, N.W.3
February 25, 1955

Dear Bill,

Every bit helps, of course, but what the hell *is* going on? We hear that the U.S. has got over its temporary recession and things are booming more than ever (they certainly are here) and I don't understand what has happened to your markets. I suppose living in Florida has something to do with it. Only the real top-notchers can afford to live so far from the publishing world; remember how you used to complain that Staatsburg was too far out?

Unless matters improve in the next couple of months, I shall have to get hold of a lawyer again, I suppose. Lord knows I don't want to. But what choice are you giving me?

I'll send you a copy of the English edition of *Smoke*, with Jack's preface.[6] Didn't know you wanted one, or I'd have done it before.

Do you remember whether both the boys have had mumps, or was it only Davy? There are three cases at their school, and all who haven't had it are quarantined. Very dull for them; the weather's been frightful for two weeks, continual snow and cold. Doug writes me that you have sent them "very pathetic letters." As I haven't seen the letters, I don't know what he means; but please don't do anything to upset them; I want to give them as much security as possible in circumstances like ours. I have told them to write to you.

Two weeks ago I took them to the Tower for the day (it was a free day) at their request; they lingered over every stone, every sword, every suit of armour. Poor Doug lamented that it made him feel envious — there was a boy's suit of armour that would just have fitted him, and he wanted it very much! I'd be glad if I could buy him an overcoat, let alone a steel suit.

Picked up the paper the other day and saw a dispatch from Clinton Corners, N.Y.; a Mrs. Hayes had been arrested and brought to trial for refusing to get off the party line when the fire warden was trying to report a

---

6. *Smoke on the Mountain: An Interpretation of the Ten Commandments* (London: Hodder & Stoughton, 1955).

fire! There ought to be a short story in that somewhere. By the way, I heard from Grace Kelly a while back; she had a baby by Bud and I believe they're finally managing to get married.

I've finished typing Jack's book and am back at work on my own; Bernice thinks it's a good idea and will try to sell it on three or four chapters. I wish it weren't such slow going — mountains of research still to do.

Regards to your family.

Yours,

Joy

Source: Wade

To William Lindsay Gresham

14, Belsize Park
London, N.W.3
March 16, 1955

Dear Bill,

Thanks for the $100; I was very glad it came when it did. The boys had a day out and came back here with me just in time to find it, and it reassured them a great deal. They are now old and sensible enough to understand the meaning of money; in fact, I fear they understand only too well and are worrying more than they ought to at their ages, Davy in particular. They both give up things they want willingly; and when I took them to tea at a rather nice-looking restaurant Davy hung back and said, "Won't it be too expensive?" He was relieved to discover it was only 2/6.

I'm glad you're able to get some money out of articles. The s[cience]-f[iction] boys here report the same thing — bottom dropped out of the U.S. magazine market. The market here is still good; what you hear about British prosperity is not exaggerated; there's a real boom going on. Manpower shortage, new building everywhere, meat on the table — this morning's paper complains that people are no longer willing as they were in pre-war days to eat frozen imported meat in the off-season; they want the fresh home-grown expensive article the whole year round. There are five times as many cars on the road as there were in '52, and I see a surprising number of big streamlined American-style ones in spite of the price of petrol. Not that any of this does me any good — quite the contrary!

I have managed — thanks partly to Jack — to get through this school term. The next one begins May 4th and I *must* have some more money by then for fees. Do your damndest.

I finished the index of Warnie's new book for him — he's in a nursing home with fibrositis and flu — and his publisher was so pleased with the job I did on it that she asked if I would do indexes professionally and said she'd send me some now and then. They pay from 15 to 25 pounds apiece for them, and I can do one in a week or little more if I try; so it will be very worth while, if anything comes of it. Keep your fingers crossed.

Was at Cambridge last week, delivering the ms. of Jack's book, and had E. M. Forster pointed out to me — a mousy-looking little old man.[7] Jack is already deep in literary controversy there with him and others. His inaugural address has been printed, commented on in magazines, etc; and is being put on the BBC's Third Programme (i.e. the cultural one). Meanwhile about five of his books have blossomed out in paper-backs: *Screwtape* with a highly flattering photo of him on the back cover which has already provoked at least one love-letter from an unknown female, praising his good looks. He debated whether to answer: "Dear Madam, the photograph is not at all like me." But on my advice filed the letter in the wastebasket instead.

For the first time in his life he has plenty of leisure to write — no pupils, no exams, no college meetings; just a nice quiet room and all the time in the world. So the inevitable has happened; he's dried up. He is quite worried about it, and was relieved to know it's the usual thing in our trade. I imagine, though, he'll be turning out fiction soon again.

The boys are very well, and have stood the cold weather without too much discomfort — real cold, heavy snow and so on; thank God it seems over now. Davy has got his glasses smashed beyond repair, fighting; according to the headmaster, his sharp tongue gets him into many battles, and he never can remember to take his glasses off first. He needs stronger ones, anyhow; I'll get them in the holidays. I've been rather ill with an abscessed ear, excruciatingly painful; but it's healed now. Back to *[Queen] Cinderella:* I hope to get the first chapters written soon.

Regards to your family, and I hope Renée's airline [job] holds out.

Yours,
Joy   *Source: Wade*

---

7. E. M. Forster (1879-1970) was an important twentieth-century novelist, best known for *The Longest Journey* (1907), *A Room with a View* (1908), *Howards End* (1910), and *A Passage to India* (1924).

To William Lindsay Gresham

The Kilns
Kiln Lane
Headington Quarry
March 23, 1955

Dear Bill,

Gee, thanks; this month, for once you're less than $100 behind![8] And what with eating at Jack's expense this week, I feel quite solvent. We're all hard at work here; the house is practically a book factory. Warnie's deep in the life of Gramont (dashing 17th century bloke), I'm putting Mme. M. together, and Jack has started a new fantasy — for grownups.[9] His methods of work amaze me. One night he was lamenting that he couldn't get a good idea for a book. We kicked a few ideas around till one came to life. Then we had another whiskey each and bounced it back and forth between us. The next day, without further planning, he wrote the first chapter! I read it and made some criticisms (feels quite like old times); he did it over and went on with the next.[10] What I'd give to have his energy!

He only writes *half* the day; the other half, he answers letters and writes lectures, which he doesn't count, and by the time *I* get up in the morning (about 8) he has like as not hauled the ashes out of all the stoves, dumped them outside, and gone off to early service. I begin to see the force of your contention that what a writer chiefly needs is a strong back!

I'm afraid you're only too right about the new reading public — after all, fewer and fewer Americans are actually *learning* to read. I think I told you they're giving remedial reading courses in *colleges?* There is an *educated* reading public, too, but it's smaller, and I imagine it's going to get more and more highbrow, until the division between the learned and unlearned

8. On March 17, 1955, Bill sends Joy a letter and a check, recounting the situation for writers like himself, noting that paperback pulp appears to be the way to go now (source: Wade).

9. C. S. Lewis, *Till We Have Faces: A Myth Retold* (London: Geoffrey Bles, 1956).

10. Increasingly Davidman is serving as a collaborator and shadow editor for the books Lewis is writing during this period. Lewis writes a friend on April 2, 1955, about his writing of *Till We Have Faces;* see *The Collected Letters of C. S. Lewis, Volume 3: Narnia, Cambridge, and Joy, 1950-1963,* ed. Walter Hooper (London: HarperCollins, 2006), p. 590; hereafter CL, 3.

is back where it was. Great disgust here over the publication of the Yalta papers. What the hell does the State Department think it's doing?[11]

Smoke on the Mountain has just got a rave review from the *Church Times,* the leading C. of E. newspaper — ought to help![12] I remember Nick [Renée's father] as a very nice guy. Regards to Renée. The boys are well; they'll be home for a month's holiday next week.

Yours,

Joy

Source: Wade

To William Lindsay Gresham

14, Belsize Park
London, N.W.3
April 11, 1955

Dear Bill,

In the general rush and scurry of term-end I omitted to acknowledge your last cheque for $50, which arrived two weeks ago. Look, my fine feathered friend, I appreciate your efforts, but this does not make it possible to *eat* on them. Even in England I can't bring up two boys on $1800 a year, which is about the rate of your payments. My parents have just stopped by on their way back to the States and replaced the boys' worn-out and outgrown clothes, thank Heaven, so at least I've an outfit I can send them back to school in, if I can pay the school! They also bought me a pair of new shoes and some underwear, those I had being composed largely of holes. And while they were here we ate lunch. But they're gone now, and the new term starts May 5th, and in the meantime I've got to

---

11. Davidman is referring to a series of agreements and compromises regarding a number of important issues related to the conclusion of World War II reached between Franklin Roosevelt, Winston Churchill, and Joseph Stalin during a conference held in Yalta, February 4-11, 1945. When details of their agreements and compromises became public, many people were outraged. For example, while Roosevelt "won" the argument for the creation of the United Nations, it came at the price of acquiescence to Stalin's demands that large sections of central Europe come under Communist control.

12. On April 6, 1955, C. S. Lewis wrote Dorothy L. Sayers about *Smoke on the Mountain:* "I hope you've read Joy Davidman's *Smoke on the Mountain,* an ex-Communist, Jewess-by-race, convertite, on the X Commandments and, I think, really good" (CL, 3, p. 596).

feed the cubs, no? So what do we get? Touching postcards about parakeets yet!

Not that the boys don't like postcards; they appreciate them very much. But they always look to see if there's a cheque in the same mail, and nothing you can do or say makes them feel so good as the knowledge that there's a bit more cash on hand. After all, children have to count on their fathers for something more than sweet words, and if you want them to love you (I know you do) you have to *be* a father, not just sound like one. In short, it's *not* a good idea to write that you miss them so much that you can't work. It frightened them considerably.

They are now, I think, getting old enough to read somewhat longer letters, particularly Davy. They find your handwriting a bit difficult; could you print your postcards? Their school reports have just arrived. Doug is second in his form and doing very well all round; even his math is improving. I think he has got the idea now and will forge ahead; my mother worked hard teaching him his tables while she was here and reported good progress. Davy is not doing quite as well as he was, largely because he is the lowest in the form in math, though first in English and second in history, as well as fourth in Latin and French. His great weakness is a distaste for hard, dull, patient work; he is brilliant as long as a subject interests him, but sees no reason for grinding away when it doesn't. Dates, arithmetic tables, French verbs — he rejects the lot. I hope this is just schoolboyish impatience and that he will eventually learn to take pains. But I have come to suspect that these quirks of character are not "neuroses" but innate and hereditary traits. Perhaps we can control them with practice and determination, but I no longer believe in a specious magic that can remove them painlessly.

I am, of course, unable to do more than scraps of reading for my book now that the boys are at home; at the moment Doug and Robin are walking around the room with rusty springs tied onto their shoes to give a bouncing effect. The real effect is that they fall on their faces at every third step. These month-long holidays will be the death of me!

Yours,
Joy

The boys have also written to you. *Source: Wade*

To William Lindsay Gresham

14, Belsize Park
London, N.W.3
[mid-April, 1955]

Dear Bill,

Here you are.[13] They seem to think it's a good book over here, and my publisher was moved to give me £10 expense money — so I can feed the boys for a couple of weeks! I wish it would *move you* to similar and greater efforts. I'm just about fed up, my friend.

Yours,
Joy

Source: Wade

To William Lindsay Gresham

14, Belsize Park
London, N.W.3
April 29, 1955

Dear Bill,

I dunno whether to thank you for the $100 or cuss you out because it's too little and too late, but considering the tale of woe you relate, I won't cuss you out.[14] Too bad about Bobby's tonsils; but a good thing to get it over with. He'll probably put on ten pounds in the couple of months afterward; I've seen that happen many times. I hope Renée gets a job quickly, but I'm pretty sure she will — she's got what it takes, adaptability and resourcefulness.

We were all pretty desperate a couple of weeks back — I was down ill with some complication of my period (I hope *that* doesn't happen again; it was very painful) and Doug wrote you a letter on his own hook which I suppose you've received. But as soon as I got up I went round to my publisher, who came through with £10 for expenses and a further £25 through

13. Enclosed was a copy of the English edition of *Smoke on the Mountain*.
14. On April 23, 1955, Bill writes Joy and encloses a check. He tells Joy that Renée has lost her airline job and gives an update on the health of Renée's children. He also confesses he is having trouble getting any of his ideas down on paper (source: Wade).

my agent. Unfortunately I'm already into [debt to] the agent for that, or most of it; but the £10 pulled us through.

I've sent you a copy of *Smoke* which ought to arrive soon. It's doing fairly well here — has sold 3000 already, mostly on the basis of Jack's preface and some extraordinarily good reviews in church publications. There ought to be a little money in it eventually, though since most of the sales are paperbacks it won't be much. But there's a prospect of my getting some writing to do for a church newspaper. I'll never get rich out of that market, but every bit helps — and may lead to more. What I'd like is lecturing or broadcasting, but no chance of that yet.

Pass on my good wishes to Vigie and Ann, won't you? Jay Marshall hasn't turned up at all. Chad and Eva Walsh and the two older girls are coming over in June, but they'll only be in London a week.

If you ever feel it would be any help, don't hesitate to consult me on any plot you're having trouble with, and we can maul it over all night by air-mail! I don't kid myself in these matters — whatever my talents as an independent writer, my *real* gift is as a sort of editor-collaborator like Max Perkins, and I'm happiest when I'm doing something like that.[15] Though I can't write one-tenth as well as Jack, I can tell him how to write more like himself! He is now about three-quarters of the way through his new book (what I'd give for that energy!) and says he finds my advice indispensable. Well, it's a very suitable gift for a woman.

Please do whatever you can toward the boys' school fees! I ought to have paid them already, but they'll have to wait.

Excuse please, I gotta go buy a herring and some salami for lunch. Ten bob covers our lunches for the whole week!

Yours,
Joy

Source: Wade

On May 5, 1955, David sent his father a brief newsy letter. At the bottom Joy added:

P.S. You can't imagine the labour that has gone into these few lines. Both boys are perfectionists and won't send you anything that isn't neat; Davy has done this over once, and Doug tried one twice and finally tore it up in

---

15. Maxwell E. Perkins (1884-1947) was a gifted editor, assisting in critically important ways many writers, including F. Scott Fitzgerald, Ernest Hemingway, and Thomas Wolfe.

tears, though I told him you'd like to hear from him no matter how messy it was. They like getting your cards and letters a good deal, were particularly interested in your fire-eating adventures, but they don't seem capable of adequate answers yet. Perhaps it would help if you wrote reassuring them about their letters.[16]

Joy   *Source: Wade*

On May 19, 1955, Bill writes Joy a very lengthy letter recounting his lack of money, the death of Nick Rodriguez (Renée's father), Renée's finding a job, and his opportunity to begin working for a newspaper company. He admits that he has never really tried to get a job: "It's hard for me to get a job for a reason I never thought of until I tried it — if I am not a writer or editor I am just a 45-year-old, uneducated and untrained man! All my published stuff cuts no ice on regular newspapers and doesn't impress publicists who look for a man with a long record of successful publicity jobs behind him. I have never really stopped looking but have had to turn to and beat the typewriter just to survive."

Bill also tells Joy of Renée's distressing situation after her father's death: Renée had been born in Cuba and had come to America with her parents when they immigrated to America; thus she wasn't a U.S. citizen. After her father's death this fact came out, so she had to fly to Cuba and go through the process of becoming an American citizen.

Finally, Bill compliments Joy on Smoke on the Mountain: *"It really is a contribution to the times. I hope lots of people buy it, read it and give it to their friends. It is the sort of book one wants to circulate." He expresses great interest in Zen Buddhism.*

Renée also writes in this letter, telling Joy how hard Bill is trying to come up with more money. Essentially, they are broke.

Joy, don't think for one moment that either Bill or I tend to minimize your circumstances. I know it's frightening not knowing where the next meal is coming from. I know how desperate you must feel. I wish I was all-wise and all-knowing and could give a simple solution. The only thing I can come up with is for us to keep trying, each and every one of us, to do what we can to help so at least the boys don't have to suffer. Bill continues to

16. Bill's letters to his sons were almost always encouraging and upbeat; he especially praised them whenever they wrote him.

*write and do the best he can. Of course, I am no help to him along those
lines. I have my limitations and fully realize them. I have not written to
you before about this because frankly I did not know how you would feel
about hearing from me, but I felt that at this point I should reassure you
that we are doing the best we can.*   Source: Wade

To William Lindsay Gresham

14, Belsize Park
London, N.W.3
May 23, 1955

Dear Bill,

I'm enclosing a letter for Renée; very sorry to hear of Nick's death. I
don't suppose there'll be any real difficulty about Renée's getting natural-
ised; the amazing thing is that it went unnoticed so long. You can't do that
over here — they accept nobody except refugees for permanent residence.
Was Bobby in the same position, or was he born in New York?

I'm glad that prospects for the future are better. I appreciate only too
well your situation as an untrained man; an untrained woman of forty is in
the same fix and worse. I've tried for jobs here, but no go — and probably
the Home Office wouldn't let me work anyway; there's a whole rigmarole
you have to go through to do it legally. Fortunately my publishers here are
eager for my two new books (I dreamed up another religious one called
The Seven Deadly Virtues half an hour before I had to talk to the publisher)
and are talking about giving me a contract and advances on just outlines.
I've got *SDV* outlined already, and am working on the other. They're
dreadfully stingy here; if I get 100 pounds all told I'll be lucky; but I've
learned to stretch a pound note until Britannia screams.

Jobs of your sort aren't plentiful anywhere, but New York and perhaps
Los Angeles would be more promising than Florida. As for fiction, etc.
my offer of help stands. I find it's easier to sell books, by far, than magazine
stuff, and even if they're flops it's worth it — after all, *Monster Midway*
paid $2500 for your two months' sweating, not to mention what you sold
the stories for first. The science fiction market, I learn, is dying of surfeit.
But how about a novel in the Florida circus setting, or Miami Beach, etc.?
By now you must be lousy with local colour.

Or how about, a book popularizing the Zen technique? Inspirational stuff sells like hot cakes, and I'm sure your old Technique of Courage idea could be developed into a beauty with all you've learned since.

The boys are well and happy, and I try to keep them from worrying about money, though it's not often possible when I have to refuse them everything they want. I tried to stop them from writing to you for money but they insisted they wanted to. I wish you *would* write them — and don't send expensive presents; a trifle will do to reassure them of your interest, and they'd rather you sent cash than anything elaborate. They are rather bitter about the situation, even Doug, and they feel you don't really care.

Taxes *here* are frightful too and they're even coming down on me for income tax — they've got a hope! I hope you are at least deducting the payments you make me on your tax return.

TV here (I often watch it on Phyl's screen) doesn't seem too different from the theatre. They use stage plays very little changed, and quite a lot of Shakespeare. As you say — camera with no long shots, and simple sets.

If I ever have any spare dough I will have the boys photographed and send you a copy of the result. Davy looks more like you every year, though his glasses give him a rather solemn intellectual look.

We are going to borrow Jack's house again in August, so at least there will be a decent holiday for them. I do hope things work out better.

Yours,
Joy

P.S. *Argosy* — the British one — quotes a bit of *Monster Midway* this month; the "OK, can you sing?" passage.   *Source: Wade*

To Renée Rodriguez Gresham

14, Belsize Park
London, N.W.3
May 23, 1955

Dear Renée,

I appreciate your writing to me, and I hope you'll feel free to do it whenever you like. I'm very sorry to hear of your father's death; it must have been a dreadful experience for you, combined with the mix-up over your citizenship. Astonishing that that was never found out before. One thing you *can* be grateful for is that you were reconciled to Nick in time; it must have meant a lot to him.

I can understand what your financial difficulties are like, and it seems to me you're carrying more than your share of the burden. As long as you and Bill keep me informed, and as long as Bill really tries, I'm willing to lean over backward to make things easier for you both. You can imagine that when a month or so goes by and I don't hear, and my money runs out, I naturally get desperate and think that I *must* consult a lawyer. But I don't want to do that, and won't unless I am absolutely forced to. I don't suppose it would do any good anyhow!

I needn't tell you that it isn't skipping my own meals that I mind. (Not that I do; I've discovered ways and means of making an adequate lunch for about a dime.) The important thing is the boys and their education. They are very good about doing without pleasures and luxuries — bless their hearts, they keep urging me to buy more for myself and less for them — but after all there *are* necessities which they can't do without.

I've got some prospects of selling my work over here — they don't pay much; for instance, one magazine has offered me 9 guineas for 2000 words — but every bit helps, and I'm doing all I can.

I'm glad you have another job. Perhaps things will take a turn for the better now; the run of bad luck has certainly lasted long enough!

Yours,
Joy

I enclose one of Davy's letters as a specimen of him at his best.

Source: Wade

To William Lindsay Gresham

14, Belsize Park
London, N.W.3
June 2, 1955

Dear Bill,

Boy, what a pleasant surprise *that* was.[17] I went and treated myself to a glass of beer on the strength of it. I needed something to cheer me up too; I've got to make a speech next week, so of course I pick *this* time to develop something like a small boil inside one nostril. My nose is swole up like Cyrano's, and hurts worse than his ever did.

Yes, the boys *are* in school; and with this blasted railway strike on, I can't get down to see them. Lord, what a racket the unions are over here! What *this* is about is that in the last wage raise the other railway workers got a larger proportional increase than the engineers and firemen. So the engineers' honour is wounded. So they gotta strike to keep proportionally ahead of their colleagues. So the colleagues say that if the engineers get *this* raise they'll strike for another. So railway fares are going up this week. And the government can't step in as it does with us, because the railways have been nationalized already. Shouldn't be surprised if the whole thing had been cooked up to embarrass poor Eden.[18]

Most freight is still moved by rail here, too; they haven't our sort of freight highways at all. What a mess!

Davy has been a trifle ill this week with indigestion, but is now better. Everything else seems to be going well. We're having a real summer this year; the last three days have had moments when I was almost uncomfortably warm! The flowers are even more fabulous than last year; and I notice the almond trees are loaded with almonds, little green fuzzy things exactly like peaches when they're young; but I don't suppose they'll ripen.

Hodder and Stoughton here are going to take my *Seven Deadly Virtues* book and I'll get 100 pounds advance.[19] Even minus agent's fees it'll be a big help — that is, if I can get the tax people to let me keep it! It

---

17. On May 30, 1955, Bill writes Joy and includes a check and tells her he hopes for more to come (source: Wade).

18. Robert Anthony Eden (1897-1977) was the British prime minister from 1955 to 1957.

19. This book was never published.

took them three months to pay the advance for *Smoke* — I hope they're a bit quicker this time.

I finished an outline of *Queen Cinderella* too — a mere 5000 words long — and sent it out. Keep your fingers crossed!

Hope you have some luck with the job hunting; and I'm glad the carnival mine still has some ore in it. Regards to Renée.

Yours,
Joy

Source: Wade

To William Lindsay Gresham

14, Belsize Park
London, N.W.3
July 11, 1955

Dear Bill,

Herewith a letter Doug asked me to forward. In case any of it needs translation, may I say that "Absolutely wizard!" is the highest praise a British schoolboy knows, even higher than "Super!" His letter to me is also full of constellations and contains the information that Betelgeuse is pronounced Beetle Juice. Unfortunate, if true.

What's happening with you?[20] I am still living in expectation of my contract and cheque from Hodder and Stoughton, blast them. They explain the delay as due to last month's railway strike; God knows how or why. I'll be having the boys back here again on July 25th, so do your stuff as soon as possible. Thank Heaven, anyhow, Jack pays on time — I've just collected for typing his last book [*Surprised by Joy*].

We're having a real Heat Wave here — that is, it's often 75 degrees or even 80 and I have several times felt slightly too warm, particularly after walking two miles in the sun. I'm just back from a week at Oxford, and the countryside is beautiful beyond belief. We went swimming in the Thames at Godstow, accompanied by one swan and a whole flock of geese. There was a pub just across the way, and that's the first time I've ever tried swim-

20. On July 9, 1955, Bill writes (from Hialeah, FL) to Joy and explains why there is no check. Renée has lost her job, and they are broke again. He promises to send money as soon as he gets some (source: Wade).

ming with a quart of beer sloshing about in my inside. Improves the technique, if anything.

Macmillan, drat them, has turned down the synopsis of my *Queen Cinderella,* and so has H[odder] and S[toughton]. Looks as if I'll have to write it first. Macmillan seems to be going slightly nuts. They dillied and dallied over Jack's autobiography until his agent sold it to Harcourt Brace instead; whereupon they went wild and bombarded him with letters and telegrams, alternately accusing him of disloyalty and pleading that he was sacrificing his own best interests; finally some damn fool, forgetting the time difference, woke him up at 1:30 a.m. with a phone call to the same tune! Needless to say, it didn't work.

Regards to Renée and the kids. Hope all is going smoothly. How did Bobby's tonsil operation work out?

Yours,
Joy

Source: Wade

Davidman not only typed the manuscript for Surprised by Joy *but also served as an editorial consultant. On June 23, 1955, Lewis wrote his publisher, Jocelyn Gibbs, about needed corrections to the galley proofs of* Surprised by Joy, *advising Gibbs to get in touch with "Mrs. Gresham" for the quickest way of identifying the needed corrections (see CL, 3, pp. 622–23). On June 24, 1955, Gibbs writes:*

Dear Mrs. Gresham,

I understand from Dr. Lewis that you corrected a proof of his book Surprised by Joy, *and I am now writing to you at his suggestion as I think you may be able to help over one point which has arisen.*

Unfortunately the "official" proof has now gone back to the printer and it would delay matters for him to send it all the way back here from Somerset, where he operates. Now, Dr. Lewis thinks you will remember some correction two-thirds of the way through the book and I imagine that it was something fairly important. You will realize that I am rather at a disadvantage because the proof in which he had embodied both yours and his corrections is, as I say, down at the printer's. But if you could tell me the nature of the correction two-thirds of the way through the book I should be most grateful as Dr. Lewis thinks it may have been omitted from the printer's proof copy. I could then telephone the printer and make sure it has duly been made.

*If it would simplify matters for you to ring me up please do as I shall be
here on Monday for all the week. The only thing is that the matter is rather
urgent as we are waiting to go ahead with printing the book.*

Source: Bodleian

To William Lindsay Gresham

14, Belsize Park
London, N.W.3
July 14, 1955

Dear Bill,

Sorry to hear such a tale of woe. You do seem to be having a run of
bad luck unusual even in your life. But is it entirely bad luck? Why concentrate on these pishteppel magazine features that take so much work
and pay so little, instead of at least occasionally doing some fiction?
There's no earthly reason why you can't write fiction all by yourself without my eagle eye peering over your shoulder; you did some of your best
stuff, like "Seven Days of the Fisherman," entirely by yourself. And look,
in the name of common sense stay away from the long-distance telephone!

Anyhow, I hope Renée gets another job soon and that your various articles go through all right. I can believe it's murderously hot in New York;
this week it's pretty damn hot right here! I had to go into the City yesterday to see my publisher and nearly fainted. According to the thermometer
it's only around 80, but it's so humid that it feels like much more than that
— one can hardly breathe.

My contract [for the *Seven Virtues* book] finally arrived this morning
and I've signed it and sent it back; so I suppose I'll get my blasted advance
after the publisher and agent have dawdled over it a few more weeks, and
the tax boys taken their huge bite! No luck so far on Mme. de Maintenon;
I'll probably have to write a chunk of it on spec.

At least my *Smoke* is still selling modestly but steadily here and has
got me a few contacts. I am now trying to write an improving article in
2000 words for the *Church Times*. I'm an old woman; better they should
give me a glass [of] beer!

I notice *Argosy* here keeps quoting bits out of *Monster Midway*. This week it was the knife-thrower and pawnbroker anecdote. I suppose they don't pay for it, but anyhow it's publicity.

Chad Walsh said he'd like to write to you and I gave him your address; but he's a very bad correspondent, about one in six months, so don't hold your breath till you hear from him. I'd a lovely time showing the Walshes around — they took me to a couple of plays, the only ones I've seen since I came, and bought me some swell dinners. Also we went to Oxford and Jack did the honours in approved tourist guide style: "On your right Queen's College founded by Boadicea." They bit, too![21]

The boys are thriving. I'll be seeing them on Saturday the 16th, and their term ends July 25th. August 1st we go to Oxford. Hope you can send some dough by then! Good luck.

Yours,

Joy

Source: Wade

To William Lindsay Gresham

14, Belsize Park
London, N.W.3
July 31, 1955

Dear Bill,

Well, better $50 than nothing; but for Heaven's sake do better than $50 soon! After paying our bill for the week, I'll have nothing in my bank account — if that much. I've just enough to get us to Oxford tomorrow. (No, I haven't sold my typewriter — it's gone to Oxford in the trunk.) My advance royalties cheque for £85 came — but didn't have a Bank of England O.K. and I couldn't deposit it; had to send it back till the tax people took their slice and passed the rest. [It will clear in] probably about two months. This is one time I miss American speed!

Otherwise all is well. The boys, with their usual luck, have made friends with an amiable lady at the hotel I rent my room from, and she's

21. The Queen's College was founded in 1341 by Robert de Eglesfield, a chaplain in the household of Queen Philippa, who named it in her honor. Apparently, however, a popular rumor traced the founding of the college to Queen Boadicea, who led her Iceni people in a brave but ultimately unsuccessful war against the Romans (A.D. 61-63). She is still hailed as one of Britain's greatest heroines.

been taking them all over London in taxis and buying them lunches. They've been to the British Museum, the Zoo, and an outdoor play in Regent's Park. This morning I took them out — for a walk on the Heath. They're now able to walk the legs off me. The boxing lessons at school have borne fruit too; you should see them sparring with each other. Davy's almost as good as Doug.

The other day in the library Davy was so deep in a book I couldn't drag him away till I promised to take it out for him. It turned out to be *Indian Philosophy* by Ramakristin. He's getting to be even more expert on the East than he was on snakes, and seems to be learning Arabic steadily himself. I don't know if I told you that he won the school essay prize this year? (A 10 s[hilling] token — we haven't spent it yet.) Very good going for the fourth form!

We leave for Oxford tomorrow morning, thank Heaven. It's very hot here, there are four babies all yowling downstairs, and fifth expected any minute, and the boys are getting tired of living on fish paste sandwiches. What I'd do without Jack's house to vacation in, I don't know. Glad to hear Renée's got a job; hope times will improve.

Yours,
Joy

Source: Wade

To William Lindsay Gresham

[The Kilns]
August 19, 1955

Dear Bill,

What in Heaven's name is happening to you? I can't help fearing that you are hitting the bottle again and going completely to pieces; otherwise I cannot understand why you should fail so completely to carry out your obligations. It is hard for me to believe that you can leave your children penniless as you are doing; Heaven knows I ought to know your character, but I didn't somehow expect that.

The boys are very worried themselves. It's not much use your sending sweet letters when you keep them destitute. I have had to give up my London place and find a cheaper one here; but we can't live on nothing at all. My stay at Jack's house will be over on September 2; I have to go back to

London for a few days and arrange about moving.[22] Well, I needn't go into details.

As for my own earnings — well, you think they're slow in the States, you ought to see them here! I've besieged my agents for the money — they were supposed to be getting the Bank of England O.K., a mere formality, but weeks and months have gone by and nothing's happened. Now I find that one of them's off on a vacation and the other has pneumonia!

I don't know what you're trying to do — force me to commit suicide or force me to bring action against you; I don't want to put you in jail, as you very well know, but you're certainly asking for it, and even my indulgence is not going to hold out forever.

In short, please send some money at once. And I don't mean pennies. You are now far short of the agreed sum. Sometimes I wonder how you can bear to live with yourself at all; but I suppose you can always find some rationalization or other.

Yours,
Joy

Source: Wade

To William Lindsay Gresham

The Kilns
August 26, 1955

Dear Bill,

Of course it is better for you to write me, no matter how dolefully, than to leave me without a word, wondering what makes and whether you've forgotten us altogether or dropped dead.[23] The real news is never as bad as the things I imagine. I wish I could write you some useful ideas; but the only thing I can think of is that the book market is certainly better than the mag-

---

22. See the P.S. of Lewis's letter of August 9, 1955, to Dorothy L. Sayers about this visit (CL, 3, pp. 640-41), and especially the P.S.S. written by Davidman.

23. On August 22, 1955, Bill writes Joy another lengthy letter of apology for not having any money to send, and not criticizing Joy for the tone of her previous letter. He writes: "You must realize that I am constantly concerned about you and the boys and am doing all I can." He plans to travel to New York to scare up some work. In a follow-up letter of August 24, 1955, he sends a brief note with a check enclosed, telling her that a story finally paid off (source: Wade).

azine one. With a new generation growing up illiterate, it's only natural for the magazines to collapse. But at the same time those who *can* read seem to be buying 25¢ books by the million. Didn't you have some good ideas for that field? I hear Ballantine and a few others are putting out originals.

I wish I could get to *my* writing, but this month with the boys and shopping and some cooking, it's impossible. Jack pays the food bills, or we'd go hungry. What makes shopping so hard is that you have to walk half a mile from here to get to shops or anything else, and half a mile back with a load of stuff. The one disadvantage of this house — otherwise it's perfect, even has a small pond in the back that we can swim in, and this year the weather's hot enough to need it. Some of the white stucco housing developments around here remind me irresistibly of Los Angeles when I see them shimmering in the heat haze on a cloudless day. Not what one expects of England at all! But of course everything is greener and juicier than L.A. — even after weeks of what they call drought here.

My new place — 10, Old High Street, Headington, Oxford — is right in the middle of a shopping district. I shall have to cook and clean myself, but there are some advantages — a garden, for one thing. I've got ten quid out of my agent and am picking up a little extra money typing — so of course the typewriter picks this moment to start sticking.

It is good news that you are staying in good shape and not drinking. I hope you don't need sleeping pills as much as you did either. My own health could be a lot better but at least I stay on my feet; there's nothing wrong with me that a good rest and plenty of dough wouldn't cure!

The boys are in fine shape. They still fight each other a lot, but it's improving. Both of them are very helpful to me — I don't know how I'd live otherwise. Doug has made a lot of friends around here and goes fishing in Jack's pond with them — the other day one of them brought in a huge perch which we ate for lunch! Davy has come out of his shell a lot and begun to climb trees and go fishing and play with other boys; a great relief. I was worried about his developing into too much of a bookworm. Jack endures the constant noise of children better than one would have thought possible and is rapidly learning the fatherly approach; he's giving Davy daily lessons in Latin. I imagine he'll be glad to escape to Ireland next week though!

The gypsies in Brooklyn sound like a good idea. There *was* a long article on them years ago, I think in the *New Yorker*, which was later reprinted in a book — was it the same guy who did McSorley's? I suppose you will have to go back to New York eventually; Florida sounds like a desert. Judging by reports of the hurricanes, the prospect isn't inviting.

Must go and feed the kids some breakfast now — not to mention myself. We're all confirmed kipper eaters, which is lucky, kippers being less than sixpence apiece.

Good luck to all.

Yours,
Joy

Source: Wade

To William Lindsay Gresham

[The Kilns]
August 28, 1955

Dear Bill,

Gott sei Dank[24] — my prayers musta been so strong they jumped clean over the Atlantic and bopped Ralph Daigh on the noggin. (I hope they raised a bump.) I was feeling pretty limp and dead yesterday morning, but it's amazing how I recovered when that cheque fell out of the envelope. The boys were equally pleased and relieved; Davy's first impulse was to ask for a bicycle, but almost at once he interrupted himself and said, "I don't really need it; get something you need." Actually a lot of it has to go on shoes and new school clothes. Jack was very pleased to hear you'd come through, but is insisting anyway on paying the school fees, and I can't afford to refuse. I hope it won't be necessary again.

The boys like their cards very much. Davy has sent you an answer.

I'm very glad to hear you're having a crack at television; it certainly seems to be the big thing these days. Even England has commercial television now.

Didn't know you were on such good terms with Rose [Renée's mother]! Ah, well, you can all sit around and agree in blaming your past quarrels on my well-known difficult disposition; I couldn't care less.

I can't write much more of this letter because a) I'm going for a walk with Jack, and b) the typewriter, as you can see, now has to be spaced by hand. Here goes another 30 bob!

24. God be thanked!

Weather here's lovely, between 75 and 80 degrees; we go swimming in Jack's mudhole, the old quarry pond. Davy has laid a rough causeway of bricks so I don't have to walk out through the mud. Jack is teaching Davy his Latin and Davy is studying the history of magic. Even Doug has suddenly developed into an ardent reader.

Yours,

Joy

Source: Wade

To William Lindsay Gresham

10, Old High Street
Headington
Oxford
September 17, 1955

Dear Bill,

Thanks for the cheque; it came very handy, as I've had a lot of expenses in moving into our new place. We are now at 10, Old High Street, Headington, Oxford; so please send future letters there, not to the Kilns.[25]

The new place is small but cozy — a great improvement over London, and the boys are delighted with it. We've got the use of the garden and I've already baked an American apple pie! We rode up on the moving van to save fare, much to the boys' delight and my discomfort — we shared the drivers' cab with 2 moving men and one large talkative Australian customer. A blistering hot day, too! But we all stood it well, even Sambo the cat who traveled in the van.

We now have a plum tree, as well as the apple trees, and a budgerigar which an acquaintance of Doug's sold us for ten bob — letting me in for buying a cage too, but I couldn't disappoint Doug; he was too thrilled. Later today I start making plum jam. Gosh it's good (even though tiring) to be cooking again. The crummy meals we were getting at our London flophouse had got me down.

25. Warren Lewis writes about this: "[After she moved to Headington] she and Jack began to see each other every day. It was now obvious what was going to happen" (*Brothers and Friends: The Diaries of Major Warren Hamilton Lewis*, ed. Clyde S. Kilby and Marjorie Lamp Mead [San Francisco: Harper & Row, 1982], p. 245).

I'm writing this in the garden of the White Hart, our nicest local pub — it's warm enough to sit outside, and you can bring the kids and give 'em ginger beer. The garden manages to look subtropical with fuchsias and aloes and tamarisks. Amazing what you can grow in this country. Our own garden (about the size of our Dutchess County living room) is more plebian — cabbages and runner beans and cabbage butterflies. This year they've been so thick that looking down a suburban street gave the illusion of looking at a snowfall of large, sparse flakes.

I'm glad to hear you are working on the novel. It ought to make a big difference.

Well, back to the grind. One week more and the boys go back to school — and I think I'll spend a day or two in bed! What with moving, cooking, mending clothes, shopping, feeding cats, feeding budgies, and making fires (we need them at night), I'm something less than fresh. Also I've broken a tooth — it hurts like hell and I haven't the time to find a dentist till the boys have gone off.

Sorry this letter's such a scribble — [I'm writing] on [an] uneven table. By the way, Doug has suddenly turned literary and is devouring Shakespeare!

Yours,
Joy

Source: Wade

To William Lindsay Gresham

10, Old High Street
Headington
Oxford
October 10, 1955

Dear Bill,

Thanks for writing to let me know how things are going; I feel much easier when I get regular letters, even if there isn't always a cheque in them.[26]

26. On October 5, 1955, Bill writes Joy and reports that his trip was productive, leading he hopes to several commissioned pieces. He is working on several different kinds of articles, and he will be happy to feed David's interest in magic. He is interested in their new living quarters in Headington. He ends by promising to send money as soon as he gets any (source: Wade).

And you sound much more optimistic; I'm glad the New York trip went so well. Sounds as if things are on the up-grade again. I wonder if the rise and fall of McCarthy has had anything to do with the bad period? They tell me the heat's slowly coming off in the U.S., thank heaven.

Oxford is about 60 miles from London — an hour and a quarter in a fast train. It's a large and active city; taken together with Cowley and the other suburbs, I think its population is well over 125,000. The English dislike of flats means that all round Oxford, and every other city, are spread out miles and miles of monotonous little brick or stucco houses; ugly enough, but somewhat redeemed by their gardens. I've got half a brick one, and am going to spend this afternoon putting in iris and tulip and daffodil bulbs all round it. You could tuck this whole place into our Staatsburg living room, but it's surprisingly cozy. I've hardly needed a fire yet, the weather's been so warm; and when I do, two tons of soft coal will take care of me for the winter.

I'm still picking tomatoes in the garden, and the rose bushes are blooming their heads off. But we've just this minute had a minor tragedy. Sambo got the budgerigar. He must have learned how to turn a doorknob, for I had the room shut; but I came downstairs just now to find the door open, the cage knocked over and wrenched open, the bird totally vanished. Oh, well, it was a nasty budgie anyhow. It bit me when I tried to talk to it. I feel bad though; and I'll have to explain it to the boys and get them a new one. Sambo is a most amiable cat ordinarily — Oh, Oh, take it all back. A loud chirp just interrupted me and I found the budgie lurking unharmed in the window curtains. Chased him round the room for ten minutes, caught him by the tail, whereupon he nipped my finger as hard as he could; but I've got him back in the cage now. Sambo is keeping out of sight. He is always adopting kittens; he's brought home a half-grown tom as black as himself, provisionally named Snowball, and the two wrestle together all day long. Sambo has the usual green eyes, but Snowball has queer eyes that are almost red; perhaps I ought to name them Stop and Go.

I've reverted to housekeeping with absolute delight — food is so cheap here that 75¢ worth of steak provided me with dinners for three days — and I've made lots of jams and jellies — blackberry, apple, plum, mint, etc. Have also started my new book; I hate writing on theological subjects but it seems to be going all right, and Jack is being very helpful with it.

I wish you had my research opportunities! Here, of course, we're crawling with bookshops and libraries; in addition to Bodley, there's

Blackwell's, a gigantic several-story bookshop in which you are encouraged to stay all day reading and not buying, if you like. A great deal of research gets done there.

The boys are both well. Yes, Davy got quite interested in magic, though I gather he doesn't believe a word of it; it seems he and Doug do a little amateur fortune-telling in the dorms at night. Doug, as I think I told you, is now getting quite literate; he reads Shakespeare for preference. Davy, stimulated by Jack, is doing a little Greek on his own. His spelling has suddenly improved miraculously. I hope you will send enough money soon so that I can buy him a warm overcoat this winter; he's been wearing a mackintosh the last two seasons, but he complains of the cold.

My father, poor fellow, is in the hospital getting all sorts of check-ups. It seems his doctor put him on a low-salt diet to get his blood pressure down. He and Mother, with their usual rigid literalness, interpreted this as no salt at all; so that's what he got, even when he was sweating at garden work in the summer. Result, of course, violent colitis, dehydration, and collapse; but he's recovering now. How tough those two must be to survive their constant attention to their health!

Jack's *Surprised by Joy* is getting good reviews and doing well — 10,000 sold before publication, out two weeks and already being reprinted. Has it come to the States yet, do you know? I forgot to ask him this weekend, and by now he's back in Cambridge. There is also another children's book about to appear; and he's sitting on a finished novel.[27] Does it all on beer, too. Regards to the lot of you.

Joy   *Source: Wade*

On October 25, 1955, Bill writes Joy excitedly: "There is just one magazine editorial job in the state of Florida. I now have it!" He tells her that Renée can now give up her job and they are moving to Ocala, "321 miles north of Miami." He says they have found a house to rent and he is busy at work: "I dug into the job on Saturday and found that the editor who had preceded me had let manuscripts pile up unread and unreturned at an alarming rate. I will be working day and night for several weeks to unscramble things. Also there is a brand new art di-

---

27. Davidman is referring to *The Last Battle* (London: Bodley Head, 1956), which first appeared March 19, 1956, and *Till We Have Faces* (London: Geoffrey Bles, 1956), which first appeared September 10, 1956.

*rector and a brand new publisher so we'll all start together." Of the magazine
itself, he writes:*

> All Florida *is an insert-type of publication similar to* This Week *or*
> American Weekly *and is devoted to happenings in the state of Florida. It
> is just the sort of little magazine I have always wanted to have to pilot and
> much can be done with it. New ideas are not only welcome, but necessary.
> So the future looks bright for all of us. . . . As soon as I can I will send you as
> much as I can but wanted to dash this off to let you know what was going
> on. I am very happy about the job and the regular income will give the
> nerves of all of us a good rest.*   Source: Wade

To William Lindsay Gresham

10, Old High Street
Headington
Oxford
October 29, 1955

Dear Bill,

I'm delighted to hear of the job, for your sake as well as my own; I
know you've always wanted something like this and can do it to perfection. Congratulations! Before you know it, the national magazines will be
picking up stuff from you; I bet you make the *Reader's Digest* inside of two
years. And we're all getting too old to stand the strain of freelancing.

The boys will be home for half-term this week; over next weekend, that
is. It's Guy Fawkes Day on the 5th and I've bought some fireworks, so we'll
have quite a show. They are both well and lively; Doug is on the under-
elevens football team and they've won a match; Davy is corresponding with
Professor Tolkien (the philologist and author of *The Hobbit*) about runes,
and has referred to an article called *Runenschrift* in Reallexikon der
Germanische Altertumskundle — he spelled it all quite right, too, which is
more than I'm able to do on this cold and frosty morning.

It *is* cold, now; my hands are numb, as I'm sitting without a fire to save
coal. For the love of Heaven, do send some money soon! The poor kids
don't even have proper winter coats, and Davy in particular suffers very
much from cold. I've sent an appeal to my parents, but my father's down
with combined diarrheas, high blood pressure, kidney complications, can-

cer phobias, and nervous collapse; and they're spending all their money on doctors. He must be pretty bad, for they're even consulting a psychiatrist, though Heaven knows what one can do for you at 70! It seems he was told to go easy on salt because of his blood pressure; so the poor silly thing went on a no-salt diet altogether, and he worked in his Maine garden sweating merrily. Result, of course, collapse; it's a wonder he didn't kill himself altogether, and it'll be months before his digestion is right. To make it worse, he thinks the doctors are lying to him when they assure him he hasn't got cancer; a logical result of the modern well-meaning medical practice of lying to you when you *do!*

I appreciate your financial difficulties at the moment; but after all, Rose doesn't need the dough immediately and I do. And I will *not* go to Jack with my hand outstretched! Once was enough. So come across, please! At least with a steady job you can pay regularly.

Warnie has been reading and enjoying *Monster Midway* — though the carny world rather horrifies him. I enclosed a clip from today's *Daily Telegraph* — the London opposite number of the *Herald Trib*. How far a good wisecrack can travel! Regards to the family.

Yours,
Joy

Source: Wade

On October 30, 1955, Lewis wrote his lifelong friend, Arthur Greeves, that he was planning to marry Davidman, ostensibly in order to extend to her British citizenship: "The other affair [his intention of marrying Davidman in a registry office] remains where it did. I don't feel the point about a 'false position.' Everyone whom it concerned wd. be told. The 'reality' wd. be, from my point of view, adultery and therefore mustn't happen" (CL, 3, p. 669). Lewis is referring to the fact that while he intends to marry Joy in order to extend to her British citizenship, he would not live with her; at this time he held to the position of the Anglican Church that divorced persons who remarried and had sexual relationships with their new spouse would nonetheless be committing adultery. Obviously he later changed his mind.[28] Davidman makes no mention of the intended marriage in her letters to Bill.

28. For more on this, see Warren Lewis's letter to George Sayer and his wife of January 2, 1957, in George Sayer, *Jack: C. S. Lewis and His Times* (San Francisco: Harper & Row, 1988), p. 223.

To William Lindsay Gresham

10, Old High Street
Headington
Oxford
November 11, 1955

Dear Bill,

Well, every bit helps — mercy drops falling around me, etc; but O for the showers I need! I notice you don't say how much you are being paid; I conclude it is at least $100 a week and probably more. I appreciate the fact that you've other obligations, but please don't put us last on your list.

This bit won't buy much coal — but never mind, I've just bought a quid's worth of old road blocks — the tar-impregnated wood blocks from the London streets. They burn beautiful. And the weather's turned warm again anyhow. Last weekend we had our lunches outdoors, and didn't even need coats.

We had a terrific Guy Fawkes weekend — fireworks are very cheap here; the boys shot them all off themselves and were very careful — no casualties except to some of the marigolds that are still blooming in the garden. Both boys are in fine shape. Doug cooked the breakfasts and even baked cookies; Davy, somewhat to my surprise, seized the hoe and demolished nettles in the garden.

There's not much other news except that I'm slogging away at my book. My father seems to be very ill, judging by the letters I get, but I can't make out that it's anything worse than nerves and high blood pressure. According to Mother, he'll be all right if he doesn't worry himself to death. But constant diarrhea is a weakening business, as I need not tell you; and he has a lot of pain.

Did I tell you that I've been asked to address undergraduates at Pusey House (not a college, some sort of religious foundation) by its Principal? I'm supposed to tell them about Charles Williams! It's funny enough that I should be lecturing to Oxford students; but still funnier that I should be talking about Williams here, where he lived for years and so many people knew him. What a world!

I forgot to ask you to send me complimentary copies of *All Florida*, if you can spare them. The more I think of that job, the more I like the sound of it; all the right contacts, etc.

Yours,
Joy

Source: Wade

To William Lindsay Gresham

10, Old High Street
Headington
Oxford
November 28, 1955

Dear Bill,

Last two cheques received.[29] You know, I get tired of labouring the obvious; you know as well as I do that $20 a week isn't enough for me to bring up two boys on even in England, and that it isn't even the legal minimum (one-third of your income) you'd be expected to pay if there were no settlement. It's too bad you haven't got a new car; but busses are good enough for us, and I live a week on a pot of soup — I'd be surprised to hear that you do.

Make it $30 a week, and I won't kick, and I'll hold on in hopes of a magazine sale that will even the score. But at this rate I'm going to be forced to see what the law can do.

Isn't it possible for Renée to get some work — part-time, perhaps — on *All Florida*? Your boss ought to understand the circumstances.

The boys are well, according to their letters; Davy is playing with the Erse alphabet and Doug is doing wonders on the Under-Elevens football team. I gather you sent them some cheques, which Doug writes that Davy is sending to me. They haven't come yet — I'll hold them till the holidays and buy the kids something. Come to think of it, perhaps the cheques were from their grandparents; they don't say.

I'm struggling ahead on my own book; slow going — I hate this sort of writing, but I'll get there. Finally had to break down and order a ton of coal — the weather is at last Novemberish, gray and clammy. But one ton will easily see me through the winter. What do you use for heat in Florida?

Have you sent me any copies of your magazine? I would like to see it. Did I tell you Warnie (who is now T[ee]T[otalling], by the way) had been

29. On November 20, 1955, Bill sends $20. He writes that he is making $88 a week and that his job has been hectic as he has had to clean up the mess left by the previous editor. He still wants to do freelancing since his job just meets regular bills. Both he and Renée need extensive dental work and can't afford it. He is also concerned about his old Oldsmobile and may be forced to buy something newer. He is very optimistic about the future (source: Wade).

reading *Monster Midway?* He didn't much care for the carnival background, though. He's enthusiastic about *Limbo Tower.*
Regards to the family.

Yours,
Joy

Don't forget I am always available for rewrite work; why not?

Source: Wade

To Renée Rodriguez Gresham

10, Old High Street
Headington
Oxford
December 13, 1955

Dear Renée,
Well, you are certainly a good wife — it isn't every woman who will make her husband's excuses to a previous wife for him![30] It seems to me that Bill has had a lucky break with this job; one doesn't get these chances often in middle life, and I don't want to spoil the opportunity for him in any way. Even if *All Florida* can't be saved, doing a good job on it will

30. On December 6, 1955, Renée writes Joy: "Enclosed you will find Bill's check for $25 which is all he can manage at the present time." She then details the difficulties of living in Ocala, the lack of work for her, the poor prospect of Bill getting any extra money by writing, and their desire to send over winter coats for David and Doug. She adds: "It was on my suggestion that Bill sent the boys each a check for Doug's birthday thinking that you could use the money to buy them some needed clothes and it would be more practical than toys or any other gift. You don't need to tell me the difficulties of raising two children on limited amounts of money. I fully sympathize with your situation. Believe me, Bill is just as much concerned about the boys and he is trying his very best." Renée then relates that the previous editor of the magazine appears to have done very little, except play golf. This has left it to Bill to organize the magazine, essentially from the ground up. Because the magazine pays so poorly, it can't attract other writers, so Bill is left to write almost everything as well as run the business side of things. Though both of them expect the magazine to fold, Bill hopes that his hard work will win him another position with the owners, the John Perry newspaper chain. She ends the letter noting the mild weather and how it is good for Bill (source: Wade).

make a name for him not only with the Perry newspapers but with news-papermen in general; these things get around. Has he thought of running contests? There ought to be lots of aspiring young talent in Florida, with local angles on good stories, and there's nothing like contests for building circulation, let alone getting material. Look at what the *Ellery Queen* magazine has done with its detective story contest; the hope of a big prize fetches stories out of first-class professionals who wouldn't dream of submitting a story for the magazine's ordinary rates — then the magazine buys most of the stories at the ordinary rate! No writer can resist a contest.

As to money, what it comes to is that I will give you all the leeway I can, but when it comes to the pinch I must put the boys' welfare, and my own, above yours. I sincerely hope I'll never have to consult a lawyer again; I hate the whole tribe and I know damn well *they* always end up with most of the dough, no matter what else happens. But it is really up to you two and not to me.

No, thanks and all that, but I'd just as soon not get clothes from your mother for the boys. And in any case American clothes would not do; styles here are quite different and the boys won't even wear the few things we brought with us that are still good. But don't worry about the winter coats; I've got an unexpected royalty cheque for *Smoke* from the States that will cover it, though I don't know where their next school fees are to come from! Or rather I fear I know only too well; and I don't like it.

We're having a very mild winter here so far, thank Heaven, and I think my one ton of coal will see me through — what a change from Staatsburg! My life here has its comic contrasts. I'm beginning to know people and get invited out; last Sunday I had a very swanky lunch (venison and Burgundy) at a country club, in company with Jack and among other people Sir John and Lady Rothenstein, he being the director of the Tate Gallery. Hah — this and tuppence'll get me a ride on a bus. So I come home and stretch hamburger for supper! Also Jack is going to give a dinner in Magdalen to introduce me to people; thank God I've still got my nine-year-old Hollywood evening dress.[31] It's out of style and I've had to let it out at the seams, but among don's wives is this bad? I feel like a Southern aristocrat after de waw [sic], starving in the grand manner. Not that I'll starve, though, as long as there's more water to put in the soup.

31. There is no mention of this in Lewis's letters; the fact that he wanted to introduce Joy to his friends suggests a growing intimacy between the two.

Remember us all to Bobby and Rosemary, and good luck — it'll be my good luck too!

Yours,
Joy

Source: Wade

To William Lindsay Gresham

10, Old High Street
Headington
Oxford
December 21, 1955

Dear Bill,

Gosh, I wish *American Weekly* would make up its mind![32] But we won't have too bad a Christmas, in spite of our poverty; we're going to have a Christmas dinner with all the trimmings at the Kilns. My contribution is the cooking, and Jack's is everything else! Turkey, plum pudding, mince pies, etc., but I wish you could get pumpkins in this country; I miss pumpkin pie. I've managed a Christmas tree too — though there's no one to do tricks with picture wire and eyelet in the mantel; we'll just have to wedge it with stones. They sell 'em here with a lot of roots on, so you just stand them in a pail and pile stones on the roots. And they all use candles; but not me!

Doug wants a football for his present, which I have managed. I offered him something more and he said firmly, "No! Don't be so extravagant. I don't want to be a spoiled child!" Davy wants to be turned loose in Blackwell's, the bookshop where they let you browse all day.

They came all the way from London by themselves yesterday, the first time they had traveled alone; it didn't bother them at all. They knew the way perfectly, and I'd supplied them with their tickets, a timetable, and emergency money; it was only a matter of getting from Waterloo to Paddington by the Tube and getting on the right train. I knew they'd be all right, but all the same I had a bad moment on Oxford station when a train

32. On December 13, 1955, Bill writes that he is working hard to generate cash to send to Joy and the boys: "The *American Weekly* is still sitting on the [story he had written on] the gypsies! But no cash. If something doesn't come through it's going to be a slim Xmas but when it does I will send something for the boys' presents. I will write them and explain how it is" (source: Wade).

I took for theirs came in without them! Jack reassured me in great style, but he said afterwards he'd been as worried as I. Fortunately a porter told us the right train would be along a bit late.

Funny to remember that when I was all of nine I rode the Third Avenue L to school for miles, every day; and yet one worries about a pair of strapping boys! Actually I think they could take a spaceship to Mars without turning a hair.

They are both well, pink-cheeked and plump. Neither of them can be kissed in public; Douglas, however, relents when he's in his pajamas. They have now been home twenty-four hours and have so far not broken, burned, or spilled a single thing, which is practically a record. But you should see the kitchen! Chocolate pudding fills the air. We lunched on ninepence worth of sprats — which is a pound of little silver fish, sardine size, that you fry and eat entire; while there's a sea round England we won't starve.

Merry Christmas to the lot of you, and I hope Ocala works out better.

Yours,
Joy

Source: Wade

To William Lindsay Gresham

10, Old High Street
Headington
Oxford
December 31, 1955

Dear Bill,

Thanks for the $50 cheque; it made a big difference to our Christmas. Where did it come from — that is, has the story gone through? I hope so.

Our Christmas dinner went off very well, and since then Jack took us to the *Wizard of Oz* (being revived again) and went book shopping with Davy, so there's been some fun for the boys. The weather here is still mostly warm and bright for the time of year — all the spring bulbs are coming up — and we don't regret having missed the white Christmas New York State had! Today Davy scrubbed the kitchen floor for me and Doug baked a cake, complete with icing and many coloured sprinkles on top; then we all listened to a BBC programme on the American Civil War, complete with Fort Sumter, the Gettysburg Address, Grant's whiskey and Appomattox

Court House. They even had some Civil War songs I've never heard along with the familiar ones — Goober Peas, Stonewall Jackson's Way, Stonewall Jackson's Requiem, Life on the Vicksburg Bluff, and a Northern anti-draft one, Grafted into the Army. Not Lorens, though. Douglas wanted to know which side won! I shall have to give them some Lectures on American History. I found myself going all nostalgic over the Battle Hymn of the Republic — it's always the *past* of one's country that wakes these emotions; I read a long article in *Reader's Digest* by Paul Gallico celebrating the present prosperity of America which left me entirely cold. Bigger and faster cars, shinier motels, and refrigerators, more television sets per head (if you can call them heads) than anybody in history! Hooray.

But I suspect Gallico didn't like it either and that's why it came out so sour. *He* lives in Luxembourg, a good place for a writer with a large income.

News from New York: my father found himself finally recovering from his assorted ailments, so what did he do but go shopping in Macy's just before Christmas! Relapse, [of] course — me, I wouldn't do it well.

Though I've only been here four months, this house is such a success that it feels like the old family homestead; the boys are much happier in it than they were in London. I'm rather sorry I stayed in London so long, though I didn't have the strength to look after a house at the beginning. Oxford, for all that it is a modern industrial city, is a much more relaxed and countrified place. Our local pub, the White Hart, sits in a garden full of aloes and fuchsia and other exotics; I don't suppose it's more than three hundred years old — dons and Cowley factory workers exchange views over a pint of mild-and-bitter, and on Thursday nights the bellringers practice like mad in the church across the way, quite like Dorothy Sayers' *Nine Tailors*.[33] The church has a Norman arch, dating from 1100 and something, but the main part of it is a mere novelty of a couple of centuries.

Carol singers came along the street for two weeks before Christmas, being quaint and cheery and hallelujish till I could have choked them — holly berries and mistletoe are all over the place; in fact, all I need to be living in a Christmas card is a bit of snow, *that* we don't get. Don't think there's any news to report. Happy New Year to you.

Yours,
Joy

Source: Wade

33. Dorothy L. Sayers, *The Nine Tailors: Changes Rung on an Old Theme in Two Short Touches and Two Full Pearls* (London: Gollancz, 1934).

The Sword of Damocles

Letters 1956

To William Lindsay Gresham

10, Old High Street
Headington
Oxford
January 8, 1956

Dear Bill,

The two cheques came and were much appreciated.[1] I'm glad to hear the job is straightening out; though it doesn't sound thrilling to learn that you're operating on a shoestring, and I wonder why your publisher doesn't do a better job on the financial side. There's no surer way to kill a paper than starving it to death. I suppose your predecessor lost 'em so much dough they don't want to lose any more.

Did the *American Magazine* ever buy that story, and how about the boys' school fees if so? They'll be due in ten days. I saved by buying Davy a fleece-lined mackintosh instead of an overcoat — Doug has one already and they insist they find them warm enough. You've probably read, though, that we're having a real spell of bad weather now; fog and frost everywhere. The fog was not too bad in Oxford, no worse than a fairly thick mist such as we used to have often in Staatsburg; London was paralyzed,

---

1. January 1, 1956, Bill writes Joy, sends her two checks, and says things are going well for them all. Also, he says he has heard from David and is glad the boys are well. He adds that work on the magazine is maddening but necessary in the short term (source: Wade).

though. The frost has been quite keen, however, and the whole place is iced like a wedding-cake; strange to see green hedges and lawns and the winter flowers all feathered with frost. We cuddle together round the fire. Temperatures just at or just over freezing can seem cold enough when you've no storm windows and only a small open hearth! What makes it bad is the damp; I made the mistake of hanging clothes out to dry a few days ago, when the sun was shining — instead of drying they froze solid and glassy, and came in wetter than they'd gone out. I have had to dry them one at a time in front of the electric heater.

The other night I came upstairs and Doug called out to me from his bedroom, "I've made up a poem!" He promptly recited it and here it is:

> A golden peacock flies
> Like a second sun
> In and out of pale blue skies,
> And does with brightness shine
> To all human eyes.

Surprising from Doug the Demon Footballer! Davy — who is again first in the form in English and last in maths — doesn't write poetry; his latest effort is a long story about an Anglo-Saxon boy and the heathen Danes attacking with witchcraft and treachery.

Warnie didn't need the AA programme — though I bombarded him with AA propaganda and literature, and it may have helped to convince him that he couldn't be a normal drinker. At any rate, he finally admitted this and just stopped! He's been on the beam for about four months now, and is working hard on his new book. He's found a non-alcoholic ginger cordial which tastes more like a strong cocktail than you'd believe possible — powerful stuff!

Jack had a letter the other day from a Dubliner now living in Birmingham, wanting to know what he thought of dianetics! It seems various groups, especially the screwy "scientology" ones, are still going strong. Jack passed it to me for answering and I told the lad what little good I could find to say about dianetics — that it was effective with psychogenic illnesses and in some cases with early traumas, but that it could be dangerous in the wrong hands.[2] After this lapse of time I really wonder at our credulousness and our temerity; a technique in which the auditor is so much

2. This letter has not survived.

more active than the traditional psychoanalyst obviously requires something special in the way of balance, intelligence, and good will.

Have you seen the life of Elinor Glyn that has just been published?[3] Amazing story. I always thought she was some old hack with a lower middle-class background and a fancy pen-name — by no means. She belonged to the top level of Edwardian country gentry, called queens by their first names, and was the mistress of a cabinet minister! And the name was her own. Just goes to prove there's always room at the top — for vulgarity. The damn woman really lay around on tiger-skin rugs.

The boys are now listening to the Children's Hour on the wireless, Davy under protest and Doug by choice — the next hour won't be worth living — oops, the battle has already started. Goodbye now!

Joy   *Source: Wade*

To William Lindsay Gresham

10, Old High Street
Headington
Oxford
January 22, 1956

Dear Bill,

Latest cheque received; it does feel good to get money regularly, I must say![4] The boys are back in school now and in fine shape; they helped with the packing, working like Trojans at getting their clothes ready. Doug has developed a taste for ironing, believe it or not; he insisted on doing his own things and was quite good at it. Davy, when he wants to be, is a good house-cleaner. Both of them are well, except that Doug developed a strained Achilles tendon — too much football, I suppose — and is not allowed hockey, etc. until it's better. Nothing serious — I had him to the doctor, who said it only needed rest.

I've been having a fairly rough time myself, what with an exposed

---

3. Elinor Glyn (1864-1943) was a novelist and screenwriter; her plots were often sexually charged.

4. On January 13, 1956, Bill writes Joy, telling her his job still is hectic and they are moving to a more affordable apartment. He also tells her the *American Weekly* did finally pay him for his story on gypsies (source: Wade).

nerve in one tooth, a touch of intestinal flu, and a peculiar hop-skip-and-jump rhythm my heart has been experimenting with; according to the doctor, this is only incipient middle age and a touch of strain, but it's a startling thing to experience. Feeling a bit better now, though.

Right now we are having our first real snow of the season; there must be a good quarter-inch of it on the ground. On the whole, our weather has certainly been no colder than yours; some days I hardly need a fire. Davy says his new coat is more than warm enough.

The *All Florida* copies have arrived too. I like some of the fact articles, particularly the wildlife stuff, very much; but I can see what a job you've got ahead of you. There's a general amateurishness of style in most of the writing that cries out for a good rewrite man. And what is the matter with your photographic reproduction? Much of it is far too pale; and I do think the colour you use is awful. I suppose nothing can be done about that. Zipping up the copy, however, is something you won't have much trouble doing. Can that ball of fire you've got scorching around your office be put to work pulling in some more ads? Can you put in some jokes and a cartoon or two? And no doubt I am being pedantic, but I wish you would tell your lady columnist to put a cedilla in Façade; no point in spreading more illiteracy than you can help. Better stick to English than get your French wrong.

Not, I suppose, that you need to be told any of this!

Don't think there's any real news here, except that I've been asked to address a London church on the Problem of the Christian Jew — mmm, the Goyim should have my problems yet! The snow has stopped; I've gotta go shopping, so goodbye for now. Glad to hear you've got a better place to live. Regards to the family.

Joy

Hey, wasn't the French election a beaut? Merde alors!   *Source: Wade*

To William Lindsay Gresham

10, Old High Street
Headington
Oxford
February 14, 1956

Dear Bill,

For this relief much thanks; delay plays the dickens with the female constitution, as you probably have noticed by now.[5] The job sounds really lively now. I gather that you've cleared up the muddle you inherited and are hitting your stride; there's quite a difference between the disgusted detachment of your first letters about the magazine and your present proprietary tone.

Here are the best ideas I can dream up: have you explored the high schools and colleges for writers, cartoonists, etc.? Most people write better at that age than they ever will again; and you don't have to pay them much if anything; they're only too delighted to get their names in print. A contest, *or* just a search for material, can be set going in these schools at almost no expense; all you need is a leaflet distributed to English and Art departments, for class reading and bulletin boards. I remember lots of such things in my teaching days; the schools are usually delighted to cooperate, gives 'em some hope of encouraging literacy. And college students, esp. of journalism, can make good volunteer correspondents whom you don't have to pay.

Also, if you can't find an experienced assistant editor, how about a bright young college graduate with ambition, energy, and perhaps some background on the school paper? That's where a lot of good journalists come from after all. You would have to put in some time training him, but it would probably be worth it, and you'd have a disciple and admirer instead of a possible rival.

About cartoons: would it be possible to reproduce jokes and cartoons clipped from other sources? Plenty of newspapers do that, with or without

---

5. On February 7, 1956, Bill writes Joy with lots of news about the magazine and the future. Since they can't afford good cartoons, he is leaving out the sad few he gets. He adds: "What the job has boiled down to is that I write the lead story — or do such a complete rewrite on it that it amounts to the same thing. This increases the quality of the [magazine] but runs me ragged. After all, I only know one way to write which is the very best I can. In all the desperate years of free-lancing I longed for a chance to write on a salary and now I've got it. But with all the routine editorial chores along with it, it is rugged. However, I seem to be thriving on it as long as they let me alone and trust me to get out the [magazine] without any interference from topside." He has enjoyed a nice letter from David (source: Wade).

credits. I could send you clips from here, even; might get some new jokes into the American press that way!

Glad to hear you're using Baynard Kendrick's stuff; you wrote me he was having a rough time.[6] Have you heard the latest on Borley Rectory, that was supposed to be so thoroughly ghosted up? The Psychical Research people here have just published a report of a long and patient study — and it seems old Harry Price ghosted for the ghost — rigged up most of the effects himself. Whaddaya know!

Did I tell you I saw your Gresham's Law joke in a newspaper here not long ago?

I'm having a hard time myself trying to write my *Seven Deadly Virtues* book, which I don't in the least feel like doing — how did I get into this theology racket anyway? The trouble is that while I like Christianity well enough, I hate Churchianity; as far as I can see, every organized church in the world ends either by missing the point and tangling itself in trivialities, or by contradicting the point altogether. And certain of my past experiences have left me suspicious of *all* organization. I got on well enough with the Episcopalians; but the C. of E. is another matter; it's dead on its feet and full of perverts, eunuchs, and Manichees. I've just got an article by one of its bright boys attacking Charles Williams as pornographic! I'm gonna tear him to shreds in my Charles Williams speech on the 26th, and Jack is plotting to bring him to the meeting and watch the sparks fly.

Afterthought on the school contest idea; you can even get the teachers to do the weeding out for you!

The boys seem to be doing well; Doug reports building a snowman. We're having constant snowfalls, but the weather changes so rapidly that they melt almost at once. Something I don't remember seeing at home is an everyday occurrence here — snow from one cloud in the middle of a blue sky with the sun shining, a startlingly beautiful effect. But O God it's cold!

Got lots more letters to write so goodbye for now. Glad to hear Bobby's so much better.

Yours,
Joy

How's your new house?   *Source: Wade*

---

6. Baynard H. Kendrick (1894-1977) was a writer and the founder and first president of the Mystery Writers of America.

To William Lindsay Gresham

10, Old High Street
Headington
Oxford
February 29, 1956

Dear Bill,

Glad to hear the job is promising so well, and sorry to hear about Renée.[7] Thyroid certainly seems to run in our family. When she gets the exact dose she needs figured out, the migraines will probably stop; it's difficult to strike a balance at first, and too much thyroid is likely to bring on headaches and nerves and whatever other ill one is constitutionally subject to. Watch her fingertips; if they tremble, she's getting an overdose.

Look, my friend, I am just as bored with saying this as you are with reading it, but $50 is not enough to live on for two weeks. Try to do a bit better. I have learned to live on things like crumpets and tea and fish paste (except when Jack takes me out, and do I tuck in then!) but my rent here is $15 a week and there are plenty of extra expenses. Right now my landlady is after me to buy a vacuum cleaner, no less. Short of giving up food for Lent, I don't see where else I can save.

The newspapers here always give Southern treatment of the Negroes a big play; right now they are concentrating on Autherine Lucy and the Negro boycott (or do *you* get any of that news in your press?).[8] What a lot

---

7. On February 25, 1956, Bill writes Joy and encloses a check. His job is calming a bit and he has taken up photography to help enhance his own stories. He is pretty desperate to find an editorial assistant. Renée has been ill, so he is thankful for the medical insurance his job provides. He responds to Joy's complaints about the Church of England: "I would probably agree with you about the Church of England. Here in the Sunny Southland it is a church-infested, God-forsaken spot. Not forsaken *by* God but where God has long been forsaken by a good many of the people. There are groups that have plenty of spirituality — such as the Girl Scouts, surprisingly enough, and, of course, AA. But among Southerners the real test of Christianity would be their attitude toward Negroes ('inasmuch as ye have done it to the least of these ye have done it unto me') and here they don't have enough charity to stick in a gnat's eye. But charity is hard to come by in large bunches, north or south, I suppose. Religion is, after all, a direct experience — anyone who has ever grabbed aholt of that hot wire never forgets it. But few have and they won't find that wire uninsulated in the modern churches" (source: Wade).

8. In February 1956 Autherine Lucy (1929-) enrolled as the first black student at the University of Alabama in Tuscaloosa; her arrival on campus sparked riots, and Lucy was hounded mercilessly.

of good all this does American prestige in the brown and yellow countries, not to mention most of Europe. In England they seem to class our Southerners along with the Russians in East Germany. I could no more live where you are than in South Africa. By the way, Phyl [Haring] is planning definitely on going back there; she's about through with her analysis and is rarin' to go out and get a job. She seems to be over the worst of her difficulties. Sel, who used to be as calm and solid as the Rock of Gibraltar, is not so good — *her* analysis has stirred up a lot of stuff without settling it. But that may be partly thyroid too.

My Charles Williams speech last Sunday went off very well indeed.[9] I was a little nervous about addressing an audience of Oxford undergraduates, expecting them to be hypercritical; but I needn't have worried. I never had such a good audience, light as Viennese pastry, in contrast to those lumps of soggy dough I used to handle in New York. They got all my jokes, even the hints of jokes, instantly, and roared aloud; instead of sitting back and waiting to be amused or edified, they came all the way to meet me. Jack and the Principal of Pusey House were very complimentary afterward. I'm all the more pleased as I was taking a bit of a chance — I attacked Manichaeism and prudery in the Church. Nobody liked it better than the parsons! I suspect I wronged the C. of E. in my last letter; it isn't as bad as its bishops.

Saw *The Bacchae* done in Greek by Cambridge undergraduates last week. The Oxford and Cambridge productions are up to Broadway standards and then some; no professionals could have improved on this. It was a tremendous experience — acting and direction and above all music. I'd boned up on the Greek beforehand, so I could follow it fairly well.

Doug and Davy have both had brief stomach upsets at school, but were only out of circulation about half a day; otherwise all is well. Doug has sent me a letter to you which I will forward by ordinary mail. He still hates writing letters; Davy, however, has begun to love it and writes almost like an educated grownup. That kid is apparently going to be a writer (oy, chosen for what? chosen for tzores) and I am going to try my level best to get him qualified for an academic career so that he can write on the side. It's the only place for one of his temperament. He's got the brains for it and the tastes; I'm not sure that he has the application, though — at present he gets enthusiasms and leaves them with great rapidity, very much as you do (or did?). Still, it's nothing to worry about; he's only going to be twelve next month. If I could only get a bit of money to spare I'd have the

9. There is no official record of this lecture.

two boys photographed and send you a picture of them; perhaps you'll do something to help in the spring holidays.

I have just nursed my cat Sambo through cat flu and pneumonia and we nearly got thrown out of the place because of the smell he made.[10] All is well now, however. The weather is warm again and I can stop cowering in front of the fire and do a little writing. Glad to hear you're at last going places with photography; I remember you always wanted to.

Yours,

Joy

To William Lindsay Gresham

10, Old High Street
Headington
Oxford
March 14, 1956

Dear Bill,

Same old Inflexibill — ignore everything I say and go on paying as little as you please.[11] What's the use? I'm too tired to argue. When you've been kicked around as much as I have, your psyche develops calluses.

---

10. On February 28, 1956, Lewis writes Chad Walsh: "Joy G. is very down on her luck at having just been given notice to quit her house: more depressed than I have ever known her — as a comparatively small knock does sometimes have a surprisingly severe effect when it comes after many harder ones and a period of what looked like being settled weather has intervened. You know the feeling. So a cheery letter [to Joy] wd. be a charitable act" (*The Collected Letters of C. S. Lewis, Volume 3: Narnia, Cambridge, and Joy, 1950-1963*, ed. Walter Hooper [London: HarperCollins, 2006], p. 713; hereafter CL, 3).

11. On March 10, 1956, Bill writes Joy that he has no money to send her and is still rather desperate for an editorial assistant. He got back the original ms. of *Nightmare Alley* and, before throwing it away, he asked if the Miami Public Library wanted it. They snapped it up. He says that he has sent David a birthday present, that Renée is better, and that he bought a copy of *Surprised by Joy:* "I couldn't afford it really but didn't think the Ocala library would ever get it. I have not finished reading it yet but I imagine that the Joy he sought was mystical experience. Jack seems to have a good burden of unreduced grief. He must have made wonderful strides in erasing some of it by means of [his] analytical mind but you could probably find enormous grief changes and ally losses if you [hunt for them]. Everyone, even the healthiest seeming people, have them I am sure" (source: Wade).

Why the hell everybody in Florida wants to be a writer I wouldn't know; better they should stay in bed. But your various projects sound like great fun as well as good for the prestige. I'd like to see the faces of an Oxford audience if anyone waved a cobra at them — though undergraduates are quite capable of it. Tell me how it goes.

The boys are sure to like the presents. I've been carrying around a letter to you from Douglas which I've forgotten to forward — sorry, but I've been snowed under with a million difficulties, tooth troubles and what not. I'll send it along.

Glad to hear Renée's improving. Don't let her slim too much — that way comes the woist dizzizzizz. A gal with a gorgeous figure like hers worries more about ten ounces than I would about ten pounds. (Though I seem to stay about the same, thank God.)

You're right about Jack's autobiography; I don't think he's ever got over his grief and horror at his mother's death — who would?[12] There'd be no point in stirring up trouble by hunting for grief charges, though — even if he'd let me! Why disturb a satisfactory adjustment? Jack's sorrows, instead of breaking him down, seem to have strengthened him, made him something like a saint. And if he had any *more* energy he'd take off and fly.

I've already got my garden started; it's a lovely feeling to have one again after four years! No glacial pebbles and corkscrew-shaped carrots here — the soil's so soft and fine a baby could deal with it. Every day I go take a look to see if the radishes are up yet. I draw the line at the cabbage family, though — England is one vast expanse of cabbage, diversified by brussels sprouts. Except where it's an expanse of dormitory suburbs with every house exactly alike.

No, that's not fair when I'm living in Oxford; the other day I walked round New College garden, where crocuses and snowdrops were blooming under the ancient city wall with its arrow slits and watch turrets. One never gets tired of Oxford.

After all these years I've finally succeeded in mastering the large recorder you bought me — the lowest note eluded me for a long time, but I've got it now. I sit here and tootle to myself for hours.

No more news. What's the American opinion of Cyprus, if any? The Press is sizzling over it here, and also over the abolition of the death pen-

---

12. C. S. Lewis, *Surprised by Joy: The Shape of My Early Life* (London: Geoffrey Bles, 1955). Chad Walsh's review of *Surprised by Joy* appeared in *The Saturday Review of Literature* 39 (March 3, 1956): 32-33.

alty — what nitwits. The underworld here is growing tougher all the time; it will mean they'll have to arm their police and the police will take to indiscriminate shooting, as ours do, in self-defense. Nowadays, if a cornered man shoots a bobby, someone goes to the police station and comes back with *one* gun. They then announce through a megaphone "We have a revolver. We think you had better surrender, please."

Oh yes — the boys say they've done well in their exams. Davy is mastering the Hebrew alphabet, and the Latin master is teaching him Greek in his spare time — quite a compliment. I hope to God Davy can get a college job when he grows up; nothing else will suit him.

Hope to hear from you, especially in pieces of paper with dollar signs on it!

Yours,
Joy

Source: Wade

To William Lindsay Gresham

10, Old High Street
Headington
Oxford
April 5, 1956

Dear Bill,

Better late than never; I was beginning to think you'd dropped dead. It's a pretty poor Easter holiday you've given us. The birthday presents or whatever you sent haven't turned up at all. Fortunately my parents sent Davy $5 and Jack gave him a present too, so it wasn't a completely blank birthday. He baked his own birthday cake with a package of ready mix, bless him, and it was a great success.

Both boys came home from school with bad colds, complicated in Doug's case by sinuses, so we are taking things easy anyway. The weather's quite warm now, there are flowers in the front garden, and vegetables sprouting in the back one, and we do get a lot of gardening; Doug puts his rows in scientifically with a cord stretched between two sticks to keep them straight. Both of them are a great help around the house, enabling me to earn a quick ten pounds by typing a book for Kay Farrer.[13] This isn't

13. Katherine Dorothy Farrer (1911-1972) was the wife of Lewis's friend, Austin Far-

the first time I've made ends meet with odd typing jobs, but it isn't very adequate.

Davy needs a new suit; the one I bought him when we first came to England is in ribbons. Just for once, could you do without nylon shirts or whatever and pull your weight?

Doug has learned to play God Save the Queen on the recorder, quite quickly. He is increasingly musical and wants to learn the piano, but I don't see how that will be possible.

No other news that I can think of. Did the Blizzard reach Florida? From what my parents write, New York really had a bad time.

Yours,
Joy

Source: Wade

To William Lindsay Gresham

10, Old High Street
Headington
Oxford
April 13, 1956

Dear Bill,

Skinamalinkadoolium, hi ho jorum! That's more like it.[14] Now I shall take the pins out of those nice lil wax images I've got stuck away in the cupboard. I was really scraping the bottom of the barrel; got three dinners out of 28¢ worth of hamburger. Got a birthday present cheque from my parents and used it to buy Davy a much needed new suit — his last one, which he's worn ever since we've been in England, was completely gone on the elbows and much too small. The new one has long trousers, grown-up style; all the other boys in the Fifth Form have long trousers and he's been feeling it bitterly, poor lamb, though he insisted he didn't want me to spend money on him. He's still a bit small for them but it looks very well.

None of Bernice [Baumgarten]'s frantic letters and cables ever

---

rer. She was a detective novelist and a good friend to Joy. The book Joy was typing was probably Farrer's *Gownsman's Gallows* (London: Hodder & Stoughton, 1957).

14. On April 9, 1956, Bill writes Joy and sends a brief note with a check enclosed. Renée is hobbled a bit with a hip injury. He is fighting off the IRS but doesn't seem very worried (source: Wade).

reached me; God knows where they were sent. I know I gave Brandt this address a long while ago! My London agent finally told me she was trying to get me and I wrote to her. It's all about the *Deadlies,* which aren't finished yet on account of various troubles.

Sorry to hear about Renée's hip. I can sympathize, as I've been going through something similar; did something to my leg on a walk with Jack some weeks ago and it isn't right yet. For a day or two I was quite lame; now it's just a bit weak and wobbly and painful. I hope it ain't rheumatism!

The boys and I are having a quiet but pleasant enough holiday; Doug does a great deal of gardening and Davy is reading the Greek Testament Jack bought him with a Greek grammar and the Authorized Version to refer to. The other day we explored the Oxford Botanical Garden, which is a beauty and pleased us all very much. We are hoping to make a quick visit to Cambridge next week; the boys have never seen it yet. Jack will be back there then and will do the honours. It is at its best in this season, with the daffodils out in the Backs.

My own daffodils are blooming merrily and I've got some well grown pea plants in the garden — Doug has covered them with wire very professionally to protect them from the blackbirds. The great menace to gardens here is the jay — even larger than our blue jay, with a brownish-grey head and body and blue wings. They will tear open all the pea and broadbean pods and eat every seed. Hence the need for netting all season. Last year I found a terrified and exhausted jay with his feet tangled in the netting in Jack's garden; he must have been hanging there for hours. I had to take him into the house to cut the last strip of netting off with a scissors — he screaming bloody murder all the time and making dabs at me with a very wicked-looking beak. But neither of us was any the worse for the experience; he flew away, sat in a tree, and made ungracious remarks.

Jack has been offered $250 by *This Week* for 300 words — to him that hath shall be given, eh? — and was much impressed by the figure, but is afraid they may find his contribution "subversive" because he suggested that all forms of government are really oligarchies in actual operation! What the hell *is* going on in the States these days, anyway? We read the craziest reports from the South — old man Faulkner prophesying civil war from his Mississippi back road, etc.[15] Black niggers running around with white —

15. William Faulkner (1897-1962) was a major twentieth-century novelist whose stories explored the decline and decay of the lifestyle of the aristocratic American South.

It's pouring cats and dogs at the moment, rather unusual this spring. I'll be picking radishes in a week. Good luck with your own writing as well as *All Florida*. Send some more copies, huh?

Yours,
Joy

Source: Wade

On April 23, 1956, Joy and Lewis were privately married in a civil ceremony at the registry office, St. Giles, Oxford.[16] *Warren Lewis writes: "J[ack] assured me that Joy would continue to occupy her own house as 'Mrs. Gresham,' and that the marriage was a pure formality designed to give Joy the right to go on living in England: and I saw the uselessness of disabusing him. Joy, whose intentions were obvious from the outset, soon began to press for her rights, pointing out with perfect truth that her reputation was suffering from J's being in her house every day, often stopping until eleven at night."*[17] *Davidman makes no mention of this marriage to Bill.*

To William Lindsay Gresham

10, Old High Street
Headington
Oxford
May 2, 1956

Dear Bill,

Cheque received; also the presents for the boys arrived at Dane Court shortly before they returned, and Davy writes that they are enjoying them a lot. Davy has discovered the old-fashioned "s" that looks like an "f" and is now using it in all his letters, so don't be surprised at anything you get. Both of them are well and happy, and Davy looks very handsome indeed in his grown-up suit. Like you, he's quite good-looking when he's in a good mood and smiling, but when he's in a temper —

16. For more details on the marriage, see Walter Hooper, *C. S. Lewis: A Companion and Guide* (London: HarperCollins, 1996), pp. 77-83.

17. Warren Lewis, *Brothers and Friends: The Diaries of Major Warren Hamilton Lewis*, ed. Clyde S. Kilby and Marjorie Lamp Mead (San Francisco: Harper & Row, 1982), p. 245.

Gordelpus, Grubblegruff to the life. One can see what his grown-up face will be like, but not Doug's — Doug still has a pixyish baby face, though in manner he is more mature than ever. He has your facility at picking up accents; when he's home on holiday he soon begins to talk Oxfordshire (e.g. Turrible, ennit?).

Glad to hear the incometaxniks aren't getting you down. Maybe they breed them tougher in Florida — cross them with alligators? Our New York ones were always polite enough. After all, I don't suppose they can *do* you much, and you can always play both ends against the middle; tell 'em all about your wicked ex-wife who threatens to throw you into jail. (Will write threatening letter if required, and it'll be a beaut.)

Your report on desegregation (what a word!) confirms what I've been trying to tell people here and is very heartening. There is an amazing amount of interest in it here, and we get the most sensational reports — civil war breaking out any minute and so on. Several trials of white men for murdering Negroes, in which the whites were freed with loud cheers, have been reported in the papers. From all one reads, the Negroes seem to have all the brains and dignity in the South. This ain't the NAACP we used to know!

Don't think I told you of my glimpse of Khrush[chev] and Bulge [Bulganin] when they visited Oxford.[18] It was really very funny. I'd taken the boys to Cambridge and Jack showed us the town; on Saturday morning the train back to Oxford took four hours and was very hot. We arrived exhausted, put the boys on the bus for home, ran some errands in town and then got a bus ourselves — we live in the same suburb. Only to have the bus stopped for half an hour near Carfax (centre of Oxford) because of the reception, while the air in it grew hotter and smellier and Jack's expressed opinion of Russians grew more and more sulphuric. Finally we couldn't stand it and got out, walking the half-mile to Magdalen College by back streets, intending to get a pint of beer each in the buttery and wait until a taxi could get through to us. We got our beer; when what should happen but the Russians followed us in! There was a terrific official reception going on, and poor Jack had to run and hide in the Fellows' Building, because as an honorary Fellow he daren't appear without a gown. I stayed, however, and got a good look at 'em as they trotted past on the lawn with their poor little legs (they're both very short) pumping like mad to keep up

18. Nikita Khrushchev (1894-1971) was the Premier of the Soviet Union. Nikolay Bulganin was his predecessor as Premier.

with all those tall dons; the Vice-Chancellor, who had them in tow, looked like a greyhound chaperoning a couple of piglets. All in all they were having a very hectic afternoon, and looked it; the undergraduates had sung Poor Old Joe (to the tune of Old Black Joe) at them, and in New College someone shot off a huge cannon cracker. Khrushchev won some hearts, though, by remarking that Epstein's statue of Lazarus in New College Chapel was a revolting example of bourgeois decadence! Most of Oxford feels the same way — I rather like the statue myself, though; at least I don't dislike it as much as most of Epstein's stuff.

Very warm here now and I've just eaten my first home-grown radishes. I'm nearly finished typing Kay Farrer's new detective story for a little extra money; painful job — she writes like an angel but plots like — well, I'm always remembering your contempt for the artificial whodunit with no knowledge of real crime and real police. Her detective is a Scotland Yard inspector; Scotland Yard oughta sue. Back to work.

Yours,
Joy

Source: Wade

To William Lindsay Gresham

10, Old High Street
Headington
Oxford
May 23, 1956

Dear Bill,

Glad to have the cheque, and sorry it's not going better.[19] Can't you twist the arm of those bosses of yours and make them relax enough to give Renée a job? You're doing a grand job with the magazine and they ought to be willing to yield a point. I got the copies you sent and was much impressed with them; it's improved a great deal from the first specimens I saw — more literate, more generally interesting, and fine pictures. And thank God that imbecile female column is gone.

---

19. On May 19, 1956, Bill writes Joy and delivers ominous news regarding Renée's lack of a job, the IRS, Florida heat, and his job. He is also very disturbed by the racial prejudice in Ocala (source: Wade).

I dunno why the boys' presents took so long — ordinary surface mail only takes about eight days — unless they were held up either by customs or by dock strikes. This is the strikingest country on earth; the British workingman will go out if he's spoken to slightly rough. And about the only way you can tell his working from his striking is that when he's working he takes more time out for tea.

But a grand country anyway, as I realize when I read your description of the South. The Negroes hereabouts would make the average American Negro look like a bad case of leukemia — they're Jamaicans and lads fresh from Africa, you'd never notice any difference in the way they're treated in the pubs etc. — though they *do* get charged high rents in the cities. Of course hereabouts you never know whether they're bus conductors or just Balliol students. I admit there's less of a problem than you have; the English have done the Negro far less harm than the American Southerner has and aren't guilt-haunted about him. I suppose that is really the trouble: "Forgiveness to the injured does belong,/He never pardons who has done the wrong!" as Jack quoted when I recounted your letter to him.[20] Your Ocala crackers sound like meat for the anthropologist: xenophobia among them alligators. There seems no doubt that the future is with the Negroes, from your description; they have the vitality — and they can stand the climate. I hope you can!

Even here the weather is freakishly hot and dry; no rain for all of May, and a succession of golden days just right for walking. Oxford is even more flowery than Hampstead was; I'll spare you the datalogue, but you ought to see the wisteria on our local library — thousands of blossoms and a trunk like a tree. The bluebells are nearly over, the lilac and laburnum just in, and the may in blossom everywhere. The river is full of students in punts and the college eights are having a lovely time on the Isis.

The boys are well; Doug has been down briefly with flu but is now over it. Davy is learning to read music and wants to play the piano — you can rent one here for $4 a month; the students do it.

Hope things pick up. Are we down 'earted? Naow!

Yours,
Joy

Source: Wade

20. This quote is from John Dryden's *Conquest of Granada:* "Forgiveness to the injured does belong,/But they ne'er pardon who have done the wrong" (part II, act I, scene 2).

To William Lindsay Gresham

10, Old High Street
Headington
Oxford
June 15, 1956

Dear Bill,

The boys, who have just come home for half-term, tell me that you are leaving your job and going north again.[21] You might have had the courtesy to tell me yourself. But I'm not at all surprised; I could see signs of restlessness in your last letters, and I didn't imagine that job would hold you for long. Of course I can understand the inadequacies of both the job and Ocala for a man of your temperament.

But I confess a certain amount of anxiety about what we're going to eat while you are indulging your temperament, particularly as you've sent nothing for the last few weeks. No doubt you'll be able eventually to get something better in New York, and certainly Renée won't have much trouble finding a job there. But what happens to us meanwhile?

Doug, with his usual enterprise, had suggested that he can earn some money helping the local commercial florist in his garden, but I hardly think that will take us far.

Meanwhile, fortunately, there are plenty of vegetables in the garden and the weather's warm. The boys are both in fine shape. Davy is practicing on a little miniature piano which I have rented — there's a firm here which rents them to students at 30 bob a month, and Davy is very eager to learn; he gets lessons at school. Doug is outside pulling nettles out of the garden.

Me, I've got fibrositis in one leg, my back, and my chest, which means I walk about all crippled up and it HURTS.[22] The fault of the climate, of course; but I'm told it will pass. The quicker the better; I have to take pills to get any sleep and I can't so much as open a window without a yelp of pain.

Much amusement here over the Khrushchev speech. I wonder what

---

21. On June 13, 1956, Bill writes Joy that they are moving back to New York because he is making too little money at the magazine. He is excited about returning: "I really belong in New York where the libraries and editors are" (source: Wade).

22. This pain was a result of the unrecognized advancing bone cancer Joy was experiencing.

the American comrades are making of it? I don't suppose it has dawned on any of them that a system under which such things *can* happen and go unpunished is not quite the earthly paradise they dream of, but perhaps there are no American communists any more except Paul Robeson, who (I hear) has been making an exhibition of himself before Congress.

Let me know your plans — and please send some dough to go on with!

Yours,
Joy

Source: Wade

To William Lindsay Gresham

10, Old High Street
Headington
Oxford
August 1, 1956

Dear Bill,

I had your letter last Friday, but this is my first chance to write; over the weekend I saw Phyl and Sel off to South Africa, visited the boys' school, and rushed back home in time to receive them here for the summer holidays.[23] I'm very glad you've found your way to Island House! Couldn't help wondering how you could manage to exist in the New York summer with two children; I read a *New Yorker* article not long ago which said the overcrowding in the city was now so great that it has the worst slums in the Western hemisphere. But Island House, however cramped your quarters, is a pleasant place. Is Katrine still there? Give her my love, if so; also all our love to Mary. The boys still remember her well. And if the young man who took Doug boating is still around, best wishes to him. Our two weeks there were rather an idyll for both boys.

I'm not surprised you're having better breaks now that you're on the spot; you never had any difficulty getting assignments until you left for Florida. TV sounds promising, too. I figured you would not be able to

---

23. On July 23, 1956, Bill writes Joy (from New Rochelle, NY) and relates details of the move. He is optimistic about getting freelance work, including perhaps writing some TV scripts. He apologizes for not sending any money but he just doesn't have any to spare (source: Wade).

send any money for a couple of months and have been setting my teeth and holding on. Fortunately my little bit of garden is now producing enormous quantities of beans, sugar peas, and marrows — squash to you. I'm living on borrowed money and home-grown vegetables for the moment; but with the boys home I need more, so do what you can.

Davy seems finally to have got the hang of mathematics; he won no prizes this term but has risen to 3rd place in his form and was congratulated for working really hard. He has begun to talk seriously about his studies, more like a man than a boy, and kept me up last night to discuss the attributes of God. In the school play, "Joseph and His Brethren," Davy played one of Pharaoh's magicians who failed to interpret the dreams. His performance got special commendation; it was really brilliant, his use of his eyes, hands, and shoulders was remarkably expressive. He can't manage his voice yet, but that will come. Doug carried a spear adequately.

Their holiday now will last till about Sept. 20. Winter holiday, approx. Dec. 20–Jan. 20; spring holiday varies, but about all of April. I've ordered a copy of the school picture this year and will send it to you.

Thanks to Jack and Kay Farrer, we're having quite a gay holiday so far. Kay has invited the boys to swim in Trinity College's little pool and will take us driving; Jack is taking us to a film today and to Studley Priory for tea tomorrow. At Studley they have two very tame fox cubs, so you can imagine the attraction. I've held both of them on my lap several times; they are about the size of a fox terrier, but very soft and cuddly and amazingly gentle. They don't try to snap or scratch even when frightened; they just nestle. A kitten is much rougher.

Hope there's been no more of your asthma and flu. I've still got fibrositis myself; not badly enough to stop me working or walking, just bad enough to take all the fun out of both. It's now very wet here, which doesn't help; we had a real American-style heat wave last week, though. By the way, I saw your "Devil's Looking Glass" story — when was it you wrote that, back in the Ossining days wasn't it? — in *Ellery Queen* last week. It packs a wallop of the Raymond Chandler sort, but you've grown infinitely better since.

No more news — except I've just heard that a choral-speaking group has been doing bits of my *Smoke* in a London church! That and tuppence'll get me a ride on the Tube.

Yours,
Joy

Source: Wade

To William Lindsay Gresham

10, Old High Street
Headington
Oxford
August 12, 1956

Dear Bill,

Mon dieu, le chutzpah de ce goy-la — *he* worries because he didn't hear from *me!* How could I write when I didn't know where you were? And my last letter to your Florida address remained unanswered. Well, at least the $50 will put meat on the table — in fact, it has; I went out and got a roast of beef that will feed us half the week.[24]

I see you've got a place to live; hope it's a nice one. As to your questions, gifts *are* taxable in customs here. But there's no telling; most of the time things that are mailed come through quite free, only now and then they open one. Doug's exerciser was heavily taxed, Davy's microscope hardly at all. I think you can find out better than I can; I should have to look up the Customs people and put them on their guard.

Might be able to tackle television if I ever get my book job done. I am making no progress at all just now, what with the boys home and ill health — I've had mild indigestion all this week and fibrositis is acutely painful. About all I'm up to is cooking, gardening, and threatening small fiends with hockey sticks. As ever, they are good in every way but their consistent battles with each other; but these get me down. Thank Heaven, at least they go out alone nowadays. Doug has innumerable friends in the neighborhood, too. Davy is still rather solitary in his tastes. He's extremely fond of cooking; baked a fine lot of biscuits the other morning as a surprise and cooked himself eggs in cheese sauce for lunch today. He has just this moment gone off to the Kilns to hunt for snails in the quarry pond there.

Glad to have news of the New Rochelleniks. Regards to Jim Putnam too, if you ever see him — I've meant to write for ages, only I lost his address, can't remember it, and don't even know if he's still there. Phyl and Sel *may* come back to England after they've had a bellyful of apartheid — they think of a trip in a couple of years. Phyl has improved enormously

---

24. On August 7, 1956, Bill writes Joy a lengthy letter, sends a small check, and says he hopes more will be on the way — "TV is our Great Hope." He asks questions about import duties since he wants to send the boys some gifts (source: Wade).

under analysis and is now determined to get a job and support herself; she feels guilty for living on other people all these years. Sel is none too eager to go back, but is tagging along with Phyl. Robin is rather immature for his age and hasn't a voice; I think he is rather unintellectual and will probably go in for something mechanical. He is very tall but still quite thin.

Your report on the litry [sic] scene has all the liveliness of a man who's just come back from seven years on a desert island and is rediscovering civilization; Ocala *must* have been dreary. Sorry to hear of the death of magazines, esp. *Bluebook;* they oughta let you edit it. I saw *A Catered Affair* (retitled *Wedding Breakfast* here) and was much impressed (also with its predecessor on Bronx life, *Marty*).[25] The only trouble with the Bette Davis film was that all those supposed Irish talked like Jews! Some even were. Talk about the passing of time; I can remember Davis as a slim kid in her first film, maybe thirty years ago. The film had an extra kick for me through being shot in streets where I grew up — but the effect was *not* to make me homesick. If I never see the Concourse again it'll be too soon.

The weather here is cold and wet for August; but at least the garden is yielding tons of sugar peas and beans and marrows. The boys got your letters and enjoyed them; they'll answer soon. The fox cubs were a huge success and very gentle; sat in my lap and nestled. We've been out to tea with friends a bit, and so on; but Jack is leaving for Ireland next week and the rest of the holidays will probably be quite dull. I think I can afford a couple of local sightseeing bus trips, though!

Regards to Naome and Paul, the Elliots, Bernice and Carl, etc. Got to stop now and go shopping.

Yours,
Joy

Source: Wade

---

25. *A Catered Affair* was a 1956 film starring Bette Davis (1908-1989), legendary actress of the 1930s to the 1950s.

To William Lindsay Gresham

10, Old High Street
Headington
Oxford
September 13, 1956

Dear Bill,

Look, cookie, I'm sorry as hell about the cataract.[26] I'm sorry (though not surprised) that *True* is behaving like a bunch of jerks. Sorry about the shortage of furniture, kids in one bed, etc. But I am also sorry for ME. And for Davy, all of whose shoes are at least a size too small, so that he can't bear to walk. And for Doug who picks up a bit of small change mowing lawns and minding animals for the neighbours. And for the diet of beans — baked and green — we are living on. It continues to rain here and the only thing that thrives in the garden is runner beans, tons of them. A monotonous diet. So for God's sake quit expecting us to live on $50 a month! Even with all the help I can get and all the extras I can earn, it simply can't be done.

I've always hated the thought of suing you to collect some of what you owe me; for one thing, it might kill the goose that lays the golden eggs. But *this* goose has got to the point where it only produces a few brass farthings. What can I lose?

As to the cataract, is it certain that Dee Ray [radium] produced it? If so, I'm lucky; nearly twenty years ago I had Dee Ray all over my face for sinuses, and the eyes still work. Altogether I now regard radium as something to stay away from; you should have heard the thyroid specialists in the London clinic when I told 'em how I'd been treated. Shall you have the cataract operated [on] when possible?

Davy has been to the oculist and needs slightly stronger glasses (oops, very non-U; I must learn to say spectacles) but nothing to worry about; thank God all children's treatments here are absolutely free. I'm twisted in

26. On September 6, 1956, Bill writes another lengthy letter filled with news of living arrangements and common acquaintances. He encloses a check from borrowed money, and he is quite excited about the possibilities of writing for TV. He notes that the latest madness is "refusal by thousands of teen-agers to believe that the highly gifted and sensitive actor, James Dean, really died in the auto wreck a few weeks ago which undoubtedly killed him. They are forming 'Dean Still Lives' clubs." He ends by telling Joy he has a cataract in his left eye (source: Wade).

knots with fibrositis but there's nothing to be done about that, and I get about all right with a stick.

I was just thanking Heaven that in England we don't have crazy teen-agers like the James Dean fans, and then I picked up the paper and saw reports of riots everywhere the film *Rock Around the Clock* has been playing![27] It started with jiving in the aisles and ended with free fights in the theatres and the streets; policemen with truncheons, arrests, etc. Most places are now banning the film; it must be rather hysterical.

But most people here are worried about nothing except Suez; the general feeling is that there will have to be fighting if Nasser doesn't back down.[28] England can't do without that canal. Also, there is considerable disgust over the usual US election-year paralysis. Nasser sure picked his moment! I suppose it's Eisenhower again, if he can manage not to drop altogether dead in the next two months?

And how about the Negroes in the South?

The boys go back to school on the 24th; somehow I've got to get their outfits into decent shape. I'm knitting new socks, but the rest of their stuff can't be home made. Their shirts — three years old now — are nearly in ribbons, but will have to last a bit longer.

If you grow tomatoes next year, get somebody to take a snapshot of you working at 'em and send it to me. This I gotta see!

Yours,
Joy

Source: Wade

27. James Dean (1931-1955) was a popular screen idol whose premature death led to his achieving legendary status. The 1956 film *Rock Around the Clock* celebrated the first rock band, Bill Hayley and the Comets.

28. This refers to the Suez Canal Crisis, when Egyptian president Gamal Abdel Nasser (1918-1970) nationalized the canal that had largely been constructed by the British and French.

To William Lindsay Gresham

10, Old High Street
Headington
Oxford
October 19, 1956

Dear Bill,

You timed that one well — another day and I wouldn't be here. I have got something really hellish the matter with my left hip and am being carted off to the hospital this afternoon on a stretcher. I've been increasingly lame for a long time but could walk painfully till last night. Then I fell and wrenched the leg, and now can not use it at all — can only move it with great pain. I've had some X-rays. . . .

Oct. 20, continued in the Wingfield Hospital, Headington, Oxford

I was going to tell you about the X-rays. The other night I fell which left my leg totally useless and in agonizing pain; then the ambulance came and carted me off here. I am now resting comfortably and it's a lovely place — all on one floor, acres of green grass and flowers, one whole window of my room glass.

But the prospects are not good. I shan't know definitely for a few days, till they get finished with blood cultures and urine tests. But the X-rays showed the bone looking "moth-eaten" — and they are talking of carcinomas or leukemia. In short, it is fairly probable that I am going to die.[29]

I am only moderately afraid for myself. I've been very tired for a long time. But I am alarmed for the boys (I have told them nothing yet, of course). My will appoints Jack and his lawyer as their guardians, and I think it is essential for them to finish their education here — a break now would upset them irreparably. Jack has promised to see to their schooling,

---

29. Lewis's letter of October 20, 1956, reveals that he is very worried for Joy (see CL, 3, p. 798). In his October 25 letter to Kay Farrer, Lewis indicates that she, and now several other friends, know about Lewis's earlier civil ceremony marriage to Joy on April 23, 1956 (see p. 801). In his November 9 letter to Chad Walsh he reports that Joy has cancer (see p. 804). He writes yet another friend on November 14: "Pray hard for a lady called Joy Gresham and me — I am likely v. shortly to be both a bridegroom and a widower, for she has cancer. You needn't mention this till the marriage (wh. will be at a hospital bedside if it occurs) is announced" (CL, 3, p. 805). See also in CL, 3, his letters of November 16 (p. 808), November 25 (p. 812), December 12 (p. 817), December 24 (p. 819), and December 30 (p. 820).

and of course I know you will contribute what you can. *Please, please* don't try to get them back to the States. You will be the first to admit you're in no position to look after two *more* children; and they never got on with Renée. If they want to come back when they're men, that will be a different matter.

Meanwhile I am not doing too badly. Jack's at Cambridge during the week but has come back for the weekend and visits whenever possible; my friends, the Farrers, rescued me when I fell the other night and couldn't get up again — thank God the telephone was nearby. My material needs are admirably looked after.

I'll know by Wednesday what the word is probably and shall write you at once. I think the specialist takes a negative view of my chances. Sorry your eyes are so bad. If this *is* leukemia, I suppose it might also be a delayed effect of Dee Rays — goddammit!

Hope you don't find this too distressing. Best wishes.

Yours,
Joy

I like the photographs — thanks!

Source: Wade

In a letter that has not survived, probably written soon after this one, Joy tells Bill she does not have leukemia. On October 29, 1956, Bill replies and tells her he is relieved to hear that whatever is affecting Joy's health is not leukemia. He has returned to attending AA meetings, not because he was drinking too much, but because

> *I did notice a definite alcoholic pattern which accompanied drinking — not insane behavior but a gradually thickening wall between me and other people and, of course, God. This was not noticeable so much while drinking as at other times. It is a subject to which I have, as you know, given a lot of thought and about which I have done a lot of reading in the past eight years. I came to the conclusion that while dianetics and the [Karen] Horney pride-self therapy had cleared away a great many of the bogies, I still preferred the AA program to living outside of it. There is a spiritual warmth within AA which cannot be found anywhere else — for an alcoholic, anyhow. And while for me a single social drink does not necessarily lead to a drunk, it has on occasion when in the presence of free liquor. . . . The ther-*

*apy I have had has done wonders in giving me a firmer foundation but af-
ter all therapy of this sort does nothing for the spiritual side of man except to
clarify to himself his own need of spiritual life. I doubt very much if I could
ever feel at home among any group of people who were not alcoholics. Certainly not in the average church, which, to me, is an unlit lamp.*

Source: Wade

*Also, he writes on November 20, 1956, and offers comfort to Joy now that
the diagnosis of cancer has been confirmed. He can't send her any money since
"this is just about the dryest spell I have ever had." He is grinding out short
pieces and has not had any nibbles on TV work.*

Source. Wade

To Chad and Eva Walsh

Wingfield Hospital
Headington
Oxford
December 3, 1956

Dear Chad and Eva,

Bless you both. One good thing has come of all this — I can now
tell you that Jack and I are married; have been for a few months, and are
going to publish an announcement soon.[30] When I come out of here I
shall go to the Kilns as Mrs. Lewis.[31] I know you'll be glad for us and
will not worry unduly about the ecclesiastical difficulty! We've been try
ing to get the Bishop to rule my former marriage invalid but he daren't.
So Jack and I have been married only civilly; but I don't feel it matters a
scrap, though I should like a friendly and independent clergyman to add

30. In a letter that has not survived, Joy tells Bill that she has married Lewis. On December 3, 1956, Bill writes: "Mazeltov! It was not exactly a surprise for the tone of your letters spoke of a happy frame of mind, and I could guess the reason." He also asks about Warren and what is happening with him. He hopes to send the boys some Christmas money
soon. He adds: "Give my congratulations to Jack and best wishes to you both" (source:
Wade).

31. On December 24, 1956, the following announcement appeared in *The Times:* "A
marriage has taken place between Professor C. S. Lewis, of Magdalene College, Cambridge,
and Mrs. Joy Gresham, now a patient in the Churchill Hospital, Oxford. It is requested that
no letters be sent."

something. Jack's love and strength are carrying me through this bad time miraculously.

As to my health, this is a breast cancer; I've had three operations and am now ready for radiation treatment on my affected hip and shall be walking again in a couple of months. The parent cancer was tiny and they've left me my breast, thank Heaven. No sign of any further spread, and I've quite a good chance of getting away without further trouble, they say. I'm in fine health aside from the hip, which doesn't hurt too often now. They nipped out my ovaries as a precaution this week, and I'm already back to normal in spite of the row of stitches up my tummy.

There were three bad days of vomiting after the op. during which physical agony was combined with a strange spiritual ecstasy; I think I know now how martyrs felt. All this has strengthened my faith and brought me very close to God — as if at last I knew all the answers. Jack is terribly upset himself partly because of a lifelong horror of cancer; but he's recovering a bit now. Warnie has been very good and the Lewis relatives are all writing from Ulster, offering good wishes and vacation care for the boys — bless 'em.[32] And you'll be glad to hear that I've made it up with my brother Howard, who's written very friendly and solicitous letters. Even my parents are at their best offering any help I want. It's wonderful what a thing like this does for people!

Love to all the girls. The boys are well and looking forward to holidays at the Kilns — Jack's fitted up an old cottage in the garden for them for daytime use. All my troubles but one are over!

Love,
Joy

Source: Wade

On December 16, 1956, Chad Walsh writes Joy:

Your letter relieved us enormously. I suppose it did so on two scores: it made us realize that the objective situation wasn't quite as grim as we had pictured, and it gave us a vivid awareness of how high your morale is. (Funny

---

32. In *Brothers and Friends* Warren Lewis writes: "I have never loved her more than since she was struck down; her pluck and cheerfulness are beyond praise, and she talks of her disease and its fluctuations as if she was describing the experiences of a friend of hers. God grant that she may recover" (p. 245).

that you should have to be building up our *morale. But of such is the Communion of Saints, I guess.) Last Sunday I offered prayer for your recovery in church, and there is a prayer cell in Ann Arbor praying for you. If love and prayer on the part of your friends can join with your own faith — and I think they can — you are going to be out of the hospital soon, and ready for the new life.*

But it is the new life that makes us happiest of all. It probably won't come as any surprise to you to know that Eva and I had suspected — and devoutly hoped — that something was brewing. When we were in England, we thought we detected matrimony in the air, and it was all I could do to keep from volunteering my clerical services on the spot. No news in a long time has given us as deep a sense of rightness and just plain joy. How wonderful for both of you! I'm going to be writing Jack soon, but meanwhile I wish you'd tell him how happy he has made us by making you and himself happy.

When will we be at liberty to start spreading the news? So far we haven't peeped to a soul, but we are dying to share the good tidings with a great many people.

I can understand why you would like the formal blessing of the Church, though you know also that a timid bishop can't keep this from being a thorough, Christian, and sacramental marriage. Thank God for the blessed fact that the ministers of this sacrament are the man and woman who marry. What is the canon law in England? Can a bishop keep a priest from marrying you? I had the vague impression that it was completely up to the individual priest. Lord, you know, I think that I take a rather strict view about the permanence of marriage, but I can't see much that's sacramental or inwardly valid about your marriage with Bill; if ever there was a situation that called for exercise of pastoral discretion by bishop or priest, this is it. . . . Please give our love to Jack, and to the boys (lucky boys, to acquire such a father!), and take a very large chunk for yourself, sweet and beloved friend.   Source: Wade

To William Lindsay Gresham

Churchill Hospital
Ward 7
Headington
Oxford
December 7, 1956

Dear Bill,

Thanks both for the mazeltov and the mazuma! The boys will be at the Kilns in a couple of weeks and it's nice to be able to pay their way a bit. Did I tell you Jack had fixed up a cottage in the yard for their work and play house?

W.'s off again. He *still* won't hear of AA and tries will power. It worked for about nine months, then he started a series of slips and now he's nearly as bad as ever. His pattern is a bit unusual; he drinks by himself about two quarts of gin, sitting up night and day; then feels terribly ill; then, gentle as a lamb, submits to a nursing home — or even goes there himself, though he may try to smuggle a bottle in. His conversation remains lucid, even scholarly, and perfectly polite, but he can't walk. I wish he'd listen to AA talk! After a bout he is usually all right for a week or more. He stayed heroically sober for about a month to look after me (run errands, etc.) while Jack was in Cambridge, but the prospect of a visit to some friends finally set him off. Jack is far more patient with him than any wife could be and I suppose he'll never really *need* to stop except for physical reasons — that hasn't happened yet; his health is good, and it doesn't take much alcohol to satisfy him.

Davy got your birthday present. I've got the Angel Chimes; thanks. My own condition progresses as well as possible. Had a tough time after the ovarectomy as I swallowed about a pint of anaesthetic, but that was only vomiting; fine now and the wound healed like lightning. No more operations, hooray! They've moved me to this hospital, a ramshackle ex–American Army place, for the radiotherapy it specializes in; they expect rapid results and back to the Wingfield for Christmas. It seems I've got a partial fracture of the weak bone, too, like [drawing included here of her femur and where the cancer and the fracture appear]. Where it is broken it's like a chopped tree crumpling towards the missing bit. But that's already healing, and they promise the pain will stop for good soon. All my insides are healthy; they're definite about my being able to walk well again

— it really looks as if I might get away with this, though only time will show! Meanwhile I've Jack, who's an angel. Love to all of you.

Joy

Thanks for the dianetics dope; I remain convinced there's *something* in it.

Source: Wade

On December 30, 1956, Lewis writes Bill Gresham a brief, friendly letter about Joy's condition and the boys. About the latter he says: "The boys are of course with me and I'm learning a lot! They're a nice pair and easy to get on with — if only they got on better with one another: but of course they are v. different types and have no tastes or interests in common. According to school reports both have brains (David more) and are both disinclined to work hard. (Who isn't?)."[33]

33. For more see CL, 3, pp. 821-22.

Agape, Phileo, Eros

Letters 1957

On January 20, 1957, Bill writes Lewis a lengthy letter thanking him for writing and for showing such care for the boys. He tells Lewis: "I would not be too alarmed at the way the boys fight; I think it is natural for brothers who differ greatly, as you pointed out."

Source: Wade

To Chad and Eva Walsh

Wingfield Hospital
Headington
Oxford
February 5, 1957

Dear Chad and Eva,

I'd have written long ago, but was waiting to be free of this hampering plaster and report that I could walk. I'm afraid that's not going to happen, though. They X-rayed my leg and removed the old plaster last week, but the results were very disappointing — the fracture had not healed. There are still six weeks before they can be sure, but it looks as if the cancer is resisting the X-ray; in which case there is nothing they can do but make my last months as easy as possible.

I am in rather a bad state of mind as yet — they had promised me definitely that the X-rays would work; I'd pinned all my hopes to having a year or so of happiness with Jack at least — and instead it seems I shall lie about in hospital with my broken femur waiting for death, and unable to do anything to make my last shreds of life useful or bearable.

I am trying very hard to hold on to my faith, but I find it difficult; there seems such a gratuitous and merciless cruelty in this. I hope that all we have believed is true. I dare not hope for anything in *this* world.

Miracles may happen, but we mustn't count on them. The worst of it is I feel perfectly well aside from mild intermittent pain in the leg. I fear all this will be horribly depressing for you; I shall go on praying for the grace to endure whatever I must endure, and perhaps I'll be more cheerful next time I write. Jack is terribly broken-up.[1] How horrible that I, who wanted to bring him only happiness, should have brought him this! Perhaps it would have been better for him if he'd never known me though he says not.

Liked your review of *T[ill] W[e] H[ave] F[aces]*, Chad.[2] I wish all the reviewers wouldn't first say it's an allegory and then complain that the allegory is obscure. Of course it isn't an allegory in the strict sense at all, but a romance with touches of parable here and there. Love to all.

Joy   *Source: Wade*

To Chad and Eva Walsh

Wingfield Hospital
Headington
Oxford
February 13, 1957

Dear Chad and Eva,

It is no longer so hard to write letters; in fact at this moment I'm sitting up in a wheelchair and shall catch up on a lot of them. Everything looks much brighter than it did before.[3] For one thing my prayers for

---

1. See in *The Collected Letters of C. S. Lewis, Volume 3: Narnia, Cambridge, and Joy, 1950-1963*, ed. Walter Hooper (London: HarperCollins, 2006), hereafter CL, 3, Lewis's letters of January 5, 1957 (p. 825), January 10 (p. 825), January 17 (p. 826), January 23 (p. 827), January 29 (p. 829), February 5 (p. 830), and February 11 (p. 831).

2. Chad Walsh, review of *Till We Have Faces, New York Herald Tribune Book Review*, January 20, 1957, p. 3.

3. In Lewis's letter to Walsh of February 2, 1957, he writes: "After a severe attack on her

grace have been answered. I feel now that I can bear not too unhappily what is to come, and the problem of pain just doesn't loom so large. I'm not at all sure I didn't deserve it after all, and I'm pretty sure that in some way I need it. Then, too, it seems they are planning to patch me up sufficiently to send me home whatever happens, and I may be able to hobble for a while even at worst. Also, I've now been allowed in chairs for a week, and it is going better than any one expected — a hopeful sign. Jack pointed out to me that we were wrong in trying to accept utter hopelessness; uncertainty is what God has given us for a cross. And from the questions I ask, it does seem that no one really knows what this cancer will do next; the leg cancer is not *of itself* likely to kill me, though others may — and no others have made themselves known as yet. What I dreaded most, lying helpless in hospital for months or years waiting for it, we can avoid. I'll get up, by the aid of will-power and sweat and grace; and if God will let me, I shall walk.

Our family doctor, Humphrey, had been talking to me before I wrote last time, and after a chat with him you always want to rush out and order your coffin. He lost *his* wife by cancer and always takes the darkest view, but even he admitted there was no knowing.

I was very merry last weekend and Jack and I had a gay time in my room with lots of sherry and kisses. *What* a pity I didn't catch that man younger.

I wish you luck with the fellowships. Will they permit a flying visit here? Poor Eva — and the second grade is generally considered the school sinecure! It will get much easier with practice — in a couple of months she won't mind it, though a sub always has a much harder time than a regular teacher. The watchword is No Self-Expression in *My* Classroom! Scare the daylights out of 'em by talking in a quiet silky sinister voice like Boris Karloff and they'll love you; be a martinet and make them pick up every scrap, do homework in identical notebooks, shine their shoes and button all their buttons — they'll learn like magic.[4] Treat 'em with tender love

morale and even her faith Joy has made a marvelous psychological and (please God) spiritual rally. During my two last week-ends in Oxford she has been in wonderful peace and even in high spirits. . . . You wd. hardly believe how much happiness, not to say *gaiety*, we have together — a honeymoon on a sinking ship" (CL, 3, p. 832; emphasis Lewis's). See also in CL, 3, his letters of February 17 (p. 834), February 19 (p. 835), March 6 (pp. 837-38), March 7 (pp. 838-39), April 13 (p. 846), April 15 (p. 847), April 21 (p. 848), May 8 (p. 851), and May 25 (p. 855).

4. Boris Karloff (1887-1969), born William Henry Pratt, became a screen icon for his portrayal of the monster in *Frankenstein* (1931).

and care and common sense and they won't. Why should they? They're happy without. No sane child will work to please a teacher who's pleased with everything in any case!

Gosh, imagine Demie going starry-eyed about a boy — and how good you are being; *my* parents would instantly have forbidden all further contact, opened all letters, etc. Love to all. Must write Jack a valentine now.

Joy   *Source: Wade*

To William Lindsay Gresham

Wingfield Hospital
Headington
Oxford
February 28, 1957

Dear Bill,

What a couple of old crocks we're getting to be! Can't those cataracts be removed yet?[5] As for me, I shall apparently be a cripple for life, but the life probably won't be long enough to matter, so why worry? That is, we don't know yet whether the deep X-ray has done the trick on my left leg or not, and if not — well, sooner or later dat ole debbil guine git me. The leg is suspiciously slow to heal. *But* general health first-rate and improving, I'm able to sit in a wheelchair, [and] I'm starting to relearn walking — or at least hopping on my right leg, which strengthens daily. I suppose crutches come next with a lighter plaster, and they're talking of sending me home soon with a nurse. If I get really well, I'll graduate to a caliper and perhaps in the end to a built-up shoe (my left leg is 3 or more inches shorter than the right) and *still* have to worry about the cancer coming back. All I really care about is having a bit of life with Jack and getting adequately on my feet for it. He has been growing more attached to me steadily — is now, I think, even more madly in love with me than I with him, which is saying plenty — and give dear Georgie Sentman my love

5. On February 21, 1957, Bill writes a newsy letter that ends with: "Had a nice note from Jack and wrote him but know how jammed up he gets with correspondence and don't want him to bother answering in a hurry. But am always glad to hear from him, of course. I like *Till We Have Faces* very much and will write him about it. Let us hear from you when you can and best wishes for everything" (source: Wade).

and tell him he was wrong about the intellectual Englishman's supposed coldness. The truth about these blokes is that they are like H-bombs; it takes something like an ordinary atom bomb to *start* them off, but when they're started — Whee! See the pretty fireworks! He is mucho hombre, my Jack!

The burst of Spanish comes of having the distinguished Professor Trueta and a friend over on the other side of my sitting room as I write, both of 'em talking anti-Franco politics at nineteen to the dozen. (I can understand enough Spanish to get that; nobody could miss it.) Trueta is one refugee from the Fascists that's done all right; he is the great Plaster King in orthopedics and Regius Professor of it here. I'm dying to ask him about the old days but haven't the nerve.

I've been out in my wheelchair for walks, have no pain in the bad leg, and on the whole have a fairly good time — except that at the moment I am suffering agonies from having my rear rammed into a chair arm by a clumsy orderly! The rear is *not* protected by plaster and I feel as if I'd been kicked by a mule.

Drat those sons of yours — they rejoiced in the magic tricks, performed with brilliant success among all neighbours' daughters — and when they said they'd written you I made sure they'd have had the sense to say thanks! But I fear Doug, at least, will never be an acceptable writer. His letters are all alike: "Dear Mother, I hope you are well. We played Burford Grammar School and won 11-9. I made three goals. I am enjoying soccer, riding, gardening, running, and jumping very much, hoping you are the same. Douglas" (don't worry about his future; he's gonna be a farmer, and neither you nor I have any say in the matter; unshakeable as a rock, and when new lands are opened to agriculture Doug will be there). Both boys, thanks to Jack, are getting piano and riding lessons now and doing well at both; I'm glad to see Davy developing an outdoor interest.

Sorry to hear Eileen's marriage went poof — or should I be? Why not marry her to Georgie? Kick *Argosy*'s teeth in for me.

Yours,
Joy

By the way, can't anyone in the U.S. see Ike is an idiot?   *Source: Wade*

On March 20, 1957, after Joy had to return to the Wingfield Hospital, Lewis contacted one of his former pupils, the Rev. Peter Bide, and asked him to come to the hospital to lay hands on Joy and to pray for her healing; on March 21, 1957, Bide went to the hospital and, at Lewis's request, first married Lewis and Joy and then laid hands on Joy and prayed for her healing.[6]

On April 2, 1957, Bill writes, sympathizes with Joy's prognosis, and offers comfort through the twelve steps of Alcoholics Anonymous. Then he "drops a bomb" by saying that he plans to have the boys come live with him after her death. He explains that he will finally be able to take care of them and give them the love and companionship they need. He goes on:

> *My big financial difficulty during the last few years was in supporting my-self and trying to send you and the boys enough for your support. If the boys are with me we will get along fine — not in luxury but with plenty to eat and enough to wear which is the main thing, in addition to love. I have plenty of love to give them. . . . The only thing I can say to you now, in view of the medical decision, is to take it 24 hours at a time. The Twelve Steps are a guide for everyone, as you know. They are nothing but Chris-tianity in its simple, by-the-waters-of-Galilee form. They work wonders for anyone approaching them with honesty. There is no other way to face up to death or life either. Making a decision to turn our will and our lives over to the care of God is a daily task, or so I have found it. Don't forget the quo-tation from St. Theresa . . . 'Let naught trouble thee, let naught frighten thee; all things pass. God alone changes not. Patience can do all things. Whoever has God has everything. God alone suffices.'"*

He also offers other bits of comfort and AA spiritual truisms. He sincerely tries to help Joy confront the reality of death. He adds: "I know how you must feel at the thought of leaving Jack — it would be the same with Renée and me. . . . If you have finally found love with Jack you have something the great

---

6. For more on this, see Davidman's letter of March 2, 1959, herein; see also CL, 3, pp. 841-42; and especially Lewis's letter to Dorothy L. Sayers of June 25 (pp. 860-62); his letter to Don Luigi Pedrollo of January 8, 1958 (p. 913); his letter to Phoebe Hesketh of December 20, 1958 (p. 1001); and his letter to Bernard Acworth of September 18, 1959 (p. 1088). See also Lyle Dorsett, *And God Came In: The Extraordinary Story of Joy Davidman* (New York: Macmillan, 1983), pp. 125-26; Walter Hooper, *C. S. Lewis: A Companion and Guide* (London: HarperCollins, 1996), pp. 631-35; and Warren Lewis, *Brothers and Friends: The Diaries of Major Warren Hamilton Lewis*, ed. Clyde S. Kilby and Marjorie Lamp Mead (San Fran-cisco: Harper & Row, 1982), pp. 245-46.

mass of men and women live and die without ever knowing. . . . Any love — if only for a week or an hour — makes all the rest worthwhile." Source: Wade

On the same date Bill sends the following letter to Lewis:

Dear Jack,

Joy wrote me that the prognosis for her hip was quite unfavorable. I shall try to offer her such comfort and encouragement as I can. The only spiritual path I know is that outlined by the Twelve Steps of the Alcoholics Anonymous program. It is such a simple and practical day-to-day design for spiritual growth that it applies equally well to war, illness and disasters of any sort, not alone to the specific problem of alcoholics.

In her last letter Joy was quite anxious to know what I intended to do about the boys in the event of her death. Up until now I have always been very cautious in what I wrote her for fear she would misinterpret what I said or would get upset but I cannot write that I am resigned never to see my boys again; quite the contrary.

Ever since she took the boys with her to England Joy seems to have had the idea that I had no intention of supporting them. She never seems to have believed me when I explained to her how things were with me, the magazine business going through upheavals and changes, etc. I have sent her every dollar I could lay hands on and this is the plain fact. But Joy's opinions and beliefs about me in recent years have been very puzzling and disturbing.

I think that I should tell you my side of the story.

In 1952, before she left for her first trip to England, Joy was in a very unsettled state of mind. What existed between us was really no more than a very close intellectual friendship. I knew that she was disturbed, restless and needed a vacation. When she discussed a trip to England I was all for it, "if we could swing it." Sometimes it seems a good idea to do something one has always wanted to do and consider the practical aspects of it later — or so it seemed to us. I tried to help her all I could, taking care of the boys when our part-time maid was not on hand, so Joy could finish her Ten Commandments series for Presbyterian Life *magazine. They took several days a week out of my working schedule but I saw no other way for her to finish the articles and she so wanted to make the money for the trip herself. She had never made very much out of her writing and I thought that this would be good for her self-confidence. Actually we could not, at the time, afford to have her go. For one thing, we borrowed money from her parents* *and I wanted to pay them back and not be indebted to them but I did not bring this up. There was also a bill of over $900 at a department store for things needed for her trip and this I had to pay when she was gone but I did not mention it to her as I did not want to spoil her trip. As the time for her sailing drew nearer she began telling people that she was not coming back. This was usually said after she had had a few beers. I tried to be calm and reassuring, telling her over and over, "No need to make any vital decisions now, just wait."*

She often told me, when she was upset, that she felt she was dying and had to get to England to see you. She said many times that she was in love with you and had to get to know you, although at the time she had no hope of ever marrying you. I was not the only one she confided in — she had long talks with her cousin, Renée, who was keeping house for us and told her the same thing. She also made it quite clear to Grace Kelly, our maid, how she felt, and possibly to other people as well.

I thought that when she got to England and did meet you that she would think differently about the whole thing — not that you wouldn't be a good person for her to marry, but as far as I knew you were well-settled and happy in a bachelor routine, not the marrying sort of chap at all. I pointed all this out to Joy before she left and she admitted the logic of it but still said she had to go to England and meet you. As you know, she stayed away five months. The boys were naturally quite alarmed, though they did not say much about it. I tried to reassure them that their mother would eventually come back but Christmas came and no Mommy; they were sad little chaps. Word had spread among the neighbors that Joy was in love with "some Englishman" and wasn't coming home. I had nothing to do with the rumors but country and small-town folk love to gossip and I had to keep denying them.

When Joy did return she was so violent and bitter in her resentment of me that I simply could not make her understand that I had no intentions of leaving her and the boys unsupported. She may have projected some of her own strong emotions outward — her desire to leave me becoming, in her mind, a fear that I would abandon her and the boys. I don't know just what she thought for I could not follow her ideas. She was so upset that it seemed wisest for me to take a job away from home which I did. On several weekends when I could get home I found an empty house — Joy had taken the boys away visiting so she would not have to see me.

When she sailed for England with the boys in the autumn of 1953 I knew that she, herself, had no intention of ever coming back. But at the same time I felt that little boys needed their mother. I did not know what to do, or what was best to do. I begged her to stay at home and told her that I would do anything she wanted as long as she kept the boys in this country where I could visit them but she refused. I still hoped that after a while she would come back with Davy and Doug and this hope kept me going through some pretty rough times. She seems never to have realized what losing the boys meant to me. I tried to carry on as best I could but was too upset to get fiction organized and decided to concentrate on articles for the time being. I have missed the boys every single day since they went away and it has grown more intense as the years go by. My marriage to Renée has been a wonderfully happy one; she is a sweet, warm-hearted girl and has tried to make up for the loss of the boys by her sympathy, encouragement and understanding. Without her I might have turned into a sorry mess indeed. Although she has to work to support her own children, she has made a comfortable home for us all. I have tried to keep up my end of it financially and it has certainly been much more economical than if I were living in a furnished room and eating out.

If I had the boys with me now we could all get along very well — not in luxury but we could make out well enough.

In the event of Joy's death, I would naturally want the boys to live with me. They do not have to be educated at an expensive private school — plenty of bright children are growing up in American public schools and they turn out quite well. I don't know how I can make Joy understand that with me the boys will have a home and they will have my love. There has never yet been a boarding school that could take the place of a father, or at least the kind of father I keep trying to be even by correspondence. I believe in helping the boys with whatever hobbies and interests they choose, educating them for self-reliance and self-knowledge and guiding them along their own pathways, in whatever constructive direction they wish to go in life.

Don't think that I am ungrateful for the financial help you have given Joy toward the boys' schooling. I do appreciate it. I appreciate deeply anything good which is done for them more than I can say. But while riding lessons and music and other advantages are fine things for boys to have, I can give them something no one else on earth can give them. They are getting to an age when more than anything else in the world they need their Dad.   Source: Wade

Lewis responds to Bill's letter with two very gracious letters of his own on April 6, 1957. In the first letter he says: "I cannot judge between your account and Joy's

account of your married life; nor is it perhaps the chief point." Instead, Lewis says the chief point is deciding what is best for David and Douglas, and he urges Bill not to try to bring the two boys back to the U.S.: "Wait, Bill, wait. Not now. A bone that breaks in a second takes long to heal. The relation between you and your sons has been broken. Give it time to mend. Forcible surgery (without anaesthetics) such as you are proposing is not the way" (emphasis Lewis's). In the second letter, "a ticklish job" written at Joy's request, Lewis appeals to Bill's sense of compassion for the psychological and emotional pain his intentions are causing Joy, but then goes on to state clearly that he will "place every legal obstacle in your way." (For the complete text of these letters, see CL, 3, pp. 843-45.)

To William Lindsay Gresham

The Kilns
April 7, 1957

Dear Bill,

I am now momentarily well enough to write to you and come down to cases. Let's skip the minor reasons why you are unfit to have the boys — your history of alcoholism, neuroses, sexual and financial irresponsibility, etc.; apparently you don't think they matter. Let's not argue about the destruction of the boys' education — you say that doesn't matter either, and apparently you don't mind subjecting a pair of completely Anglicized schoolboys to the utter misery and confusion a shift to the American system would bring them. All this you brush aside.

But there is one thing you won't be able to brush aside; the boys both loathe you. They always disliked and despised you; Davy, as you ought to remember, could never stand your touch, and even Doug used to tell Jack Keator that you were crazy. During the years we lived together I tried constantly to defend you to them — "Daddy's not himself today" — and so on. After we separated and I let them speak freely, I was startled myself by the fear and terror they felt, by their horror of your public and private scenes, and their contempt for your irresponsibility. It took hard work on my part to keep them civil to you. On one occasion I took a knife away from David, who was prepared to use it in my defense. On another Douglas deliberately shamed you into putting up a few storm windows — he has often told the anecdote scornfully since. How you could have missed seeing *then* what he thought of you I do not know.

In the years since it has taken constant pressure from me to make them keep up cordial relations with you by post. Both of them are horrified at the thought of living with you; they are now old enough to tell the true story in court. You haven't got a chance, my friend.

Joy

Source: Wade

To William Lindsay Gresham

The Kilns
April 7, 1957

Dear Bill,
Jack has just shown me your letter of complaint against me. I shall not go into your statements except to say that with one exception they are all false in some degree; totally false in the matter of the $900 bill I never ran up, false in every implication when you lament the "violent resentment" I somehow felt against you without mentioning that you had previously asked me to live with your mistress in a ménage a trois, slapped my face, half-throttled me, and threatened my life. You surely cannot believe the things you now write; and I am at a loss to know why you write them. The grotesque bad taste of your sending such a letter to my present husband hardly qualifies you as a fit guardian for the young; still less when the young concerned are present, articulate, and quite ready to testify to their own memories of your customary behaviour. You ought to hear 'em, Bill, you really ought; it would give you a salutary shock. I really haven't the heart to tell you any more.

As for myself, you will be delighted to know that I may live for several years yet. Don't you think it would be a good way of proving your ability to support the boys if, during this period, you began paying their full legal allowances? It would be a good way of laying the groundwork for a friendly relation with them. But don't let me influence you!

Yours,
Joy Lewis

Source: Wade

To William Lindsay Gresham

The Kilns
April 26, 1957

Dear Bill,

That's rather more like it.[7] Glad to hear that your income tax snarls are being straightened out; with both Renée and Ruth managing your affairs you ought to be kept in quite good order. As for myself, the doctors tell me my case is arrested "at least for the time being" and decline to risk any guesses as to how long that may be. I am certainly stronger, in less pain, and better able to move than I was when I left the hospital, and am now sitting comfortably in a wheelchair. I wish, though, they'd arrested the damn thing in time to leave me legs I could use! I sincerely hope you've better luck with the treatment of your cataracts than I've had with my cancer. From what I'm told, it's a slow business, but you'll end by seeing quite well again.

I have told the boys you sent a cheque and they're very pleased. If you don't mind taking my advice in dealing with them (and perhaps I'm a fool to give it) you consistently underrate their intelligence, perceptiveness, and maturity. I've come across some of your letters to them in sorting old papers, and was struck by the fact that you were writing as if to cuddly six-year-olds. These two are English schoolboys verging on adolescence — distrustful of emotion, tough, shrewd; Davy can be talked to as if he were a man — after all he's thirteen. Doug will hardly bother to read anything. You have written them long accounts of your *own* adventures; but, like most schoolboys, they are far more interested in *theirs*. And they are too mature to be impressed with expensive birthday presents if the regular allowance does not arrive; the years of uncertainty and going without things have made them a bit cynical. Besides, schoolboys of their ages — especially Davy's — had rather have money to spend as they choose themselves.

---

7. On April 22, 1957, Bill writes Joy and sends her another check based on his having sold a story. He tells her more about his IRS problems and adds that Renée and Aunt Ruth are helping him get organized in handling the problems. An operation on his cataracts is in the planning stage. He ends: "I hope that with you things have a more favorable outlook, as you hinted in your last letter that they might. If the boys will be home to the Kilns for summer vacation they should be a big help in feeding and caring for the livestock as well as helping with the garden." He makes no mention of Joy's points in her two letters of April 7 (source: Wade).

(Davy, these holidays, has bought a cage of mice, a book on the Anglo-Saxons, several teach-yourself books about doctoring, nursing, physiology, etc., and a charming marcasite lizard for me to wear on my bedjacket.) I should like your relation with them to become a real one; but this will only be possible on an adult basis. At present *you* don't seem grown up to *them*.

I'm sorry to have written as sharply as I did in my last letters; for I believe your love of the boys is a genuine one in spite of its lack of understanding. But you certainly brought it on yourself.[8]

Yours,

Joy

Source: Wade

To David Gresham

The Kilns
May 23, 1957

Dear Davy,

I wrote to Mr. Pooley as well as to you on Monday, but have heard nothing as yet about your proposed homecoming on Saturday. *Are* you and Doug coming or not? Please let us know by Saturday morning. If Mr. Pooley says no, don't be downcast — half-term isn't far off!

Love,

Mummy

Source: Bodleian

8. On May 7, 1957, Bill writes Amalia, his stepmother, who will be visiting England, and lets her know where to find Doug and David. He tells her that Joy has married Lewis. Then he adds: "Joy has written me that the outlook for her condition is quite bad and has tried to get me to agree to let the boys stay in England if she dies. This I have no intention of doing and she has written me that the boys 'hate' me and don't want to come to the United States ever again, etc. etc. She may have frightened the boys, in telling them things about me that she quite believes to be true by this time. However, I try to be of good cheer and keep up my courage; I am sure that all will come out happily in the end. Joy's opinion of me seems to vary with the amount of money I am able to send her for the boys, but I have been having trouble with my eyes (cataracts which have to be operated on) and have not been able to send her as much as I would like" (source: Wade).

Agape, Phileo, Eros

To Mrs. D. Jessup[9]

The Kilns
May 27, 1957

Dear Mrs. Jessup,

I'm venturing to answer your last letter to my husband — partly because he, poor soul, has strained his back lifting me and is very busy just now getting massage, heat therapy, and what not; there isn't much I can do to repay his loving care of me, but I *can* write letters. But mostly because I *want* to answer it. You and I seem to have much shared experience, and I'm grateful for the fellow feeling you express — as well as for the nice things you say about my book!

My husband's sore back is not, so far as we know, anything to worry about, and he's otherwise in the best of health. So am I — except for a permanently crippled and useless leg which makes it impossible for me to get out of bed. My cancer has been arrested for the time being — may become active again tomorrow or not for a couple of years. Meanwhile I try to make the best of things. There is some faint hope that my damaged thighbone may knit enough to let me walk in a caliper — which is all I ask for my last years; it's so frustrating to have to lie in bed waiting for death when you're full of energy and feel perfectly well!

What you say about Mr. Appleyard interests both of us, and we should be delighted to have him call on us here during July.[10] (Of course, it will depend on whether my health holds out.) I think he'd better telephone us when he's here. The number is 6963.

One thing I'd like to say since you mention that you've been threatened with cancer. Before I had it I had all the usual fear and horror of it, but since then I've found that it's possible to live with your cancer and still get a great deal of happiness out of life. The pain, perhaps, is usually exaggerated. I've had three operations, a frightful time with deep X-rays, three months encased almost completely in plaster, and the complication of a broken leg — and all this has involved a great deal of pain at times; but the pain came more from the treatments than from the disease, and was on

---

9. Mrs. D. Jessup was one of Lewis's frequent correspondents. This letter also appears in CL, 3, pp. 857-58.

10. According to Walter Hooper, Mr. Appleyard was a clergyman known to Mrs. Jessup. See CL, 3, p. 575, n. 95.

the whole less than I would have expected. At the moment I've no pain at all! I'm not going to play Pollyanna about the blasted disease — it's just that, bad as it is, one can take it without complete disintegration.

God bless you —

Yours sincerely,
Joy Lewis

Source: Bodleian

To William Lindsay Gresham

The Kilns
May 29, 1957

Dear Bill,

Something for your "Ghosts of Versculles" piece — Miss Jourdain had a reputation in Oxford as an accomplished liar, who was always inventing psychic experiences. Apparently everyone who knew her knew better than to believe her. A dead giveaway was the claim to have identified "themes from several operas" in *twelve* bars of ghostly music — or just enough to state *one* theme briefly! The Iremonger book has been well publicized here.

Can't say your dynamite adventure sounds exactly safe! Are your eyes good enough to travel? And did Charlie M. ever pay back the money to get them fixed with?

The boys were here last weekend to see Amalia [Bill's stepmother], who was passing through on a Cook's Tour — nine countries in thirty-one days, Hampton Court and Windsor all in one afternoon with Eton thrown in; gosh! She's as lovely as ever, quite unchanged, and was a great success with everyone. She took a lot of pictures with and of the boys — if they come out well you should have some. She's very impressed with their manners and good health and spirits.

My own health goes on improving — I've got back to full use of my right arm, though I thought that shoulder was gone for good. Leg's much better too. I don't need any painkiller now, not even codeine, and one small pill is all I need to sleep. I begin to think from its present behaviour that I may be able to hobble about on my bad leg after all before we're done! The worst difficulty now is that I can't bend the knee, which got stiffened by the plaster; but that can be dealt with if the thigh bone heals. I may last till the boys are well grown after all!

By the way, did I tell you that "Borley Rectory" has had its ghosts laid too? Seems that dear old Harry Price faked them himself.

The doctor says I can do without a night nurse now so I'm sacking her — we can't afford her, anyway. She was a nasty night nurse anyhow — just my luck that when I'm full of sedative and longing for sleep, I've got a borderline psychotic to soothe down. Getting rid of her in this now over crowded house will be like taking out the goat and chickens. Oi, Rabbi, it's wonderful.

Yours,

Joy

Source: Wade

To Chad and Eva Walsh

The Kilns
June 6, 1957

Dear Chad and Eva,

I think if I send this by surface mail it will arrive in Vermont at the right moment to greet you! And with luck I'll still be around next May to greet you in England. My case is definitely arrested for the time being. I may be all right for three or four years, they say. Meanwhile my health and strength are improving rapidly. I'm almost back to normal now except for my bad leg, and even that is stronger. There's a faint hope it may knit enough to let me hobble around a little in a caliper; if I could walk fifty feet, I could go visiting and see shows and be taken driving, oh, wonderful.

As it is, I still have to be lifted with care, but I can help a lot, and there's no pain at all — I don't even take aspirin. Jack and I manage to be surprisingly happy considering the circumstances; you'd think we were a honeymoon couple in our early twenties rather than our middle-aged selves![11]

---

11. Lewis writes Dorothy L. Sayers on June 25 and expresses a similar sentiment: "We have much gaiety and even some happiness. Indeed, the situation is not easy to describe. My heart is breaking and I was never so happy before: at any rate there is more in life than I knew about" (CL, 3, p. 862). He writes another friend on September 24: "It is nice to have arrived at all this by something which began in Agape, proceeded to Philia, then became Pity, and only after that, Eros. As if the highest of these, Agape, had successfully undergone the sweet humiliation of an incarnation" (p. 884). For more, see in CL, 3, Lewis's letters of [June? 1957] (p. 862), July 1 (p. 864), July 3 (p. 865), July 9 (pp. 866-67), August 12 (p. 875), Au-

He's quite well, except for a wrenched hip he got lifting me; it *was* very painful but is now yielding to deep heat and massage. Warnie is well too; having the responsibility of looking after me and assisting the nurse now and then seems to be doing him good. He's written his life of Louis XIV and is now cutting and rewriting. Jack is working on a projected book about the Psalms.[12] Me, I'm superintending the household and working on a crocheted rug!

I never before had the experience of keeping a fairly large housekeeping staff happy — I feel quite the lady of the manor! For ten weeks we had, in addition to the gardener, housekeeper, and daily woman, two nurses — and the night nurse fought with everyone else in the place; I spent most of my time soothing ruffled plumes. I thank Heaven I'm now well enough to do without a night nurse, so I sacked her last week amid universal rejoicing.

Glad to hear you're moving toward our camp in poetry! I warn you though: the simpler and clearer it is, the harder it is to do, which, no doubt, explains the fashion for the obscure, allusive, and involved.

Finnish sounds absolutely *terrifying;* I admire your courage! Perhaps you'll go onto Euskara; who knows? They say no one not born a Basque has ever mastered it; there's a challenge for you. And of course Mandarin awaits.

Have a lovely time in Vermont, and catch a fish in the lake and name it after me!

Love to all of you.

Joy

Source: Wade

To Mrs. D. Jessup[13]

The Kilns
July 17, 19[57]

Dear Mrs. Jessup,

I should have written before — but I've been deep in medical arrangements and exercises; I've now reached the point of being able to stand up

---

gust 21 (p. 878), September 21 (p. 884), November 12 (p. 894), November 17 (p. 898), November 27 (pp. 900-901), November 30 (p. 902), December 10 (p. 904), December 12 (pp. 905-6), December 16 (pp. 907-8), and December 23 (p. 909).

12. C. S. Lewis, *Reflections on the Psalms* (London: Geoffrey Bles, 1958).

13. This letter does not appear in CL, 3.

for a few moments and am to have more treatments with a view to getting me on my feet. It's wonderful to be able to do that, and to turn on my side, after nine months flat on my back! With luck I shall be walking in a couple of months. My husband's back, unfortunately, is not progressing so well; he was feeling fine yesterday, but then his surgical belt arrived at last (after the months' delay usual with National Health).[14] It turned out to be a fearsome contraption loaded with trick buckles, and he promptly wrenched a muscle putting it on. Such is life.

We haven't heard from your friend Bob Appleyard; I hope nothing's gone wrong with his arrangements. We *do* get telephone calls daily from quite unknown and previously unheard of American lady tourists who seem to regard my poor husband as one of the sights in Oxford which everyone must "do," like Magdalen Tower! They usually invite themselves to tea, so my life is unexpectedly lively. One of the most recent was a pathologist — she discussed all the least savoury bodily processes throughout tea, and lectured us on Higher Indian Thought afterward.

I don't know Evelyn Underhill's Letters (though my husband does) — I must look at them; I've liked what little of hers I've seen.[15] At the moment I've rather gone off reading, after the months when I could do nothing else; these days I crochet lace tablecloths instead, or knit socks, or sew buttons on pajamas — all of which keep me from feeling too useless.

I *do* like getting letters and answering them; it's an important part of my social life just now. It's awfully nice of you to offer to get me things in New York! My parents and my brother live in New York, though; so I shan't need to trouble you. I'm glad and grateful that you are praying for me, and I feel that my unexpected improvement may very well be due to the prayers of friends rather than the drugs of doctors — Best wishes from my husband.

Yours,
Joy Lewis   *Source: Bodleian*

14. Lewis was suffering from osteoporosis.
15. Evelyn Underhill (1875-1941) was a religious and mystical poet. Davidman is referring to *The Letters of Evelyn Underhill*, ed. Charles Williams (New York: Longmans, 1943).

To William Lindsay Gresham

The Kilns
August 22, 1957

Dear Bill,

Glad to hear your cataract operation was a success; your typing was perfect.[16] Will the other eye need an operation too? I've been reading up on cataracts in one of Davy's medical books — he now seems quite serious about being a doctor — and it doesn't sound like fun, but they insist that the technique is sure-fire. My own health continues to improve; I'm now having extensive deep X-ray treatments in the hope of healing my bones enough to walk. They make me a bit sickish, but I stand them better than most people. I can stand up now, and have no symptoms of illness — in fact, there is even some hope of *permanent* recovery, and in any case I may live for many years. I'm one of the lucky ones whom testosterone helps — a very new treatment.

What complications life can get into! The picture of you having to explain to your stepchildren that their real father's second wife is leaving him — oy! But as long as their own home feels secure I don't suppose it will do them much harm. Davy and Doug are profiting very much from *their* new security here. They're spending a fortnight in Kent, getting their first taste of the sea. Davy has just sent me a letter in French — very bad but quite fluent in its way — apropos of some French children at their hotel. The place is run by friends of Jack's who volunteered to look after the boys personally.

Next term Davy will be living at home and attending Magdalen College School as a day-boy — he prefers it that way, but if he can't get there in time every morning we'll change over. Doug still has two years to go at Dane Court.

Bel Goldstine [née Kaufman] will be visiting us this weekend — she's having a European tour. We see quite a number of visiting Americans; some of them are exactly like the Americans in English novels, a breed I never believed in till now. Pompous, humourless, very slow on the uptake

---

16. On August 13, 1957, Bill lets Joy know about his cataract operation and the long healing process it involves. He tells her that now he understands a bit about how the blind have their other senses sharpened. He also offers some details on Renée's children and former husband, Claude Pierce (source: Wade).

by English standards, ill-educated, full of naïve earnest "uplift" — I suppose they've all been hiding in the Middle West. I never met them in the States myself! What *has* happened to the American sense of humour? Mark Twain — or even Will Rogers — would be considered subversive today, I gather. And visiting dons tell us that even in the colleges intelligence is suspect.

Well, good luck with your recovery and more writing!

Yours,
Joy

Source: Wade

To William Lindsay Gresham

The Kilns
October 31, 1957

Dear Bill,

Davy has received the medical book and is reading it with pleasure, but claims he is too deep in logarithms, Greek, Latin, biology, physics, etc. (not to mention rugger) to write letters just now. I suppose you must have sent Doug a birthday present, but in all my experience of him he is always too busy to write letters unless seized by the scruff and held over a desk; so I'd better write acknowledgements for both and report on health, etc. Doug was one of the very few in his school to escape Asian flu; he's fine. Davy, like the rest of us, has had it, but threw it off in a day or two with no after-effects; it's really a very mild disease. He is struggling with a very exacting curriculum at his new school but seems to be holding his own.

I am slowly learning to walk again — I can get about the house with a cane and a two-inch lift on my shoe. This is little short of a miracle considering that in April I was given two months at the outside, could not shift myself in the bed and had only broken fragments of a thigh bone! There is now no predicting what the course of my illness may be.

I trust your eyes are now back in use and you can work a bit. Frankly, I don't think you are justified either morally or legally in leaving the support of your sons entirely to Jack. You are simply taking advantage of his conscientiousness and charity. Of course, he does what he can, but our expenses are enormous (I still need a nurse) and it is not possible to continue for long at our present rate. I dislike bringing any pressure on you in your

324

present situation; but you have only sent $100 this whole year, and unless things improve I shall have to consider what action can be taken. Please don't make this necessary.

Yours,
Joy

Source: Wade

To Kay Farrer

The Kilns
November 16, 1957

Dear Kay,

I'm fairly drooling at the thought of luscious housecoats, etc — and it *is* time I got some clothes to be queenly in! But no hurry. I'm getting so much more active every week that there's no telling where it will end — I'll probably be able to go to shops in a month or two! I can climb a step or two now. My dearest hope is to be able to do without a nurse — as soon as I can bathe and dress myself completely that will be possible. My present nurse is one of those good-hearted, willing, hard-working *maddeningly* typical people who set a house by the ears far more than the clever malicious ones.

It's good to hear that Caroline [Kay's daughter] is doing so well! Yes, when our prayers are granted it's always a bit of a surprise; one gets so used to expecting the worst. My doctor says he's never encountered a case like mine before; ordinarily, this sort of practice leads to further disintegration and death. Miracles all round us — and I bet Caroline will learn to be shrewd about money, and she's had a bit of experience! I'm at present praying hard for my parents' conversion and convalescence; I get the most doleful letters from my father, who simply refuses to accept the medical reports that give him and mother a clean bill of health. He is now explaining that hypochondriac symptoms are really much worse than "merely physical" ones. I suggested distracting his mind with a little social or volunteer hospital work, but he wouldn't hear of it. I don't, on the basis of worldly experience & psychological knowledge, think there's the slightest chance of a change of heart in either of them. But as a Christian I feel I mustn't give up trying.

Davy's a reformed character, making serious efforts to control his temper, stop his fault-finding, and learn his math. So am I; so is Jack. When we're all better and you have left your tooth troubles triumphantly behind, let's have a session and discuss clothes — black and turquoise, wine-red and azure, gold and green, printed and plain . . . lawsy massy, I sound like Dior![17] I'm still sizzling over the press that gave Dior columns and columns of obituary and Dunsany a supercilious few lines — did I say this last time I wrote? When I saw *that,* I decided that Western civilization deserves anything that happens to it.

Wonder if Penny cut her vegetables into giant-shapes?

Love to both,
Joy

Do I help you understand St. Paul's prickliness? Umm . . .   *Source: Bodleian*

To William Lindsay Gresham

The Kilns
November 29, 1957

Dear Bill,

Thanks for the cheque — a very pleasant surprise with Christmas approaching.[18] I'm glad to hear you can see again; it *has* taken a dreadfully long time — Bel Goldstine wrote me that you were still quite incapacitated. I'm progressing too, can now climb two or three stairs, walk fifty feet or so, sit nearly normally, and use the john like the big folks — no small triumph that! Shall soon be able to ride in a car and get another look at the outside world. I'm extremely lame even with a raised shoe, but it's a damn sight better than lying flat on my back! At present all my strength goes into building myself up and running the household, but I begin to hope I can write again.

Your AA work sounds very rewarding. Now that I've been away from the U.S. for some years what I read of life there seems madder and more

17. Christian Dior (1905-1957) was a well-known French fashion designer.
18. On November 25, 1957, Bill sends Joy money based on royalties from a second paperback edition of *Nightmare Alley:* "Bless that old war-horse, *Nightmare Alley!*" He also mentions more on his recovery from cataract surgery, some new writing ideas, and how he has been counseling some new AA adherents (source: Wade).

demoralized than ever. Saw an article in the *New Yorker* about American prisoners in Korea that was worse than my wildest fears; has it created a sensation in the States? It should! And what really goes on with Eisenhower? One gets the impression he's deep in senile decay and they keep him because his silly smile is a sort of human tranquilizer pill for the public.

Heard of Carl's death but not of Bernice's retirement. Like you, I don't think she'll stay retired.

Doug was enormously enthusiastic about his birthday present book — it really is a beauty. I hope he's written to thank you — but the pressures of archery, football, boxing, and guitar playing are heavy on him. He knocked a boy cold not long ago. Note from Davy on reverse of this.

Yours,
Joy

Source: Wade

A Sweet Season

Letters 1958-1960

To Kay Farrer

The Kilns
January 30, 1958

Dear Kay,

Ages since we met, surely? The mumps scare must be well over by now. I'd have telephoned you, but the telephone is now lost in clouds of whitewash and plaster — I'm redecorating with a vengeance. My bedroom has come out very well and I'm about to move into it, thus restoring the common room (as it's known here) for sitting purposes; do come and sit!

One pleasant surprise; underneath a horrid yellow finish like congealed egg-yolk the bedroom chests & wardrobe turned out to be nice simple oak pieces. That's always like finding buried treasure.

I grow stronger daily — can now drive about freely, and rush about the house like mad, scaring dogs and cats and making up fires and opening windows, but everywhere I go I see more things that need repair! If one moves the books, the walls fall in.[1]

We have given away all but one of our pups, thank Heaven, and I'm

---

1. Lewis comments on this time in several letters; see in *The Collected Letters of C. S. Lewis, Volume 3: Narnia, Cambridge, and Joy, 1950-1963*, ed. Walter Hooper (London: HarperCollins, 2006), hereafter CL, 3, his letters of March 26 (p. 926) and April 7, 1958 (p. 933).

now training that one; he and the cat lie across my lap side by side, like a black sausage next to a white one, sizzling gently at each other.

Love,
Joy

W[arnie]'s in Restholme, I've got no nurse, I'm all alone most afternoons; come and see!   *Source: Bodleian*

To William Lindsay Gresham

The Kilns
February 4, 1958

Dear Bill,

Thanks for the cheque. You do seem to be having even more hard luck than usual, but it must be a relief to be able to work on a book — best of success.[2] If anybody can do an inspired work on Houdini it's you. Hope Renée's innards are recovered and feeling fine — I know how miserable one can be after an abdominal op.

We're all pretty well. I can hobble about fairly actively, go for drives, even shop (with someone rushing to get me a chair — thank God this is Oxford and not New York) and have been able to sack my nurse and see about getting this house to rights. Nothing has been done to it for about thirty years; the walls and floor are full of holes; the carpets are tattered rags — in fact, I think it's being held up by the books that line all the walls and if we ever move a bookcase All Fall Down. Makes our place at Staatsburg, even after the boys had done their worst, look like a palace. I'm getting some cautious painting and repair done.

Davy worried us a bit at the end of last year — he had a series of digestive upsets after flu and got very lackadaisical and disagreeable, so I had him checked all over by specialists, stomach X-rayed and all — I take no chances on National Health these days! It cost only $25 and gave him a

2. On January 28, 1958, Bill sends a check and tells Joy that Renée had a bad fall and lost her job, but they took advantage of the opportunity to have a necessary operation done on her — financed by *Nightmare Alley* paperback sales and an advance on a biography of Houdini. He tells Joy more about his eyes, the Pierce children, story ideas, and his AA work (source: Wade).

clean bill of health. He is now much better in every way. Doug, as ever, is indestructible and a hero of the football field. I've some good snapshots of them which I'd have sent, but didn't know if you could see them and thought they might only annoy you. But if you would like some, let me know.

Jack's finished his book on the Psalms and is nearly through a fearsome work of scholarship — something on medieval poetry and philosophy; he goes about muttering bits of Latin and Anglo-Saxon, except when the cat trips him up, when what he says is much more vernacular. He'll have to write some more science fiction though; there's no money in Boethius. He's just done a short piece for the *Christian Herald* on the possible effect on Christian belief of finding intelligent life in space![3] The difficulties people dream up for themselves.

Has the U.S. been as silly over the Sputniks as it looks from here?[4] I keep having to explain things like Little Rock until none of it makes any sense even to me.[5]

Yours,
Joy

Source: Wade

To C. S. Lewis

The Kilns
March 8, [1958]

Dear Jack,

I'm writing early a) because it's a short week, b) because the news is good. My blood count came out quite all right, the lump is a-shrinking & Ellis is very pleased with my response to the hormone he gave me — whose purpose is to counteract the effect of X-rays. I continue to feel as sassy as a jaybird (Americanism, needless to say) in spite of the weather.

3. C. S. Lewis, "Will We Lose God in Outer Space?" *Christian Herald* 81 (April 1958): 19, 74-76. Reprinted as "Religion and Rocketry," in *The World's Last Night: And Other Essays* (New York: Harcourt, Brace & Co., 1960).

4. On October 4, 1957, the Soviet Union launched the first of a series of artificial Earth satellites; nicknamed "sputniks," these earliest space missiles inaugurated the space age.

5. This refers to the riots and social unrest that occurred in Little Rock, Arkansas, after desegregation was instituted in the public schools in 1957 and 1958.

Miss O'Connor telephoned from the Passport Bureau to say she'd forgotten my naturalization papers! That comes of letting you Irish get together. So Nurse & I got the taxi again & went back with them; also went to Blackwells & bought some books (light). Then Jean Wakeman turned up in the evening to discuss the Wales trip & stayed to dinner & ran out of petrol in the drive on the way home & had to be rescued by Jones after much telephoning & perfuffle — and I *still* felt fine![6]

Davy has repaired the couch, it only needed a spanner. The cold weather today has brought all the birds to eat, even the big woodpecker. Snip [the cat] is yelling her head off, must stop & let her in.

Love,
Joy

Source: Bodleian

To Roger Lancelyn Green[7]

The Kilns
May 23, 19[58]

Dear Roger,

Please forgive me for typing this — I'm doing all Jack's letters at the moment and being madly businesslike.

Of course Doug will be delighted to convoy Scirard; he thinks the world of him. (Did you know your son is a very determined fighter and discourager of bullies?) As it happens I'm calling at the school tomorrow to take Doug out, and I'll make arrangements with him then. If you are not going to visit tomorrow, I'll see if I can manage to take Scirard out too and debauch them both with scones and jam.

I usually send Doug £1 for the journey; it covers fares, FOOOD, and emergencies like missing the train and having to telephone. I think the actual fares both ways come to a bit less, but somehow I never get any change.

6. Jean Wakeman was a writer living near Oxford who befriended Davidman; after Joy's death, Douglas Gresham lived with her for a time.

7. This letter also appears in CL, 3, pp. 947-48. Roger Lancelyn Green (1918-1987) was a scholar of Victorian children's books; he was one of the first persons to read the manuscript of *The Lion, the Witch and the Wardrobe* (London: Geoffrey Bles, 1950), and he offered Lewis helpful feedback on several of the later Narnian stories.

I'll make whatever arrangements are necessary with Peter Bayley.[8] By the way, the Kilns is now a real home, with paint on the walls, ceilings properly repaired, clean sheets on the beds . . . we can receive and put up several guests, and could have Scirard here another time, not to mention you and June! I've even got a fence round the woods and all the trespassers chased away; I shoot a starting-pistol at them and they run like anything! We'd love a visit.

Poor Jack comes up for air and blows a few feeble bubbles now and then, but is sinking in waves of Tripos.

Yours,

Joy

Source: Bodleian

To Mary Shelburne[9]

The Kilns
June 6, 19[58]

Dear Mary Shelburne,

Perhaps you won't mind a letter from me this time, instead of Jack? He is having his first go at examining for the Cambridge tripos, and is fairly drowning in examination papers — apparently very silly ones. He comes up for air now and then, blows a few pathetic bubbles, then submerges again. He can't even get home for the next fortnight; our longest separation since our marriage, and we're both feeling it badly!

I am sorry you've been having that nasty time in the hospital. I know only too well what even the nicest hospital is like; how the nurses all vanish at the one moment of the day when you really need them, how the televisions and wirelesses all around make night hideous, how the night nurse wakes you from the first really refreshing sleep you've had in a month, at midnight, to give you your sleeping pill. And you, I suppose, have been the subject of demonstrations to medical students as well! In Oxford they give students their examinations at some poor patient's bed-

---

8. Peter Bayley (1921-) had been a pupil of Lewis; at the time of this letter he was Fellow and Praelector of English at Oxford University.

9. This letter also appears in CL, 3, pp. 951-53. Mary Shelburne was one of Lewis's many correspondents.

side; examiners and student alike all done up in their mortar-boards and gown, and scaring the patient half to death. But I'm told that experienced patients have been known to whisper the correct diagnosis to the student if he gets stuck.

Well, I hope you're home again now, and that it wasn't too bad and they found the right answers. I can share too in your thwarted desire to be useful. We women feel that more than men, I think. There are a million things that need doing around this house. Once I would have pitched in and helped my housekeeper — but now, because I have to walk with a stick and have only one hand free, I'm more nuisance than help and can only sit on the sidelines and give advice and be a pest. It is difficult having to accept all the time! But unless we did, how could the others have the pleasure and the spiritual growth of giving? And — I don't know about you, but I was very proud; I liked the superior feeling of helping others, and for me it is much harder to receive than to give but, I think, much more blessed.

Then, too, it's only since I've been ill and helpless that I've realized just how good people in general are, when they have a chance. So many people have taken trouble over me, and gone out of their way to give me pleasure or help! It's very heart-warming — and humbling, for I remember how cynical I used to be about humanity and feel a salutary shame.

Is your pet a cat or dog? I've found that cats stand these changes and separations pretty well — one of mine, when I was ill, took possession of a new home and mistress and had them completely under his thumb in a week. (If one can speak of a cat's thumb?)

Can you do any sort of work? I've found that making crocheted rugs and tablecloths, or knitting socks, was an amazing help with my spiritual difficulties when I was feeling low. One can work off so many frustrations by stabbing away with a knitting needle! It's better to make pretty things, I find, than just useful ones.

Of course we're both praying for you — and don't be too afraid, even if you turn out to need an operation. I've had three, and they were nothing like so bad as my fears.

Blessings,

Yours,
Joy Lewis

Source: Wade

To Mrs. D. Jessup[10]

The Kilns
June 12, [1958]

Dear Mrs. Jessup,

Just a hurried and flurried note, I fear — I've got one boy coming home for his half-term holidays this afternoon and another in bed with German measles! and some American friends visiting with three as yet uninfected young daughters, not to mention repairs and redecorations going on indoors and out, bills to pay, and two articles of my husband's I promised to type for him and have sinfully neglected for a week. If this letter gets a trifle incoherent, do forgive me!

The Appleyards must have made a mistake in telephoning, or else our line was out of order, for at the time they were here I never got out at all. But I'm much better now — almost normal. I can walk quite a long way, go for drives, scramble about in the woods, even do bits of light housework; and I've plunged into running the house and getting it all done over from top to bottom. The place hadn't been touched in twenty-five years, and you can imagine how much was needed! And the woods were overrun with trespassers; we had to put up a barbed-wire fence, and I've been patrolling the boundaries with the dogs to warn people off. So you can see I don't feel useless any more! Quite the contrary — there's so much to do, and to catch up with, that I feel like butter which is spread too thin over too much bread. But it's wonderful to be able to do all this. I take a positive pleasure in making beds and clearing tables. Though quite lame, I'm very active and my bones showed up solid and healthy on my last X-ray; the doctors are calling my recovery miraculous.

I believe there *is* a Reading for the Blind foundation here, or something of the sort; at all events, I know some women in Oxford who regularly read to blind students. I don't think they use recordings, but as each student's work is individual, tapes might not be so much use. It's a wonderful idea and of course we will pray for its success and expansion. I must suggest recordings to people here; now I come to think of it, there are certainly standard texts which could be done.

We're often asked to come to the States, but my husband's job at

---

10. This letter also appears in CL, 3, pp. 858-59, dated there (incorrectly, I believe) June 12, 1957.

Cambridge and my health both make it doubtful whether we'll ever be able to. Still, I hope to make it some day!

It is good to read of your happiness. We too are far happier now than we've ever been before. Two vans have just driven up at the door; I must fly — God bless you.

Yours,
Joy Lewis   *Source: Bodleian*

To William Lindsay Gresham

The Kilns
July 2, 1958

Dear Bill,

Sorry your eyes are no better; but, though it can't be much comfort to you, you *do* sound far stronger and more serene than you used to, and I shouldn't wonder if the challenge of those cataracts had roused you to a better response than you were formerly able to make to life's problems.[11] All the same, it would be nice if you could get your eyes straightened out! Much as I'd appreciate some contribution to the boys' upkeep, which grows more costly daily now they're in their teens, I do think that second operation should take precedence. I hope Houdini will pay for it.

I am very well myself; my last X-ray showed that my bones are now solid as rocks, and I am able to scramble about in the woods almost as well as I used to.

My only complaint lately has been a strained back — which I got by rushing after a wood-pigeon too recklessly with a shotgun! Missed him too, drat it. They're very good eating — and I'm getting to be quite a good shot.[12]

Lord, no; Jack is about as likely to turn Roman Catholic as I am to be

11. On June 22, 1958, Bill tells Joy that, in spite of continued eyesight problems, he finished the Houdini book (*Houdini: The Man Who Walked through Walls* [New York: Henry Holt, 1959]) in ten weeks, citing his AA beliefs as extremely helpful. Renée has recovered from the surgery but the bills have been expensive. He has heard rumors that Jack has converted to Roman Catholicism (source: Wade).

12. Lewis comments on Joy's shooting in CL, 3, in his letters of August 28, 1958 (p. 966), March 11, 1959 (p. 1029), and April 27, 1959 (p. 1041).

made Pope.[13] *That* canard is a hardy perennial; the Romans always indulge in wishful thinking about anyone who has theological influence. But Jack isn't even High Church. He's a tough Ulsterman, after all, half Scot and half Welsh, with the sort of views you expect of an Orangeman — though in his case they're half humorous. His maternal grandfather (name of Hamilton) kept a diary, and records his horror, on landing in England, to find that the churches had crosses on them — this seemed to him downright Papish! As to the Virgin as mother-substitute, well, haven't you discovered yet what rot popular psychology is? Tolkien, who *is* RC, explained Jack's refusal to be converted to Rome as a dislike of the Virgin based on misogyny! One's as likely as the other. Thank Heavens, the fashion for all forms of analysis is about over here. I read the other day, though, that casting any doubt on psychoanalysis in the States practically gets you accused of UnAmerican activity.

Had a brief visit from Eddy and Bess Rosenthal, still as full of energy as ever, who were doing seven countries in four weeks; the American idea of travel seems to be making it as much like a screen travelogue as possible. Then the Walshes turned up, fresh from a year in Finland, with three of the girls, grown large and lovely. Demmie, now 19, was still at home; she's getting married this August! Chad and Eva were very well and enjoyed their Oxfordshire stay a good deal; this has been a wet and cold spring, but a miraculously flowery one.

The boys are thriving. Davy has an occasional bad moment as a result of mixing Chinese food, chili, and raviolis, or some such (from whom he's loining dis?) but keeps well on the whole and is beginning to grow tall and strong. He's taken to shooting and fishing and assorted outdoors adventures — collects insects, etc. Doug slips away from school to help at a nearby farm, weaning calves.

I'm beginning all sorts of new social activities; had G. B. Stern, a very lively old lady, to dinner,[14] and [W. H.] Auden, now a rather limp middle-aged man with the face of a sad bloodhound, to tea. He's the only person I ever met who not only *likes* living in New York but has chosen St. Marks' Place (remember that?) to do it in! I'd sooner live in hell. And this week-

13. Although Lewis had several close Roman Catholic friends, including J. R. R. Tolkien and Don Giovanni Calabria, he never contemplated following the road to Rome. For perhaps his most definitive statement on this, see his letter of May 8, 1945, *The Collected Letters of C. S. Lewis, Volume 2: Books, Broadcasts and War, 1931-1949*, ed. Walter Hooper (London: Harper Collins, 2004), pp. 645-47.

14. Gladys Bertha Stern (1890-1973) was a writer of popular short stories and novels.

end we're flying to Ireland for a fortnight — Jack and I, that is; our first vacation trip together. Shall be motoring through the Mourne Mountains [in Ireland]; it ought to be fun if it doesn't rain the whole time![15]

Jack's halfway through *another* book.[16] That makes his third this year, in addition to newspaper articles, shorts, etc. — and to lecturing and examining. There is no slowing him down. The man really *likes* to write! Warnie is in good shape and starting research on a new one, too. Everybody writes but me; and I'm too comfortable just living. Jack sends his best wishes for your recovery and the success of the Houdini book by the way — you might send us a copy?

Yours,
Joy

Source: Wade

To William Lindsay Gresham

The Kilns
August 8, [1958]

Dear Bill,

Well, you seem to be getting a lot out of life for a man with almost no eyesight![17] Hope it can be fixed soon. Davy was interested but disapproving about your witchcraft theory — he's going through a stage of science-worship — and judging by the words he asked me to spell, his answering letter must be a pip. He's a frightful pedant at the moment; Jack says I must remember that in this family I'm not the only pedant on the beach! Between Davy botanizing, trotting out Latin names and nuclear chemistry formulae and gruesome medical details and Doug discussing with great expertise different car models, planes, soccer, rugger, cricket, horses and fishing, our dinner table is varied and lively.

15. Lewis writes about this trip in CL, 3; see his letters of August 28, 1958 (pp. 966-67), September 23 (p. 974), and December 15 (p. 1000).

16. Davidman is probably referring to *Reflections on the Psalms* (London: Geoffrey Bles, 1958); it appeared September 8, 1958.

17. On August 2, 1958, Bill tells Joy (from New Rochelle) that it was good to hear her bones are healing (source: Wade). Lewis writes about her improved health in several letters in CL, 3; see his letters of April 15, 1958 (p. 935), April 26 (p. 940), May 12 (p. 945), and May 30 (p. 949).

Doug's terms run roughly from Sept. 20–Dec. 20, Jan. 20–Mar. 20, April 20–July 25. The rest of the time is holiday. I'm hoping to take both boys to Wales for a week in September — a friend with a car has offered to drive us — but it depends on finding an inn.

Don't remember if I wrote you since we came back from Ireland. We had a heavenly time; beautiful sunny weather, miraculous golden light over everything, clear air in which the mountains glowed like jewels — there isn't a speck of dust in the whole country. We drove about in a leisurely way through the Carlingford Mountains, the Mourne Mountains (*not* the mountains of "Mora," but they do sweep down to the sea) and finally Donegal. The country is all rocks — granite hillsides like the roughest of New England, and dry stone walls everywhere — and completely lacks the lush garden quality of England; there's a good deal of austerity in its beauty, but it is the most beautiful place I've ever seen. Certainly the greenest! Other colours too — gold and blue and purple, and all as bright as jewels. Dunsany described it best, I think. The hedges are honeysuckle and fuchsia, with great masses of flowers; the hills are *really* purple with heather or rosy with wild thyme; the peat bogs have a curious dark, enchanted beauty of their own; there are little grey donkeys everywhere. Not so many pigs, but plenty of sheep and cattle. I found I could walk on the hills or the beach quite actively — I can do about a mile now.

We liked flying too; it was the first time for both of us, and we're quite converted. It only takes about an hour and a half, and I should have liked a much longer trip.

Well, is there going to be a war? I notice the threat of one sent the N.Y. stock market up! The papers here say quite plainly that the U.S. is ducking summit meetings because Ike is too irresponsible mentally to be exposed so publicly. But it's also suggested that the U.S. wants a small war in the Middle East to pull itself out of the recession — got to do *something* to rescue the auto industry! Sounds plausible. Hold onto your hat; this is where we came in.

Got to stop now and send this off to the post via Warnie. Regards to any old pals of mine you meet — Naome and Paul and so on.

Yours,
Joy

Source: Wade

To William Lindsay Gresham

The Kilns
October 29, 1958

Dear Bill,

Golly! You *do* have consistent bad luck; or is it just that *bad* luck's all *I* ever hear about?[18] Anyhow, I hope the Houdini book's working out all right now. We're all doing well here. My health continues to improve; I can get about almost normally now, cook a meal or go shopping or walk about a mile! I tend to wrench muscles and tire rather easily but no real trouble. Did I tell you I'd taken the boys to Wales for a week in September? A fishing village called Solva in Pembrokeshire with impressive cliffs; very beautiful, and I love the Welsh. They're the friendliest and most intelligent people. I even asked for road directions — they *tell* you! Just enough, perfectly clear, with the landmarks stressed. We went out in fishing boats to the bird sanctuary island of Skomer, climbed cliffs, saw gannets and puffins and skuas and seals. The boys loved it all. Doug, of course, made friends with all the fishermen and helped work the lobster pots. Both of them went fishing — we came home with a dozen mackerel!

Davy, who was rather a goblin-child last year (showing *all* the family vices on both sides and a few of his own invention) is now miraculously improved. He's finally begun to grow to his own and everyone's relief — how old were *you* when you finally sprouted? I remember your telling me it was late and sudden — and is now nearly my height. Outgrows his clothes every two months, drat him! He's beginning to take his school work seriously, and becoming good-humoured, cooperative, and amusing company. A great relief. He appreciated [your gift] and will write soon. He collects live mice and voles at present; they are always escaping, and he puts little piles of grain around the house for them. Fortunately Snip, my Siamese cat, is a mighty hunter. Doug, as ever, is well, strong, sweet-tempered, football minded, and a total loss at his school work. Who cares! If you're like Doug, you don't need books. He'll be home for half-term weekend tonight, bringing a friend, and we've got a mighty Guy Fawkes celebration planned.

Jack's *Psalms* book is off to a good start, thank Heaven — we go broke

---

18. On October 19, 1958, Bill responds to Joy's letter describing her trip to Ireland with Jack. He also tells her about his writing and problems with the Houdini book (source: Wade).

each year paying last year's income tax. It's the surtax that does it; they soak you 19 bob in the pound; otherwise we'd have no money worries! Oh well, there's a chance for a *Reader's Digest* article — Regards to Renée and the kids, etc.

Yours,
Joy

Source: Wade

To Chad and Eva Walsh

The Kilns
December 29, 1958

Dear Chad and Eva,

Thanks for the card. We don't send 'em ourselves; they're one of the few things Jack loses his temper over as they descend by thousands from all sorts of people we don't know from Adam and all ordinary life is suspended till they're dealt with.[19] He was just finishing a book, too! But we love the kind that have real letters from real friends inside.

All the same we are feeling deeply injured and would dunk you in the pond if you were available for dunking! *Why* did you get my poor Jack mixed up with the ineffable Rakestraw or whatever her name was?[20] She began by criticizing his opening words — "Today I want to discuss. . . ." "Professor Lewis, couldn't you say instead *'Let us think together, you and I about . . . ?'" No,* he couldn't. "*But* we want you to give the feeling of *embracing* them." Jack said if they wanted an embracer they had the wrong man. "Well, perhaps I mean a feeling of involvement. . . ." Ugh! At the end she made him sit absolutely silent before the microphone for a minute and a half "so they could feel his living presence." I told him he oughta

19. For more on this, see C. S. Lewis, "What Christmas Means to Me," *Twentieth Century* 157 (December 1957): 517-18. Reprinted in *God in the Dock: Essays on Theology and Ethics,* ed. Walter Hooper (Grand Rapids: Eerdmans, 1970).

20. Caroline Rakestraw (1912-1993), in conjunction with the Episcopal Church, founded the Episcopal Radio-TV Foundation in 1954. Through Chad Walsh, she made contact with Lewis and asked him to make recordings that would be broadcast during the "Episcopal Radio Hour." Lewis agreed to talk on the four loves; however, as Joy's letters here and later suggest, the experience was one Lewis did not altogether enjoy. For more on this, in CL, 3, see Lewis's letter to Rakestraw of August 8, 1958 (p. 964), Hooper's comment on p. 965, and Lewis's letter to Walsh of October 22, 1959 (p. 1097).

charge double rates for that — C. S. Lewis being silent, a unique listening experience. He came home rather shattered with all this; and now we learn — not from the organization, but through a friend — that they've decided to suppress the whole series because of Jack's "startling frankness" on sexual matters! Needless to say he wouldn't have startled anyone over the age of sixteen and the I.Q. of 80.

I'm feeling rather sour about the U.S. in general, though the last elections were rather reassuring. One gets a lopsided view from here, perhaps? I've now been away so long I can't claim to understand the present political set up. But the general effect of brutal materialism and overweening wealth is not pleasant. Nixon made a surprisingly good impression here; it was a relief to have an American politician who could talk spontaneously without sounding like the village idiot, but people wonder if he can be trusted.[21] Ike's goodwill message from the Sputnik was considered appallingly bad taste — "Hark the Herald Yankees Sing" commented one newspaper.

Glad to hear Demmie's enjoying marriage! So am I — Love from us all, and a Happy New Year.

Yours,
Joy
Source: Wade

On January 2, 1959, Walsh writes:

> *I'm ready to be dunked.*
> *Can you send me this Rakestraw's full name and address? (I failed to keep her letters.) I want to write her and ask for a full explanation, and then I'll be in position to give them the kind of Holy Hell they deserve. Not that this will change anything, but they've asked for it, and I want to have my say. Jack is the one who has been principally betrayed, but in a secondary way I have real reason to be sore. After all, I was the go-between, and I served as a go-between on the basis of the favorable things I'd heard about that program. If they are a bunch of timid prudes, it was their duty to spell out their taboos in advance. So, for the sake of my blood pressure, do send me that name and address. And ask Jack's Christian forgiveness for me.*

21. Richard M. Nixon (1913-1994), later thirty-seventh president of the United States, was at this time serving as vice-president under Eisenhower.

Strange, strange, how one can act with such unsullied motives and yet contribute to the most stupid situations.

I think there is creeping prudery abroad in the land. Last winter some of the faculty at Beloit accused the Poetry Journal *of being anti-Christian and indecent and kicked up enough of a rumpus so that the trustees, to avoid "controversy," I suppose, withdrew the college support. It is now an independent mag. Then this summer a juvenile writer whom I know found that her recent novel was on the "don't buy" list in the public libraries of a large city because she described an eleven-year-old girl becoming aware that she was developing.*

The elections encouraged me. There seems at least a slight swing away from the fairyland mentality of Eisenhowerism toward more awareness of the world as it is. The old kind of McCarthy hysteria no longer gathers in many votes or much publicity. More and more people will talk sense about China. I don't want to paint too rosy a picture, but things have indeed improved.

Write me air-mail, won't you? And much love to you and Jack and the boys. Source: Wade

To Chad Walsh

The Kilns
January 10, 1959

Dear Chad,

Goodness gracious! Never saw you so angry. I think you're quite right; they behaved very shabbily. They *did* pay for the lectures, thank Heaven, but I don't think $300 is an adequate return — and they actually wanted Jack to let them *publish* the lectures too, for no additional fee! He turned *that* down, of course.[22]

The address of the Episcopal Radio:

Mrs. Caroline Rakestraw
2744 Peachtree Road, N.E.
Atlanta, Georgia

22. Actually the recordings became the basis for C. S. Lewis, *The Four Loves* (London: Geoffrey Bles, 1960).

I enclose the clipping we were sent. It's strange to find this prudery surviving in a country whose sexual morals seem to have broken down completely — or am I judging too much by the press and the best-sellers? Pornography is certainly a Great American Industry these days. But of course the pornographers don't use any taboo *words,* and that makes all the difference.

I'm glad there are some signs of improvements politically — it is hard to feel otherwise than appalled at a nation that takes an Eisenhower seriously instead of retiring him to the Old Folks' Home. Nixon made a good impression here, you know, largely because he was able to answer questions spontaneously and coherently — a novelty in American statesmen. I wish something could be done about the American belief of giving ambassadorships as social plums to rich party-supporters! A recent envoy to Spain responded to toasts and boasts at a public dinner by saying that for him the strength and pride and dignity of the Spanish character were symbolized by "your magnificent Rock of Gibraltar!" Ouch. And the envoy to South Africa, usually tongue-tied, opened his mouth the other day in praise of Nasser! I *do* see that they're shifting him to Afghanistan or somewhere like that.

How extraordinary it is for us lifelong fantasy and sci-fi readers to have *real* spaceships flying past the moon! I can't resist the temptation to yell, "Yak! I told you so!" at all who jeered me for predicting it. But there's a curiously anticlimactic feeling when one's been reading the stuff so long; life is slower than the imagination and seems only a blurred copy.

Have you seen the new *Horizon?* Ed Fuller apparently is doing a study of Jack in it! They sent us a [specimen] and it seems very intelligent but over priced and too pretentious.[23] The *Atlantic* has degenerated dreadfully, judging by the last copy I've seen. Love to all.

Yours,

Joy

Source: Wade

---

23. See Edmund Fuller, "The Christian Spaceman: C. S. Lewis," *Horizon* 1 (May 1959): 64-69.

To Chad Walsh

The Kilns
January 29, 1959

Dear Chad,

Herewith the latest from Caroline Rakestraw — you seem to have marched through Georgia to some purpose! I'd find her protestations more credible if they had come spontaneously. Jack has sent a politely noncommittal answer.

We're having rheumatic aches and pains (weather's horrible) but otherwise doing well.[24] Jack is busy (among other things) revising the Psalter, along with some slightly woffly bishops who wanted to do it at committee meetings.[25] That brute [T. S.] Eliot, who is also on the committee, has fled to the Bahamas leaving Jack holding the bag; I guess he's met bishops before.

How's everyone? Love to Eva and the girls.

Yours,
Joy   *Source: Wade*

On March 5, 1959, Walsh writes Joy: "Just a note to thank you for sending me the letter from Caroline Rakestraw. I am glad that she finally got around to writing Jack. I still do not like the smooth taste of everything, but I guess that is the way the world operates nowadays. One nice by-product of the whole thing is that Mrs. Rakestraw lent me a copy of Jack's manuscript, and I had a chance to read them. They are strong stuff and magnificent."   *Source: Wade*

24. On January 1, 1959, Lewis wrote a friend: "We are all well. It is almost as if we had died and were in a new life" (CL, 3, p. 1008).

25. For more on this, see CL, 3, pp. 988–89, 1015, 1228, 1594, and 1595.

To William Lindsay Gresham

The Kilns
March 2, 1959

Dear Bill,

Hope the series of disasters that plagues you is now nearly over![26] Tell Renée she'll feel much better now she's had the works out; no more curse, no more worry, more energy, calmer nerves, no change-of-life problems ahead, and just as female as ever; the operation does *not* age or chill a woman, whatever popular superstition says! My laying-on-of-hands service was by an ordinary C. of E. clergyman, and friend (and convert) of Jack who had cured someone else the same way. Doctors here are by no means so rigidly hostile. The ignorant materialism which still prevails in America is regarded as quaintly nineteenth-century in educated circles here. It is no longer thought necessary to choose between religion and science; God knows why it ever should have been![27]

You do meet weird people — your list makes my tranquil Oxford life seem very quiet by contrast — thank Heaven! I like it this way. Woods, garden, books, pets, intelligent company, and lots of love — no wonder I continue to grow stronger. I admire the AA work you're doing, but I'm very glad to be out of the Westchester loony bin. I don't find England perfect (especially the taxes, which are keeping us broke) but it's a lot saner than America.

Don't envy you the Jean Harlow assignment.[28] What finally happened

---

26. On February 25, 1959, Bill writes Joy that Renée is back from the hospital, having had a hysterectomy. He is working on a story on Jean Harlow and also reports extensively on his AA projects. He notes: "Jack's article in the *Atlantic Monthly* on 'The Efficacy of Prayer' has caused a good deal of comment and I gathered that the miracle healing referred to your hip. I have some English friends who are mightily interested in prayer and divine healing and I sent them a copy of the article. There is a faith healer over here named Oral Roberts who has received the usual treatment from the news magazines but who seems to produce some miraculous cures though I have never had a chance to observe them myself. . . . Some friends of mine saw a goiter reduce in size in a few minutes after Roberts had prayed and laid his hands on the woman who bore it" (source: Wade).

27. Lewis's essay regarding prayer is partially autobiographical and refers to the laying on of hands and prayer for healing performed by the Rev. Peter Bide; see C. S. Lewis, "The Efficacy of Prayer," *The Atlantic Monthly* 203 (January 1959): 59-61. Reprinted in *The World's Last Night: And Other Essays*. Lewis also refers to the prayer for healing in his letter of January 26, 1959 (CL, 3, p. 1016).

28. Jean Harlow (1911-1937) had been a popular screen actress.

about the Houdini book? We had a funny contretemps with the Southern Episcopal Radio foundation that recorded Jack's talks on *The Four Loves* for broadcasting — it seems he actually mentioned sex, shocking them so much they decided not to broadcast the talks except to some college program! Chad Walsh gave them hell for it. He says there's a nasty new prudery getting started — purely verbal, I suppose; the worse you behave, the less you can say about it.

The boys are very well. Davy has already written you. *He* is now in a materialist, science-is-all phase, so I fear your mystical letter was wasted on him. We have his phases to time; he changes like the moon. He has outgrown all his clothes *again* and is active, merry, and hard working. Even Doug is now a dormitory prefect at school and has begun to pay some attention to his school work! Wonders never cease!

Regards,
Joy

To William Lindsay Gresham

The Kilns
July 14, 1959

Dear Bill,

Very glad to hear your eyes are behaving as they should.[29] I hope this means you'll be doing a lot better in the future — for your sake as well as ours! It *would* be nice if you were ever able to contribute something, even a little. Doug has just failed his Common Entrance exam and will have to have a term's expensive and intensive cramming if he's to get into a decent school; he's intelligent enough, but simply will not work at books — he works like a demon at everything else. Davy is doing a good deal better at Magdalen School than he did at first, but still tends to spread himself out too thin and to be carried away by new enthusiasms — he'll study any new subject hard for about a month and then drop it. He's improving a great deal physically — getting taller and broader — and looks quite well in his Cadet uniform. Both of them are now old enough to expect more of a fa-

29. On July 11, 1959, Bill writes Joy and tells her he is having success with a bifocal lens (source: Wade).

347

ther than occasional presents, and if you ever hope to have any sort of relation with them you would be wise to do something for them now.

I still have not been able to get Jack's affairs untangled from the lifetime charitable trust he set up, which takes nearly all his royalties; so we are
by no means well off. The money flows in all right, but we don't keep it!

You know, however, that I'd have to be pretty desperate before I took
any legal action to collect what you owe me. I can only leave the matter to
your own conscience.

Thanks for the news of the Science Fiction boys. I had heard that
Henry Kuttner was dead and wondered about it.[30] I hope Cat is bearing
up! We don't see many people here except our own circle and visiting
American admirers — there was a lovely one yesterday with white hair
and a little pointed beard, the Old Suhtha Cunnel to the life — only he
discussed the philosophy of Plotinus and the physics of Heisenberg. T. S.
Eliot has invited us both to dinner next week, though (he and Jack are
both on the official committee for revising the *Psalter*) and I'm looking
forward to that a great deal; I've always wanted to meet him.

Phyl [Haring] often asks about you. She's in South Africa now, working hard and sending Robin to college — has got over her worst troubles
and is trying to write children's stories. I now have the job of writing her a
detailed criticism of one which is all talk and no action with a clumsy
tacked-on moral. As she has all the touchy pride of the amateur, it won't
be fun. She is also flirting with Buddhism and seems to have the impression that Christianity rejects the world while Buddhism affirms it, but
she's a nice girl all the same.

I'm now so well that I'm able to do a good day's work in the garden
(we've enormous quantities of peas, beans, corn, squashes, turnips, lettuce,
etc. all needing picking) or go shopping on a bus like any other housewife.
I hope to start writing this autumn, if the cares of the household leave me
any time!

Regards to everyone.

Joy   *Source: Wade*

---

30. Henry Kuttner (1915-1958) was a science fiction and fantasy writer.

To William Lindsay Gresham

The Kilns
September 26, 1959

Dear Bill,

The cheque couldn't have come at a better time — I've just had to spend about 50 quid on new clothes for both boys.[31] They outgrow their old ones at a fearful rate now, and Davy has graduated from schoolboy stuff into mansize tweed jackets and trousers. As for Doug, he has just left for a terrific school in Wales which undertakes to get him through his Common Entrance exam — at about $390 a *term;* and he had to have a lot of new stuff to go with. His address is: Lapley Grange, Glandyfi, Machynlleth, Montgomeryshire, Wales. I've forwarded your letter to him. He will never be much of a scholar, but if he's to have the agricultural training he wants and needs he must get into a decent public school first. I hope to get him into Magdalen College School with Davy, who is doing passably well though not brilliantly there. Did you happen to see a recent article in the *Sat[urday] [Evening] Post* about British vs. American schools? The British school illustrated was Magdalen C[ollege] S[chool] and the masters and boys in the pictures are all friends of Davy — they came in for a terrific ribbing! I gather from American visitors that the praise of American schools was entirely undeserved. But Magdalen's a good place and they don't really wallop them at all.

Jack has just sold *Sat[urday] [Evening] Post* an after-dinner speech by Screwtape, denouncing (among other things) "democratic education." I bet it'll make the fur fly.[32]

We've had a fabulous summer here — in fact, it's not over yet; the squash and gourd vines are still bearing, roses and nasturtiums are flowering etc. The lawn is burned brown like an American one; there's been hardly any rain for four months. I tried all sorts of American vegetables and they came through with a bang — oh, yellow tomatoes and miniature

---

31. On September 21, 1959, Bill tells Joy that they have moved into a new apartment across the street — bigger for them. Enclosed are a check and his explanation for why it is not more — IRS problems. He says his Houdini book is selling steadily and that both of his eyes continue to have problems (source: Wade).

32. C. S. Lewis, "Screwtape Proposes a Toast," *The Saturday Evening Post* 232 (December 19, 1959): 36, 88-89. The "Toast" is now also published in most editions of *The Screwtape Letters.*

tomatoes and eggplants and artichokes and peppers and pumpkins and sweet corn and fancy squashes; my garden's a neighbourhood sensation. My one extravagance these days is bulbs and plants.

We'd a heavenly week in Wales at the beginning of the month; Doug got taken on free trips by fishermen and allowed to steer the boat, as he did a man's work. He caught oodles of lobster and mackerel. Davy went in for marine biology and filled his room with weird worms and whelks; he brought back three eels alive, packed in seaweed, and they are now happily swimming in the aquarium. (Very *small* eels, I hasten to add.) He also keeps live voles and mice, and raises interesting greenhouse plants: cacti and coleus and various oddities. He is going through an intense Jewish-nationalistic phase (a bit of a bore but a great deal better than his earlier Mohammedan period!) and takes trips to London's East End, coming back laden with books on Jewish life and parcels of gefillte fish. I have taught my plain English cook to make borscht and schav and gehackte leber . . . yummm.

I stay miraculously well and active; my latest X-rays showed a few holes here and there in my bones that won't quite vanish, but at least they don't grow. I can walk for miles now, climb hills, garden, and so on. I *do* have a lot of pain, on and off, with rheumatism and strained muscles — it's not easy walking about with one thigh more than three inches shorter than the other — but I'm assured these aches don't mean a thing (damn them!).

Jack's juveniles have a steady, small sale, larger here than in America, but we'll never get rich from *those* (Jack guesses three to five hundred pounds a year). The good thing about them is that they don't dwindle with time — but I think it's only the most successful juveniles that go on for ever.

Our meeting with [T. S.] Eliot was great fun all round. He turns out to be a sweet, genial, but rather vague old boy (he's almost seventy!) — quite unlike the rather bleak and unhappy tone of his work. He's got a statuesque blonde young wife who obviously adores him and is no doubt mellowing him a good deal.

Glad to hear Thel Greenhaus is back among the living. More power to your elbow and AA.

Yours,
Joy

Source: Wade

To William Lindsay Gresham

The Kilns
December 15, 1959

Dear Bill,

Well, that's a pleasant surprise for Christmas![33] Thank you for all three of us. Doug is home now for the holidays and he wrote you a letter the other day thanking you for his birthday present. He's been having a wonderful time assembling the knights. I think you are right to send money though — things are so much cheaper here, and the boys now like to do their own shopping. Davy buys books, pet rodents, and their equipment and food; fancy delicatessen and cakes are his passion. Doug buys tools, guns, etc. His first day home from school he got two pigeons in the woods. Davy traps mice and rats in the house and rears them with loving care (last night there was a huge rat in W's bedroom! It was hurt in the trap, so the boys etherized it on the dining-room table and Jack said it was like the evening spread out against the sky).

Doug is doing very much better at his new school, thank goodness. He came back with twice as much pocket money as he left with — result of buying cheap and selling dear all sorts of schoolboy junk.

We did get the Houdini book; thanks very much. Davy and I have both been reading it with interest. We agree Houdini was a horrid little man, though, and the whole show-business and newspaper-stunt world you describe has a grubbiness that puts one off. What a terrific job of research you did on it! I confess I like your serious style better than your journalistic one; but you know best which one sells. Did I tell you Jack has sold a Screwtape speech to the *SEP*? His publisher got a request the other day for a copy of "Screwed up Letters!"

I'm not as well as I was — a few new spots on my bones and lumps here and there — but so far they melt away beautifully before X-rays. I've attacks of pain — my skeleton is now such a haywire job that the slightest strain jerks something loose — but am usually fairly comfortable and able to get about, and should be able to live another year or two at least.[34] They

33. On December 8, 1959, Bill sends Joy a check for $230 plus $15 each for the two boys. He shares that his Houdini book has gotten good reviews, that they watched several old Houdini movies recently, and that he is still working with AA (source: Wade).

34. Lewis's letters from this time forward express his sense that "the tide has turned"

tell me I'm one of their great triumphs and exhibit me to visiting doctors. On the whole life's not too bad; except for my egregious parents who make nuisances of themselves by post. They are now nagging each other to death apparently. Dad writes begging for pity on the ground that he is actually 72 (he's in perfect health as far as the doctors know) and his wife, boohoo, expects him to wash the dishes and shop for groceries. *She* gets a check-up about eight times a year for some imaginary disease but is always disappointed — strong as a horse and lazy as a cow. Dad thinks Jack and I ought to come to New York to help him look after her. I think not.

Regards to Renée and the children — Happy Christmas.

Yours,
Joy
Source: Wade

To William Lindsay Gresham

The Kilns
March 30, 1960

Dear Bill,

I think the boys have both written you thanks for their presents, though I must check up on Doug who vanishes into the woods with a gun at the first hint of letter-writing. I have temporarily bagged *Tros* and am rereading it with interest, though it isn't up to my early memories of it. Too much talk; but the worst thing is that he keeps the full pressure going in the boiler all the time. Never a quiet moment, never a chance to draw breath, always *vivacé* and *fortissimo*. Gets very dull after a while.

I'm still on my feet and not in more pain than codeine can control, though I've now got so many cancers at work on me that I expect them to start organizing a union. Fortunately I have enormous resistance to X-rays and lose ground only very slowly. Jack and I are flying to Greece for a fortnight this week — a big chance in my condition, but the doctors say OK

for the worse in terms of Joy's health; see CL, 3, October 18, 1959 (p. 1092), October 22 (p. 1097), November 25 (p. 1101), December 3 (p. 1102), December 8 (p. 1105), December 22 (p. 1112), Christmas Day (p. 1116), December 31 (p. 1119), January 9, 1960 (p. 1122), January 17 (p. 1123), January 25 (p. 1126), March 5 (p. 1138), March 12 (p. 1139), March 26 (p. 1141), May 16 (p. 1146), and June 14 (p. 1161).

and I'd rather go out with a bang than a whimper, particularly on the steps of the Parthenon.

Doug is just back from a visit to friends in Kidderminster — up in midlands. He's become an experienced traveler by now. They went boating on the Severn all day. When I fetched him from his school in Wales, we drove back through Shropshire — over Hemlock Edge, down Only and Teme and Clun — lunch at Ludlow, which was always a beautiful city and has escaped modernizing. I wish I had time to see more of England. I've never been to Cornwall or Devon or the Lakes, but at least I know our own Cotswold country pretty well now. In Wales we visited Plynlimmon and Cader Idris — grim country, full of abandoned slate quarries — great hills of broken slate everywhere. Wonderful lakes and seashores, though.

I see your Houdini book has been published over here; good luck. Jack's latest two are off to a good start.[35] Doug has been made Second Head Prefect at his school and is actually *learning* something. He has saved up about £25 and is planning to buy a gramophone! Poor Phyllis has picked *this* moment to borrow money and buy a house in Jo'burg for a swimming school. Davy has become a terrific cook and Hebrew scholar!

Yours,
Joy

Source: Wade

Lewis and Joy flew to Greece with Roger and June Green April 3 to 14, 1960; although both knew it was risky and could actually have accelerated Joy's deteriorating condition, the trip turned out to be a lifelong dream delightfully realized.

35. Davidman is probably referring to *Reflections on the Psalms*, which appeared September 8, 1958, and *The Four Loves* (London: Geoffrey Bles, 1960), which appeared March 28, 1960.

To William Lindsay Gresham

[postcard from Greece]
April 10, 1960

Dear Bill,

This is the real of which Southern California is a shoddy mock-up. Rhodes is pure Garden of Eden; Attica is pale, bare, stony, austere, with tremendous mountains — all much bigger than one thought. Usually I can only walk about 100 yards, but Athena got me up the Acropolis and all round it! I hope I last long enough to go back there.[36]

Yours,
Joy

Source: Wade

On April 23, 1960, Bill tells Joy he was glad to hear of her trip to Greece, but for him "there are few places I really want to visit now — my exploring is all done inside Gresham." He sympathizes with her pain and says that he is ready for death himself, but is still heavily into AA work. He also says he might come over to visit the boys.

Source: Wade

To William Lindsay Gresham

The Kilns
May 2, 1960

Dear Bill,

The boys' holiday starts about the last week in July — they'll be home permanently after that, as we're going to send Doug to school in Oxford. Unless I am busy dying or having my pituitary clipped out (both of which are on the cards) we could put you up here for a bit. Let us know when you'll be coming, and for how long. I think one *can* still travel by tramp

36. In CL, 3, Lewis writes letters about the trip; see those of April 19, 1960 (p. 1147); May 13 (pp. 1151-52); and May 23 (pp. 1153-54). See also Walter Hooper, *C. S. Lewis: A Companion and Guide* (London: HarperCollins, 1996), pp. 95-97; and Douglas Gresham, *Lenten Lands: My Childhood with Joy Davidman and C. S. Lewis* (New York: Macmillan, 1988), pp. 122-25.

freighter, but it takes forever and they are not allowed to charge less than tourist-class on liners so what's the point? In your place I'd fly. I've fallen quite in love with flying — it was wonderful on this last trip looking down on the Alps and the Aegean.

Greece was beyond all expectation. We went, of course, with our heads full of the ancient country and the ruins. But one soon is captured by the modern country instead — it's all so much bigger and more splendid than one thought: incredible mountains, shimmering mists of olive trees, herds of black goats, donkeys and women spinning in the sun and the burning blue sea. They still build well — they seem incapable of making an ugly building. A box of a peasant cottage has one pillar at the corner and a touch of contrasting paint or ornament and becomes a house. And what elsewhere is the drearest modern "functional" style is given a variation — ironwork balcony or egg-and-dark moulding — that brings it to life. The Greeks are splendid people too — friendly but never servile or greedy; and how they work! Both of us went mad over the food and drink as well — octopus, squid, stuffed vine leaves, artichokes, ouzo, and retsina.

I came back barely able to walk at all — used my legs up on the Acropolis and Mycenae and Rhodes — but the damage isn't as bad as we feared at first; I can just about hobble on two sticks at present, but I hope to improve. I admire the lofty fortitude with which you endure my cancer; for me, however, the problems are more mundane — how to scheme for each step I take, how to sit down in the john and worse yet manage to get up again, how to run a house when I can't so much as get to the telephone — how to keep going with a grin in spite of pain, and not make myself a dreary nuisance to everyone else. Anybody can die with fine theological sentiments, Bill; it's the daily living that hurts.

The boys are both in good form; Doug has been made Second Head Prefect and is much praised by his headmaster. Davy has taken a sudden leap into manhood and is much nicer than he's ever been before.

If by some miracle I recover sufficiently (I'm such an unpredictable case the doctors have given up guessing) we shall want to do another trip to Ireland this summer. So better let us know as soon as possible when to fit you in. I enclose a review of your Houdini book from the *Oxford Mail*. Regards to Renée — Phyl's address: 51 Eden Rd., Bramley, Johannesburg, S. A.

Yours,
Joy

Source: Wade

In mid May, Joy was readmitted to the Acland Nursing home and had her right breast removed on May 20. Although she was able to return to the Kilns in early June, on June 19-20 she had to be rushed back to the Acland. When Douglas Gresham arrived home from school fearing for his mother's life, his mother greeted him by saying: "Doug, congratulations on passing your Common Entrance examinations.' I held her in my arms and merely wept. I was now taller than she would have been had she been able to stand, but as usual it was she who comforted me."[37] Yet Joy did eventually return to the Kilns on June 27, confounding even the doctors who thought she would not.[38]

On June 9, 1960, Bill writes and says he will fly into England on August 2 and gives other details of his travel plans. He also expresses frustration with his continuing IRS and eyesight problems. On June 20, 1960, Bill writes and asks the exact date of Joy's marriage to Jack; it may help him with IRS issues since he may have deductions he can take for alimony. "You gave as the date April 23, 1956 but this must be an error for I recall the time we got your letter saying you and Jack had been married and it was in 1957, for my eyesight was very dim at the time." Also, he welcomes the idea of David coming over for a visit.

Source: Wade

To William Lindsay Gresham

Acland Nursing Home
Headington
Oxford
June 27, 1960

Dear Bill,

April 23, 1956 *is* the correct date of my marriage; you are thinking of the religious ceremony, which came long after. Taxes they're complaining about in the *States* yet; you should see the way it's got here — and *our* taxniks you can't even bribe. But the British public, in its quiet way, have simply learned to go round *all* available corners, and tax evasion has become respectable.

---

37. Douglas Gresham, *Lenten Lands*, p. 121.

38. For more see Warren Lewis, *Brothers and Friends: The Diaries of Major Warren Hamilton Lewis*, ed. Clyde S. Kilby and Marjorie Lamp Mead (San Francisco: Harper & Row, 1982), pp. 248-49; and Hooper, *C. S. Lewis: A Companion and Guide*, pp. 97-100.

It's all off about Davy's trip to the States. His grandfather can't face having him (the old boy's blood pressure is up to about 170 and with that and nerve-strain he imagines himself sicker than he is). Anyhow, it would have been at a summer cottage not the Bronx. And I collapsed last week in a terrifying vomiting attack, which lasted all night, and strained all my weak places — was carted off to hospital apparently dying. The first guess was that the cancer had now reached the liver and I'd be leaving shortly. But as usual I fooled 'em by recovering with lightning speed and am now able to eat a full meal and get out of bed a bit — hope to go home again this week. Latest guess is that I was just having a storm in the adrenal latitudes as a result of the operation. Still, with this touch and go situation neither Davy nor I want him away. Your idea of taking the boys to London seems a good one — they can show you things, too. Davy knows London well by now.

Doug has passed his Common Entrance exam with surprisingly high marks and been accepted at Magdalen College School here, so we'll have *him* living at home too, much to everyone's delight!

Glad you've got a really good subject like Henry Morgan; the carny is getting very corny. Alas, our baby budgerigar has died of parental neglect; see you (I think) on the 3rd Aug; telephone us and we'll have a meal. Goodbye for now.

Joy   *Source: Wade*

To William Lindsay Gresham

The Kilns
July 2, 1960

Dear Bill,

    After thoughts, requests, suggestions:
1. It's *cold* here. Bring an ordinary suit and a mack!
2. Could you buy for us 2 nice Tarot packs?
3. Don't bring American whiskey or cigarettes. We hate.
4. Any Dunsany books to spare? I'm dying to read *Idle Days on the [Yansee]* again and can't get it here.
5. If planning to take boys to London, better book bed and breakfast rooms ahead on your first night there.

A. Do you, like all other Americans, want to visit Stratford? Only the theatre is worth it; if you like we'll try to get seats, but of course it'll be full of coachloads of Middle Western schoolmarms.

B. Are your eyes good enough for scenery? I thought of a car trip through the Cotswolds and another to the Vale of the White Horse; and of course the boys can show you Oxford. OK?

C. I've been wondering if you would welcome or the reverse, advice in dealing with the boys. It doesn't seem decently Christian to let you meet two English public school boys unprepared; and your letters to them, I fear, have been arrows very wide of the mark. Begin by summing up everything that is commonly said of American adolescents — *then tear it up and throw it away!* They are, I think, far less developed sexually than American boys their age; and they are rather prudish and austere — my mildest jokes shock Davy. Doug as Head Prefect has been energetically stopping smutty talk at his school. I do not venture to discuss their own feelings with them.

In every other way — emotional and intellectual — they are far *more* advanced than American boys, indeed many American men. "Integrated" might be the word, especially for Doug. Remember talking about raising them as tigers? No tigers; but Davy is something like a leopard (not so beautiful though!) and Doug is certainly a lion. Or, you might reread Kipling's *Stalky and Co.* as a preparation.[39] They are more civilized than those boys, but Davy is not unlike the egregious Beetle and Doug is quite a good Stalky. One could trust him to take a regiment into action right now, I think!

Above all, they are emotionally very reserved — for God's sake, don't try to kiss them; *I* don't. They are full of enthusiasms — Davy for Hebrew studies and small animals, Doug for hard work and discipline — and very lively, uninhibited companions. But they are not children to be petted — After thought: any chance of smuggling in a pair of box tortoises? Davy'd love it.[40]

Yours,

Joy

Source: Wade

39. Rudyard Kipling, *Stalky & Co.* (London: Macmillan, 1899).

40. On July 6, 1960, Bill thanks her for her advice on meeting the boys and will try to bring the items she requests (source: Wade).

Joy seemed to be recovering, but on July 13 she awoke in agonizing pain and was moved to the Radcliffe Infirmary. Warren Lewis captures the end most poignantly, writing in his diary:

> *I heard J[ack] come into the house [near midnight] and went out to meet him. Self: "What news?" J: "She died about twenty minutes ago." She was, he tells me, conscious up to the last, just before Till called J out of the room to say she was dying rapidly. J went back and told Joy, who agreed with him that it was the best news they could now get. During the afternoon and evening she dozed from time to time, but was fully sensible whenever she was awake. Asked during these final hours that she should be cremated, left her fur coat as a parting gift to K. Farrer, and was able to receive Absolution from Austin, whom she asked to read the funeral service over her at the crematorium. Once during the afternoon she said to J, "Don't get me a posh coffin, posh coffins are all rot." God rest her soul, I miss her to a degree which I would not have imagined possible.*[41]

July 15, 1960, Lewis writes to Bill: "Joy died on the 13th July. This need involve no change in your plans, but I thought you should arrive knowing it."[42]

Joy Davidman's funeral was on July 18, 1960, and her body was cremated.[43] *The plaque at the Oxford Crematorium is inscribed with a poem Lewis wrote for Joy:*

> *Remember*
> *Helen Joy*
> *Davidman*
> *D. July 1960*
> *Loved wife of*
> *C. S. Lewis*

> *Here the whole world (stars, water, air,*
> *And field, and forest, as they were*

---

41. For Warren's complete account, see *Brothers and Friends*, pp. 249-50.

42. CL, 3, p. 1170. Other letters offer insights into Lewis's grief after Joy's death; see those of July 14, 1960 (p. 1169), July 15 (pp. 1170-71), July 21 (p. 1174), July 25 (p. 1175), August 5 (p. 1177), August 20 (p. 1179), August 30 (p. 1181), September 20 (p. 1185), September 23 (p. 1187), September 24 (p. 1188), and October 18 (p. 1199). See also Douglas Gresham, *Lenten Lands*, pp. 125-29.

43. Warren Lewis offers a poignant account of this in *Brothers and Friends*, pp. 250-51.

Reflected in a single mind)
Like cast-off clothes was left behind
In ashes yet with hope that she,
Re-born from holy poverty,
In Lenten lands, hereafter may
Resume them on her Easter Day.[44]

Sometime during August 1960 Lewis began making notes about his grief,
which culminated in what some consider one of his most powerful books, A
Grief Observed, *first published under a pseudonym. There he writes:*

For a good wife contains so many persons in herself. What was H. not to
me? She was my daughter and my mother, my pupil and my teacher, my
subject and my sovereign; and always, holding all these in solution, my
trusty comrade, friend, shipmate, fellow-soldier. My mistress; but at the
same time all that any man friend (and I have good ones) has ever been to
me. Perhaps more. If we had never fallen in love we should have none the
less been always together, and created scandal. That's what I meant when
once I praised her for her "masculine virtues." But she soon put a stop to that
by asking how I'd like to be praised for my feminine ones. It was a good ri-
poste, *dear. Yet there was something of the Amazon, something of Penthe-*
sileia and Camilla.[45]

44. This poem appears as "Epitaph for Helen Joy Davidman," in *The Collected Poems of*
C. S. Lewis, ed. Walter Hooper (London: Fount, 1994), p. 252. For more on Lewis's life after
Joy's death, see Douglas Gresham, *Lenten Lands,* pp. 130-39 and 146-59.
45. *A Grief Observed* (London: Faber and Faber, 1961), p. 39. The book was first published under the pseudonym of N. W. Clerk.

Bibliography

A Chronological Bibliography of Joy Davidman's Works

"Clair de Lune" (Translation of Verlaine) and "Odelette" (Translation of H. De Regnier). *Hunter College Echo* (Christmas 1932).

"Reveal the Titan." *Hunter College Echo* (May 1934): 26-36.

"Apostate." *Hunter College Echo* (November 1934): 17-26. This story was Winner of the Bernard Cohen Prize.

"My Lord of Orrery." MA Thesis. Columbia University, 1935 (unpublished).

"Resurrection" and "Amulet." *Poetry* 47 (January 1936): 193-94.

"Variations on a Theme," "The Half-Hearted," "Shadow Dance," and "Odi Et Amo." *Poetry* 49 (March 1937): 323-27.

Letter to a Comrade. New Haven, CT: Yale University Press, 1938. Winner of the Russell Loines Memorial award for poetry given by the National Institute of Arts and Letters.

"Strength through Joy." *New Masses* 27 (April 5, 1938): 5.

"Spartacus — 1938." *New Masses* 27 (May 24, 1938): 19. Reprinted in *Letter to a Comrade*, 22-23.

"Prayer Against Indifference." *New Masses* 28 (August 9, 1938): 17. Reprinted in *Letter to a Comrade*, 31.

"Apology for Liberals." *New Masses* 28 (August 16, 1938): 4. Reprinted in *Letter to a Comrade*, 90.

"Near Catalonia." *New Masses* 29 (October 18, 1938): 18. Reprinted in *Letter to a Comrade*, 67.

"Arcadia, Kentucky" (Book review of *Black Is My Truelove's Hair* by Elizabeth Madox Roberts). *New Masses* 30 (December 27, 1938): 25.

"About Spain" (Book review of *Salud! Poems, Stories, and Sketches of Spain by*

American Writers, edited by Alan Calmer). *New Masses* 30 (January 31, 1939): 24-25.

"Kansas Poet" (Book review of *The High Plains* by Kenneth Porter). *New Masses* 30 (February 7, 1939): 26-27.

"Nazi Classroom" (Book review of *The Age of the Fish* by Odon von Horvath). *New Masses* 30 (March 14, 1939): 24-25.

"The Power-House" (Book review of *The Power-House* by Benjamin Appel). *New Masses* 31 (May 16, 1939): 23-24.

"The Devil Will Come." *New Masses* 32 (June 27, 1939): 6.

"Jews of No Man's Land." *New Republic* 99 (July 5, 1939): 248.

Anya. New York: Macmillan, 1940.

"For the Gentlemen." *New Masses* 38 (December 31, 1940): 23

"Prophet without Honor." *New Masses* 38 (January 14, 1941): 14.

"For the Happy Man." *New Masses* 38 (February 18, 1941): 36.

"Marxist Mania" (Movie review of *Go West*). *New Masses* 38 (March 4, 1941): 27-28.

"Blunted Edge" (Movie reviews of *Tobacco Road* and *The Lady Eve*). *New Masses* 38 (March 11, 1941): 30-31.

"Humdrum Cinema" (Movie reviews of *Come Live with Me* and *So Ends Our Night*). *New Masses* 38 (March 18, 1941): 29-30.

"Pacific Shore." *New Masses* 39 (March 25, 1941): 24.

"Pepe le Moko" (Movie reviews of *Pepe le Moko, Andy Hardy's Private Secretary, The Mad Doctor,* and *Cheers for Miss Bishop*). *New Masses* 39 (March 25, 1941): 29.

"Huey Hooey" (Movie reviews of *Meet John Doe* and *Rage in Heaven*). *New Masses* 39 (April 1, 1941): 30-31.

"Rover Boys on Wings" (Movie reviews of *I Wanted Wings* and *Topper Returns*). *New Masses* 39 (April 8, 1941): 28-29.

"Soviet Love Story" (Movie reviews of *The New Teacher* and *That Hamilton Woman*). *New Masses* 39 (April 22, 1941): 28-29.

"Citizen Kane" (Movie reviews of *Citizen Kane* and *The Sea Wolf*). *New Masses* 39 (May 13, 1941): 28-29.

"Three Films" (Movie reviews of *That Uncertain Feeling, The Flame of New Orleans,* and *Penny Serenade*). *New Masses* 39 (May 20, 1941): 30-31.

"Volga-Volga" (Movie review of *Volga-Volga*). *New Masses* 39 (May 27, 1941): 25.

"St. George Pets the Dragon" (Movie reviews of *Major Barbara, A Woman's Face,* and *Proud Valley*). *New Masses* 39 (June 3, 1941): 28-29.

"Poet of the Poor." *New Masses* 39 (June 10, 1941): 12.

"Neptune's Pets" (Movie reviews of *Washington Murderdrama, Power Dive,* and *Border Vigilantes*). *New Masses* 39 (June 10, 1941): 28-29.

"Dayspring." *New Masses* 39 (June 17, 1941): 17.

"Shining Screwballs" (Movie reviews of *Love Crazy* and *Shining Victory*). *New Masses* 39 (June 17, 1941): 28.

"Monopoly Takes a Screen Test." *New Masses* 39 (June 24, 1941): 28-30.

"Tripe and Taylor" (Movie reviews of *Billy the Kid, She Knew All the Answers*, and *The Face Behind the Mask*). *New Masses* 40 (July 1, 1941): 30-31.

"Here in the City." *New Masses* 40 (July 8, 1941): 20.

"The Face of China" (Movie reviews of *Ku Kan* and *Out of the Fog*). *New Masses* 40 (July 8, 1941): 27, 29.

"Soviet Frontiers" (Movie reviews of *Soviet Frontiers on the Danube* and *Underground*). *New Masses* 40 (July 15, 1941): 27-28.

"Three Movies" (Movie reviews of *The Big Store, Blossoms in the Dust*, and *Tight Shoes*). *New Masses* 40 (July 22, 1941): 29-30.

"The Movies: Stern, Gay, and Otherwise" (Movie reviews of *The Bride Came COD, In the Navy*, and *They Met in Bombay*). *New Masses* 40 (August 5, 1941): 28-29.

"Fantasy and Fun" (Movie reviews of *Million Dollar Baby* and *Singapore Woman*). *New Masses* 40 (August 19, 1941): 30.

"Studies in Pathos" (Movie reviews of *Honky Tonk* and *Hold Back the Dawn*). *New Masses* 41 (October 14, 1941): 27.

"The Maltese Falcon" (Movie reviews of *The Maltese Falcon, It Started With Eve*, and *The Man Who Seeks the Truth*). *New Masses* 41 (October 21, 1941): 28.

"Recent Movies" (Movie reviews of *Musical Story* and *This Woman Is Mine*). *New Masses* 41 (October 28, 1941): 28-30.

"Other Movies" (Movie reviews of *Dumbo, All That Money Can Buy*, and *Target for Tonight*). *New Masses* 41 (November 4, 1941): 27-28.

"Scorched Valley" (Movie reviews of *How Green Was My Valley* and *Le Roi*). *New Masses* 41 (November 11, 1941): 26-27.

"Horror with Subtlety" (Movie reviews of *Ladies in Retirement, The Chocolate Soldier, Never Give a Sucker an Even Break*, and *My Life with Caroline*). *New Masses* 41 (November 18, 1941): 28-29.

"Perfect Landing" (Movie reviews of *Wings of Victory* and *The Land Is Bright*). *New Masses* 41 (November 25, 1941): 26-27 and 28-29.

"Forgotten Village" (Movie reviews of *The Forgotten Village, International Lady*, and *This England*). *New Masses* 41 (December 2, 1941): 27-28.

"A Rake Reforms" (Movie reviews of *Suspicion* and *Skylark*). *New Masses* 41 (December 9, 1941): 27-29.

"New Movies" (Movie reviews of *The Feminine Touch* and *The Men in Her Life*). *New Masses* 41 (December 23, 1941): 28.

"B Becomes A" (Movie reviews of *Among the Living, Birth of the Blues*, and *Blues in the Night*). *New Masses* 41 (December 30, 1941): 26.

"The Girl from Leningrad" (Movie review of *The Girl from Leningrad*). *New Masses* 42 (January 6, 1942): 26-27.

"Thumbs Down" (Movie reviews of *Two-Faced Woman, The Shanghai Gesture,* and *The Wolf Man*). *New Masses* 42 (January 13, 1942): 26-28.

"Dinner Knives" (Movie reviews of *The Man Who Came to Dinner* and *Louisiana Purchase*). *New Masses* 42 (January 20, 1942): 29-30.

"Ingratiating Comedy" (Movie reviews of *Ball of Fire* and *Pacific Blackout*). *New Masses* 42 (January 27, 1942): 27-28.

"Paris Calling" (Movie reviews of *Paris Calling, I Wake Up Screaming,* and *Mr. and Mrs. North*). *New Masses* 42 (February 3, 1942): 27-28.

"Quack, Quack" (Book review of *Hollywood: The Movie Colony — The Movie Makers* by Leo Rosten. *New Masses* 42 (February 10, 1942): 24.

"This Week's Films" (Movie reviews of *Sullivan's Travels* and *Joan of Paris*). *New Masses* 42 (February 10, 1942): 28-29.

"Cabbages and Kings" (Movie reviews of *King's Row* and *All through the Night*). *New Masses* 42 (February 17, 1942): 28.

"Our Russian Front" (Movie reviews of *One Day in Soviet Russia* and *Woman of the Year*). *New Masses* 42 (February 24, 1942): 29-30.

"The Shadow" (Movie reviews of *Mr. V, Nine Bachelors,* and *Design for Scandal*). *New Masses* 42 (March 3, 1942): 28-29.

"Superb Screen Satire" (Movie reviews of *Roxie Hart, Crime and Punishment,* and *The Brothers Karamazov*). *New Masses* 42 (March 10, 1942): 28-29.

"Tanya's Glass Slipper" (Movie reviews of *Tanya* and *Invaders*). *New Masses* 42 (March 17, 1942): 29-30.

"Zola Revival" (Movie review of *Zola* and further discussion of *How Green Was My Valley*). *New Masses* 42 (March 24, 1942): 30.

"A Spirited Ghost" (Movie reviews of *The Remarkable Andrew* and *Alexander Nevsky*). *New Masses* 42 (March 31, 1941): 29-30.

"Tragic Laughter" (Movie review of *To Be or Not to Be*). *New Masses* 43 (April 7, 1942): 29-30.

"Fourth Down" (Movie reviews of *The Male Animal, The Bugle Sounds,* and comments on the reissuing of *Gone with the Wind*). *New Masses* 43 (April 14, 1942): 28-30.

"Guerilla Brigade" (Movie reviews of *Guerilla Brigade* and *The Ghost of Frankenstein*). *New Masses* 43 (April 21, 1942): 28-29.

"Shadows and Percy" (Movie reviews of *Joe Smith, American, Dangerously They Live,* and *My Favorite Blonde*). *New Masses* 43 (April 28, 1942): 30.

"Before the Talkies" (Movie review of the reissue of *The Gold Rush*). *New Masses* 43 (May 5, 1942): 28-29.

"Low Ebb" (Movie review of *Moontide*). *New Masses* 43 (May 12, 1942): 30.

"Native Land" (Movie review of *Native Land*). *New Masses* 43 (May 19, 1942): 28-29.

"Shadows in a Fog" (Movie reviews of *Tortilla Flat, This Above All,* and *The Thirty-Nine Steps*). *New Masses* 43 (June 2, 1942): 29-31.

"This One's a Dud" (Movie review of *Ships with Wings*). *New Masses* 43 (June 9, 1942): 31.

"Exciting Soviet Film" (Movie reviews of *Red Tanks* and *Take a Letter, Darling*). *New Masses* 43 (June 16, 1942): 27-29.

"Under the Bombs" (Movie reviews of *Mrs. Miniver*, *Nazi Agent*, and *Ring of Steel*). *New Masses* 43 (June 30, 1942): 29-30.

"This Is the Enemy" (Movie reviews of *This Is the Enemy* and *Laugh, Town, Laugh*). *New Masses* 44 (July 7, 1942): 30-31.

"Women: Hollywood Style." *New Masses* 44 (July 14, 1942): 28-31.

"Peter the Plowman." *New Masses* 44 (September 15, 1942): 15.

"Heroes Are Human Beings" (Movie reviews of *In the Rear of the Enemy, Desperate Journey, Manilla Calling,* and *Tales of Manhattan*). *New Masses* 45 (October 13, 1942): 30-31.

"Two Films, One Revue" (Movie reviews of *Inside Britain* and *Panama Hattie*). *New Masses* 45 (October 20, 1942): 28.

"The Will and the Way." *New Masses* 45 (October 27, 1942): 28, 30-31.

"Fun with Russell" (Movie reviews of *My Sister Eileen* and *The Devil with Hitler*). *New Masses* 45 (November 3, 1942): 29-30.

"The Moon and Sixpence" (Movie reviews of *The Moon and Sixpence* and *Now, Voyager*). *New Masses* 45 (November 10, 1942): 29-30.

"Dutch Underground" (Movie reviews of *One of Our Aircraft Is Missing, George Washington Slept Here, A Yank at Eton,* and *Iceland*). *New Masses* 45 (November 17, 1942): 29-31.

"The War Film: An Examination." *New Masses* 45 (November 24, 1942): 29-30.

"Those Fighting Britons" (Movie reviews of *Target for Tonight, Soviet School Child,* and *Listen to Britain*). *New Masses* 45 (December 1, 1942): 29-30.

"Cameras as Weapons." *New Masses* 45 (December 8, 1942): 28-29.

"Real Boy Meets Real Girl" (Movie reviews of *Mashenka, Casablanca, The Avengers,* and *I Married a Witch*). *New Masses* 45 (December 15, 1942): 29-30.

"Screen Spookery" (Movie review of *The Cat People*). *New Masses* 45 (December 22, 1942): 31.

"Poems Against Hitler" (Book review of *Untergrund* by Hans Marchwitza). *New Masses* 45 (December 29, 1942): 25-26.

"Battered Formulas" (Movie reviews of *The Palm Beach Story* and *Life Begins at Eight-Thirty*). *New Masses* 45 (December 29, 1942): 29-31.

"Little Margaret's Journey" (Movie reviews of *Journey for Margaret* and *Fortress on the Volga*). *New Masses* 46 (January 5, 1943): 29-30.

"Crowds in the Rain" (Movie reviews of *The World in Action* and *Flying Fortresses*). *New Masses* 46 (January 12, 1943): 29-30.

"In Which We Serve" (Movie reviews of *In Which We Serve* and *Arabian Nights*). *New Masses* 46 (January 19, 1943): 29-30.

"A Film Goebbels Would Love" (Movie review of *Tennessee Johnson*). *New Masses* 46 (January 26, 1943): 29-30.

"The Camera as Narrator" (Movie reviews of *The Black Room* and *Shadow of a Doubt*). *New Masses* 46 (February 2, 1943): 29-31.

"Commandos Strike at Dawn" (Movie reviews of *Commandos Strike at Dawn* and *China Girl*). *New Masses* 46 (February 9, 1943): 27-28.

"Drama Roundup" (Play review of *The Barber Had Two Sons* and movie reviews of *Air Force* and *Random Harvest*). *New Masses* 46 (February 16, 1943): 27-28.

"Margaret Walker: Negro Poet." *New Masses* 46 (February 23, 1943): 24-25.

"Siege of Leningrad" (Movie review of *The Siege of Leningrad*). *New Masses* 46 (February 23, 1943): 29-31.

"Saludos Amigos" (Movie review of *Saludos Amigos*). *New Masses* 46 (March 2, 1943): 30.

"Mr. Chadband's Ghost" (Movie reviews of *The Human Comedy* and *Counterattack*). *New Masses* 46 (March 16, 1943): 29-31.

"Goebbel's Missing Link" (Comment on forthcoming movie *Captive Wild Women*). *New Masses* 46 (March 23, 1943): 29.

"False History" (Movie review of *Young Mr. Pitt*). *New Masses* 46 (March 23, 1943): 30-31.

"Stephen Vincent Benét." *New Masses* 46 (March 30, 1943): 23-24.

"Keeper of the Flame" (Movie reviews of *Keeper of the Flame*, *Chetniks*, and *Hitler's Children*). *New Masses* 46 (March 30, 1943): 28-29.

"With Bullet and Whip" (Movie reviews of *Diary of a Nazi* and *Forever and a Day*). *New Masses* 47 (April 6, 1943): 28-30.

"The Moon Is Up" (Movie review of *The Moon Is Down*). *New Masses* 47 (April 13, 1943): 29-30.

"Script and Screen" (Commentary by screenwriter Lester Cole disagreeing with Davidman's earlier article "The Camera as Narrator"; Davidman answers). *New Masses* 47 (April 20, 1943): 28-30.

"Prayer for Every Voyage." *New Masses* 47 (April 27, 1943): 16.

"Sword's Edge" (Movie reviews of *Edge of Darkness*, *Desert Victory*, and *Heart of a Nation*). *New Masses* 47 (April 27, 1943): 28-30.

"But the People Live" (Movie review of *Hangmen Must Die*). *New Masses* 47 (May 4, 1943): 28-29.

"Journey into Truth" (Movie review of *Mission to Moscow*). *New Masses* 47 (May 11, 1943): 28-30.

"Deaths and a Warning" (Movie reviews of *The Ox-Bow Incident* and *Next of Kin*). *New Masses* 47 (May 18, 1943): 30-31.

"Mission of Sabotage." *New Masses* 47 (May 25, 1943): 29.

"Assignment in Brittany" (Movie review of *Assignment in Brittany*). *New Masses* 47 (May 25, 1943): 31.

"Let the People Sing" (Book review of Aaron Kramer's *Till the Grass Is Ripe for Dancing*). *New Masses* 47 (June 1, 1943): 26-27.

"Masquerade" (Movie review of *Masquerade* and continuing discussion of *Mission to Moscow*). *New Masses* 47 (June 1, 1943): 29-31.

"Canvas and Film" (Movie reviews of *The More the Merrier, Desperados, I Walked with a Zombie,* and *Leopard Man*). *New Masses* 47 (June 8, 1943): 29-31.

"Seamen in Battle" (Movie reviews of *Action in the North Atlantic, This Land Is Mine,* and *Five Graves to Cairo*). *New Masses* 47 (June 15, 1943): 29-31.

"The Russian Story" (Movie review of *The Russian Story*). *New Masses* 47 (June 22, 1943): 30-31.

"Entertainment Goes to War." *New Masses* 47 (June 29, 1943): 30.

"Young Defenders" (Movie review of *Boy from Stalingrad*). *New Masses* 48 (July 6, 1943): 28-29.

"Two Films about Bataan" (Movie reviews of *So Proudly We Hail* and *Bataan*). *New Masses* 48 (July 13, 1943): 29-31.

"At the Canteen" (Movie reviews of *Stage Door Canteen* and *Background to Danger*). *New Masses* 48 (July 20, 1943): 31.

"The Equivocal Bell" (Movie review of *For Whom the Bell Tolls*). *New Masses* 48 (July 27, 1943): 30-31.

"For Odessa" (by Boris Veselchakov, adapted by Joy Davidman). *New Masses* 48 (August 10, 1943): 14. Reprinted in *War Poems of the United Nations,* edited by Joy Davidman. New York: Dial Press, 1943.

"The Young Pioneers" (by A. Bezmensky, adapted by Joy Davidman). *New Masses* 48 (September 7, 1943): 12.

"Anti-Fascist Vignettes" (Book review of *A Garland of Straw* by Sylvia Townsend Warner). *New Masses* 49 (October 19, 1943): 28-29.

"Fairytale" and "Trojan Women"; "For My Son" (under the name Megan Coombes-Dawson); "Four Years after Munich" and "Peccavimus" (both under the name Haydon Weir); "For Odessa" (by Boris Veselchakov, adapted by Joy Davidman) and "The Young Pioneers" (by A. Bezmensky, adapted by Joy Davidman); and "Snow in Madrid" (reprinted from *Letter to a Comrade*). All in *War Poems of the United Nations,* edited by Joy Davidman. New York: Dial Press, 1943.

"The Language Men Speak" (Book review of *The Fourth Decade* by Norman Rosten). *New Masses* 49 (November 30, 1943): 26-27.

"Foreword." In *They Look Like Men,* by Alexander F. Bergman. New York: Bernard Ackerman, 1944.

"Spartacus 1938" (from *Letter to a Comrade*), "The Dead Partisan," "Dirge for the Suicides," "For the Nazis," "Elegy for Garcia Lorca," "Trojan Women," and "New Spiritual," all in *Seven Poets in Search of an Answer,* edited by Thomas Yoseloff. New York: Bernard Ackerman, 1944.

"Dialogue for D-Day." *New Masses* 51 (June 20, 1944): 15.

"No Sun, No Stars" (Book review of *No Beautiful Nights* by Vassili Grossman). *New Masses* 52 (August 1, 1944): 28.

"Poem for Liberation." *New Masses* 52 (September 12, 1944): 8.

"The Nessus-shirt" (Book review of *The Mocking Bird Is Singing* by Louise Malley). *New Masses* 52 (September 12, 1944): 26-27.

"Sonnet to Various Republicans." *New Masses* 53 (December 19, 1944): 10.

"Without the Reason Why" (Book review of *The Journal of Mary Hervey Russell* by Storm Jameson). *New Masses* 55 (April 10, 1945): 24-25.

"Life with Mother" (Book review of *The Ballad and the Source* by Rosamund Lehman). *New Masses* 56 (July 10, 1945): 26-27.

"Quisling at Twilight." *New Masses* 56 (July 31, 1945): 4.

The last time Davidman appears on the masthead of *New Masses* as a "contributing editor": *New Masses* 59 (April 16, 1946): 1.

"Materialism vs. Romance (letter to editor)." *The Saturday Review of Literature* 31 (December 25, 1948): 23.

"Theater Party." *Bluebook* 88 (February 1949): 16-17.

Weeping Bay. New York: Macmillan, 1950.

"The Longest Way Round." In *These Found the Way: Thirteen Converts to Protestant Christianity,* edited by David Wesley Soper. Philadelphia: The Westminster Press, 1951.

"A Little Bird Told Her." *McCall's* (February 1951): 44, 112, 115-17.

"It's Right to Marry Young." *Redbook* (November 1952): 40-41, 72-73. With William Lindsay Gresham.

"Into the Full Light." *Presbyterian Life* 6 (April 4, 1953): 12-13, 26-29.

"God Comes First." *Presbyterian Life* 6 (May 2, 1953): 12-14.

Smoke on the Mountain: An Interpretation of the Ten Commandments. Philadelphia: Westminster Press, 1954; London: Hodder & Stoughton, 1955.

Critical Bibliography

Book Reviews

Letter to a Comrade

Blackmur, R. P. "Nine Poets." *Partisan Review,* Winter 1939, p. 112.

Emerson, Dorothy. "Three Young Poets." *Scholastic* 34 (May 27, 1939): 27E.

Hawkins, Desmond. Review of Joy Davidman's *Letter to a Comrade. Spectator* 162 (May 19, 1939): 868.

Lechlitner, Ruth. Review of Joy Davidman's *Letter to a Comrade. New York Herald Tribune Books,* December 25, 1938, p. 2.

Millspaugh, C. A. "Among the New Books of Verse." *Kenyon Review* 2 (1940): 363.

Review of Joy Davidman's *Letter to a Comrade. Times Literary Supplement* [London], October 14, 1939, p. 599.

Rukeyser, Muriel. Review of Joy Davidman's *Letter to a Comrade. New Republic* 98 (March 8, 1939): 146.

Ulrich, Dorothy. Review of Joy Davidman's *Letter to a Comrade. New York Times Book Review*, August 6, 1939, p. 4.

Williams, Oscar. Review of Joy Davidman's *Letter to a Comrade. Poetry* 54 (April 1939): 33.

Anya

Cournos, John. Review of Joy Davidman's *Anya. New York Times*, July 14, 1940, p. 7.

Frye, Dorothy. Review of Joy Davidman's *Anya. Boston Transcript*, August 10, 1940, p. 2.

Kazin, Alfred. Review of Joy Davidman's *Anya. New York Herald Tribune Books*, July 14, 1940, p. 2.

Review of Joy Davidman's *Anya. Christian Century* 57 (July 10, 1940): 879.

Review of Joy Davidman's *Anya. New Republic* 103 (August 12, 1940): 222.

Rothman, N. L. Review of Joy Davidman's *Anya. Saturday Review of Literature* 22 (July 13, 1940): 10.

Weeping Bay

Breaden, R. P. Review of Joy Davidman's *Weeping Bay. Library Journal* 75 (February 1, 1950): 171.

Derleth, August. Review of Joy Davidman's *Weeping Bay. Sunday Chicago Tribune*, March 12, 1950, p. 4.

Hicks, Granville. Review of Joy Davidman's *Weeping Bay. New York Times*, March 5, 1950, p. 30.

Hilton, James. Review of Joy Davidman's *Weeping Bay. New York Herald Tribune Book Review*, March 12, 1950, p. 6.

Jackson, J. H. Review of Joy Davidman's *Weeping Bay. San Francisco Chronicle*, March 7, 1950, p. 18.

Review of Joy Davidman's *Weeping Bay. Kirkus* 18 (January 1, 1950): 8.

Review of Joy Davidman's *Weeping Bay. New Yorker* 26 (March 11, 1950): 103.

Review of Joy Davidman's *Weeping Bay. United States Quarterly Booklist* 6 (June 1950): 156.

Sandrock, Mary. Review of Joy Davidman's *Weeping Bay. Catholic World* 171 (June 1950): 171.

Walsh, Chad. "First Things First: How Does One Come to Know God?" *Presbyterian Life* 3 (May 27, 1950): 36-38.

Wolfe, A. F. Review of Joy Davidman's *Weeping Bay. Saturday Review of Literature* 33 (March 18, 1950): 16.

Smoke on the Mountain

Miller, L. R. Review of Joy Davidman's *Smoke on the Mountain*. *Library Journal* 79 (September 1, 1954): 1496.

Review of Joy Davidman's *Smoke on the Mountain*. *Christian Century* 72 (February 16, 1955): 72.

Review of Joy Davidman's *Smoke on the Mountain*. *Journal of Bible and Religion* 23 (April 1955): 157.

Review of Joy Davidman's *Smoke on the Mountain*. *Kirkus* 22 (September 15, 1954): 661.

Review of Joy Davidman's *Smoke on the Mountain*. *Saturday Review of Literature* 38 (March 5, 1955): 31.

Review of Joy Davidman's *Smoke on the Mountain*. *Times Literary Supplement* [London], May 6, 1955, p. iii.

Articles and Books

Aaron, Daniel. *Writers on the Left*. New York: Harcourt, 1961.

Allego, Donna M. "The Construction and Role of Community in Political Long Poems by Twentieth-Century American Poets: Lola Ridge, Genevieve Taggard, Joy Davidman, Margaret Walker, and Muriel Rukeyser." Dissertation, Southern Illinois University at Carbondale, 1997.

Belknap, Michal R. *Cold War Political Justice: The Smith Act, the Communist Party, and American Civil Liberties*. Westport, CT: Greenwood Press, 1977.

Benét, William Rose. "Assumption." *The Saturday Review of Literature* 30 (May 10, 1947): 35.

———. "The Phoenix Nest" (column). *The Saturday Review of Literature* 32 (January 29, 1949): 42-43.

———. "The Phoenix Nest" (column). *The Saturday Review of Literature* 32 (July 23, 1949): 28-29.

———. "To a Communist." *The Saturday Review of Literature* 31 (October 23, 1948): 39.

Borhek, Mary. "A Grief Observed: Fact or Fiction?" *Mythlore* 16 (Summer 1990): 4-9, 26.

Bradley, George, ed. "Introduction." In *The Yale Younger Poets Anthology*. New Haven: Yale University Press, 1998.

Christopher, Joe. "Joy Davidman, Laundress?" *Lamp-Post of the Southern California C. S. Lewis Society* 27 (Summer 2003): 26-27.

Christopher, John. "Notes on Joy." *Encounter* 68 (April 1987): 41-43.

Dorsett, Lyle. *And God Came In: The Extraordinary Story of Joy Davidman*. New York: Macmillan, 1983.

————. "The Search for Joy Davidman." *Bulletin of the New York C. S. Lewis Society* 14 (October 1983): 1-7.

Edison, Edward R. *The Worm Ouroboros.* London: Jonathan Cape, 1922.

Edwards, Bruce, ed. *C. S. Lewis — Life, Works, and Legacy.* 4 vols. Westport, CT: Praeger, 2007.

Engels, Friedrich. *Ludwig Feurbach and the Outcome of Classical German Philosophy.* New York: International Publishers, 1941.

Ferrari, Arthur C. "Proletarian Literature: A Case of Convergence of Political and Literary Radicalism." In *Cultural Politics: Radical Movements in Modern History,* edited by Jerold M. Starr. New York: Praeger, 1985.

Fitzpatrick, John. "*Shadowlands:* Moving, Beautiful . . . and True? *Bulletin of the New York C. S. Lewis Society* 18 (June 1987): 1-7.

Foley, Barbara. "Women and the Left in the 1930s." *American Literary History* 2 (Spring 1990): 150-69.

Folsom, Franklin. *Days of Anger, Days of Hope: A Memoir of the League of American Writers, 1937-1942.* Boulder: University Press of Colorado, 1994.

Folsom, Michael, ed. *Mike Gold: A Literary Anthology.* New York: International, 1972.

Glyer, Diana Pavlac. "Helen Joy Davidman Gresham Lewis." In *The C. S. Lewis Reader's Encyclopedia,* edited by Jeffrey Schultz and John West, 248-49. Grand Rapids: Zondervan, 1998.

————. "Joy Davidman Lewis: Author, Editor and Collaborator." *Mythlore* 22 (Summer 1998): 10-17, 46.

————. *The Company They Keep: C. S. Lewis and J. R. R. Tolkien as Writers in Community.* Kent, OH: Kent State University Press, 2007.

Gold, Mike. "Go Left, Young Writer." *New Masses* 4 (January 1929): 3-4. Reprinted in *Mike Gold: A Literary Anthology,* edited by Michael Folsom, 186-89. New York: International, 1972.

————. "Notes of the Month [On Proletarian Realism]." *New Masses* 5 (September 1930): 4-5. Reprinted in *Mike Gold: A Literary Anthology,* edited by Michael Folsom, 203-8. New York: International, 1972.

Gornick, Vivian. *The Romance of American Communism.* New York: Basic Books, 1977.

Green, Roger Lancelyn, and Walter Hooper. *C. S. Lewis: A Biography.* London: Collins, 1974.

Greenfield, Dean Robert. "Recollection of Joy Davidman Lecture." *The Chronicle of the Portland C. S. Lewis Society* 5 (January-March 1976): 4-5.

Gresham, Douglas. *Jack's Life: A Memoir of C. S. Lewis.* New York: Broadman & Holman, 2005.

————. *Lenten Lands: My Childhood with Joy Davidman and C. S. Lewis.* New York: Macmillan, 1988.

Gresham, William L. "From Communist to Christian, Part 1." *Presbyterian Life* 3

(February 18, 1950): 20-22 and 35-36; "From Communist to Christian, Part 2." *Presbyterian Life* 3 (March 4, 1950): 22-23, 46; and "From Communist to Christian, Part 3." *Presbyterian Life* 3 (March 18, 1950): 21-24. The articles were later combined as "From Communist to Christian" and appeared in *These Found the Way: Thirteen Converts to Protestant Christianity*, edited by David W. Soper, 63-82. Philadelphia: The Westminster Press, 1951.

————. *Houdini: The Man Who Walked through Walls*. New York: Henry Holt, 1959.

————. *Limbo Tower*. New York: Rinehart & Co., 1949.

————. *Nightmare Alley*. New York and Toronto: Rinehart, 1946.

————. *Monster Midway: A Book about Circus Life and Sideshows*. New York: Rinehart & Co., 1953.

Griffin, William. *Clive Staples Lewis: A Dramatic Life*. San Francisco: Harper & Row, 1986.

Healey, Dorothy, and Maurice Isserman. *Dorothy Healey Remembers: A Life in the American Communist Party*. Oxford: Oxford University Press, 1990.

Hicks, Granville. *Granville Hicks in the New Masses*. Port Washington, NY: Kennikat Press, 1974.

Hooper, Walter. *C. S. Lewis: A Companion and Guide*. London: HarperCollins, 1996.

Howe, Irving, and Lewis Coser. *The American Communist Party: A Critical History*. New York: Praeger, 1957.

Isserman, Maurice. *Which Side Were You On? The American Communist Party During the Second World War*. Middletown, CT: Wesleyan University Press, 1982.

Jerome, V. J. *Culture in a Changing World*. New York: New Century Publishers, 1947.

Kaufman, Bel. "A Joy Observed." *Commonweal*, March 25, 1994, pp. 6-7.

Kidd, Noelene. "*A Grief Observed:* Art, Apology, or Autobiography?" *The Canadian C. S. Lewis Society* 97 (Spring 2000): 4.

King, Don. "Finding Joy: A Comprehensive Bibliography of the Works of Joy Davidman." *SEVEN: An Anglo-American Literary Review* 23 (2006): 69-80.

————. "Fire and Ice: C. S. Lewis and the Love Poetry of Joy Davidman and Ruth Pitter." *SEVEN: An Anglo-American Literary Review* 22 (2005): 60-88.

————. *Hunting the Unicorn: A Critical Biography of Ruth Pitter*. Kent, OH: Kent State University Press, 2008.

————. "Joy Davidman and the *New Masses:* Communist Poet and Reviewer." *The Chronicle of the Oxford C. S. Lewis Society* 4, no. 1 (February 2007): 18-44.

Kirkpatrick, Ken, and Sidney F. Hunter. "Women Writers in the Proletarian Literature Collection, McFarlin Library." *Tulsa Studies in Women's Literature* 8 (Spring 1989): 143-53.

Klehr, Harvey. *The Heyday of American Communism: The Depression Decade*. New York: Basic Books, 1984.

Kramer, Aaron. *The Alarm Clock*. Privately printed, 1944.

―――. *The Glass Mountain*. New York: Beechhurst Press, 1946.

―――. *The Thunder of the Grass*. New York: International Publishers, 1948.

Lenin, V. I. *Materialism and Empirio-Criticism: Critical Comments on a Reactionary Philosophy*. New York: International Publishers, 1927.

Leopold, Paul. "The Writings of Joy Davidman Lewis, Part 1." *Bulletin of the New York C. S. Lewis Society* 14 (February 1983): 1-10; "The Writings of Joy Davidman Lewis, Part 2." *Bulletin of the New York C. S. Lewis Society* 14 (March 1983): 1-9.

Lewis, C. S. *The Allegory of Love: A Study in Medieval Tradition*. Oxford: Clarendon Press, 1936.

―――. *The Case for Christianity*. New York: Macmillan, 1943.

―――. *The Collected Letters of C. S. Lewis, Volume 2: Books, Broadcasts and the War, 1931-1949*. Edited by Walter Hooper. London: HarperCollins, 2004.

―――. *The Collected Letters of C. S. Lewis, Volume 3: Narnia, Cambridge, and Joy, 1950-1963*. Edited by Walter Hooper. London: HarperCollins, 2006.

―――. *The Collected Poems of C. S. Lewis*. Edited by Walter Hooper. London: Fount, 1994.

―――. "De Descriptione Temporum." In *Selected Literary Essays*. Cambridge: Cambridge University Press, 1969.

―――. "The Efficacy of Prayer," *The Atlantic Monthly* 203 (January 1959): 59-61. Reprinted in *The World's Last Night: And Other Essays*. New York: Harcourt, Brace & Co., 1960.

―――. *English Literature in the Sixteenth Century Excluding Drama*. The Oxford History of English Literature, Vol. 3. Oxford: Clarendon Press, 1954.

―――. *The Four Loves*. London: Geoffrey Bles, 1960.

―――. *The Great Divorce: A Dream*. London: Geoffrey Bles, 1945.

―――. *A Grief Observed*. London: Faber and Faber, 1961.

―――. *The Horse and His Boy*. London: Geoffrey Bles, 1954.

―――. *The Last Battle: A Story for Children*. London: Bodley Head, 1956.

―――. *Letters to Malcolm: Chiefly on Prayer*. London: Geoffrey Bles, 1964.

―――. *The Lion, the Witch and the Wardrobe*. London: Geoffrey Bles, 1950.

―――. *The Pilgrim's Regress: An Allegorical Apology for Christianity, Reason and Romanticism*. London: J. M. Dent, 1933.

―――. *Reflections on the Psalms*. London: Geoffrey Bles, 1958.

―――. *The Screwtape Letters*. London: Geoffrey Bles, 1942.

―――. "Screwtape Proposes a Toast." *The Saturday Evening Post* 232 (December 19, 1959): 36, 88-89.

―――. *Surprised by Joy: The Shape of My Early Life*. London: Geoffrey Bles, 1955.

―――. *That Hideous Strength: A Modern Fairy-tale for Grown-ups*. London: Bodley Head, 1945.

―――. *Till We Have Faces: A Myth Retold*. London: Geoffrey Bles, 1956.

————. "What Christmas Means to Me." *Twentieth Century* 157 (December 1957): 517-18. Reprinted in *God in the Dock: Essays on Theology and Ethics.* Edited by Walter Hooper. Grand Rapids: Eerdmans, 1970.

————. "Will We Lose God in Outer Space?" *Christian Herald* 81 (April 1958): 19, 74-76. Reprinted as "Religion and Rocketry," in *The World's Last Night: And Other Essays.* New York: Harcourt, Brace & Co., 1960.

————, ed. *Essays Presented to Charles Williams.* Oxford: Oxford University Press, 1947.

Lewis, Warren. *Brothers and Friends: The Diaries of Major Warren Hamilton Lewis.* Edited by Clyde S. Kilby and Marjorie Lamp Mead. San Francisco: Harper & Row, 1982.

————. *The Splendid Century: Some Aspects of French Life in the Reign of Louis XIV.* London: Eyre & Spottiswoode, 1953.

————. *The Sunset of the Splendid Century: The Life and Times of Louis Auguste de Bourbon, Duc de Maine, 1670-1736.* London: Eyre & Spottiswoode, 1955.

MacDonald, George. *Phantastes: A Faerie Romance for Men and Women.* London: Arthur C. Fifield, 1905.

Madden, David, ed. *Proletarian Writers of the Thirties.* Carbondale, IL: Southern Illinois University Press, 1968.

Martindale, Wayne. "Shadowlands: Inadvertent Evangelism." In *C. S. Lewis: Lightbearer in the Shadowlands,* edited by Angus Menuge. Wheaton, IL: Crossways Books, 1997.

McGuire, Damaris Walsh. "Memories of Joy, Jack, and Chad [Walsh]." In *Chad Walsh Reviews C. S. Lewis.* Altadena, CA: Mythopoeic Press, 1998.

Musacchio, George. "Fiction in *A Grief Observed.*" *SEVEN: An Anglo-American Literary Review* 8 (1987): 73-83.

North, Alfred, ed. *New Masses: An Anthology of the Rebel Thirties.* New York: International Publishers, 1969.

Ottanelli, Fraser M. *The Communist Party of the United States: From the Depression to World War II.* New Brunswick, NJ: Rutgers University Press, 1991.

Pilat, Oliver. "Girl Communist [Joy Davidman]: An Intimate Story of Eight Years in the Party." *The New York Post,* October 31; November 1-4, 6-11, and 13, 1949.

Porter, Kenneth. *Pilate before Jesus and Other Biblical and Legendary Poems.* North Montpelier, VT: The Driftwood Press, 1936.

————. *The High Plains.* New York: The John Day Co., 1938.

Prendergast, Alan. "One Man's Nightmare: The Noir Journey of William Lindsay Gresham." *The Writer's Chronicle* 38 (May/Summer 2006): 14-19.

Rideout, Walter. *The Radical Novel in the United States, 1900-1954.* Cambridge: Harvard University Press, 1956.

Root, Jerry, and Jennifer Trafton. "The Great Iconoclast." *Christian History and Biography,* Fall 2005, pp. 39-40.

Santamaria, Abigail. "Joy Davidman: The Honest Fingers of My Hand." *Sacred History*, December 2005, pp. 32-34.

Sarrocco, Clara. "The Three Phases of Joy Davidman." *Bulletin of the New York C. S. Lewis Society* 34 (May-June 2003): 1-9.

Sayer, George. "C. S. Lewis and Adultery." *Bulletin of the New York C. S. Lewis Society* 21 (June-July 1990): 4-7.

————. *Jack: C. S. Lewis and His Times.* San Francisco: Harper & Row, 1988.

Sibley, Brian. *C. S. Lewis, Through the Shadowlands: The Story of His Life with Joy Davidman.* New York: Macmillan, 1985.

Turney, Ruth. "Joy Davidman's *Weeping Bay*." *Bulletin of the New York C. S. Lewis Society* 17 (January 1986): 1-3.

Wald, Alan M. *Exiles from a Future Time: The Forging of the Mid-Twentieth-Century Literary Left.* Chapel Hill, NC: University of North Carolina Press, 2002.

Walsh, Chad. *C. S. Lewis: Apostle to the Skeptics.* New York: Macmillan, 1949.

————. *The Literary Legacy of C. S. Lewis.* New York: Harcourt Brace Jovanovich, 1979.

Williams, Charles. *The Greater Trumps.* London: Victor Gollancz, 1932.

Wixson, Douglas. "In Search of the Low-Down Americano: H. H. Lewis, William Carlos Willaims, and the Politics of Literary Reception, 1930-1950." *William Carlos Williams Review* 26, no. 1 (2006): 75-100.

Wolfe, Thomas. *Look Homeward, Angel: A Story of the Buried Life.* New York: Charles Scribner's Sons, 1929.

Wood, Ralph. "The Tears of Things" (Review of *Shadowlands*). *Christian Century* III (February 23, 1994): 200.

Index

Boldface indicates that the poem or essay in question
is reprinted on the pages indicated.